GAY VOICES
OF THE
HARLEM RENAISSANCE

GAY VOICES
OF THE
HARLEM
RENAISSANCE

A. B. CHRISTA SCHWARZ

INDIANA
University Press
Bloomington & Indianapolis

Publication of this book is made possible in part with the assistance of a Challenge Grant from the National Endowment for the Humanities, a federal agency that supports research, education, and public programming in the humanities.

Quotations from the Claude McKay Papers are courtesy of the Literary Representative for the Works of Claude McKay, Schomburg Center for Research in Black Culture, The New York Public Library, Astor, Lenox and Tilden Foundations.

Quotations from Langston Hughes are from *The Collected Poems of Langston Hughes* by Langston Hughes, copyright © 1984 by The Estate of Langston Hughes. Used by permission of Alfred A. Knopf, a division of Random House, Inc.

This book is a publication of

Indiana University Press
601 North Morton Street
Bloomington, Indiana 47404-3797, USA

http://iupress.indiana.edu

Telephone orders	800-842-6796
Fax orders	812-855-7931
Orders by e-mail	iuporder@indiana.edu

The paper used in this publication meets the minimum requirements of American National Standard for Information Sciences—Permanence of Paper for Printed Library Materials, ANSI Z39.48-1984.

Manufactured in the United States of America

Library of Congress Cataloging-in-Publication Data

Schwarz, A. B. Christa, date
Gay voices of the Harlem Renaissance / A. B. Christa Schwarz.
p. cm. — (Blacks in the diaspora)
Includes bibliographical references and index.
ISBN 0-253-34255-4 (cloth : alk. paper) — ISBN 0-253-21607-9
(pbk. : alk. paper)
1. Gay men's writings, American—History and criticism.
2. American literature—African American authors—History and criticism.
3. Homosexuality and literature—United States—History—20th century.
4. American literature—New York (State)—New York—History and criticism.
5. American literature—20th century—History and criticism. 6. American literature—Male authors—History and criticism. 7. African American gays—Intellectual life. 8. African American men in literature. 9. Gay men in literature.
10. Harlem Renaissance. 11. Sex in literature. I. Title. II. Series.
PS153.G38 S39 2003
810.9'9206642—dc21
2002153777

1 2 3 4 5 08 07 06 05 04 03

CONTENTS

ACKNOWLEDGMENTS   vii

LIST OF ABBREVIATIONS   ix

Introduction   I

ONE.   Gay Harlem and the Harlem Renaissance   6

TWO.   Writing in the Harlem Renaissance: The Burden of Representation and Sexual Dissidence   25

THREE.   Countée Cullen: "His virtues are many; his vices unheard of"   48

FOUR.   Langston Hughes: A "true 'people's poet'"   68

FIVE.   Claude McKay: *enfant terrible* of the Negro Renaissance"   88

SIX.   Richard Bruce Nugent: The Quest for Beauty   120

Conclusion   142

NOTES   145

BIBLIOGRAPHY   187

INDEX   203

Acknowledgments

Completing this project has proven a true challenge, but I mastered it—with the support, advice, and kindness offered to me by a great number of people who presumably deserve more than a mere thank-you. First of all, I would like to express my sincerest gratitude to my parents, Ursula and Carlpeter Schwarz, who supported me in too many ways to be recorded here. Without their help, I would not have been able to carry out this research project. My research trips turned out pleasant, amusing, interesting, and successful because of the library staff at the Beinecke Rare Book and Manuscript Library at Yale University, the Rare Book and Manuscript Library at Columbia University, the Library of Congress, the Schomburg Center for Research in Black Culture, The New York Public Library, and particularly the Moorland-Spingarn Research Center at Howard University. While undertaking research in the United States, I benefited from financial assistance of the Graduate Research Centre in the Humanities of the University of Sussex, for which I am very grateful. I owe my outstanding research experience to Thomas Wirth, who was willing to spend an enormous amount of time to introduce me to writer and artist Richard Bruce Nugent, whose papers he holds. It has been a pleasure working with him, and I have always enjoyed his support, suggestions, and conversations.

For her support and patience, Maria Lauret, my supervisor, deserves special mention. I guess that guiding me through earning my doctorate was no easy task, and I thank her for her kindness, interest, and energy. Also from the University of Sussex, I would like to thank Michael Dunne for his convincing display of interest in my dissertation. For scholarly advice, I would particularly like to thank George Hutchinson, who not only has been generous in providing helpful comments on chapters but also, though of course only in a positive sense, is responsible for this study insofar as he enlightened me and other students at Bonn University about the Harlem Renaissance. His teaching has been inspiring and his support unfailing.

A special thank-you goes to Susan Tomlinson for her encouragement, moral and research support, and her hospitality. Seyhan Karabulut has been extremely generous in offering me her friendship—despite the distance that separated us. Many other people assisted me in ways too numerous to mention here—Mrs. Patawaran, Ligaya Salazar, Pınar Karabulut, Silke Rumpf, Alastair Dingwall, and Oswald Jochum. I certainly cannot forget to mention that I am grateful to Indiana University Press and its staff for offering me the opportunity to publish this book.

This leaves me with the impossible task of thanking Wigan Salazar, who deserves mention as the one person who had to suffer through the lack of sleep, social life, and leisure time with me but who still managed to not only keep me going but also to make me laugh. I still do not know how he has managed to endure all these years with me, but I appreciate everything he has done for me and dedicate this book to him.

Abbreviations

AASP	Arthur A. Schomburg Papers, Manuscripts, Archives and Rare Books Division, Schomburg Center for Research in Black Culture, The New York Public Library, Astor, Lenox and Tilden Foundations
ADP	Aaron Douglas Papers, Manuscripts, Archives and Rare Books Division, Schomburg Center for Research in Black Culture, The New York Public Library, Astor, Lenox and Tilden Foundations
AGC	Alexander Gumby Collection, Rare Book and Manuscript Library, Columbia University
ALP	Alain Locke Papers, Moorland-Spingarn Research Center
ARC	Amistad Research Center, Tulane University, New Orleans, Louisiana
BRBML	Beinecke Rare Book and Manuscript Library, James Weldon Johnson Memorial Collection, Yale University, New Haven, Connecticut
CCP [ARC]	Countée Cullen Papers, Amistad Research Center
CCP [BRBML]	Countée Cullen Papers, Beinecke Rare Book and Manuscript Library
CMKP [BRBML]	Claude McKay Papers, Beinecke Rare Book and Manuscript Library
CMKP [SCRBC]	Claude McKay Papers, Manuscripts, Archives and Rare Books Division, Schomburg Center for Research in Black Culture, The New York Public Library, Astor, Lenox and Tilden Foundations
CURBML	Columbia University, Rare Book and Manuscript Library, New York, New York
GCP	Glenn Carrington Papers, Moorland-Spingarn Research Center
GDJP	Georgia Douglas Johnson Papers, Moorland-Spingarn Research Center
JWJP	James Weldon Johnson Papers, Beinecke Rare Book and Manuscript Library
LC	Library of Congress, Manuscript Division, Washington, D.C.
LHP	Langston Hughes Papers, Beinecke Rare Book and Manuscript Library

MSRC	Moorland-Spingarn Research Center, Howard University, Washington, D.C.
RBNP	Richard Bruce Nugent Papers, Thomas H. Wirth, Elizabeth, New Jersey
RBNP/Notes	Richard Bruce Nugent Papers, Notes
RBNP/Tapes	Richard Bruce Nugent Papers, Tapes
SCRBC	Manuscripts, Archives and Rare Books Division, Schomburg Center for Research in Black Culture, The New York Public Library, Astor, Lenox and Tilden Foundations
SSVP	Society for the Suppression of Vice Papers, Library of Congress
WPC	Writers' Program Collection, Manuscripts, Archives and Rare Books Division, Schomburg Center for Research in Black Culture, The New York Public Library, Astor, Lenox and Tilden Foundations
WTP	Wallace Thurman Papers, Beinecke Rare Book and Manuscript Library
WWP, NAACP	Walter White Papers, NAACP Collection, Library of Congress

GAY VOICES
OF THE
HARLEM RENAISSANCE

Clockwise from top left ❧ **Claude McKay**. Yale Collection of American Literature, Beinecke Rare Book and Manuscript Library. ❧ **Countee Cullen**. Yale Collection of American Literature, Beinecke Rare Book and Manuscript Library. ❧ **Richard Bruce Nugent**. Alexander Gumby Papers, Rare Book and Manuscript Library, Columbia University. Image courtesy of Thomas H. Wirth. ❧ **Langston Hughes**. Yale Collection of American Literature, Beinecke Rare Book and Manuscript Library. Reprinted by permission of Harold Ober Associates Incorporated.

Introduction

Any enumeration of leading figures of the African American cultural movement known as the Harlem Renaissance gives evidence of the dominant position held by men in its definition and creation. This, however, does not imply that the Renaissance was exclusively male-defined. Research undertaken by such scholars as Cheryl Wall and Gloria Hull has led not only to an acknowledgement of the participation of numerous women in the movement but also to various explorations of works that had, from the Renaissance time, been regarded as inferior to male writing.[1] A closer examination of the biographies of the movement's male protagonists sheds light on the central position occupied by men-loving men, who, as artists and writers but also, as evident in the case of Alain Locke, within the movement's leadership, were at the heart of the Harlem Renaissance. Henry Louis Gates acknowledges that the Harlem Renaissance "was surely as gay as it was black,"[2] yet the scholarship in the field does not reflect the strong presence of same-sex-interested men or women within the movement. This relative neglect needs to be seen in the context of the main debates addressed by critics writing on the Renaissance. Most works on the period pivot on the question of the movement's success or failure, a debate closely intertwined with that about the autonomy of black cultural production from white "interference."[3] In the context of these preoccupations, the issue of the significance of same-sex-interested men and women for the Renaissance was—either deliberately or inadvertently—sidelined.

The reluctance or refusal to establish a link between the Harlem Renaissance and homosexuality on the one hand implies a neglect of biographical research; on the other, a link between writers' creative output and their sexuality is ignored or denied. As Alan Sinfield points out, the claiming of a text's "gay significance"[4] represents a contested undertaking, as literary critics frequently treat literary value and homosexuality as mutually exclusive issues. Against this background, it is not surprising that when, particularly in less recent critical works, a connection between writers' same-sex desire and Renaissance writers' works was established, it was, maybe fitting an overall narrative of failure, often envisaged in a negative context linking homosexuality with despair.[5] Significantly, the rare instances of a recognition of the presence of men-loving men in the Harlem Renaissance triggered a backlash, as is evident in the work of Gerald Early, who denies same-sex desire on the part of Countée Cullen despite clear indications to this effect in Cullen's personal correspondence.[6]

Since the 1980s, some explorations of the Harlem Renaissance's gay dimensions, superseding homophobic notions of same-sex desire, have been undertaken. Eric Garber's 1983 essay "T'ain't Nobody's Bizness: Homosexuality in 1920s Harlem," which includes a brief discussion of Renaissance writers and their works, deserves special mention in this context.[7] More recently, Kevin Mumford has highlighted interracial same-sex spaces in Chicago and 1920s Harlem, thereby venturing beyond a strict racial dichotomy and forcefully arguing that gay life in black districts also needs to be viewed within the context of a shared experience of marginalized black and white men and women.[8] Although the presence of women-loving women in the Harlem Renaissance seems harder to recognize because of stronger social policing and pressures that concerned particularly female writers, sexually dissident readings of Renaissance works seem to have been first suggested regarding female Renaissance writers such as Nella Larsen and Angelina Weld Grimké.[9] In recent years, the apparently more contested area of male Renaissance writing has been entered by critics such as Alden Reimonenq and Gregory Woods, who are willing to explore sexual dissidence in the cases of writers such as Langston Hughes, Claude McKay, and Cullen.[10]

Interestingly, some scholars' reactions to "gay" Harlem Renaissance projects evidence a sense of boredom with an issue which, as seems to be claimed, has been the focus of allegedly exaggerated or even faddish attention in recent years. Yet the number of explorations of the gay dimensions of the Harlem Renaissance and their content reveal an altogether different picture. Particularly in the case of Hughes, an iconic figure within the field of African American literature whose public image is highly contested, a focus on what can be described as a biographical project can be recognized. Against a history of neglect and denial of Harlem Renaissance writers' same-sex interests, gay readings are frequently presented as "evidence" for writers' homosexuality. This approach not only implies a questionable equation of author and text but, similar to heterosexist readings of literature, the multiplicity of meanings contained in literary works is negated as sexual, or in this case, specifically homosexual textual coherence is claimed. Potentially contradictory readings or alternative lines of thought that do not contribute to the argument pursued are consequently negated or subordinated to what are presented as "true" readings. Because literary texts, as Sinfield underlines, are "sites of struggle" and literary criticism means the participation in a "cultural contest," writers are subject to "cultural hijacking"—the exclusive claiming of a writer for a political project.[11] In the context of the claiming of gay identities, this process entails a potential pitfall—ignorance of what Thomas Yingling describes as the "materiality and historicity of homosexual practices and cultures"[12] which may result in an uncritical transfer of the concept of a modern gay identity to an earlier period. As George Chauncey points out, the binary of homo-/heterosexuality did not yet govern most people's perception of sexual relationships during the 1920s. Numerous homosexually active men and women did not identify as gay or lesbian, while others accepted a gay identity.[13] While informed cross-cultural and trans-historical identifications are valuable, ignorance of historical circumstances appears to lead some critics to equate sexual practice with identity, thereby neglecting potential sexual ambiguity that can also be reflected in writers' works. In short, there is a need for more varied and nuanced gay readings of Harlem Renaissance texts that place works in a historical and biographical context.

As Reimonenq asserts with reference to his readings of Cullen's works as sexually dissident formations, "Tracing where and how his gay life intersected and shaped his creativity is an integral part of historicizing Cullen's art."[14] This applies equally to other Renaissance writers from whom, in addition to Cullen, I have selected two further Renaissance "stars"—Hughes and McKay—and the still relatively unknown Richard Bruce Nugent, who can, with reservations, be described as the only openly gay writer of the Harlem Renaissance. Although McKay was somewhat older than the other writers chosen, this study reflects the pivotal role of a younger generation of writers within the Renaissance movement. Moreover, the choice of writers that includes the movement's "poet laureate" Cullen, the "poet of the masses" Hughes, its so-called *enfant terrible* McKay, and its most distinct bohemian Nugent, offers a wide range of positions toward sexuality, literature, and the Renaissance movement. I largely exclude female writers because a joint discussion of the sexual dissidence of male and female Renaissance authors that pays tribute to their distinct sexual and writing experiences is beyond the scope of this project.

This study is an exploration of Renaissance writers' gay voices via a biocritical approach which entails readings of Renaissance works in the context of archival material such as writers' personal correspondence and unpublished manuscripts. While the focus is on works created during the Harlem Renaissance, which is here loosely defined as starting in the early 1920s and ending in the early to mid-1930s, I will also include earlier or later pieces of interest for this project. The gay readings produced in this study are by no means definitive interpretations to be grasped only by a specific—for example, gay—readership; instead, they represent what Sinfield terms "haunting possibilities." They are instances that open up new dimensions of texts, thereby revealing subtexts so far ignored.[15] The mapping of homosexuality onto race within the Harlem Renaissance, thus an exploration of points where "racial" discourses meet "gay" discourses, producing gay literary codes with a difference and a multiple overlapping (black/white/gay/straight) rather than what Renaissance intellectual James Weldon Johnson described as black writers' "double audience"[16] (black/white), will be of significance in this context.

Acknowledging the contentious potential of the term *gay*, I will use this term to describe men who define their identity as men-loving—within or outside a context of gender inversion. The term *lesbian* will be employed correspondingly. Other terms to be used will indicate same-sex desire or attraction which is not necessarily linked to an exclusively man- or woman-loving identity. Despite the need to address the sexual identity of each of the four writers discussed in this study, my focus is on an exploration of their "gay voices." As employed in this study, the term denotes Renaissance writers' voices of sexual dissidence—in the sense of a literary voice that relates to writers' same-sex interests but also in the context of their portrayal of sexually dissident characters, a category that includes varieties of sexual "deviance" in a male and female context. It is noteworthy that the term implies neither a sympathetic nor a favorable representation of transgressive sexualities and particularly homosexuality.

Before this book embarks on gay readings of Harlem Renaissance works, the first two chapters serve to illuminate the sociohistoric background of Harlem and the Harlem Renaissance. Chapter 1, "Gay Harlem and the Harlem Renaissance," explores the geographical site of Harlem during the 1920s and early 1930s. There, the emphasis is on the status of sexuality and homosexuality against the backdrop of the area's development into a sexual/homosexual pleasure center attracting numerous white visitors. In this context, gay formations within the Harlem Renaissance and African American bohemian circles surrounding it are of interest. Joining this exploration of living conditions particularly for gay and lesbian or same-sex interested Renaissance artists, I focus on the Renaissance movement as a site of ideological struggle in chapter 2, "Writing in the Harlem Renaissance: The Burden of Representation and Sexual Dissidence." Central in this regard will be the politics of representation as advocated by different actors—Renaissance writers, the group of intellectuals leading and defining the Harlem Renaissance, and contemporary literary critics—and the position sexual dissidence occupies in this context.

Starting off with the writer deemed the poet laureate of the Harlem Renaissance, chapter 3, "Countée Cullen: 'His virtues are many; his vices unheard of,' " focuses on Countée Cullen's poetry. This chapter serves to reveal the somewhat solitary status Cullen, a gay-identified yet closeted author, occupied among the group of younger Renaissance writers. Cullen's special position needs to be seen in the context of his formal literary approach, social pressure, and his identification with the "burden of representation" as defined by the group of Renaissance leaders, which clearly shaped his gay literary voice. Langston Hughes's identification with working-class African Americans occupies a central position in chapter 4, "Langston Hughes: A 'true "people's poet." ' " The development of his gay voice is explored against the background of his self-defined representative function in a black working-class context which implied a need for credibility with the black masses. Displaying a similar interest in the black working class, Claude McKay is an intriguing figure as an outsider yet simultaneously an influential figure of the Harlem Renaissance. Particularly his involvement in a primitivist discourse is explored in chapter 5, "Claude McKay: '*enfant terrible* of the Negro Renaissance,' " in the context of his literary sexual dissidence. Chapter 6, "Richard Bruce Nugent: The Quest for Beauty," presents Richard Bruce Nugent as the only openly gay literary contributor to the movement. Nugent is reclaimed from the position of important eyewitness of the Harlem Renaissance to that of an artist in his own right whose gay voice represents an alternative to those audible in the works created by other Renaissance protagonists. Finally, I summarize the results of my study, thereby returning to the question of writers' employment of a coded language in which discourses of race and sexuality merge.

ONE

Gay Harlem and
the Harlem Renaissance

A specific time frame for the Harlem Renaissance seems hard to establish, as neither its "beginning" nor its "end" can be pinned to a specific date or event, yet for the purpose of this book, it is defined as starting around the beginning of the 1920s, reaching its end in the early to mid-1930s. This period evokes contradictory images in the context of U.S. cultural history. For the period before the Great Depression, the pervasive cliché is that of the "roaring twenties" and the "Jazz Age" with its "key image . . . of a fast life, propelled by riches and rapidly changing social values. . . . Flappers dancing the Charleston and participating in a sexual revolution, . . . and speakeasies trafficking in illegal liquor, all suggested a world far removed from Victorian restraint."[1] Although only a minority of predominantly white middle- or upper-class Americans could indulge in this lifestyle, less privileged Americans could still taste the new pleasures. The image of joyful abandon, experimentation, and a relaxation of traditional morality, however, reflects only one side of an era equally shaped by racism, epitomized by a regrouping of the Ku Klux Klan, and fears about developments in the field of sexuality and gender—particularly the changing role of women and the more open discussion of topics relating to sexuality. A key indicator of the climate of anxiety regarding sexual morality was an intensification of anti-vice movements' policing efforts. Organizations like the New York Society for the Suppression of Vice (SSV) and the Committee of Fourteen (COF) focused on clamping down on prostitution and, to a lesser extent, homosexual activities and, moreover, concentrated on the censorship of "indecent" literature and entertainment.[2] While the Depression shattered most Americans' vision of prosperity, a white financial elite continued its lifestyle into the 1930s. George Chauncey observes that attitudes toward sexuality were strongly influenced by the deteriorated economic situation. Policing efforts intensified, yet change did not come overnight: The early 1930s saw a "pansy craze," in which cross-dressing, effeminate men were sought-after entertainers in cabarets and theaters.[3]

THE EMERGENCE OF HARLEM
AS A SEXUAL PLEASURE CENTER

Before venturing on an exploration of Harlem as a sexual/homosexual pleasure center, it is important to historicize same-sex relations to shed light on their complexity. While numerous homosexually active men and women, who could from today's perspective be described as gay or lesbian, lived in New York and Harlem, their self-perception varied. From the 1890s, sexologists, observing changes in sexual behavior, developed theories which diverged from earlier concepts according to which same-sex desire was inextricably linked to gender inversion. They increasingly stressed sexual as opposed to gender identities, thereby giving rise to the modern concepts of hetero-/homosexuality.[4] During the 1920s, this binary, however, had not yet become a well-established category governing the perception of sexuality.[5] Consequently, various identities involving same-sex contacts coexisted: gay-identified men and lesbian-identified women; men and women who explored the realm of sexuality and in the process also experimented in a homosexual context but did not identify as gay or lesbian; men and women who engaged in both hetero- and homosexual relationships without viewing these in the context of homo-/heterosexuality; and men and women who represented "inverts" and displayed a gender inversion which, as Gert Hekma describes, was generally "very partial and seldom ostentatious,"[6] but which could also extend to cross-dressing. As Chauncey points out regarding male homosexuality, "fairies"—"inverted," effeminate men—"constituted the primary image of the 'invert' in popular and elite discourse alike and stood at the center of the cultural system by which male-male sexual relations were interpreted."[7] Given this centrality of gender inversion, also evident in popular representations of lesbians as "mannish-looking" women, men and women who desired people of their own sex outside a context of gender inversion were to some extent protected from prosecution because of what Chauncey describes as the "straight world's ignorance of the existence of a hidden middle-class gay world."[8]

Harlem's development into a predominantly black urban district occurred in the context of a mass migration of African Americans from the South to northern cities, particularly during the first two decades of the twentieth century.[9] New York attracted the greatest number of migrants and, mainly owing to the practice of racial segregation, the previously white neighborhood of Harlem was transformed into the residential center for African Americans. The fact that African Americans for the first time lived in what at least looked like a city of their own nurtured a sense of pride and, as Alain Locke summarized, attracted

the African, the West Indian, the Negro American; . . . the Negro of the North and the Negro of the South; the man from the city and the man from the town and village; the peasant, the student, the business man, the professional man, artist, poet, musician, adventurer and worker, preacher and criminal, exploiter and social outcast.[10]

Harlem thus evolved into what Claude McKay termed the "Negro capital of the world."[11] Expressing the newly found racial self-confidence of the so-called New Negroes, who wanted to redefine African Americans' stereotypical image and sought equality with white Americans, the artistic movement of the Harlem Renaissance reached its climax during the mid-1920s.[12] The aim of the Renaissance, the integration of black America into the American nation, or "racial uplift," was formulated by race leaders such as W.E.B. Du Bois and to some extent coincided with the aspirations of the burgeoning black bourgeoisie.[13]

The existence of a large urban area inhabited almost exclusively by African Americans represented a novelty for white Americans. Although many perceived the formation of a black district as a threat, Harlem's "exoticism" attracted numerous white visitors. As Chidi Ikonné polemically suggests:

> The white man, dissatisfied with his own baby (his unprimitive civilization which could save him neither from emotional desiccation nor from wars . . .), had . . . discovered in the Negro what he thought was the opposite of the product of his own civilization—the 'primitive' being, charmingly clothed with unbridled instincts.[14]

For most visitors, this fascination with the "primitive" did not translate into an acknowledgement of African Americans' equality. Race prejudice, as Steven Watson points out, did not disappear but usually simply shifted, as evident regarding African Americans' sexual image: "The dangerously licentious, oversexed figure of earlier times was now idealized as an uninhibited, expressive being."[15] According to Nathan Huggins, the majority of white tourists were attracted by "Brown and black bodies—the color seemed lustier than white—full lips that quickened flesh to move. . . ."[16] By venturing into Harlem, visitors seemed to respond to images popularized in novels like Carl Van Vechten's best-selling *Nigger Heaven* (1926)[17] or in advertisements for black musicals or works by Harlem Renaissance artists. The manner in which the district was presented is exemplified in a leaflet advertising the play *Harlem* (1929), coauthored by Renaissance writer Wallace Thurman: "The City that Never Sleeps! . . . A Strange, Exotic Island in the Heart of New York! . . . Rent Parties! . . . Sweetbacks! . . . Hincty Wenches! . . . Number runners! . . . Chippies! . . . Jazz Love! . . . Primitive Passion!"[18]

Geographically, Harlem was located conveniently for white New Yorkers: African Americans lived "too far away to be dangerous yet close enough to be exciting."[19] Those white visitors in search of sexual and homosexual adventures had less reason to fear social ostracism or the loss of family ties and employment, as they could retain a sexually inconspicuous image in their everyday white environment. Harlem additionally promised relative safety from prosecution. The efforts of anti-vice movements in white areas of New York led to the closure of numerous establishments that offered or tolerated sexual entertainment; as such places closed down in, for instance, the Tenderloin area, Harlem's entertainment and sex industry prospered.[20] Black newspaper commentators observed that anti-vice organizations and the police generally seemed to overlook Harlem. According to an article in the *New York Amsterdam News*, "supervision was, to say the least, lax."[21] It was not until 1928 that the COF commissioned a report on conditions in Harlem. Even this decision seems to have been taken halfheartedly: Only one black investigator was appointed to inspect Harlem's speakeasies and nightclubs for four months during which he worked "only five days a week, while his four associates in other districts worked six."[22] New York's white-directed police force seemed satisfied to see Harlem as New York's premier red-light district, thereby tolerating what Kevin Mumford describes as the "racial segregation of vice."[23]

Harlem's nightlife was reputed to be outrageous and, in light of increased policing in other areas of the city, seemed to constitute the safer alternative—especially for those seeking physical same-sex encounters—since sentences for what was termed "disorderly conduct" could be harsh, varying between a fine of up to $50 and six months in prison.[24] Harlem, or maybe rather African Americans' sexual deviance, was however not completely overlooked, as Thurman and Augustus Dill, the business manager of the National Association for the Advancement of Colored People's publication *The Crisis*, learned. Both were, in separate cases, arrested for homosexual activities in public lavatories.[25] In a more general context, though apparently to a lesser degree than in white areas, establishments linked to prostitution or explicit sexual entertainment were occasionally raided. Moreover, as the *Baltimore Afro-American* reported in 1930, several cafés, which rather openly attracted same-sex-interested men, "received police attention within a few weeks of their opening."[26] Yet even if some public spaces were shut down, they frequently either regained their licenses or reopened under a new name.

Owing to white economic dominance in Harlem—according to the COF, 95 percent of Harlem's nightclubs and speakeasies were owned by whites—"black" entertainment was altered in a manner that would please white visitors, at least in those places where "the tables were reserved for whites."[27] This tendency is discernible particularly for the beginning of Harlem's invasion by white "slummers." Numerous working-class saloons closed down, were redecorated, and started to offer floor shows designed to please white customers.[28] Many of these new patrons wanted to see and experience the "exotic"—but only to a certain limit. According to Langston Hughes, "Harlem nights became show nights for the Nordics" and black entertainers employed at large cabarets catering to a predominantly white clientele adapted their repertoire, "[leaving] out a great many things they thought would offend their American brothers of a lighter complexion."[29] Young African

American female dancers, who were usually of a light complexion—another indication of a process of adaptation to white visitors' limited exoticist tastes—formed the main attraction in cabarets and clubs like the Cotton Club and Connie's Inn.[30] The COF report indicates that venues featuring revues and music shows usually offered or tolerated another, specifically sexual level of entertainment: 380 out 392 nightclubs and speakeasies investigated were "found to be definitely identified with prostitution."[31] Harlem's sex industry was dominated by black prostitutes or "hostesses," yet white women, who apparently focused on black customers, were also active in the district.[32]

GAY LIVES IN HARLEM

Entertainment exclusively arranged for white visitors aimed at the satisfaction of white male heterosexual desire, yet many white male and female tourists came to Harlem to explore "the epitome of the forbidden" by indulging in what Lillian Faderman terms "bisexual experimentation."[33] While same-sex incidents involving white men in Harlem were occasionally reported in black newspapers, information about women's same-sex experiences seems to be rare. Faderman's research on white female "slummers" in Harlem, however, indicate that their expectations and experiences were similar to those of white men.[34] Getting in touch with black same-sex-interested men in the form of "fairies" was not difficult, as they were easily identifiable and could apparently be picked up like female prostitutes.[35] Two articles from the *New York Amsterdam News* in 1928 and 1929, reporting the arrests of black cross-dressing men, suggest that the association of white men with black fairies was not uncommon. The arrested men apparently worked as prostitutes: One "had paraded up and down Lenox avenue soliciting white men only"; another "told the police that he only 'associated' with white men."[36]

By targeting white men, black fairies apparently cashed in on white visitors' curiosity and stereotypical notions. Faderman suggests that white visitors' trips to Harlem may be viewed in the context of "sexual colonialism," yet this interpretation confines African Americans to a passive role. Mumford's observation that some black gay men's sexual contacts with white men "were for pleasure only, some for financial gain, some for both" seems helpful in this context.[37] Many sexual encounters between black gay men—this seems also valid for black women—and white men in Harlem can be viewed in the context of economic necessity and prostitution, but the view of sexual colonialism denies the presence of sexual desire on black women's and black men's parts. The example of gay Harlem Renaissance artist Richard Bruce Nugent shows that black gay men's sexual relations with white partners could be a matter of choice for both parties involved. Reflecting on the 1920s, Nugent pointed out in an interview that "blacks suddenly [had] the freedom to have white sex partners."[38] Nugent himself occasionally got involved sexually with white men in Harlem, and although he was usually in desperate need of money, financial remuneration apparently was not his motivation.

Black gay men and lesbians—usually as "invert" types in "pansy" choruses and as cross-dressing female singers—frequently found employment in cabarets and similar entertainment spots where they were to attract tourists.[39] Their presence in Harlem, however, also should be seen outside the context of white exoticist desire and the Harlem craze. Mumford points out that homosexual involvement in what he terms *interzones*—interracial spaces, usually located in an African American environment—predated the 1920s. These interzones, ranging from cafés and black-and-tans—racially mixed clubs—to speakeasies, provided spaces for marginalized men and women, some of whom desired members of their own sex.[40] Significantly, white gay men and lesbians did not dominate these interzones but belonged to the "stigmatized white groups [that] temporarily inhabited [them]."[41] They thus participated in what Chauncey terms a "gay world,"[42] built by gay men and lesbians within the African American community.

Nugent always stressed his conviction that there was no distinct gay community in Harlem, yet he included the depiction of an all-male gay party in one of his novels.[43] According to Mumford, some exclusively gay and exclusively lesbian spaces existed, but gay men and lesbians usually frequented the same establishments. Particularly speakeasies were mixed in that they catered not only to black and white but also to gay and lesbian as well as to heterosexual customers. In many of these establishments, "the single unifying theme was explicit sexuality," not sexual orientation.[44] Harlem's gay world encompassed distinct networks and participants of all classes. Frequently, boundaries were blurred, as working-class, middle-class, and bohemian Harlemites—several of the latter involved in the Harlem Renaissance—shared spaces. Renaissance artists thus socialized with other African Americans and visiting residents of Greenwich Village at so-called rent parties, organized privately by Harlemites so they could afford the next rent payment, and at "buffet flats," private apartments turned into entertainment spots during some nights of the week.[45] Accounts of rent parties and buffet flats suggest that the presence of gay men and lesbians was taken for granted. Ruby Smith, a niece of the blues singer Bessie Smith, recalled that she often saw "nothing but faggots and bulldykers" at buffet flats where "people used to come . . . just to watch [a gay man] make love to another man."[46] Apart from these rougher events, Harlem offered more refined entertainment like the elegant parties organized by wealthy black heiress A'Lelia Walker, who, according to David Levering Lewis, was "especially fond of homosexuals" and attracted a "circle of handsome women . . . [and] effete men."[47]

Entertainment offered by blues singers such as Gladys Bentley and Bessie Smith had a distinctly raucous flavor. They performed songs that incorporated double entendres and often directly referred to sex, gay men, and lesbians, usually making fun of effeminate men, the so-called sissies. Though less commonplace, there were songs like "Prove It on Me Blues," in which female singers voiced their interest in, if not direct sexual preference for, women.[48] Chauncey suggests that in Harlem fairies and butch lesbians could, to a greater extent than in Greenwich Village, be seen in public and even during daytime. Moreover, although this was presumably a rare practice, some butch–femme lesbian couples married publicly, calling each other husband and wife.[49] Organized on a larger scale than in New York's white areas, Harlem's popular drag balls stand out as the district's most publicly "gay" form of entertainment. For the usually predominantly male and black participants, masked balls represented the best opportunity to display what many contemporary black newspapers admiringly described as "the most gorgeous of feminine attire," to compete for prizes, and to receive applause and admiration from thousands of spectators that included Renaissance artists, who usually watched the spectacle from the distance of their boxes.[50] Harlem's bohemians also frequented gay spaces of their own, like the studio of the gay black art collector Alexander Gumby and the apartment of the well-known same-sex-interested bohemian bachelors Caska Bonds and Embry Bonner.[51] "Niggeratti Manor," a house which was inhabited by, among others, Thurman and Nugent and which constituted the creative center of a group of young, dissident Renaissance writers, also partly served as a gay meeting place. Compared with the sophisticated meetings at Gumby's place, the meetings at Niggeratti Manor were more outrageous affairs.[52]

The correspondence of Alain Locke, Renaissance artists, and other African American bohemians points to the existence of a gay male, transnational, and, though apparently mainly black, interracial network which included artists such as Nugent and Countée Cullen. Renaissance leader Locke, a self-identified gay man who displayed a keen interest in sexology, was consulted by various young men regarding sexual problems, many of them related to same-sex desire. Locke offered advice, for instance suggesting to one of his correspondents that "repressed homosexualist emotions and fixations are primarily responsible for your condition."[53] In such letters, Locke appears very frank, discussing same-sex interest from what seems to be a scientific point of view.

Same-sex passion features differently in another layer of Locke's gay network. Here, his man-loving identity, that apparently derived from what appears to be a fusion of the Whitmanesque concept of "manly," "comradely" love with a Greek model of homosexuality in which an older man forms a "noble friendship" with a younger man, comes to the fore. In a carefully worded correspondence, in which a medical discourse on same-sex desire seems wholly absent, Locke displayed sexual interest in young men who were apparently not gay-identified. Several of his correspondents came to develop a positive identity as men-loving men. As one man wrote, his introduction to Locke's particular model of same-sex love, which usually occurred via Locke's suggestion of a canon of works that discussed the topic of male same-sex unions sympathetically, made him feel as though he had "awakened from a long sleep": "It opened a bright beautiful way for me, one that was natural and wholesome. . . ."[54] Along with a man-loving identity, Locke introduced his correspondents to a specific gay discourse. Looking at the coded terms figuring prominently in this discourse, such as "spiritual affinity," "perfect friendship," and "stimulating comaradie [sic]," it can be recognized that they denote honor, masculinity, and depth.[55] Locke thus opened up to these same-sex-interested men a gay identity without regard for contemporary dominant views linking homosexuality to degeneracy, sickness, or gender inversion. One might speculate about sexual exploitation, yet it seems that the young men involved and their parents, who, as should be added, were presumably unaware of the sexual aspect of their sons' relationship with Locke, believed that "association with [Locke] means advancement mentally and in maturrness [sic]."[56]

If Locke felt confident about his correspondents' sincerity, was sure that they understood his same-sex concept, and convinced that they would respond positively to explicit sexual advances—a state he usually reached only after a long correspondence and numerous confidential talks—he was willing to accept them into a "fraternity of friends"[57] of which he himself was a member. New members, or "new friends," as they were termed, were introduced into "the circle" through initiation ceremonies which took place twice a year.[58] While Cullen can be counted among Locke's "fraternal comrades," it seems that Nugent participated in the gay network on a different level. Gay-identified from an early age, he did not need an introduction to the topic of homosexuality, but his positive interpretation and acceptance of same-sex desire linked him to Locke and other participants. This also seems to be true for other Renaissance figures such as Claude McKay and Harold Jackman. Despite their evident display of heterosexual desire, which was apparently not uncommon among these men, they were linked to the network through their positively defined same-sex interest.[59]

An involvement in the network on whatever level could be advantageous. Locke pointed out potential sexual partners to, for instance, Cullen. Referring to Lewellyn Ransom, whom Locke asked to "look up the good friend [Cullen] whom we were last discussing," Cullen expressed his gratitude to Locke, as an intimate relationship with Ransom developed: "L. [Lewellyn] is really godsend. And I don't forget your part in directing the gift my way."[60] Moreover, the latest literature dealing with same-sex desire was discussed. Nugent, for instance, thought that Radclyffe Hall's *The Well of Loneliness* (1928) was "a superbly written and conceived work," "so very different from most novels on inversion," and Locke was unsure "whether to admire more its beauty or its quiet bravery."[61] With Locke as a pivotal figure, the men involved in the gay network formed an invisible, diverse community which was at the heart of the Harlem Renaissance. Some of its members were unrelated to the Renaissance movement, and not all same-sex-interested men involved in the Renaissance participated in the network, but it seems that at least in Locke's perception, numerous well-known and lesser-known writers—"Jean Toomer—Langston Hughes, Countee Cullen, Lewis Alexander, Richard Bruce—Donald Hayes—Albert Dunham"—counted among his "spiritual children."[62]

SEEKING RESPECTABILITY:
SEXUALITY, MORALITY, AND
THE BLACK BOURGEOISIE

Assessments of attitudes toward homosexuality within black urban communities vary widely. One line of argumentation links the existence of Harlem as what Mumford describes as a "site of homosexual leisure"[63] with Harlemites' tolerance. The fact that "black folk of every persuasion, profession, status, and lifestyle"[64] coexisted in a densely populated, racially segregated space might, as Cheryl Clarke maintains, have effected a degree of tolerance toward difference. Clarke argues that Harlemites, who were predominantly of a working-class background, resisted the definition of what was generally regarded as deviant behavior and were therefore willing to tolerate same-sex-interested men and women in their midst.[65] In a similar vein, Mumford entertains the possibility that "a tolerance for the marginalized among people with a long history of exclusion"[66] existed. These suggestions may also be applicable to the presence of white gay men and lesbians in Harlem. African Americans' and white gay men and lesbians' experiences of oppression were clearly distinct, yet, as Eric Garber suggests, they shared a marginalized social position that may have constituted a unifying factor.[67] According to Hughes, Harlemites generally disapproved of the strong presence of white visitors in their community during the 1920s: "But they didn't say it out loud—for Negroes are practically never rude to white people."[68] The toleration of white gay men and lesbians may be linked to economic dependence on white customers but also to whites' racially defined social "superiority" which presumably prevented policing efforts. Blair Niles's novel *Strange Brother* (1931), however, indicates that white gay men, like the protagonist Mark, at least felt welcome and spiritually linked to Harlem: Mark "always identified himself with the outcasts of the earth. The negro had suffered and that bound Mark to him."[69] Furthermore, he "was impressed by all they were doing [in Harlem], under such heavy odds, too—odds of a different sort. . . . In Harlem I found courage and joy and tolerance."[70] Nugent suggests that Harlemites did not display interest in others' sexual preferences. His interpretation was based on the premise that Harlemites had enough problems to cope with in their own lives because of economic pressures and discrimination but certainly also derived from Nugent's bohemian environment—"everybody did whatever he wanted to do . . . and who cared";

or, according to a popular blues song, one's sexuality was "Nobody's Bizness."[71]

Assumptions about Harlemites' tolerance may, however, be overly romanticizing. What looks like tolerance may well have been involuntary toleration: Harlemites did not have much choice but to accept or ignore the presence of men-loving men and women-loving women of whatever racial background because they lacked the power to police their district and could not rely on white-directed anti-vice forces.[72] This does not mean, however, that there was no opposition. It is difficult to assess working-class Harlemites' reactions to homosexuality in their community, because of a lack of documentation, but it is evident that the black bourgeoisie attempted to control the black community. In this context, it needs to be stressed that the black middle class in many respects differed from its white counterpart. As Sterling Brown pointed out, the African American elite was generally "only one remove—even our 'ritziest' only one and a half removes—from our masses."[73] The black bourgeoisie, for instance, included distinctly blue-collar workers like Pullman porters who were often educated but, due to racial discrimination, unable to enter other professions. A further distinction must be made in the specific case of Harlem. Since the district had only recently emerged as a major black settlement because of the migration of predominantly working-class African Americans, no single group monopolized cultural authority the way the long-established African American families of Boston, Philadelphia, and Washington did in their cities.[74]

In Harlem, as in white America, the general trend of a relaxation of rules and morals clashed with forces attempting to curb the excesses of modernity and uphold a traditional value system. Changes brought about by modernity—with urbanization at the center of criticism and attacks—were regarded as reasons for what was perceived as a threatening decline in morality, particularly in the field of sexuality.[75] Black middle-class Americans reacted to changes in very much the same way as their white counterparts, or, as seems to have been the case, even more vigorously, as at least parts of the white middle class adopted less stringent views on morality. In a somewhat sweeping statement, E. Franklin Frazier points out that the black middle class has "striven to mold themselves in the image of the white man"[76]—an aspiration which to some extent implies attempts to emulate the "best" white Americans in terms of looks, taste, morality, and value system. A more accurate analysis seems to be that the black bourgeoisie sought respectability. African Americans had been portrayed and treated as sexually suspicious and excessive in the form of sexless "darkies" and "mammies" or "oversexed studs" and "Jezebels." The black bourgeoisie aimed at sexual "normality" by means of an adherence to high moral standards that whites, who had the power to define respectability, had denied them for centuries.[77] Claudia Tate argues that "for black people, middle-class life-style became synonymous with their constructions of freedom, as attaining that standard of living became the measure of achieving social equality."[78] It is thus unsurprising that the black bourgeoisie emerged as the guardian of moral standards in Harlem, attacking anything that could be considered immoral behavior—for instance, drug or alcohol consumption, prostitution, and sexual transgression. While wealth was difficult to achieve for African Americans, it was attained by a speedily increasing number of white Americans with no outstanding academic or family background. Emphasis was consequently placed on education and moral values— categories in which, as George Hutchinson suggests, the black middle class regarded itself as superior not only to white lower but also white upper classes whom they deemed "morally inferior and vulgar."[79]

The black bourgeoisie was tied to working-class African Americans in an ambivalent relationship: By emphasizing strict sexual morality, the black middle class sought to define itself as distinct from the working class, yet it was at the same time inextricably linked to all African Americans and consequently had to aim at the moral elevation of the black community.[80] The black bourgeoisie's concerns about morality focused on urbanization, as the city was the most potent symbol of what a black newspaper described as the "modern world [that] has grown less religious and less serious and more materialistic and more pleasure-loving."[81] The main threat the city seemed to pose was an undermining of social control through anonymity—a quality that indeed attracted many gay men and lesbians to urban environments.[82] The groups deemed most vulnerable to the seductive, "corrupting" influences of the metropolis were working-class African Americans, women, and migrants, who were themselves the harbingers of change regarding gender, class, and morality. The focus was on migrants, who, as Frazier suggested in 1928, constituted "a group that has been uprooted from all forms of social control" and "set adrift in a world without a moral order."[83] For reasons of care, but certainly also out of fear of embarrassment, migrants, strangers to metropolitan life who arrived in Harlem on a daily basis, were specifically targeted in black newspapers that, as Chauncey observes, "lectured [them] on how to carry themselves properly on buses, what to wear, and how to behave in public."[84]

Particularly menacing to America's gender and power structure was the public change of women's roles within the first two decades of the twentieth century. Women had become visible elements in America's workforce and had successfully fought for suffrage. Furthermore, scientists had acknowledged that they were sexual beings with sexual desires. Many men feared that the "New Women" aspired to become "masculine" by breaking out of a gender category that traditionally assigned them to the space of the household and the task of motherhood, thereby threatening male dominance.[85] It needs to be noted that although fears about the role, position, and especially the sexuality of women existed, the situation within the black community was somewhat different. As Alice Dunbar-Nelson pointed out in 1927, "For sixty-three years the Negro woman has been a co-worker with the Negro man."[86] A black housewife rather than a black working woman represented a novelty in Harlem. Furthermore, because of the racial segregation of the labor market, employment for black men was scarce.[87] The white middle-class definition of masculinity with men as breadwinners was thus not applicable to the majority of black men, yet, as Kobena Mercer suggests, they "adopted certain patriarchal values such as physical strength, sexual prowess and being in control."[88] An extreme example of a different definition of masculinity in black working-class circles was the "sweetback" or "sweetman," who, instead of providing for wife and family, spent his time in clubs and speakeasies while receiving money from his female lover(s). This relationship that seems to invert a white-defined gendered economic power structure apparently did not clash with the concept of black masculinity but rather asserted it. In his novel *The Blacker the Berry* (1929), Wallace Thurman underlines what appears to be the basis of a sweetback's success: he had to "[remain] master of all situations."[89] As long as a man managed to psychologically and sexually dominate a woman, making her appreciate his presence as her lover and keeping her from realizing his actual dependence, his masculinity remained intact.[90]

For the black bourgeoisie, Tate points out, "the highly noticeable exercise of conservative Victorian gender roles was a candid sign of [its] claim on respectable citizenship."[91] Consequently, an emphasis on men's economic roles corresponded to a celebration of the cult of "True Womanhood"—a white nineteenth-century construct that defined "true" women as righteous and moreover stressed their maternal role. Opposing the lascivious stereotype of black women, the ideal African American woman was, as Anne Elizabeth Stavney observes, "constructed . . . as nonsexual, devoted, demure." Motherhood was assigned central significance—an oppressive situation focused on in Nella Larsen's novel *Quicksand* (1928).[92] The growing number of black single migrant women was therefore perceived as a threat to the black bourgeoisie's aspirations. Hazel Carby notes the emergence of "fears of a rampant and uncontrolled female sexuality . . . and fears of the assertion of an independent black female desire that has been unleashed through migration."[93] The fact that migrant women were often unmarried meant that they not only stood outside a family structure, regarded as fundamental to black America's "racial uplift," but also seemed to reject the role of motherhood. In reference to white Victorian attitudes toward sexuality, Christina Simmons suggests that "reproduction represented the payment, the sacrifice that symbolically drained female sexuality of its frightening powers"[94]—an observation that clearly seems applicable in this context. An apparent refusal to partake in reproduction seemed to be of particular significance against the backdrop of a steady decline in birth rates—a development also evident in white America.[95]

Lesbians were viewed as particularly deviant. According to bell hooks, the "prevailing assumption was that to be a lesbian was 'unnatural' because one would not be participating in child-bearing."[96] Same-sex-identified women were thus represented as the epitome of sexual and moral aberration and degeneracy—images at least partially based on medical writings from the turn of the nineteenth century. Although, as Erin Carlston asserts, "the medical discourse on homosexuality was never uniform," it seems that American readings particularly of Havelock Ellis's but also of Sigmund Freud's theories, according to which lesbianism signified a "retreat not only from adult female sexuality but from the maternal and marital roles and responsibilities conventionally attached to it," dominated popular views on homosexuality during the 1920s.[97] Although Ellis and other sexologists aimed at lifting homosexuality out of the sphere of sin and morbidity, their writings often seemed to point in the opposite direction. Ellis linked particularly female homosexuality to violence and morbidity, starting off his discussion of lesbianism with a "typical invert" who murdered her female lover.[98] This image of lesbianism was also conveyed in other sexologists' works in which homosexuality was often linked to degeneracy and disease—a depiction that triggered or supported the close association of homosexuality in general, but lesbianism in particular, with morbidity in popular discourses.[99] As old moral attitudes toward lesbianism persisted, the danger lesbians were presumed to pose to society was consequently judged to be even higher.

Concerns about female sexuality were mainly voiced in black middle-class circles, but a woman's choice of a female sexual partner was presumably equally perceived as a serious threat in a black working-class environment. In this social context, lesbians were, evoking an "inverted," masculine image, derogatorily known as "bulldaggers" or "bulldykers." Significantly, their gender role inversion seems to have met with far less favorable reactions than that of their male counterparts, the fairies. While this is not to imply a sympathetic treatment of fairies, it seems that, for instance, in newspaper reports on drag balls, cross-dressing men were favored: Fairies and their elaborate costumes were often described in detailed, long columns as "gorgeous beyond words," whereas cross-dressing women were mentioned only briefly, if at all.[100] While their costumes were certainly fundamentally different and men's clothes, as could be argued, can only to a limited extent be admired for their fabrics or colors, it is noteworthy that usually any tone of admiration is lacking in the description of cross-dressing women. They appear to be implicitly blamed for their lack of colors and elegance or, in short, their lack of femininity.

The circulation of negative images of homosexuality and of lesbianism in particular was part of the anti-vice propaganda disseminated in Harlem. The prominent black Reverend Adam Clayton Powell, for instance, launched a campaign against homosexuality, intending to either alert the black community to the "problem" or strengthen its rejection of the issue.[101] In his newspaper column, black critic and writer George Schuyler particularly criticized permissiveness, bemoaning that "the mention of [lesbianism] no longer elicits horrified comment among the sophisticated moderns."[102] According to Frazier, the black middle class "[held] strategic positions in segregated institutions and create[d] and propagate[d] the ideologies current in the Negro community."[103] Although this assessment seems to overstate the black bourgeoisie's ideological power, one can, in the case of lesbianism, assume that it at least managed to intensify existing negative images. The key to achieving this aim was the black press. Members of the black middle class owned the majority of newspapers circulating in Harlem, and, according to Frazier, these publications consequently "represent[ed] essentially the interests and outlook of the black bourgeoisie."[104]

Male homosexuality and, to a lesser extent, lesbianism, were regular topics in black newspapers during the 1920s and into the 1930s. As indicated in the aforementioned reports on drag balls, the topic of gender inversion was not always portrayed without sympathy or amusement, and some reports on social life in Harlem had a distinctly camp flavor. Yet negative images seem to have dominated the media discourse on homosexuality and particularly on lesbianism. An example of the similarity between this discourse and that of sexologists and a very explicit portrayal of lesbianism as the epitome of sickness and violence is a 1926 report of a murder story with the telling headline "Women Rivals For Affection of Another Woman Battle With Knives, and One Has Head Almost Severed From Body."[105] Emphasizing the link between the murder and lesbianism, the main suspect is described as a woman "Crazed with gin and a wild and unnatural infatuation for another woman."[106] Another piece of "information" can be gathered from the article: "it is said that no men had attended the affair."[107] This statement gains in significance considering that homosocial gatherings increasingly began to be looked on with suspicion from the turn of the century as heterosexual socializing gradually became the norm. The all-female nature of the gathering described in the article was therefore strongly indicative of the "lesbian" character of the party and furthermore hinted at the popular perception of lesbians as "man-haters."[108]

The most significant threat lesbians posed to society and womanhood was perceived to be their "intention" to convert other women. This alleged trait, which, as is discussed later, also existed concerning gay men, was taken up in white and black newspapers: "This group [of masculine women] preys upon inexperienced girls. Its members tempt the girls with clothing, marihuana and liquor and if successful add their victims to the group."[109] Thurman plays on the stereotype of the preying older lesbian woman in *The Blacker the Berry*, thereby ridiculing, however, what could be termed "uplift" housing projects, which, as Carby points out, were to protect single migrant women's sexual "purity." Searching for a new room, the novel's black protagonist, Emma Lou, meets a landlady, a "spinster type,"[110] who runs a boarding house for women. Thurman nowhere explicitly mentions lesbianism, yet it is evident that the older woman, who "insisted upon sitting down beside her" and "placed her hand on Emma Lou's knee, then finally put her arm around her waist," displays sexual interest in Emma Lou.[111] Emma Lou rejects the woman's passes, but the house's other young female inhabitants, who significantly "have parties among [them]selves" instead of socializing with men, appear to have fallen victim to her wiles.[112]

Not only girls or young women but also boys were seen as potential targets for older "perverts." Although media coverage of sexual child abuse particularly by older men peaked only from the 1930s, this topic had already surfaced in newspaper reports during the 1920s. A 1926 *New York Amsterdam News* article with the headline "Uncle Held for Special Sessions Charged with Corrupting Boy's Morals" reports the case of a boy forced to indulge in an "unnatural practice" and found "in a dangerous condition."[113] Behind the fear of male and female "homosexuals" as abusers and corrupters of youth was not only the aim to "protect" young people; there was also the perception that, fitting the age of mass culture, the "third sex is flooding America" and that "Homo-sexuality and sex-perversion among women . . . has grown into one of the most horrible, debassing [*sic*], alarming and damning vices of present day civilization . . . [and] is increasing day by day."[114]

Discussions surrounding the topic of homosexuality in newspapers evidence a curious blend of moral and medical discourses. In the course of the wider dissemination of medical findings about homosexuality, distortions and simplifications of theories were commonplace. In 1930, the *Baltimore Afro-American* published an article titled "Are Pansies People?" which reported that "experiments [with hens] had proved that a change in the activity of certain sex glands could change the sex," and that "the key to this transformation . . . is as much physical as it is mental."[115] But what did this mean? How and why could people be "inverted" into "fairies," "bulldaggers," or what was called the "third sex"? Many drew their own conclusions, thereby neglecting sexologists' theories regarding the congenital nature of homosexuality: According to the Reverend Powell, "much of the prevalence of these vicious habits is due to contact and association and not to inherent degeneracy."[116] The view of homosexuality as a communicable disease was convenient, as it not only offered the option of "redemption" but also seemed to account for what was perceived as an increase in the number of gay men and lesbians. This reasoning, however, neglected the possibility that not so much the number but rather the visibility of gay men and lesbians had increased. It seems that, similar to venereal disease, which was increasingly seen as a medical rather than a moral issue, homosexuality came to be regarded as a contaminating illness.[117] This interpretation of homosexuality as a health and contamination issue might have struck a chord in Harlem, where the majority of inhabitants lived in congested housing and where infant mortality and deaths from tuberculosis by far exceeded the average rate for New York.[118]

Explanations of white and black Americans accounting for the potential source of contamination varied. Publicized comments convey the impression that the formerly "pure" United States were "infected" in two stages. White Americans located the origin of homosexuality in Europe—an idea which coincided with contemporary xenophobia. European immigrants "swamped" the country, and, as seems to have been argued, imported "European" diseases.[119] A 1932 *Brevities* article—sections of this piece were reprinted in a black newspaper, indicating a shared view on the issue—conveys the sense of danger felt regarding immigration and questions of sexuality. It describes the alleged threat homosexuality posed to the United States, suggesting that drag balls originated in Europe. Americans who had traveled to Europe "swore that men passed themselves off as women and women aped the manners of men so well that they even made love to other females."[120] Following this reasoning, homosexuality originated in "decadent" Europe. As the article explained, "[Americans] did not believe them. They were sure that nothing existed in their country which was at all comparable,"[121] yet America had apparently already been "contaminated." In a different interpretation of how the United States "contracted" homosexuality, Europe was also seen as the source. According to the COF, "American boys undoubtedly became familiar with perverse practices while in France."[122] Although other theories were considered, a clear link was established between a recorded "increase in perversion" and the return of American soldiers from Europe.[123]

Comments voiced by African Americans about the spread of contagion to black America seem to outline a second stage in the overall contamination of the United States. Just as white America assumed that the country had been innocent before Europe "infected" it, it was argued that nothing initially linked Harlemites to homosexuality. While a direct connection to Europe may have been implied, it seems that white America was primarily pointed at. James Weldon Johnson, one of the leading Renaissance intellectuals, suspected that "sex has gone to the white man's head" and claimed that "Sex with us is, in a large measure, still in the lusty, wholesome stage."[124] The view of African Americans as "healthy" and "natural" corresponds to primitivist notions that prompted white visitors to go to Harlem: African Americans purportedly possessed a "pristine superiority of spirit and character invulnerable to the contaminating decadence of Western civilization."[125] Against the backdrop of an increasing stream of visitors, African Americans increasingly deemed Harlem's existence as a "wholesome" community threatened. It was proposed that white Americans contaminated the black community—not only with homosexuality but also with other "vices." As the majority of Harlem's clubs were owned by whites and attracted white visitors, it was argued that "the greater part of Harlem's vice is not indigenous, but is forced upon the community by outsiders."[126] Harlem, it was claimed, was thus in the process of being sexually undermined: White men came to have sex with black women, thereby turning them into prostitutes; black men were seduced by white prostitutes working in Harlem; and white gay men and lesbians came to Harlem to "convert" Harlemites.

As evident in black newspapers, the "Queer People of Greenwich Village" were identified as the source of contamination.[127] Another newspaper article, which threateningly asked, "Will the Plague Spread?" reiterates this argument: "Greenwich Village is bad enough for New York to stomach but now the poison has spread and Harlem is infected."[128] The connection between the occurrence of homosexuality in Harlem and the presence of Villagers was also made in other articles, one of which claimed that "some of the most notoriously degenerate white men in the city" were present at Harlem's drag balls and that "judges were imported from Greenwich Village especially for this occasion."[129] By blaming "perverts" from the Village, the black bourgeoisie tried to achieve several aims: to insist on the state of innocence of the black community, display its moral superiority over white Americans, and establish a level on which it was linked with its white moralist counterparts who also rejected Village bohemians. Yet while Villagers were cast as villains, no reports in black papers about arrests of white Americans for indecent disorderly conduct seem to exist—a fact that can be attributed to the lack of power of Harlem's anti-vice forces. This meant that black lesbians but, judging from newspaper reports, particularly black same-sex-interested men—predominantly in the generally recognized form of "inverts"—were left as targets for anti-vice campaigners.[130]

Because of the police's and anti-vice movements' neglect of Harlem, the bourgeoisie, frequently supported by clergymen, attempted to supervise morality. Ministers warned their congregations about the dangers of "vice" and "crime," including homosexuality, and actively sought police cooperation to "clean up the city."[131] At times such attempts were successful: Owing to the efforts of the Reverend Hightower in Pittsburgh, "twenty-five Federal prohibition agents swept through the Hill district twice within six hours and raided 23 alleged moonshine dives."[132] Powell's aforementioned 1929 campaign in Harlem, which focused on sexual issues, yielded a similar result. Harlemites also arranged anti-vice crusades of their own and managed to chalk up successes. In one case, complaints prompted a police raid on a club that led to the arrest of "more than 30 men dressed as women."[133] However, cases like these were, particularly due to the reluctance of white policing agencies, probably rare. In the above-mentioned example, Harlemites had to file numerous formal complaints to prompt the magistrate to take action. The Reverend Hightower, as was claimed, encountered even greater obstacles: "Officials responded [to his complaints] by flashing warrants against him and warned him to keep quiet and cease his efforts to clean up Pittsburgh."[134]

Insisting on respectability, the black bourgeoisie managed to exert pressure on the black community. It was thus best to evade policing attempts and gossip by either behaving "decently" or by at least publicly displaying a respectable image in which marriage played a central role. Faderman suggests that a number of marriages during the 1920s were "front marriages,"[135] yet the situation could be more complicated if one of the parties involved in a marriage was unaware of the other's same-sex desire. This was apparently the case with Renaissance writer Cullen, who got married, embarked on what one might call a honeymoon with his intimate friend Harold Jackman, and shortly afterward divorced his wife. Cullen, who fulfilled most of the black bourgeoisie's expectations, got away with relatively few remarks about his failed marriage, since, as Lewis points out, "Harlem always ignored or forgave everything of its best and brightest."[136] Thurman, another same-sex-interested Renaissance writer, encountered greater difficulties. Similar to Cullen, he got married, a separation following shortly afterward. But his wife, Louise Thompson, then blackmailed Thurman, threatening to disseminate the information that he had once been arrested for soliciting gay sex. The rumors about his sexuality upset Thurman, who deplored "with what relish a certain group of Negroes in Harlem received and relayed the news that I was a homo. No evidence is needed of course beyond the initial rumor. Such is life."[137] One can suspect that Thurman was a more likely target for gossip than Cullen, as he in terms of his writing and lifestyle did not fulfill the black bourgeoisie's expectations. Although marriage obviously could not prove a "normal" sexual status in Cullen's case (there were, as Langston Hughes reported, "a lot of amusing jokes that went around Harlem at wedding time"[138]), it served as a fundamental symbol of respectability.

To some extent, male same-sex-interested Renaissance artists enjoyed a greater degree of freedom than other Harlemites who desired members of the same sex. They could partake in all aspects of Harlem's gay world—the lower-class world with speakeasies and buffet flats, the bohemian parties and studio meetings—and had their own gay networks offering protection, intimacy, and support. As evident in their correspondence, however, they never felt completely safe faced with vigilant black moral forces demanding performances of respectability in what Locke generally described as a "dangerous environment."[139] Same-sex-interested female Renaissance writers were in an overall less privileged position. Gloria Hull points to the existence of black lesbian circles, yet while these could offer support, they lacked the powerful presence of Renaissance "stars"—usually crowned by predominantly male critics and Renaissance intellectuals—and Renaissance leaders who could offer personal advice and boost careers. More significantly, same-sex-interested female authors such as Angelina Weld Grimké and Georgia Douglas Johnson were forced to guard their reputation and were furthermore geographically restricted. They were thus often unable to move to the center of Harlem Renaissance activities, as they were "likely to be tied to place via husbands, children, familial responsibilities, parental prohibitions, lack of fresh opportunities or the spirit of adventure."[140] It seems true that indiscretions on the part of male Renaissance artists were usually overlooked by the guardians of Harlem's morality if general standards of decency were adhered to —their homosexual inclinations were generally treated as "open secrets."[141] The black bourgeoisie was not interested in scandals and moreover hoped that Renaissance artists could accelerate the integration of black Americans into white America.[142] Yet although it may seem as if same-sex-interested Renaissance writers led a largely carefree existence, they, as shown in the next chapter, frequently encountered conflicts regarding their literary works.

TWO

Writing in the Harlem Renaissance: The Burden of Representation and Sexual Dissidence

While their elevated social position and the relatively lax policing of Harlem allowed especially male same-sex-interested Harlem Renaissance artists what looks like a rather unrestrained lifestyle, their works were subject to close scrutiny as they were presented publicly. In this context, the private–public dichotomy does not merely signify the distinction between "within the privacy of home" and "outside home" but has the extended meaning of "within the black community (of Harlem)"/"before a white audience." Writing conditions for African Americans in the 1920s and early 1930s need to be examined within the framework of the Harlem Renaissance because they were largely determined by the definition of a "movement" and its specific "aims," undertaken by a group of African American intellectuals. They were furthermore shaped by publishers, patrons, the reading public, other contemporary writers, and critics—groups that were neither racially nor politically homogenous and that often had overlapping interests.

CREATING THE HARLEM RENAISSANCE

Leading Renaissance figures were keen to point out that there had been African American literary figures like Phillis Wheatley, Charles W. Chesnutt, and Paul Laurence Dunbar prior to the Harlem Renaissance. By presenting these "creative workmen" as "pioneers and path-breakers in the cultural development and recognition of the Negro in the arts," Renaissance leaders evoked a linear tradition of black literature.[1] Through the anthology *The Book of American Negro Poetry* (1922), James Weldon Johnson made this literary tradition visible to readers, linking the older and the younger generation of black writers.[2] The earlier African American writers were, however, individual achievers whose works failed to make a significant impact on America's literary scene. This was to change fundamentally with the advent of the Harlem Renaissance. Crucial to the Renaissance's construction as a literary and artistic movement was a group of intellectuals who were instrumental in defining its aims and in guiding, supporting, and promoting its protagonists. An enumeration of the group's key figures—W.E.B. Du Bois, James Weldon Johnson, Charles S. Johnson, Walter White, and Alain Locke—exposes the movement's predominantly male character. There were, however, also important female Renaissance figures. Writer Georgia Douglas Johnson was particularly supportive of young male and female writers and stands out as an organizer of literary soirées, but she did not significantly shape the character of the Renaissance in terms of defining and leading it.[3] Jessie Fauset serves as another example, as she was not only a prolific writer but moreover held a key editorial position at *The Crisis* during the early Renaissance years. Her success in this position is indicated in Hughes's comment that she, alongside Charles S. Johnson and Alain Locke, "midwifed the so-called New Negro literature into being."[4] Yet since she lacked extensive contacts with publishers, editors, and sponsors and was furthermore subordinate to more powerful male figures like Du Bois, she cannot be counted among the Renaissance leaders.

With the exception of Locke, the leading promoters of the Renaissance were affiliated with one of the two leading African American reformist groups. Du Bois served as director of publicity and research for the National Association for the Advancement of Colored People (NAACP), whose magazine *The Crisis* he edited. James Weldon Johnson was the association's field secretary; White, its assistant executive secretary; and Charles S. Johnson was editor of *Opportunity*, the monthly publication of the National Urban League (NUL). These two periodicals contributed significantly to the definition, interpretation, and development of the Harlem Renaissance. The notion of a movement in African American arts and letters was brought to the fore explicitly in *The Crisis* with Du Bois's 1920 announcement that "A renaissance of American Negro literature is due. . . ."[5] One of the first initiatives to give concrete public expression to the burgeoning literary activities of African Americans was the organization of the Civic Club Dinner in 1924, during which aspiring writers were formally introduced as a group to white publishers, intellectuals, writers, and editors.[6] Against the backdrop of an increase in publishing activities by African Americans after World War I, the Renaissance promoters' initiative seemed sensible. Their vision of a movement was shared by writers like Langston Hughes, who wrote to Locke in 1923: "You are right that we have enough talent now to begin a movement."[7] By 1924, several African American writers already met "with some degree of regularity, to talk informally about 'books and things.' "[8]

By offering space in their magazines and reviewing writers' work, Renaissance leaders promoted young black artists and writers. Their attempts to create a market were apparently so successful that, as Locke commented, "[t]he demand as far as the artistic material already available in drama, music, painting and the decorative arts is even now outstripping the supply of competent interpreters and producers. . . ."[9] Given its freshly gained status as "Negro capital" and its location within Manhattan, the intellectual as well as the publishing center of the United States, Harlem seemed suitable as the movement's focal gathering place. Some writers, like Hughes, came to Harlem on their own initiative, while others were encouraged to move there or, as in the case of McKay, who lived outside the United States during much of the Renaissance, to return to Harlem with the promise that "unlimited opportunity" awaited them.[10] Once writers had settled down, Renaissance entrepreneurs, along with influential white figures like novelist Carl Van Vechten, served as connecting links to publishers, critics, and magazine editors. They could also offer support concerning financial matters—for instance, by assisting writers in their search for employment. More significant for the development of the movement, however, was the insight that black artists' "contributions [to art, literature, and life] demand incentives."[11] Starting in 1925, literary and artistic contests designed to encourage young black artists and the production of artistic material on the subject of African American life were organized. Competitions were, though on a modest level, financially rewarding and could furthermore boost careers, as winning entries were published in *The Crisis* and *Opportunity*.

Renaissance promoters' ambitions and values could, however, prove problematic. This was the case with Du Bois, who, apparently because of his growing disillusionment with the Renaissance, increasingly restricted competition rules and selected works without consulting other judges, thereby measuring material solely by his rather genteel aesthetic standards.[12] Personal interests also played a role regarding the securing of usually white financial sponsors for younger writers. Locke, for instance, did not only look for potential patrons but was himself the protégé of elderly white sponsor Charlotte Mason, for whom he fulfilled the role of talent scout.[13] Charles Scruggs points out that Locke "became uncharitable to writers he felt had betrayed him"[14] and let personal preferences influence his proposals to Mason. Gloria Hull suggests, moreover, that Locke "behaved misogynistically and actively favored men."[15] Locke, however, promoted Zora Neale Hurston and suggested her name to Mason. He nevertheless might, as Hull puts it, have let "bedroom politics" affect his decisions; his possibly sexual relationship with Hughes might have influenced his decision to introduce him to Mason.[16] However, caution must be exercised when linking Locke's discriminatory politics to misogyny and his sexual preference for men. While Hull suggests that Richard Bruce Nugent enjoyed privileges since he belonged to Locke's gay network, Nugent gives a different account, indicating that negative aspects of "bedroom politics" perhaps also applied to men. According to Nugent, Locke displayed sexual interest in him: "I was in Locke's house. . . . I came into the room where he was [and] he was lying there [and] said, 'You can do whatever you like.' I was shocked. He was the professor of philosophy. . . . I did indeed do what I liked, which was to leave."[17] In hindsight, Nugent interpreted this scene as having earned him Locke's malevolence, especially as Mason later disclosed that Locke explicitly advised her not to sponsor him.[18] Although Nugent's assertions cannot be verified and Locke's decision might have rested solely on aesthetic preferences, this possibility is worth considering. It must be added that not only access to sponsorship through patrons could prove problematic. As the cases of Hughes and Hurston indicate, patronage could involve sponsors' attempts to influence and restrict Renaissance writers' creative works.[19]

ART AND AIMS

While the NAACP and NUL initially concentrated on social, economic, and political issues, their aforementioned officials sponsored, or, as might be said, created the Harlem Renaissance, opting for "the art approach to the Negro problem"[20] by integrating art into the organizations' goal of racial advancement. In 1922, Du Bois disclosed general reasons for this novel approach: "We Negroes have gone fast forward in economic development, in political and social agitation; and we are likely to forget that the great mission of the Negro to America and the modern world is the development of Art and the appreciation of the Beautiful."[21] Cultural production was regarded as a field African Americans had not entered to a sufficient degree. Chances for success in this area were assessed optimistically in the belief that "the fields of art and letters are, fortunately, ones which hold no racial limitations for Negroes."[22] The decision to promote art and specifically literature reflects a trend in the United States, as the 1920s saw a steep increase in the country's general literary output.[23] The literary scene changed decisively with the rise of new publishing companies like Alfred A. Knopf and Harcourt, Brace & Co., who were willing to take risks and publish material ranging from H. L. Mencken's essays to Sigmund Freud's studies in the field of psychoanalysis.[24] Additionally, periodicals like the *Liberator* and the *New Republic* offered a variety of material, from political discussion to poetry and book reviews. Publishers and magazine editors, who increasingly sponsored and emphasized American as opposed to Anglocentric culture and literature, were consequently inclined to consider works by African Americans.[25]

Publishers' interest in black writers' works was linked to an increased curiosity about African Americans in general and Harlem in particular. Among white Americans, Renaissance leaders detected "a healthy hunger for more information—a demand for a new interpretation of characters long and admittedly misunderstood."[26] The focus was not, however, exclusively on white readers. A black readership was targeted with schemes like *The Crisis*'s "Buy a Book" campaign.[27] Comments in numerous black publications, however, indicate that black readers displayed no sustained interest in Renaissance works, thereby representing mainly an "imagined" audience.[28] It therefore is not surprising that Renaissance leaders in the first instance seemed to target the white section of what was termed Renaissance writers' "double audience," defining art largely as a "vehicle for recognition."[29]

The mere participation of African Americans in the field of cultural production had an impact on white America, affecting and challenging basic assumptions about African Americans' intellectual inferiority. Although writing during the Harlem Renaissance no longer meant proving one's humanity, as it had for earlier black writers, African Americans who displayed writing skills still managed to astonish white critics and readers. Renaissance leaders, however, had greater aspirations and consequently rejected the notion of a "double standard of competence"[30] applied to black writers, aiming at the creation of art that could compete on equal terms with that of white authors. This target was set because, as James Weldon Johnson put it, "no people that has produced great literature and art has ever been looked upon by the world as distinctly inferior."[31] By adhering to "universally" acknowledged artistic standards, he proposed, African Americans' cultural contributions would stand out because they possessed "the emotional endowment, the originality and artistic conception"[32] American culture needed.

The conclusion Renaissance entrepreneurs wanted white America to draw was that African Americans' cultural contributions were essential for the nation. This proposition was advanced by means of what Jonathan Dollimore in his study on sexual dissidence terms a strategy of *double affirmation* that serves not only to validate but also to posit as superior what is generally deemed nonexistent or inferior by dominant society.[33] James Weldon Johnson thus claimed that not only could the African American contribute to American art but that he was "the creator of the only things artistic that have yet sprung from American soil and been universally acknowledged as distinctive American products."[34] Without the inclusion of cultural contributions by African Americans, there would be no basis for a national art and culture—a promising proposition particularly in light of the more general redefinition of the body of American culture. The aim was to firmly inscribe African Americans into America's artistic scene and, more significantly, into the American nation. Again, a double affirmation can be observed: According to Charles S. Johnson, black Americans were not only as American as white Americans, but "With the exceptions of the Indian and the Appalachian Mountaineer, no man in America is so entirely native to the soil [as the African American]."[35] African Americans were thus authenticated as "original" Americans, deserving a say not only in the nation's artistic but also in its social and political spheres. Claims for a positioning of African Americans in the American nation have been interpreted by, for instance, Houston Baker as conscious manipulations by Renaissance leaders who actually followed a black nationalist agenda. It seems, however, that unlike Marcus Garvey, who had won the support of large masses of America's black population with his back-to-Africa movement, Renaissance entrepreneurs saw the future of African Americans in integration and the attainment of "full and unlimited American citizenship."[36]

THE POLITICS OF REPRESENTATION

As Walter White pointed out, literary representations of African Americans were traditionally white-dominated:

> For many years the only fictional treatment of the Negro that has gained any wide circulation has been that in which we are painted either as good old humble servants or as comedians or as degenerate brutes. The average American has formed his ideas of us through reading Thomas Dixon or Octavus Roy Cohen or Irvin Cobb.[37]

The Harlem Renaissance was thus interpreted as "an opportunity . . . for Negroes themselves to replace their out-worn representations in fiction faithfully."[38] Black writers were to participate in what was recognized as the politically significant arena of representations, thereby contesting white dominance and disrupting what Richard Dyer describes as "the process of [a minority's] oppression, marginalization or subordination."[39] There was accord that an elite, the so-called Talented Tenth, was to shoulder the task of representing African Americans. According to Locke, "the black masses [should be] going gradually forward under the leadership of a recognized and representative and responsible élite"[40] that was to interact with its white American counterpart. This contact was to lead to an exchange of ideas on an elite level and eventually to a transformation of attitudes toward all African Americans.[41] Renaissance writers were thus placed in a highly responsible position that implied a view of their creative work as not only individual but also racial achievements.[42]

Opinions about the nature of representations to be created by Renaissance artists varied widely. A more genteel group that included Du Bois and many other prominent black critics favored the production of art that would facilitate recognition through its propagandistic power. The reaction of white readers was thereby given priority over aesthetic considerations—which were, however, not totally neglected. A more liberal camp, which included James Weldon Johnson, Charles S. Johnson, and Locke, espoused what George Hutchinson terms a "pragmatic aesthetic theory"[43]—the judging of art by its aesthetic merit, but simultaneously an aiming at appraisal and recognition by white Americans. At the core of the debate was the question of what was to be defined as "art." Du Bois once famously asserted that "all Art is propaganda and ever must be," adding that he "[did] not care a damn for any art that is not used for propaganda."[44] Locke and the two Johnsons strongly opposed this stance. Although the views of the Johnsons were not identical, it seems that both rejected an equation of art and propaganda yet viewed propaganda as a complementary element.[45] Locke, who became Du

Bois's direct opponent, rejected propaganda and was satisfied that African American writers had "passed from poeticized propaganda and didactic sentiment to truly spontaneous and relaxed lyricism."[46]

This fundamental disagreement is also evident in the two camps' politics of representation. Locke and the two Johnsons largely abstained from prescribing "representative" material, convinced that "the Negro today wishes to be known for what he is, even in his faults and shortcomings."[47] Tolerance or approval were therefore usually displayed toward writers who, according to Locke, were "thoroughly modern, some of them ultra-modern" and in "alignment with contemporary artistic thought, mood and style."[48] At this point, it is necessary to briefly discuss the term modernism as applicable to the Harlem Renaissance. Hutchinson points out that the fact that most Harlem Renaissance protagonists "considered themselves participants in, and the potential vanguard of, an American modernist movement"[49] seems at odds with dominant Eurocentric definitions of modernism as white, Western, and elitist, defined by such figures as T. S. Eliot. Several critics have suggested that the concept of modernism needs to be revised, if not redefined, to encompass nonwhite and non-elitist experiences.[50] Hutchinson suggests that in contrast to a "high modernism" which, because of its separation of the personal and the social, was not feasible as a means for empowerment, some Harlem Renaissance writers embraced a "low modernism." They opted for "different modes of expressive modernity," focusing on realism and naturalism, which, particularly owing to these writers' subject matter, can be viewed as "modern."[51] This does not mean, however, that avant-gardist literary forms, evident in, for instance, Nugent's stream-of-consciousness piece "Smoke, Lilies and Jade" (1926),[52] did not figure in Renaissance writing.

A turn from traditional romanticism toward realism could be a positive development, as noted by Charles S. Johnson, who praised Hughes's work as "without doubt the finest expression of this new Negro poetry," adding that "Like Sandburg he has shocked polite circles by daring to search for beauty in things too commonplace for dignity and exaltation."[53] Despite the emphasis on artistic freedom within the liberal group of Renaissance intellectuals, the writers' task of representation was never forgotten, and tolerance was consequently limited. Naturalism and realism were accepted, while other literary forms, such as an 1890s' decadent style, were—particularly by Locke— rejected as insincere. Renaissance writers were reminded of the significance of their task that did not allow for individualism or an "art for art's sake" approach, and neglect or a rejection of the representational task was branded "exhibitionist."[54]

Du Bois and other more genteel critics viewed the younger Renaissance writers' interest in literary modernism as an unwillingness "to conform to any academic standards in the matter of construction, expression or finish."[55] It seems that it was believed that the literary form chosen had to be "inoffensive" and impressive in terms of its display of a mastery of "white" traditional form to deliver a "positive" message to a white American mainstream. As Wallace Thurman pointed out, these black critics resembled "those American whites who protest against the literary upheavals of a Dreiser, an Anderson, or a Sandburg."[56] There was agreement among genteel critics that "This is called the age of realism or naturalism in literature, and the Negro is not ready for it."[57] Many critics expected Renaissance writers to create "epical, heroic, romantic literature."[58] To achieve this type of work, as noted black literary critic Benjamin Brawley, speaking for other genteel critics, stated, "we commend [Alfred Tennyson's] example to the young writers of the Negro race."[59]

Statements regarding formal aspects constituted only a small part of reviews, however; far greater attention was paid to the question of "representative" subject matter. This emphasis was based on the conviction that white readers would regard literature by African Americans as "information" about the "race"—an assumption which seems partially justified in light of a white reviewer's description of Claude McKay's novel *Home to Harlem* (1928) as "not so much a novel as a social document about a race that few of us have tried to understand."[60] The genteel group therefore championed literary works which reflected what Jack Moore in the context of discussing Du Bois describes as a truth that "had to be carefully modeled to further a positive view of black life and attack racism."[61] Although Du Bois conceded that "[w]e are seriously crippling Negro art and literature by refusing to contemplate any but handsome heroes, unblemished heroines and flawless defenders,"[62] he preferred the portrayal of middle-class or "moral" characters. Interestingly, the usually conflicting agendas of the black bourgeoisie and Garvey's camp converged at this point. Both groups, it seems, desired writers to depict "what the race hopes and aspires to," convinced that "this better side is just what the average Negro wishes to read about."[63] Seeking a "full and positive image of black life"[64] in Renaissance art and literature, many black critics favored a covering up of negative aspects of black lives. It was thus deplored that articles on contested issues, such as intraracial conflicts, were published in white magazines: "[These] contributions would have served their purpose better if they had been published in Negro magazines" instead of being "paraded before a white reading public."[65] Renaissance entrepreneurs' interpretations of the movement clearly varied widely, yet by agreeing on the representative role and responsibility of Renaissance writers, they collectively placed a burden of representation on writers' shoulders.

THE BURDEN OF REPRESENTATION: WRITERS' POSITIONS AND CRITICS' RESPONSES

The construction of a burden of representation had profound implications for individual Renaissance artists and their literary works. There was an interplay between critics' attacks, which sometimes assumed the character of policing efforts, the identification of individual artists with the Harlem Renaissance, their attitude toward the task of representation, and the works they created. Before turning to the younger and male generation of writers on which this study focuses, the positioning of older writers and the majority of female authors should be addressed. Cary Wintz remarks that "the lines between the various types of participants [in the Harlem Renaissance] were not clearly drawn," and that a number of older writers like James Weldon Johnson and Du Bois often simultaneously acted as promoters, writers, and critics.[66] Their allegiance to the movement and acceptance of the task of representation is not surprising. In the case of a number of female Renaissance figures like Fauset and Nella Larsen, an identification with the movement and acceptance of the responsibility of representation seems similarly evident. Although their works frequently rise above the middle-class respectability often ascribed to them, their dissidence regarding, for instance, the portrayal of black female sexuality, usually remained hidden "behind the safe and protective covers of traditional narrative subjects and conventions," as they were forced to live up to higher standards of respectability than were their male counterparts.[67]

In the group of writers including McKay, Nugent, Hughes, and Cullen, attitudes ranged from an identification with the movement and acceptance of the burden of representation to a straightforward rejection of the Renaissance. The writer standing out in this group is Cullen, whose use of traditional poetic forms was lauded and who, as Steven Watson comments, "was a figurehead New Negro, playing strictly by the rules and exemplifying . . . the racial and moral values of the Talented Tenth."[68] Demonstrating acceptance of the task of representation, Cullen commented that "we who have been given voices must not remain apart from our obligation."[69] He thus intended to contribute to a project that set out to "improve race relations"[70] through the creation of art. Cullen generally managed to navigate smoothly between the two groups of black critics and Renaissance leaders. He seemed close to Du Bois, stating that "whether they relish the situation or not, Negroes should be concerned with making good impressions."[71] Additionally affirming his willingness to portray literary "types that are truly representative,"[72] Cullen secured his predominantly positive reception by black genteel critics. He did not, however, share this group's heavy reliance on propaganda. His insistence on aesthetic standards endeared him to Locke, yet Cullen found some of Locke's aesthetic proposals problematic. Believing that literary merit should have priority over the factor of race, Cullen voiced "serious doubts" about Locke's proposal that "the present-day Negro poet regards his racial heritage as a more precious endowment than his own personal genius."[73] He insisted that he wanted to be measured solely by artistic standards, irrespective of the factor of race.[74] Yet despite such conflicts, Cullen appeared to be a model Renaissance artist, displaying control, sincerity, and an ever-present consciousness of the black writer's task.

For the other three writers, an identification with the Renaissance, and with it an acceptance of the burden of representation, was more problematic, leading to encounters with what Henry Louis Gates terms the "thoughtpolice"[75]—in a Harlem Renaissance context, those groups that focused on the issue of representation. Nugent, who published only few works, apparently never commented on or displayed any kind of identification with the movement. McKay, in contrast, was vocal in his refusal to identify with a black cultural movement. Spending most Renaissance years in Europe and North Africa, he mainly relied on letters to judge developments in Harlem. What he read convinced him not to get closely involved with any of the Renaissance factions, for he had "settled down on the individualistic wagon and [was] not going to be used as brushwood for any of the selfish propaganda fire of *any* of the gangs."[76] He not only rejected being claimed as a Renaissance writer but, being West Indian, moreover denied membership in an American-defined "Negro society."[77] Hughes shared McKay's individualistic notions, stating in 1927: "I do not pretend . . . that I officially represent anybody or anything other than myself."[78] He never ceased to believe, however, that advantages for black Americans could be achieved through a black cultural movement; but, as he stated retrospectively and in accordance with McKay, he could not believe that "the New Negro would lead a new life from then on in green pastures of tolerance created by Countee Cullen, Ethel Waters, Claude McKay, Duke Ellington, Bojangles, and Alain Locke."[79]

In an effort spearheaded by Wallace Thurman, who arrived in Harlem in 1925, several artists, including Nugent, Hughes, Aaron Douglas, and Zora Neale Hurston, formed the provocatively named Niggeratti. They claimed to stage a "second renaissance" in which the Renaissance leaders' "New Negro" was replaced by what Hughes described as "a brand new nigger."[80] Owing to his physical absence from Harlem, McKay did not have the opportunity to join this formation, but he to some extent shared its views.[81] Instead of accepting a task of representation, the Niggeratti proclaimed that they were "primarily and intensely devoted to art," and McKay commented that black writers should create works that "will hold ground besides the very highest white standard."[82] Claiming to digress from what they presented as the black bourgeoisie's and Renaissance leaders' focus on a white audience, the Niggeratti insisted that their creations would interpret black Americans to themselves. The aim of black writers therefore had to be, as Thurman stated in his editorial for the short-lived magazine *Harlem* (1928), to

> impress upon the literate members of the thirteen million Negroes in the United States the necessity of . . . reading the newer Negro authors, . . . the necessity of sublimating their inferiority complex and their extreme race sensitiveness and putting the energy, which they have hitherto used in moaning and groaning, into more concrete fields of action.[83]

In spite of their emphasis on individuality, this statement indicates that the Niggeratti to an extent accepted responsibility toward black Americans. As Thurman commented in a 1927 interview, the younger writers were aware that they were "gaining recognition not only for [themselves] but also for [their] race"—a realization that linked them with Renaissance leaders of both camps.[84] The Niggeratti were unwilling, however, to accept restrictions of their creative freedom and insisted that "characters are characters—not the whole Negro race."[85]

Given this stance, conflicts between these younger writers and Renaissance entrepreneurs, as well as black critics, seemed inevitable. Even encounters with the more liberal camp of black critics and Renaissance leaders could, in case of an opposition to or neglect of the task of representation, have negative consequences for writers. Occasionally, Renaissance leaders could influence editorial matters. Editing contributions for his anthology *The New Negro*, Locke, for instance, changed the title of a poem by McKay because, as described by Scruggs, it otherwise "did not fit his own aesthetic program for the Harlem Renaissance."[86] Particularly during the disillusioned final years of the Renaissance, writers were reprimanded if their works failed to meet Renaissance leaders' expectations. Thurman, as the leading figure of the Niggeratti, was specifically targeted by Locke, who complained that "his novels turn out to be prolonged orgies of exhibitionism."[87]

Clashes with the larger group of genteel black critics were more frequent and violent. Receiving a mainly sympathetic response to his first volume of poetry *The Weary Blues* (1926), Langston Hughes had to endure predominantly harsh reviews from the black press for his subsequent work. As Thurman sarcastically commented, black critics were initially

> too thrilled at the novelty of having a poet who could gain the attention of a white publisher to pay much attention to what he wrote. Quietly, and privately, however certain of them began deploring the author's jazz predilections, his unconventional poetic forms, and his preoccupation with the proletariat.[88]

With Hughes' second poetry volume, *Fine Clothes to the Jew* (1927), the boundaries of what many regarded as tolerable literary expression were obviously crossed. As Hughes reported, "Colored critics raged [the book] to death."[89] Many critics shared J. A. Rogers's view that Hughes' poems were "Trash," and furthermore regarded them as "unsanitary, insipid and repulsing."[90] Hughes's subsequent publication, the novel *Not Without Laughter* (1931), also encountered moral criticism, with Brawley refusing to even review the book on grounds of "the very unsavory tone of individual passages."[91] Thurman and McKay experienced a similar barrage of criticism: Thurman's novel *Infants of the Spring* (1932) was dismissed as a "hodgepodge of punk literature," and in a review of McKay's novel *Home to Harlem* (1928), Du Bois declared that it "for the most part nauseates me, and after the dirtier parts of its filth I feel distinctly like taking a bath."[92]

Another critic complained about McKay's "sordid imagination," and Marcus Garvey stated in his front-page headline: " 'Home to Harlem,' Claude McKay's Damaging Book, Should Earn Wholesale Condemnation of Negroes."[93]

When dismissive reviews are examined closely, a pattern stands out: Writers were accused of rejecting their task of representation as a consequence of giving in to the seductions of white America. It seems that Renaissance writers were criticized for pandering to the "wrong," for example exoticist type of white audience; they should have instead focused on a white audience that would ideally concentrate on literary craftsmanship. Almost symbolizing exoticism in 1920s Harlem, Van Vechten and his novel *Nigger Heaven* constituted repeated points of reference for critics. Younger Renaissance writers were frequently termed "Van Vechtenites" and were, like Van Vechten, believed to "[seek] to express all of Harlem life in its cabarets."[94] To some extent, this view was informed by white Americans' "discovery" of Harlem, as it was feared that this development would perpetuate the stereotyping of black Americans. Renaissance promoters seemed ambiguous about white Americans' interest in the Harlem Renaissance: While channeling their efforts into raising awareness of a black literary movement, they were concerned about the Renaissance's development into a "fad to be discarded in a few seasons."[95]

On the one hand, many black critics suspected corruption of black writers on an ideological level. Renaissance writers were claimed to be seduced into primitivism and exoticism by white artists and intellectuals who incited them to "hold up [their] own race to ridicule and contempt before the Caucasian world" by, for instance, proclaiming an "atavistic yearning for the African jungles."[96] In reference to Hughes, whose first volume of poetry was dedicated to Van Vechten, the latter was accused of having "misdirected a genuine poet" to create works focusing on black cabarets rather than what genteel critics viewed as the "average Negro"—an "everyday laborer, attending church, lodge and movie and as conservative as ordinary working folk everywhere."[97] On the other hand, a form of corruption based on writers' commercial interests was suspected. These allegations hinged on the perception that white publishers or, more generally, an economically potent white audience seduced Renaissance writers into representing stereotypes of African Americans by offering "subsidies and bribes."[98] Critics sometimes suggested that Renaissance authors could not help writing to "suit a white audience" for want of a black readership, yet the blame was continuously placed on the writers, who were claimed to be "solely after shekels, shekels and still more shekels."[99]

Judging from Renaissance writers' correspondence, hostile reactions and accusations were largely anticipated. Just as critics were conscious of the dissident spirit linking many young writers, the latter were acutely aware of their critics' predominantly genteel outlook.[100] By 1926, many writers' patience with what they perceived as the Renaissance's elitist and assimilationist direction had apparently run out. Particularly the Niggeratti were keen on provoking the black bourgeoisie and the more genteel members of the Renaissance leadership by consciously transgressing these critics' aesthetic and moral limits. The creation of the magazine *Fire!!* (1926), according to Thurman a publication "purely artistic in intent and conception" that was to expose the "vices and stupidities of the race," constituted the epitome of the Niggeratti's transgressive efforts and, as Watson suggests, "an alternative manifesto to *The New Negro*."[101] The Niggeratti hoped for a strong, condemnatory critical reaction which however never materialized. Many critics ignored *Fire!!*, and among the few, generally short comments on the publication, positive reactions outnumbered negative criticism.[102] In light of critics' refusal to take up the young writers' challenge, the critical outrage that greeted Hughes's *Fine Clothes to the Jew* only a few months later might have come as a surprise.

According to McKay, genteel black critics were instrumental in the creation of a "peculiar racial opinion [that] constitutes a kind of censorship of what is printed about the Negro."[103] This assessment must be viewed in light of these critics' potential influence, as they were greater in number than the usually moderate Renaissance leaders and, moreover, had access to publishing outlets whose circulation by far exceeded that of magazines like *The Crisis*.[104] Their comments therefore not only affected writers personally but, significantly, also influenced attitudes current in African American society. Young black writer Donald Hayes, for instance, suggested that Hughes's *Fine Clothes to the Jew* only "reached about one-tenth the sales it warranted" due to bad reviews—an assessment that at first glance seems corroborated by Rogers's appeal to the black public to "discourage the marketing of such books."[105] Considering, however, that African Americans generally ignored black writing even if it was praised in the black press, the effectiveness of such appeals is doubtful. Sometimes, as was apparently the case with Thurman and William Rapp's play *Harlem*, propaganda against works by Renaissance authors proved successful: As Thurman informed Hughes, *Harlem* "flopped terribly in Chicago before closing. Thanks to Negro propaganda."[106] Because black critics personally attacked writers in their reviews and other articles, resentment of specific writers could be fueled. Thurman was a popular target and had to endure frequent attacks, as he related to Rapp:

> I wish you could take my place in Negro society for about a week. Even on the train I was beset by a Pullman porter for my bastardly propaganda against the race. And here at home—a delegation of church members . . . flocked in on me and prayed over me for almost an hour, beseeching the Almighty to turn my talents into the path of righteousness.[107]

Feeling its consequences even in their private lives, it seems that no matter how much these Renaissance writers rejected the burden of representation, they could not evade it, as it remained an issue against which they were constantly forced to define themselves.

THE BURDEN OF REPRESENTATION
AND SEXUAL DISSIDENCE

During the 1920s and 1930s, articles focusing on sexuality and specifically homosexuality were regularly run in the black press, reflecting an interest in these topics also evident in white America. This occupation in the black press with sexual issues should not necessarily be seen as an indication of a new sexual freedom, as it also constituted a reaction to what was perceived as the negative development of Harlem into an entertainment center catering to white visitors' sexual/homosexual interests. In contemporary criticism of Renaissance works, sexuality and homosexuality figured on various levels. Renaissance promoters indicated awareness of a development of new attitudes toward sexuality which were at least partly related to the recognition that "[t]he subject 'Negro' like the subject 'sex' has been tabooed in polite circles, and the stripping off of the veil . . . follows with stern consistency our modernistic trend in literature as well as in life."[108] It was recognized that the white American liberal forces pushing for a relaxation of sexual norms also supported the Renaissance. Locke's hope that "the literary artist will deal with sex without ceremony or prudery, without affection or timidity"[109] was therefore by no means astonishing. Even Du Bois seemed willing to acknowledge this trend and in 1923 defended Hughes against charges of vulgarity, replying to a letter of complaint: "Mr. Hughes in his strikingly beautiful poems . . . talks about prostitutes frankly but does not make the cabarets of Harlem beautiful and desirable."[110] In 1924 he even went so far as to state that Jean Toomer in his novel *Cane* (1923) "first dared to emancipate the colored world from the conventions of sex."[111] Clearly, Du Bois did not object to sexual themes in literature—as long as he deemed the context "morally correct." His tolerance regarding representations of sexuality by Renaissance writers waned, however, in the face of the growing white interest in Harlem and the more challenging approaches the younger generation of writers opted for.

As many younger Renaissance writers were to produce works in which not only working-class characters predominated but which also included homosexual, sexually promiscuous, and adulterous characters, the topic of sexuality and the policing of sexual norms, as was the case generally within black bourgeois circles, gained significance for black critics. It may thus come as a surprise that sexual issues rarely figured prominently in black critics' articles and reviews. If such topics were addressed, the inclusion of sexual subject matter was usually placed in the context of other material deemed offensive. Distinct issues were thereby linked, as evident in Du Bois's criticism that in *Home to Harlem* McKay "used every art and emphasis to paint drunkenness, fighting, lascivious sexual promiscuity and utter absence of restraint."[112]

In other instances, black critics simply referred to subject matter they did not approve of as "degenerate stuff."[113]

A closer look at critics' enumerations of undesired portrayals reveals that their main concern was about what they regarded as the perpetuation of stereotypes of African Americans, ranging from sexually to intellectually derogatory images typical of white representations of blackness. The compounding of transgressive sexual and nonsexual issues additionally must be seen in light of the fact that these were usually viewed in a working-class context and the environment of speakeasies and cabarets. What Chauncey in a nonracial context describes as a degeneration theory embodying "middle class assumptions about the class nature of sexual morality"[114] seems also recognizable in black middle-class critics' comments. The association of sexual degeneration with the lower classes is aptly illustrated in George Schuyler's statement that "[t]he environment in which the poorer classes vegetate in our large cities is admirably adapted for the turning out of prostitutes, perverts, criminals, drug addicts and bums."[115] As indicated in Schuyler's comment, issues pertaining to what was regarded as sexual "deviance"—for instance, prostitution and homosexuality—were also linked. Reviewing McKay's novel *Banjo,* Aubrey Bowser, for instance, deplored that the black characters' "haunts are known as Bum Square, Boody Lane and the Ditch, places whose population is composed entirely of pimps, prostitutes and degenerates."[116] Bowser went on to complain that "All the Negro bums' sweethearts and all the women in the story are frankly prostitutes."[117] In another article, Bowser declared that "[the African American] is tired of seeing himself depicted as a pimp, a gambler, a degenerate or other reptile of the underworld."[118]

The one sex-related topic standing out in critics' comments is black female sexuality. Hughes, for instance, was specifically attacked for his poem "Red Silk Stockings" about a black prostitute, and McKay was reprimanded for his sexualized portrayal of black women in *Home to Harlem.*[119] William Ferris deplored that McKay "conjure[d] up in his sordid imagination things which never happen in the West Indies or Harlem"—the passage in question describing two black women who, as Ferris summarized, were "stripping stark naked and fighting . . . in broad daylight before a crowd of spectators over the love of a man."[120] Ferris seems to have been the only critic to comment on lesbianism as alluded to in Renaissance works: Though only in a passing reference, he complained that McKay used "phrases like 'bull diker,' which are only bar-room terms."[121] Literary references to lesbianism, like other sexual portrayals of black women, were clearly regarded as unacceptable—a reflection of the black bourgeoisie's desire to challenge and transform the sexualized stereotype of African American women as explored in more detail in the preceding chapter. Bowser's condemnation of the journal *Fire!!* as a "prostitute's directory"[122] gives an indication of the importance attached to the representation of black women, yet this reduction of the magazine's content to the issue of prostitution is astonishing considering that

Fire!! contained Nugent's "Smoke, Lilies and Jade," the first overtly homo-erotic story published by a black writer.

The critical reception of *Fire!!* is instructive for an analysis of reactions displayed toward sexually transgressive subject material. Although Thurman in retrospect claimed that *Fire!!* "caused a sensation the like of which had never been known in Negro journalism before,"[123] few critics, as mentioned earlier, actually commented on its publication in 1926. This refusal to re-spond to the Niggeratti's provocation in itself constituted a silencing. The majority of critics who commented on *Fire!!* either failed to recognize, or, as seems more plausible in view of the explicitness of Nugent's story, carefully avoided to mention its inclusion of a piece featuring same-sex desire. Braw-ley's critical reaction stands out: Singling out Nugent's story as an example of black writers' "preference for sordid, unpleasant, or forbidden themes,"[124] he quoted a longer section that highlights the protagonist's idleness but does not reveal the text's homoerotic content. Through this exercise in omission, Brawley gives the impression that "unwillingness to work" is the story's main theme.[125]

Reactions to *Fire!!* were friendlier in Renaissance circles—Du Bois and Cullen surprisingly endorsed it. Cullen's reaction is clearly linked to his own participation in the project, a move maybe indicative of his desire to be closer to other younger Renaissance writers.[126] Du Bois, in contrast, was privately distraught by the Niggeratti's move. A reporter who interviewed him inti-mated to Cullen that his mere mentioning of *Fire!!* "hurt [Du Bois's] feelings so much that he would hardly talk to me."[127] Maybe intending to deny the Niggeratti the pleasure of observing his outrage or wishing not to further es-trange the younger writers from the movement, Du Bois went so far as to state in *The Crisis*: "We bespeak for [*Fire!!*] wide support."[128] In his *Oppor-tunity* column, Cullen proclaimed the magazine to be the "outstanding birth of the month."[129] Like Brawley, he singled out Nugent's story but commented that "ample extenuation for what some may call a reprehensible story can be found in the beautifully worded *Smoke, Lilies, and Jade*,"[130] thereby cau-tiously hinting at the story's transgressive content while focusing on its aes-thetic level. The only more outspoken critic was Locke, whose review article trailed the publication of *Fire!!* by eight months—an indication of his un-willingness to respond to the Niggeratti's challenge. Mentioning the "strong sex-radicalism of many of the contributions" and commenting on Nugent's homoerotic story by discussing it in what might be termed a literary code, Locke dismissed what he described as the writers' "hectic imitation of the 'naughty nineties' and effete echoes of contemporary decadence," criticizing their "left-wing pivoting on Wilde and Beardsley."[131] Given the scandal that surrounded Oscar Wilde's arrest in 1895, many readers of Locke's review could certainly comprehend the allusion to homosexuality.

Black critics' rejection of "decadence" and their refusal to explicitly ac-knowledge a link between sexual transgression and the Renaissance movement could perhaps also be viewed in the context of contemporary sexologists' linking of blackness, sexual "deviance," and "decadence" that was contrasted with a link between whiteness and authorship. Against this background, a story like "Smoke, Lilies and Jade," combining blackness in the form of the author with a decadent style and homosexuality as a literary theme, ran against Renaissance leaders' aim of inscribing literary works created by African Americans into the canon of American literature.[132]

Fire!! can also serve as the background against which to examine younger writers' views regarding the portrayal of sexuality in literature. Although the journal brought together various factions of young black writers, the separation into the Niggeratti wing on the one hand and Cullen on the other remained stable. As Eleonore van Notten emphasizes, Thurman approached Cullen for a contribution not to demonstrate unity among the younger writers but to emphasize the ideological and artistic gulf that separated them.[133] Cullen's position on the topic of sexuality was distinct from that held by the Niggeratti: He employed a romantic, partially sexually charged imagery within a mainly heterosexual or gender-unspecified context, and usually veiled transgressive sexual desire by literary codes. As pointed out in the preceding chapter, Locke was a decisive influence in the formation of Cullen's sexual identity, pointing out a white literary canon featuring male same-sex love for him to study.[134] One might thus argue that Locke shaped Cullen's gay literary voice, indicating that same-sex desire could, if presented cautiously and in specific cultural codes, constitute suitable subject matter.

For the Niggeratti and McKay, "deviant" sexualities, which also included homosexuality, seemed a valid subject matter. Addressing conservative critics, Hughes illustrated this point in a heterosexual context: "College boys, as you know, do have affairs with loose women."[135] In a similar vein, McKay explained that he "[did not] make virgins of [his] colored girls," insisting that he was justified in doing so: "I think I'm nearer the truth and tragedy and gaiety of Negro life than Miss Jessie Fauset."[136] For the Niggeratti and McKay, "truth" and sexuality, as depicted in works like *Home to Harlem*, seemed intrinsically linked.[137] As Notten suggests, "sexual taboo functioned as the leading image of [the Niggeratti's] rebellion."[138] This is clearly evident in *Fire!!*, in which almost all contributions, particularly Thurman's story "Cordelia the Crude"[139] and Nugent's "Smoke, Lilies and Jade," which explicitly dealt with sexual issues, were designed to offend. As observed by Michael Cobb, the Niggeratti thus created "rough," uncomfortable narratives, thereby "enabl[ing] queer and race to exist within the same literary articulation"[140]—something that had never been achieved so openly and controversially before in African American literature. As Nugent recalled, he and Thurman "flipped a coin to see who wrote bannable material. The only two things we could think of that was bannable material were a story about prostitution or about homosexuality."[141] Presumably to ensure critics' outrage, they eventually included both topics. Maybe aware of critics' compounding of sexually transgressive with nonsexual transgressive material, Thurman and Nugent ensured that their stories offended on more than a sexual level. Thurman's protagonist Cordelia is not only a prostitute but is also only 16 years old and portrayed in a "low-life" setting featuring cinemas, parties, and alcoholic excesses. Nugent's story is not only overtly homoerotic: Its protagonist Alex is portrayed as spending his time doing nothing apart from smoking, thinking, and indulging in sex and sexual visions.

Sexual dissidence was thus clearly part of the younger Renaissance writers' transgressive strategies and their rejection of the burden of representation. How far the portrayal of sexuality in works other than those included in *Fire!!* was infused with an intent to shock is debatable but offers interesting possibilities for interpretation. While, as evident in the meager critical response to *Fire!!*, consequences of explicit portrayals of transgressive sexualities could not be foreseen, literary sexual dissidence for Renaissance writers meant that they were counted among what Thurman dubbed the "damned"[142] group of writers who rejected the task of representation—an option unavailable to a writer like Cullen.

RACE, SEX, AND MODERNISM

Mirroring the pattern observed for other "sordid" subject matters, many black critics saw a direct link between white America and Renaissance writers' breaching of sexual themes. Against the background of the black bourgeoisie's condemnatory reaction to Harlem's development into a sexual entertainment center, it is not surprising that sexual artistic representations of black life were seen as pernicious developments brought into Harlem from without. White publishers were accused of exercising a kind of censorship of black writing—a censorship that did not weed out what black critics deemed offensive literature but one that tended to exclude "wholesome" black writing. According to James Weldon Johnson, the main complaints of genteel critics were

> that the leading white publishers have set a standard which Negro writers must conform to or go unpublished; that this standard calls only for books depicting the Negro in a manner which tends to degrade him in the eyes of the world; that only books about the so-called lower types of Negroes . . . find consideration and acceptance.[143]

Sometimes, though rarely, the topic of sexuality was mentioned directly in this context. Jessie Fauset, for example, declared: "The publishers best preferred Negro literature that bordered on the pornographic."[144] Shifting the focus onto the predominantly white audience of Renaissance writers, Rogers recognized, however, that publishers were "only caterers to the public."[145] An emphasis on sexuality, black critics argued, was part of the primitivist image of black Americans. By stressing particularly sexual aspects of African American lives, it was feared, Renaissance writers played into the hands of those white Americans who preferred "cultural as well as residential separation."[146] Many critics felt that an insistence on racial distinctiveness—particularly in the field of sexuality—would forestall black America's integration into the American nation.

Primitivism, realism, naturalism, and a choice of subject matter with which writers were seen to be "play[ing] up the sex element"[147] were specifically condemned by black critics. Implying that McKay had merely copied the currently fashionable inclusion of explicitly sexual material in white writers' works, Ferris dismissed *Home to Harlem* as the "bottom of the hill"[148] of that trend. The Niggeratti and McKay rejected being characterized as victims of white modernist intellectuals or conscious exploiters of their race. Responding to the charge of having been "misdirected" by Van Vechten, Hughes emphasized that "if the poems which [*Fine Clothes to the Jew*] contains are low-down, jazzy, cabaret-ish, sensational, and utterly uncouth . . . the fault is mine—not Mr. Van Vechten's."[149] McKay also publicly justified his fictional portrayals of African Americans, stating that the material claimed to be primitivist and allegedly written at the behest and pay of whites was written of his own volition, as he "prefer[red] virtues that are colorful to the sepulchral kinds."[150] The impression conveyed in this statement, however, is that McKay deliberately held back to appease critics. His private correspondence reveals that he genuinely subscribed to primitivist notions: He expressed his belief that "Negroes . . . have more of primitive rhythm than [white people]," and that "[s]ex is a primitive, natural, unlawful thing," thereby indicating the foundation of his depiction of sexuality in his fictional works.[151] Yet, as will be explored in greater depth later, McKay's example shows that far from "riding the bandwagon of primitivism," Renaissance writers could, as Wayne Cooper points out, genuinely endorse primitivism and thereby appropriate "white stereotypes if they contained aspects of black existence vital to the black man's character and survival."[152] In their attempts to reclaim black culture, some Renaissance writers were clearly willing to endure criticism of stereotyping and pandering to exoticism.

Renaissance leaders such as James Weldon Johnson and Locke—both singled out for praise by the Niggeratti for their profession "to understand and to aid in anyway [*sic*] possible those in revolt"[153]—frequently came to the assistance of Renaissance writers. Like some publishers, these intellectuals refuted the notion that only works with "derogatory" material were accepted, listing books "depicting Negro life on the 'upper' levels or shedding a favorable light on the race," and concluding that the "complaint against the publishers is not in consonance with the facts."[154] It is important to mention, however, the case of Renaissance writer Arna Bontemps, who was apparently pressured by publishers into rewriting his novel *God Sends Sunday* (1931). Describing an early version of the novel, Harold Jackman wrote to Cullen that "Arna has avoided all the sensational side of the Negro's life that has been portrayed in so many books. . . ."[155] Reviewing the final version, in contrast, Du Bois concluded that the novel was only about "sordid crime, drinking, gambling, whore-mongering and murder."[156] As Hutchinson however points out, such interferences by publishers were apparently rare.[157]

The Niggeratti expressed varying views on supposed material gain to be had from pandering to a white audience. Hughes strictly denied that his writing brought him financial rewards, stating that he could "make much more money as a bell-hop than as a poet."[158] Nugent, rarely publishing any material, equally could not be claimed to write for financial gain. Far from desiring to be celebrated by white readers, many younger Renaissance writers held white Harlem enthusiasts in contempt yet were not above exploiting exoticist desires for their own purposes. Thurman, who occasionally guided white visitors around Harlem for cash payments or at least a provision of food and drink, spoke of his white audience as "morons";[159] but he, as one of the few Renaissance writers who attempted to earn a living from literary activities alone, sometimes explicitly wrote for the demands of his predominantly white audience. Planning a piece with Rapp, Thurman predicted that "[t]he morons should eat that up especially in the movies, if given a deal of darky dancing, nigger comedy, and coon shouting."[160] Even critics' claims about the role transgressive sexuality played in young writers' alleged pandering to a white audience seem corroborated by Thurman's plan to "[center] largely around the [theatrical group], exposing the usual jealousies, lack of talent (subtly of course), and the queer types which abound in this milieu."[161] Thurman obviously had no scruples about giving in to the demands of a white audience but apparently distinguished between works—usually written in collaboration with white writers—produced in response to the public's demand and more personal creations like his novels *The Blacker the Berry* (1929)[162] and *Infants of the Spring* (1932).

As indicated earlier, a central issue separating the Niggeratti, including McKay, from genteel black critics was their attitude toward modernism, a topic closely linked to the matter of literary representations of sexuality. Although Baker asserts that Cullen should not be excluded from discussions on modernism solely on the grounds of his adherence to traditional form and subject matter, the Niggeratti clearly regarded him as "the symbol of a fast disappearing generation of Negro writers."[163] In contrast to Cullen, they intended to "burn up a lot of the old, dead conventional Negro-white ideas of the past."[164] In terms of the politics of sexual representation, *Fire!!* was of central significance. As Notten points out, this publication can be regarded as a "move away from what [the Niggeratti] considered the old guard's constraining idealism,"[165] a rejection of prescribed "appropriate" literary forms and subject material, and a decisive push into a modernist direction as the Niggeratti attempted to carve out a niche in America's literary avant-garde. Although interest in the white literary scene varied—Hughes did not seem particularly interested, while Nugent, for instance, was closely involved in white avant-gardist circles—current trends were pursued with interest. Correspondence between various younger Renaissance figures reveals that modernist works were frequently discussed and that an explicit interest was shown in works that had caused scandal because of their portrayals of sexuality. Gwendolyn Bennett, a *Fire!!* contributor, tried to obtain a copy of *Ulysses* and showed interest in Frank Harris's *My Life and Loves*, intending to "add [them] to [her] library of pornography." [166] McKay, Thurman, and Nugent shared this interest and particularly noticed works with homosexual references, a fact that can be linked to their same-sex interest but that also demonstrates to what extent sexual issues were part of what is described as 1920s writers' "rebellion against Victorianism." [167]

The Niggeratti and McKay thus deliberately opted for what they regarded as the "modern," explicit way of representing sexuality. *Fire!!*, as Locke noted in his review, could in this context indeed be said to be "an exhibit of unifying affinities in the psychology of contemporary youth." [168] However, as James Levin points out, "Despite the new sexual freedom in the 1920s, in fiction the closet door remained tightly closed on discussion of homosexuality." [169] Explicit references to homosexuality were rare in publicly available literature. As the reports of the SSV indicate, some privately distributed novels, magazines, and stories dealing explicitly with homosexual themes were circulated during the 1920s. The SSV's records offer only a selective insight into what type of same-sex related material was available, yet it seems that the number of works featuring homosexuality was significantly lower than that of works containing other sexually explicit material recorded and confiscated. [170] Viewed in this context, the inclusion of Nugent's "Smoke, Lilies and Jade" in *Fire!!* seems all the more remarkable, as it stands out not only in the field of black writing but also in the larger framework of 1920s American literature.

Inspired by white writers' literary ventures like the *Little Review*, *Fire!!*, as Notten asserts, constituted part of Thurman's "strategy for achieving the transformation to modernity . . . by way of shocking his readership." [171] It must be noted, however, that *Fire!!* not only was intended to provoke the black bourgeoisie and Renaissance leaders but was also to have effects on a larger scale. Nugent and Thurman wanted the magazine to be banned by Boston's Watch and Ward Society—a process which, in light of the anticipated publicity and the expectation of an eventual lifting of the ban, could be financially rewarding. [172] From the writers' viewpoint, a ban would furthermore elevate them to the level of such authors as James Branch Cabell and H. L. Mencken, who had both been subject to censorship. [173] Where white avant-gardists had shocked by serializing James Joyce's *Ulysses*, the Niggeratti were to surpass them by publishing "Smoke, Lilies and Jade," which, interestingly, was presented as the first installment of a novel.

Fire!! undeniably reflected trends in white literary avant-gardism, if only in its form as a little magazine. However, as Thurman explained, it represented more than just an imitation:

Hoping to introduce a truly Negroid note into American literature, [*Fire!!*'s] contributors had gone to the proletariat rather than to the bourgeoisie for characters and material, had gone to people who still retained some individual race qualities and who were not totally white American in every respect save color of skin.[174]

With this riposte, Thurman reversed a central argument of black critics, implying that bourgeois African Americans themselves pandered to "white" tastes. Additionally, he thereby authenticated the black masses, in contrast to the black bourgeoisie, as "original" race members. In light of the specifically sexual contributions to *Fire!!*, he thereby seems to sexualize the masses, implicitly claiming that while the black bourgeoisie accepted white Americans' sexual norms and morality, the black masses held on to an unrestrained "black" sexuality. This sexual and racial authentication must be viewed in the context of the debate on assimilation that had peaked in Schuyler's rejection of notions of racial distinctiveness and "Negro Art," epitomized in his claim that "the Aframerican is merely a lampblacked Anglo-Saxon."[175] Hughes responded to Schuyler, expressing his conviction that the black masses "furnish a wealth of colorful, distinctive material for any artist because they still hold their own individuality in the face of American standardizations."[176]

Only five months after Schuyler's and Hughes' theses had sparked controversy, *Fire!!*'s general editorial line was to support Hughes's stance: "We believe that the Negro is fundamentally, essentially different from their Nordic neighbors. We are proud of that difference."[177] A glimpse at the contributions to *Fire!!* reveals a gap, however, between the rhetorical emphasis on racial distinctiveness and the magazine's content. While Hughes's and Hurston's contributions centered on "racial" subject matter, neither "Smoke, Lilies and Jade" nor "Cordelia the Crude," the two stories that figured prominently because of their sexually transgressive content, feature white or black characters with distinct racial characteristics.[178] The Niggeratti's editorial statement could thus best be viewed as an attempt to reconcile conflicting agendas for the sake of an assault on the black establishment. A common ground behind the rhetoric is nonetheless discernible. Encompassing literary styles as diverse as Hughes's socially, politically, and racially motivated poetry to Nugent's fin-de-siècle decadence, *Fire!!* is best described as an embodiment of Hughes's literary credo: "We Negro artists who create now intend to express our individual dark-skinned selves without fear or shame."[179] In *Fire!!*, this freedom of expression facilitated a fusion of transgressive sexuality, modernism, and racial self-expression. The publication stands out as a unique manifestation of the younger Renaissance writers' literary sexual dissidence; their failure to continue the publication points to their financial dependence. Though planned, a second issue of *Fire!!* never materialized, and Thurman was financially ruined for years. The magazine *Harlem* (1928), a publication that can be seen in the tradition of *Fire!!*, was compromised from the outset, as Renaissance leaders were asked for assistance and contributions.[180] After the failure of *Fire!!*, the Niggeratti slowly dissolved as a group and members began to follow their individual paths. They nevertheless continued to produce dissident work in terms of a rejection of the burden of representation—a dissidence often expressed through depictions of transgressive sexuality.

THREE

Countée Cullen:
"His virtues are many;
his vices unheard of"

Houston Baker observes that when discussing Countée Cullen, "critics are often embarrassed by the poet who is out of step with the age,"[1] because Cullen preferred a strict formal romanticism for his literary works. Yet in spite of the scant and predominantly negative critical attention Cullen attracted since his death in 1946, it must be recognized that he was regarded as the "poet laureate" during the Harlem Renaissance. Cullen excelled in his studies, graduated as a Phi Beta Kappa, and was awarded numerous prizes—in short, "he was the proper poet with proper credentials."[2] Success appeared to come easy, yet Cullen knew that building up a literary career involved hard work. He was aware of the significance of academic merits, as evident in a letter to Alain Locke: "I had such strong outstanding visions of a Phi Beta Kappa key. And then I was sort of a colored hope to you and others, wasn't I?"[3] At age twenty, Cullen, whose poems were published with increasing frequency in both white and black magazines, already felt the burden of expectation black America placed on him. Winning a citywide poetry contest while still in high school, Cullen entered the literary limelight as a child prodigy, subsequently turning into a public figure whose every step was watched and whose literary ventures, as Wallace Thurman remarked, were celebrated in "dithyrambic prose."[4] Most black periodicals covered the young poet's apparently unblemished success story, and Cullen delivered: His academic and literary merits and his persona "with his dark suit, tie, and always-ready-for-company good manners"[5] seemed perfectly shaped. Moreover, Cullen's adherence to strict measures and rhymes, his following of writers like John Keats, Alfred Tennyson, and A. E. Housman, and his preference for romantic form and imagery endeared him, as Thurman cynically commented, to "both bourgeois black America and sentimental white America."[6] Cullen was consequently seen as the embodiment of the virtues of the Talented Tenth—it seemed, as a columnist for the *Pittsburgh Courier* wrote, that "[h]is virtues are many; his vices unheard of."[7]

While it would be inaccurate to suggest that Cullen's public image was based on a myth, it is indicative of the extent to which the poet laureate Cullen was a public construct that he gave fictitious information regarding his place of birth. Cullen claimed to have been born in New York, yet while it remains impossible to determine his exact place of birth, it is certain that he was not born within the city's boundaries. Although this might seem negligible, it was significant for Cullen, who lied to uphold the larger fiction that he was born to the respected Cullens. As Cullen confided to his intimate friend Harold Jackman, he was adopted by the well-known Harlem minister Frederick Cullen and his wife at the age of eleven. Speculations about Cullen's upbringing abound, yet there seems to be a consensus that his childhood spent before adoption was unpleasant.[8] Cullen closely guarded his birth and childhood circumstances, constructing a mythical past in the belief that his origins would not fit the aura of respectability he wished to create.[9] Considered a pillar of the community, Cullen's adoptive father similarly depended on the division of a public and a private persona. He was "rumored to be a menace to choirboys and oddly fond of Mrs. Cullen's cosmetics,"[10] yet his parishioners apparently supported his position as "moral" leader. By adopting Countée, the childless Cullens may have gained as much in credibility as Countée did by entering what was described as "a simple, intelligent home environment."[11] Implying a sexual relationship, Jean Wagner suggests that the Reverend adopted Countée out of "feelings that were more than paternal."[12] This interpretation cannot be substantiated, yet the extreme closeness of father and adopted son is noteworthy and was apparently "snickered about."[13]

Befitting his general concern about his public image, Cullen was circumspect about his sexual life. When a journalist inquired how he wrote love poetry, presuming that Cullen "was scarcely on speaking terms with romance" because of his young age, a seemingly innocent Cullen responded that he learned about love "[b]y reading books and observing other people."[14] As evident from his private correspondence, however, Cullen had, at the time of the quoted interview, already had several inter- and intraracial relationships with men—some of them presumably sexual. Cullen did not aim at a wholesale denial of relationships, however: He went out with several women, and journalists eagerly picked up on this apparently "normal" development of his love life, stating that "rumor has it that he is already engaged."[15] It seems that Cullen could be attracted to women: He wrote Jackman that "One of [William S. Braithwaite's] daughters, Fiona, quite subjugated me. You know the type that interests me. . . ."[16] Yet in contrast to Jackman, who, though clearly involved in the Renaissance's gay coterie, had a sexual relationship and a child with a Viennese woman, Cullen was apparently never sexually involved with a woman. For him, women seemed mainly attractive in their representative function as potential wives. In 1923, Cullen happily reported to Locke:

"Recently I met Yolande Du Bois—and I believe I am near the solution of my problem."[17] This "problem" presumably was his need to round off his public persona with an appropriate female partner. Cullen married Yolande five years later, but the marriage deteriorated quickly and eventually damaged Cullen's reputation, as rumors about his homosexuality began to spread. Divorcing Yolande in 1929, Cullen remarried in 1940 and stayed with his wife Ida Robertson while being involved in a long-lasting secret relationship with the younger Edward Atkinson.[18]

Gerald Early insists that "nothing conclusive"[19] has been offered to "prove" Cullen's homosexuality and the existence of his gay literary voice, yet Cullen's correspondence gives clear indications of his love interest in and sexual desire for men. Countering statements by critics who, if at all referring to Cullen's same-sex interest, describe him as a writer whose sexual orientation was "a source of shame he never fully succeeded in turning into a creative strength," Alden Reimonenq emphasizes that Cullen's life and identity as a man-loving man—its negative but also its (for most scholars apparently inconceivable) positive aspects—shaped his writing.[20] A problematic homosexual relationship could deter Cullen from writing when it preoccupied him but could also enhance his creative process, as he himself acknowledged: "Depression seems to be good for my verse. . . ."[21] Satisfying relationships with men could be a motivation, as Cullen intimated to Locke: "L. [Lewellyn] R. [Ransom] was here last night, and we quite conclusively understand one another. . . . I shall write now. I am sure. . . . There is so invigorating a relief in being happy!"[22] The link between Cullen's homosexuality and his literary work—ignored, denied, and at best regarded as a stifling connection—clearly exists.

Cullen can be described as a self-identified gay man, yet while he was aware of his sexual preference for men, it was apparently not until his close relationship with Alain Locke that he was able to contextualize his emotions and desires. Locke and Cullen's relationship might have been sexual, but scholars prefer to discreetly term it a "father–son relationship."[23] Locke supported Cullen generously, advising him regarding his literary career and furthermore assisting him in developing a positive view of same-sex relationships. It is significant for a discussion of Cullen's gay voice as reflected in his poetry that his correspondence with Locke and Jackman contained coded references to homosexuality. Locke introduced Cullen to this gay discourse by recommending *Ioläus: An Anthology of Friendship,* written by same-sex-identified British radical Edward Carpenter. This work offered Cullen insights into a literary tradition of writing on male–male friendship and, as Cullen wrote Locke, "opened up for me soul windows which had been closed."[24] Like other members of Locke's gay network, Cullen found a positive interpretation of his desire and was at the same time fully initiated into the accompanying terminology of "friendship" in which terms emanating from the Greek discourse of homosexuality such as "perfect friendship" were fused with Whitmanesque expressions such as "comraderie" and "attachment."[25] Carpenter and Locke's interpretation of male same-sex love as "noble," healthy, and sexual—as opposed to what was deemed a decadent and effeminate homosexuality of a Wildean mold—was of great significance for Cullen: "[I]t threw a noble and evident light on what I had begun to believe, because of what the world believes, ignoble and unnatural."[26] Apparently sparing him from wholly internalizing homophobia and prejudices, it could not dispel all doubts, however. Despite discussing sexual issues with Locke in the language of "friendship," Cullen feared detection, stating in the postscript to the above-quoted letter: "Sentiments expressed here would be misconstrued by others, so this letter, once read, is best destroyed."[27] Through an exercise of self-censorship, concrete expressions of same-sex passion remained absent from his letters, same-sex desire constituting an omnipresent absence that could only be expressed by ellipses or codes.[28]

Cullen clearly believed that expressions like "friendship beyond understanding"[29] could be "misconstrued"—but in what sense? The impression gained here is that Cullen did not regard himself as a "homosexual." The term probably did not figure in his personal interpretation of same-sex love because of its connection in medical and public discourses with effeminacy, degeneracy, and disease—something he was not involved in, as his "noble" love constituted a "glorious feast of beauty."[30] Cullen's reasoning seems based on what Jonathan Dollimore terms "*internal differentiation*": By naturalizing and authenticizing one's own sexual behavior within the framework of the dominant system—a system that distinguishes between "effeminacy" and "manliness," "health" and "sickness"—those regarded as "inauthentic," for example, fairies, are separated and "some at least of the social stigmata of homosexuality" are displaced onto them.[31] Although initiated into the contemporary gay discourse and aware of his love for men, Cullen, who was highly sensitive to the risks involved in homosexual affairs, had a propensity to assess same-sex love negatively. Against the backdrop of his social position and artistic aspirations and particularly in light of even the pondering of the self-confident Locke over the question of whether gay men were "really an accursed tribe," Cullen's worries seem unsurprising.[32] Moreover, Cullen clearly felt depressed by what Locke described as a "dangerous environment"[33]—the homophobic United States. He therefore enjoyed spending time away from attentive American eyes from 1928 to 1930 in France, where same-sex activities were not outlawed and where, as he wrote in his poem "To France" (1935), he "found . . . / What was denied [his] hungry heart at home."[34]

Cullen's fear of being interpreted as "homosexual," his worries about even the use of a coded gay discourse in his private correspondence, and his efforts to create a perfect public persona indicate the unlikeliness of overt references to same-sex passion in his literary work. Additionally, it needs to be considered that he generally disliked explicit literary references to sexuality, accepting the term "Puritanical"[35] to describe himself and his literary taste. Nevertheless, Cullen did not exclude the topic of male same-sex attraction from his work. Although he also wrote fiction, poetry constituted his main field of literary production and is focused on here.[36] As Reimonenq suggests, attentive readers can recognize gay "sounds"[37] in Cullen's poetry. His gay literary voice is often dim and, although Reimonenq proposes that Cullen in the course of his career "fine-tuned his gay poetic voice,"[38] the readings produced in this chapter point to a softening process setting in after a stronger initial emphasis on same-sex desire in his early poetry, which seems directly influenced by his contact with Locke and his reading of *Ioläus*. Painfully aware of the outlawed status of homosexuality, Cullen veiled references to men-loving men. Romanticism, with its decorous images, served him well in this context. It is noteworthy that Cullen frequently avoided to specify the gender of characters depicted or addressed in his poetry. This was a strategy popular among gay writers who, while protecting themselves from accusations, intended to leave an undefined space open to an almost unlimited variety of readings, including gay interpretations.[39] Like Walt Whitman, for instance, Cullen might also be said to have followed a strategy of resexing pronouns to evoke a heterosexual context, yet also considering Cullen's minor but apparently genuine interest in women, this apparently was not the case.[40] Nevertheless, the possibility of his inclusion of poems about women, or the dedication of poems to women, functioning as a suitable cover should be entertained. From time to time, a less speculative gay voice can be discovered. Many more of Cullen's poems than those discussed here invite gay readings, yet fitting the scope of this study, a selection of works is divided into four groups: race and religion; *carpe diem*; love, death, and doom; courage and hope.

RACE AND RELIGION

Burdened with his persona—scion of a respected pious family and celebrated poet whose works were recited in Harlem's churches—Cullen felt a religious obligation. As he wrote to Jackman, he went to church "every Sunday, being sometimes, I fear, more of a model son than is good for me."[41] Cullen's doubts concerning Christianity emerge in his early poems, which display a sometimes violent religious skepticism that, as Nathan Huggins observes, "was always voiced as stemming from race consciousness."[42] This link between Cullen's depiction of race and religion emanated from what he confessed was his "chief problem": "reconciling a Christian upbringing with a pagan inclination."[43] The pivotal role of the Christian–pagan dichotomy in Cullen's oeuvre has attracted critical attention, yet the sexual overtones in his brand of paganism have by and large gone unnoticed. Representations of sensuality and sexuality seem crucial, however, to Cullen's discussion of race and religion and therefore central to an understanding of his participation in what could be termed the "pagan" discourse of the Harlem Renaissance. Contrasted with Christianity, as a Puritan, restrained structure, paganism denotes the heathen, "primitive," and uncontrolled. Extended to the level of sexuality, this dichotomy was assimilated into a coded gay discourse that enabled Locke, for instance, to indicate his homosexual interests by identifying himself as "pagan to the core."[44] Since black genteel critics viewed with suspicion anything that could be linked to a primitivist discourse current particularly in the works of white writers, they disapproved of Cullen's inclusion of pagan imagery and themes in his early poetry. In *The Crisis*, Allison Davis expressed dismay that "Even Mr. Cullen made especial use of the jungle urge. . . ."[45] More liberal commentators like Charles S. Johnson praised Cullen's poetry, claiming that "the spirit of the transplanted African moved through his music to a new definition."[46] Over time, Cullen turned away from racial primitivism and paganism, themes that seem wholly absent from his last poetry volume, *The Medea and Some Poems* (1935).[47]

Particularly through the lenses of white reviewers, "pagan" themes were seen as representative of Cullen's poetry and of Harlem Renaissance writing in general. A reviewer for the *New York Herald Tribune*, for instance, commented that Renaissance artists "stuff their fingers in their ears to shut out the sudden maddening memory of the sound of rain on banana leaves, of dances in the moonlight, and the tom-toms throbbing through the breathless tropic night!"[48] Although possibly appropriate for some of his poems, Cullen could not appreciate this interpretation, which ran against his aspiration of acceptance as a "POET and not NEGRO POET"[49] and jeopardized the Renaissance's integrationist aim by placing emphasis on racial difference. Darwin Turner suggests that Cullen to some extent "succumbed" to the myth of the African American as the "child of nature" in his early poetry—an explanation for Cullen's emphasis on paganism that seems more convincing than any desire on his part to cash in on exoticism.[50] Cullen himself admitted: "In spite of myself . . . I find that I am actuated by a strong sense of race consciousness . . . and although I struggle against it, it colors my writing. . . ."[51]

Cullen's racial or pagan voice is clearly audible and seems to merge with his gay voice in his well-known poem "Heritage."[52] The poem's speaker poses the question "What is Africa to me?"[53] and responds to it in seven stanzas which, owing to their regular rhyme and tetrameter, contrast starkly with the poem's subject matter of uncontrolled desire. The poem is a good example of Cullen's interweaving of paganism, Christianity, sensuousness, and homoeroticism. Exploring the significance of Africa for himself, the speaker visualizes jungle images, "Strong bronzed men," and "regal black / Women."[54] Physical beauty and attractiveness shape this vision of Africa in which only men's physical features are described in seductive terms. African women, in contrast, are depicted as honorable and almost untouchable as they are "regal" and fulfill a reproductive role.

The lure and bodily sensations linked to paganism are intensified in the second and fourth stanzas: Torn between the desire to hear "jungle" sounds and the wish to cover his ears, the speaker succumbs to urges beyond his control. The natural force of rain fuels his restlessness and his blood threatens to wash away the restraints that civilization and Christianity place on his body. As David Bergman suggests, "Africa becomes both the despised Sodom and the long-sought Eden of the homoerotic against which Cullen stuffs his ears and for which his heart sings."[55] The speaker's attempts to remain aloof by rationalizing Africa as "A book one thumbs," seem in vain as he asks what Bergman describes as the "forbidden" question: "What's your nakedness to me?"[56] In light of the poem's dedication to Cullen's intimate friend Jackman, this question may be read as directly addressing Jackman. The focus is immediately redirected to Africa, however, as the speaker tries to deny the lure of the continent's nakedness—"bodies sleek and wet, / Dripping mingled rain and sweat."[57] He apparently has no option but to surrender to his sensual black heritage, obeying his inherent pagan voice's command to " 'Strip! / . . . and dance the Lover's Dance!' "[58] At this point, a further stanza depicting the speaker's attempt to dismiss African gods is interjected. Cullen assigns seductive powers to the heathen gods: Fashioned "out of rods,"[59] their shape is clearly phallic. Moreover, they are formed by black men "[i]n a likeness like their own," thereby gaining the sexual allure of their creators.[60]

The last two stanzas feature the speaker's attempt to reconcile Christian faith with pagan impulses. Admitting to playing a "double part" by worshipping a Christian deity while "fashion[ing] dark gods," he confesses to the urge to endow God with "[d]ark despairing features" and "dark rebellious hair."[61] On the one hand, he thereby ensures God's compassion for black people; on the other, by bestowing the features of seductive black men on God, he transforms God into an object of sexual desire. The speaker's anxieties eventually prevail, as he senses the need to tame his pagan impulses. His inner conflict between Christianity and paganism, also in its racial and homosexual dimensions, therefore remains unresolved. Interestingly, a longer quote from "Heritage" is contained in Blair Niles's apologetic novel *Strange Brother* (1931). In this work, the white gay protagonist's strong identification with Cullen's "Heritage," particularly with its depiction of restlessness and inner conflict, indicates that the transference between race and sexuality could easily be made by readers. The "double consciousness" Cullen describes in "Heritage" is not necessarily exclusively racially defined.[62]

The transformation of Christ into a deity suitable to the needs of African Americans, hinted at in "Heritage," is performed in "The Black Christ" (1929).[63] Set in the South, this epic treats the tragedy and subsequent miracle witnessed by a black family that consists of a religious mother and her two sons, Jim and the speaker. Catalyst for the imminent tragedy is an incident in which a white man hurls abuse at Jim and his white girlfriend. Incensed by the distress his girlfriend suffers, Jim kills the man and returns to his family's cabin, where he is hidden in a closet. On arrival of a lynch mob, Jim emerges from the locked closet and is subsequently lynched. This event intensifies the speaker's rejection of Christianity, yet he regains faith when Jim reappears, resurrected as the black Christ.

Beneath the story's amalgam of race and religion lies a homoerotic subtext evident in the relationship between the two brothers in which same-sex desire and an appreciation of male physical beauty figure prominently. Reimonenq suggests that Jim can be seen "also as the victim of heterosexism,"[64] thereby implying Jim's same-sex interest. Jim is certainly a victim of racism, yet it seems that although he in the poem literally comes "out of the closet" to face his persecutors, only the speaker, who adores Jim's and thereby Christ's bodily qualities, is directly linked to same-sex desire. Placing himself in the literary tradition of writers like colonial American poet Edward Taylor, whose "love for Christ," as Stephen Foster asserts, "takes on homoerotic tones in its intensity and in [his] description of Christ's physical beauty," Cullen chooses to have his speaker admiringly describe Jim as "handsome in a way / Night is after a long, hot day" and as having "an ease of limb, a raw, / Clean, hilly stride."[65] Jim's effect on women—"quickened throbbings of the breast"[66]—further enhances the sense of his physical attractiveness. According to Gregory Woods, "[Jim's] death itself is . . . eroticized."[67] The scene of his lynching is replete with sexual imagery: He is the *"Groom"* of the "virgin tree," *"Love and Beloved"* are bound in *"embrace,"* Jim is "raped" by sleep, and his corpse is described as "lusty," stimulating the speaker's/brother's desire.[68] In reference to the biblical scene involving the doubting Thomas, Ellis Hanson points out that "[e]ven beyond the spectacle of crucifixion, Christ calls attention to his body, especially after his death."[69] This statement is applicable to "The Black Christ," in which Jim's brother replaces Thomas and desires physical contact with his beloved brother/Christ: He "saw," "touched; yet doubted him," and, reaching the state of intimacy necessary for a bodily recognition of his beloved, "[his] fingers faltered down his slim / Sides, down his breathing length of limb."[70] Adding the statement that Jim's body is "The form than life more dear to [the speaker],"[71] Cullen leaves no doubt that the speaker adores specifically his brother's/Christ's physical qualities.

Despite the poem's title, Cullen's depiction of Jim/Christ and his physical beauty almost completely lacks "racial" elements. While Cullen appropriates the Christ figure, imbuing Jim/Christ with what Isaac William Brumfield described as a "New Negro spirit"[72] and transforming him into a sign of "blackness," the poem's homoerotic subtext seems directly linked to Cullen's identity as a man-loving man, the construction of which was based on a white cultural tradition. Cullen's choice of a white cultural framework of homoerotic depictions is evident in the speaker's expression of grief for Jim/Christ: "My Lycidas was dead. There swung / In all his glory, lusty, young,

/ My Jonathan, my Patrocles."[73] All three figures mentioned were mourned by their male lovers: Edward King was mourned by Milton as "Lycidas," Jonathan was mourned by David, and Patrocles by his lover Achilles.[74] Although Cullen's black Christ cannot be said to be same-sex-interested himself, he obviously arouses and tolerates homosexual desire.

As a third poem in which Cullen produces a layering of the themes of race, religion, and sexuality, "The Shroud of Color" (1925)[75] should briefly be mentioned here. In this poem, neither a racial transformation nor a recreation of God seems necessary, as a black protagonist, who struggles with doubts that seem to concern not only his faith but also his sexuality and desires, is watched over by a god who seems sympathetic to his problems. Eventually, the speaker reaches happiness as the poem ends in what Reimonenq describes as the "birth and acceptance of not only race but also the soul as an expression of the homosexual self."[76]

A vision of Christianity that involves tolerance of same-sex relations, albeit not in a racial context, is put forward in "Judas Iscariot" (1925).[77] Cullen presents an unconventional interpretation of the story of Judas, portraying him as Christ's dedicated servant instead of a villainous traitor. Cullen did not entirely break new ground thereby: Patrick Cockburn points out that the idea of "seeing Judas as an essential instrument of salvation, fulfilling God's will"[78] was not new, as essayist Thomas de Quincey, drawing on earlier German sources, had already discussed this interpretation in the early nineteenth century. Cullen adds a homoerotic level to this reading of Judas's story, presenting his alleged betrayal as an act motivated by love. While in "The Black Christ" homoerotic overtones are discernible only in the speaker's love of his brother/Christ, in "Judas Iscariot" Judas's love is apparently reciprocated by Christ. This interpretation of the disciples and Christ being bound by homosexual attraction also was not unprecedented: In his privately printed book *The Intersexes* (1908), Edward Prime Stevenson entertained the possibility of Christ as the "highest type of Uranian that the world could see."[79]

Cullen focuses on the relationship between Judas and Christ, thereby offering a multitude of opportunities for gay readings. The poem's speaker imagines that Judas and Christ got acquainted at an early age: Judas "knew the growing Christ" and "played" with him—expressions that can be read in a sexual context, a central issue being Judas's "knowledge" of Christ.[80] Since the verb *to know*, as exemplified in the Bible story on Sodom, was interpreted in a homosexual context to denote "to have sex with," one can read this knowledge as "carnal knowledge."[81] The depiction of intimacy between Judas and Christ is intensified in the course of the poem. When Christ intimates his mission to Judas, the latter's reaction—"And I, though good betide, / Or ill, will go with you"[82]—is reminiscent of a wedding vow. Moreover, as emphasized through repetition, Judas "[l]oved Christ, and loved Him much."[83] The intensely intimate nature of their relationship is underscored when Christ senses that his crucifixion is imminent. After giving assignments to the other disciples, he approaches Judas, asking him to fulfill the most difficult of all tasks: "kill / One whom you love"—a duty which Judas "in his hot desire" accepts.[84] Significantly, Cullen indicates that Judas's love and desire are reciprocated by Jesus, who "loves [Judas] / As only God's son can."[85] This is clearly a love connection—though one involving suffering and pain. Warning Judas, Christ predicts that

> . . . men to come will curse your name,
> And hold you up to scorn;
> In all the world will be no shame
> Like yours; this is love's thorn.[86]

This statement reflects predominant attitudes displayed vis-à-vis the figure of Judas, but it is intriguing to compare the scornful reactions predicted by Christ to the reaction of a heterosexist society toward gay men: Homophobia and discrimination, then, constitute "love's thorn." Having fulfilled Christ's will, Judas joins the disciples in heaven, where "none shrinks from His hand, / For there the worst is as the best, / And there they understand."[87] On revisiting Cullen's correspondence, it is significant that the term *understand* had a coded meaning, denoting the realization of mutual same-sex desire among men—a hint, as could be asserted, that the disciples form a gay circle.[88] Judas, who sacrificed his own body by hanging himself from a tree, thereby "[giving] young Christ heart, soul, and limb" as the ultimate token of his love, is presented as the one who, because of the strength of his same-sex love, was able "[t]o save the creature man."[89] Same-sex desire is thus claimed to be at the very heart of Christianity, as men-loving men are presented as instrumental in the redemption of humankind.

CARPE DIEM

While Cullen depicts Christ and his disciples in eternal happiness in heaven, his view of humankind seems less optimistic, as indicated in the transitoriness of life and the need to seize the day which figure prominently particularly in his love poetry. In this context, Cullen's own stance, evident in his private correspondence, in which he counts himself among what he describes as "us erotic lads,"[90] is of interest. Possibly influenced by Carpenter's philosophy, according to which sexual encounters are "as a rule needed," Cullen had numerous male lovers.[91] He obviously felt a strong need to satisfy his sexual urges, as evident in his seeking of advice from Locke concerning a relationship which had not reached a sexual stage: "The prospect of a mutually sincere adjustment is stimulating to me, as tenuous as it is. . . . Please pardon my urgency, but I <u>must</u> have an adjustment as soon as possible, or I shall be driven to recourse with <u>E.W.</u>. . . ."[92] This sense of urgency and need of "adjustment," this term being, as Reimonenq observes, a "code word for gay sex,"[93] is reflected in Cullen's poetry. Few poems in which Cullen employs the *carpe diem* theme are set in a clearly heterosexual context, an exception being "To a Brown Boy" (1925), in which sexual impulses are stimulated through a "brown girl's swagger."[94] Yet Cullen used even this poem in a gay context: He sent the poem to Hughes with the dedication "For L.H.," thereby, as Steven Watson notes, introducing an "undeniably romantic note" into their friendship.[95]

Leaving gender unspecified in numerous *carpe diem* poems, Cullen allows for various readings. In "Youth Sings of Rosebuds" (1927),[96] the dedication "To Roberta" points to an exclusively heterosexual context. This impression is not contradicted by the poem's content: An ungendered speaker desires to kiss to gather memories of love and passion for his old age. While not dismissing this reading, it should be noted on revisiting Cullen's correspondence that the term *rosebud* is repeatedly employed in reference to same-sex interests. Its gay meaning seems based on Robert Herrick's *carpe diem* phrase "Gather ye Rose-buds while ye may" but is also linked to the gay slang meaning of the term—"anus."[97] Reporting difficulties in a letter to Locke concerning his relationship with a certain Knapp, whose departure seems imminent, Cullen resolves to make use of the remaining time: "So I must gather my rosebuds while I may."[98] He however also entertains the possibility that "there still may be roses after June."[99] In another letter, Cullen again makes a reference to the term, advising Locke "to play and 'gather rosebuds.' "[100] Against this background, Cullen's poem "Youth Sings of Rosebuds" could well be viewed as a celebration of same-sex desire.

In "Advice to Youth" (1925), a male context is established through the poem's dedication to "Guillaume"—possibly Cullen's friend Guillaume Brown —and the addressing of a "Lad," both indications for a reading of "Youth" contained in the title as denoting one particular young man.[101] In this short poem, the speaker reminds a young man that he should grasp his opportunities to kiss, as "little time" for "pride in pain or play" is given. Apart from the lack of time to indulge in sexual pleasures, sexual desire is presented as vulnerable to the attacks of time as "blood soon cools before that Fear / That makes our prowess clay." Death of passion and impotence are caused by "that Fear"—an unspecified, yet, as indicated in Cullen's use of a capital letter, distinct terror that might on one level be interpreted as the fear of death. Another interpretation of "Fear" is conceivable. Discussing difficulties in finding a suitable female partner, Cullen intimated to Locke that one woman particularly intimidated him: "[T]here are complications—her age and experience above my own, and then that fear which is always at my heels."[102] Again, the exact nature of this terror remains veiled, yet as it is mentioned in a heterosexual context, it can be interpreted as the anxiety about failing in a sexual relationship with a woman. Supposing that "Advice to Youth" is dedicated to Guillaume Brown, another link between "Fear" and the idea of marriage can be established. Brown interpreted Cullen as having "no over-romantic illusions"[103] about marriage. Cullen must have expressed his unease with his prospective marriage in a previous letter or conversation. He also indicated his discomfort with the institution of marriage in an earlier letter to Jackman: "I really believe that true friendships, instead of marriages, are made in Heaven."[104] In terms of the poem's *carpe diem* theme, Brown's opinion that marriage is part of "life's realities that cums [sic] with manhood"[105] is of interest. As E. Anthony Rotundo observes for intimate male same-sex friendships during the nineteenth century, "manhood," and specifically "the task of taking on a man's duties," including wedlock and the pursuit of a career, usually resulted in the deterioration of all-male bonds.[106] Cullen's poem seems to suggest that youth, a limited period not defined within a heterosexual framework, should be seized: "If lips to kiss are freely met, / Lad, be not proud nor shy."[107] Every opportunity to enjoy love and physical contact should be seized, because in the sphere beyond "Fear"—either the grave or, indeed, marriage— "men forget, / And undesiring lie" as impotence reigns. Cullen's dedication of the poem to Brown indicates another intriguing possibility for a gay reading: It is feasible that the poet himself offers his lips to be kissed "freely," thereby, as in the case of "To a Brown Boy," employing a poem in his courtship of a potential partner.

LOVE, DOOM, AND DEATH

Closely related to the *carpe diem* theme, the depiction of doomed love and death—in the sense of a bodily passing but also figuratively in the sense of the death of love and desire—is prominent in Cullen's poetry. Before engaging in a further exploration of Cullen's love poetry, it seems important to consider the poems "Suicide Chant" (1925) and "Saturday's Child" (1925), which can be described as forming the basis of much of Cullen's death-stained works.[108] The speaker of "Saturday's Child" describes the occasion of his birth as a scene of misery: "Death cut the strings that gave me life, / And handed me to Sorrow."[109] In "Suicide Chant," a similar notion of doom, in this case originating from an unspecified inheritance, is evident. Here the link between homosexuality, frustration, and writing that critics seem most willing to establish may be said to exist: Describing himself as "The seed of a weed / [that] Cannot be flowered,"[110] the speaker indicates his impotence and inability to reproduce, thereby possibly referring to homosexuality as the source of what seems to be his sexual inadequacy.

The connection between sexual desire and doom is made in several of Cullen's love poems, of which many, as Baker observes, are imprinted by a "dark romanticism of frustrated love and infidelity."[111] Among the poems in which Cullen concentrates on love's death, "The Love Tree" (1927),[112] whose title already evokes a phallic image, is of particular interest. In the poem, a speaker envisions how he and an ungendered lover bury their forbidden, maybe homosexual love. This undertaking curiously seems to entail making love—the lovers "plant / A seed"—yet no pleasure is involved, as they seem doomed. Through their act of "reproduction," however, the speaker hopes to produce offspring in the form of "a tree / With fruit and flowers," the phallic embodiment of their love. As imagined by the speaker, this tree will become a catalyst for a broader vision: In an envisioned scene replete with sexual imagery, "pale lovers" "pluck" and "eat" from its fruit and are subsequently enticed by it, as, moved by "[a]n unimagined tune, their shy lips meet." The love scenes can be read in a heterosexual context, yet there is space for gay readings, too: "And men / Will pilgrimage from far and wide to see / This tree." Employing a biblical trope, Cullen seems to reinterpret the "tree of life" that stands for eternal life as the "Love Tree" which becomes a symbol of eternal same-sex love.[113] The religious theme is continued with the term "pilgrimage," which evokes an image of countless men-loving men visiting the phallic shrine. According to Christian belief, the poem's protagonists have committed a "sin" for which they will be "crucified" in a homophobic society; but while the tree—a possible reference to the cross on which Christ was crucified—symbolizes men-loving men's suffering, its history of "break of heart" and pain will, as envisioned by the speaker, be forgotten over time, as its positive power prevails. In an interesting twist to Cullen's presentation of Christ as same-sex-interested in "Judas Iscariot," men-loving men here seem to become Christ figures, and same-sex love acquires a religious status, an idea echoing John Addington Symonds's description of a Whitman-based interpretation of male same-sex love as "what . . . we may now call the new religion."[114]

Death is clearly not a one-dimensional destructive force in Cullen's love poetry. In the epitaphs "For a Virgin" (1925) and "For a Wanton" (1925), death, "amorous" and seductive, can be "a constant lover," who gives rather than takes love.[115] While death might not be an obstacle to love, love itself can be cruel. In several poems that are all devoid of references to race, Cullen highlights the painful character of love. Outstanding in this respect are "Magnets" (1935) and "Portrait of a Lover" (1927).[116] In "Magnets," a speaker laments that weak and sorrowful people attract his heart like magnets. These doomed creatures, which seem reminiscent of the speaker in "Suicide Chant," are contrasted with people who appear young and fresh, who are watched with a "kind appraising eye," and who are "straight." Possibly playing on the double meaning of the term *straight*, Cullen opens up the possibility of identifying the young and cheerful people as heterosexual. Though it should be attracted by these people, the speaker's heart is "such a strange contrary thing . . . it will never cling / To any bright unblemished thing." The impression conveyed is that the speaker's heart is abnormal. Moreover, it is "contrary," pointing into the opposite direction of "straight" people. Through his intimate relationship with Locke, Cullen might have been aware of the terms *contrary sexual feeling* and *contrary sexuality*, originally coined by German psychiatrist Carl Westphal in 1869 and used by American doctors toward the end of the nineteenth century to describe that "[t]he feeling in question was 'contrary' to that erotic emotion considered proper and exclusive to males or females"—a fitting description of the heart's queer ways depicted in "Magnets."[117] Those who attract the speaker thus represent the contrary of lively and "straight" people. They are "bitter" and their love life seems dead, as their "kissing [is] done"—a condition that appears to be linked to the fact that theirs is "The loving heart that must deny / The very love it travels by." As in "The Love Tree," a forbidden, potentially same-sex love needs to be denied and concealed. Same-sex desire that is outlawed and, as suggested by the magnetic force of attraction determining the speaker's desire, uncontrollable, appears too heavy a burden to bear.

Although the impression may be gained that Cullen presents those who dare to follow homosexual desire as either heroic or pitiable creatures, facing suffering, death, or an enforced denial of their desire and love, "Portrait of a Lover" indicates that Cullen could view same-sex love and the negative aspects that in some of his poems seem inextricably linked to it with ironic detachment. In this poem, Cullen's speaker creates a portrait of a man whose love and desire cause him pain and sorrow. Although race is not mentioned, a link to Cullen's "pagan" poetry is evident in the imagery employed to describe the lover's passion: Like the speaker in "Heritage," he is "Weary, restless, now fever's minion, / furnace-hot, / Now without reason"[118] as his blood boils and he seems to lose control over his body. The lover seems to be a victim of his apparently forbidden desire which causes him to shake and shiver when he envisions as a "great dread" the consequences of giving way to his emotions.[119] Moreover, the lover's desire is presented as a haunting secret: "Trusting, doubting, prone to reveal, yet wish- / ing not / To name this malady whereby his wits are led,"[120] he seems torn between disclosing and keeping his secret. Similar to Cullen's letters, same-sex desire here remains the omnipresent void that can only be paraphrased. Interestingly, the speaker's description of the lover's transgressive desire as a "malady" is reminiscent of sexologists' interpretations of homosexual desire. Harking back to Wilde, readers are furthermore reminded of homosexuality as the "[l]ove that dare not speak its name."[121] As the protagonist does not have the courage to reveal his desire, there seems to be no escape: His desirous body imprisons him and he feels "[t]rapped in this labyrinth,"[122] the unexplainable and unspeakable structure of his desire. All he feels able to do is suffer and lament his fate, deeming himself "so much / accurst, / His plight so piteous, his proper pain so rare."[123] In spite of this detailed account of the protagonist's predicament, Cullen does not evoke compassion, underlining that the lover only "deems" himself the victim of a curse. The speaker's question "What shall we liken such a martyr to?"[124] is clearly ironic and negates the equation of the lover with a martyr. While frequently portraying men-loving men as doomed, Cullen in this poem presents an alternative by emphasizing individuals' courage as a central factor in the pursuit of happiness.

COURAGE AND HOPE

In several of Cullen's poems, love prevails and transgressive sexual behavior and courageous resistance against restrictions are portrayed in a positive light. The sexually charged "Ultimatum" (1927)[125] can serve as a good example in this respect. The poem's speaker rejects society's or fate's strictures, denying that "what must be must be." Read in light of Cullen's later mentioning of the planting of "seed," this unspecified "what must be must be" can be read in a sexual context as denoting heterosexuality, reproduction, and marriage. Cullen's speaker, for whom "[t]here is enough to meet [his] need" in himself, clearly rejects any state of heterosexual togetherness. His transgressive sexual behavior is unveiled in the last stanza. Metaphorically referring to sexual activity, he states: "The seed I plant is chosen well; / Ambushed by no sly sweven." As no "sweven" or vision—possibly of a family— motivates his sexual activity, the speaker is obviously not engaging in procreative sex. A similar attitude is evident in Cullen's epitaph "For One Who Gayly Sowed His Oats" (1925),[126] the title of which concisely summarizes the content. The poem refers to a man who spread his semen liberally, the term "Gayly" evoking a potential same-sex context.[127] In the last lines of "Ultimatum," the speaker also spreads his semen without worrying about consequences: "I plant it if it droops to hell, / Or if it blooms to heaven."[128] More than expressing carefreeness, this statement, in its reflection of society's value judgments by naming the dichotomy of hell–heaven, can be read as reflecting society's juxtaposition of procreative heterosexual sex with "sinful," potentially homosexual sex, thereby confirming the speaker's disregard for moral norms.

"More Than a Fool's Song" (1927),[129] a poem Cullen set into a gay framework by dedicating it to his intimate friend and presumable lover Edward Perry, can be read in a similarly transgressive vein. The poem's speaker urges an addressee—maybe Perry—to seek positive values, for instance beauty and honesty, in what are deemed their opposites. In the course of the poem, an acceptance of concepts such as truth, beauty, and Christianity is indicated, but Cullen, to borrow from Jonathan Dollimore's phrasing, transgressively reinscribes those whom society regards as the "other" or the "deviant" into these concepts.[130] The poem's speaker thus advises readers:

> For honest treatment seek the thief;
> For truth consult the liar;
>
> . . .
>
> In Christian practice those who move
> To symbols strange to us
> May reckon clearer of His love
> Than we who own His cross.

The binary structures fundamental to society are clearly inverted. In this context, it is interesting to revisit "Magnets" with its depressing distinction between lively heterosexuals and the near-dead homosexuals. This distinction is reversed in "More Than a Fool's Song," which offers a solution to what in Cullen's poetry often seems to be the "problem" of homosexuality: "The souls we think are hurtling down / Perhaps are climbing up."[131] Those who are expected to be damned in hell for their sins—such as homosexuality— may be on their way to heaven, where a Christ reinvented by Cullen as black and/or gay welcomes them.

Cullen could also emphatically celebrate "deviant" sexuality and love, as evident in "Love's Way" (1927).[132] Reminiscent of "Sonnet" (1935), in which the "noblest way" of love is mentioned, Cullen already in the second line seems to hint at same-sex love, stating that "love's is the nobler way," thereby evoking the coded term for homosexuality—"noble friendship."[133] The line runs on to state that "love's is the nobler way / Of courtesy"[134]—the formal separation of the line serving as a kind of safety net, further covering up the code. In contrast to most of Cullen's poems, love is here portrayed as beautiful and harmonious, uniting two people who share everything in a partnership between equals built on "perfect faith." Here again, there could be a clue for a gay reading, as the latter term seems reminiscent of the code expression "perfect friendship."[135] Cullen's gay voice here resonates in the depiction of the beauty of love between equal partners. In a 1923 letter to Locke, Cullen reported: "I have read 'Love's Coming of Age' and it has helped me immensely"[136]—a potentially significant factor for the reading of "Love's Way," since Carpenter, who praised the democratic bonds among men, in this book criticized the lack of equality in conventional heterosexual marriages, which he described as unions between a "half-grown" man and a woman who is a "serf or a parasite."[137]

The young protagonists of "Uncle Jim" (1927) and "Tableau" (1925) know and live "Love's Way."[138] A strong link between the two poems is the spirit of youthfulness that can partly be ascribed to Cullen's age. The emphasis on youth can additionally be linked to Cullen's interest in youth movements. In 1923, Locke specifically pointed out the German *Wandervogel* movement to Cullen. This movement was well known for its homosexual undercurrents, of which Locke, who was intimately involved with a male *Wandervogel* himself, was clearly aware. A trip to Germany that Locke tried to arrange for Cullen in 1923 did not materialize, but Cullen remained interested.[139] In his speech to the 1923 League of Youth Meeting in New York, in which he refers to the *Wandervogel* movement, Cullen proclaimed: "Youth the world over is undergoing a spiritual and an intellectual awakening, is looking with new eyes at old customs and institutions. . . ."[140] The young men Cullen depicts in "Uncle Jim" and "Tableau" also oppose customs by forming male couples who transgress racial boundaries. They thereby join in what

Alexander Gumby, a gay African American bohemian and, in Bruce Kellner's words, "one of [the Renaissance's] reigning dandies," described as a "strange friendship . . . / That discards geneology and creeds, / American's bigotry, that ignorenc breeds . . . " [sic] in a sonnet to an intimate male friend.[141] In his above-mentioned speech, Cullen suggested that youth movements "are being viewed with trepidation by those who desire to see things continue in the same rut."[142] This fear seems reflected in the elements of doubt and threat that endanger the happiness of Cullen's protagonists, who through their behavior challenge a heterosexual norm and a specifically American tradition—racial segregation.

"Uncle Jim" begins with a discussion between the apparently black speaker and Jim, his uncle, about "[w]hite folks."[143] Cullen depicts a clash between generations: Jim, presented as representative of an older generation, believes that race relations will never change, because "[w]hite folks is white. . . ." His skepticism is not shared by his nephew, who dismisses Jim's statement as "[a] platitude." Although the words remain unspoken, the speaker can anticipate his uncle's prophecy: "Young fool, you'll soon be ripe!" A belief in an improvement of interracial relations is obviously judged naïve. The impression gained from the third and fourth stanzas, however, is that Jim is proven wrong because the speaker is involved in a happy interracial relationship—not, as may be expected, with a woman, but with a man. While it is not explicitly stated that the speaker's "friend" is white, this can be inferred from the context because the speaker presents their friendship as evidence for his case. The two intimate friends share joy and grief, yet while lying together in the grass—a scene evocative of Cullen's poem "Spring Reminiscence" (1925), in which two "colts," two young and uncontrollable men, remember a night spent lying in clover—the speaker wonders why his mind should "stray the Grecian urn."[144]

The image of the "Grecian urn" invites multiple readings, one being that the speaker is diverted from his thoughts about displays of same-sex activities as frequently depicted on Greek vases: He cannot concentrate on the physical intimacy he and his friend perhaps planned to experience. A similar conclusion is reached if the term is read as a metaphor for the speaker's friend. The reference to Greece could point to the friend's white complexion, but more significantly, one can read "Grecian" as indicative of the friend's same-sex orientation. The latter reading seems corroborated by Cullen's use of "urn," which could constitute a hint at Urning, a term coined by German Karl Heinrich Ulrichs to denote a man-loving man.[145] There is yet another possibility: "Ode on a Grecian Urn" is a poem by Cullen's literary idol Keats. It is feasible that Cullen's speaker cannot concentrate on the poem's central chiasmus—"Beauty is truth, truth beauty":[146] Although his friend's affection is beautiful and must therefore be true, the speaker's mind is led astray to "muse on uncle Jim" and his deep mistrust of whites. This final reference to uncle Jim casts a shadow of doubt that obscures the image of an otherwise happy interracial same-sex relationship, thereby emphasizing the pervasiveness and destructive force of matters of race.

The problematic issue of interracial relations is also central in "Tableau," where a black boy and a white boy are depicted walking arm in arm along a street, being watched and talked about by disapproving white and black observers. In this "tableau" or scene, Cullen blends the topics of race and homosexuality, achieving what Woods terms "a harmonized counterpoint of the two themes."[147] Even before the beginning of the actual poem, a dedication establishes a same-sex context: The poem is dedicated to Cullen's white lover Donald Duff.[148] Following this dedication, the poem's homoerotic content is manifest in the first two lines: "Locked arm in arm they cross the way, / The black boy and the white."[149] Here Cullen already hints at the boys' transgressive behavior: They "cross the way," or, as might be said, moral and racial boundaries, by publicly displaying their intimacy. Beginning the poem with the word "Locked," Cullen could have intended a pun on Alain Locke's name, in which case, considering Locke's mediating role, it seems appropriate that two boys walk together. Cullen emphasizes the insoluble link between the boys through the formal variation of beginning the first line with an inversion of the poem's otherwise predominantly iambic meter. The physical closeness of the two boys seems striking, yet Cullen soon draws attention to racial matters. Employing metaphors—"night" and "day"—he emphasizes the visual contrast between the two boys. Yet, as D. Dean Shackleford observes, these metaphors can also be read as indicators of the boys' intimacy: They complement each other like night and day, and, additionally, it could be hinted that they spend not only the day but also the night together.[150]

A threatening element is introduced in the second stanza: "Indignant" white and black observers disapprove of the two boys' intimacy. Though united in their outrage, the onlookers are portrayed as two distinct groups. On the one hand, there are the "dark folk," who "stare" at the boys "[f]rom lowered blinds." Apparently wary of being seen, they silently hide behind their shades while closely observing the street. On the other hand, "the fair folk talk," clearly feeling no need to refrain from voicing their objection. Employing a sequence of two stressed syllables, Cullen formally emphasizes the onlookers' focus on the two boys: They watch "these two" who dare to disrespect social norms, and readers can almost visualize the pointing of fingers. What is presented as precipitating the observers' objection is that the boys "should dare / In unison to walk." Cullen here subtly interweaves the themes of race and same-sex desire, as the expression "in unison" describes male–male but also interracial bonding. Homosexuality and miscegenation could thus be said to be at issue here. The term "miscegenation" may at first seem inappropriate in this context because it usually applies only to heterosexual relationships that potentially involve reproduction and thereby an actual "mixing" of races. However, as Kevin Mumford observes, the concept of miscegenation was at the beginning of the twentieth century also applied to interracial same-sex relationships, as sexologists and prison reformers "understood black/white *homosexual* relations through reference to the ideology of miscegenation," thereby conceptualizing the absence of gender difference through racial difference.[151]

While readers may expect the two boys in "Tableau" to be intimidated by the onlookers' comments and gazes, they are instead "[o]blivious to look and word" and simply "pass" by. Apparently conscious of their transgression of social codes, they "see no wonder / That lightning brilliant as a sword / Should blaze the path of thunder." Comparing these last two lines of the poem to the preceding parts, the powerful imagery is striking. Disrupting neither meter nor the interlaced rhymes, Cullen evokes a picture of powerful movement, violence, and disruption through his figurative language, squeezing into these lines the words "lightning," "sword," "blaze," and "thunder." At first sight, this imagery appears threatening, fusing noise, striking light, heat, and possibly physical violence that can be linked to the grim faces of the boys' vigilant observers. Violent retribution might await them for their disrespect of moral codes. Reimonenq suggests, however, that when the lovers are viewed as "lightning," the term can also be interpreted as "knowledge," enlightenment that clears away the darkness of ignorance—not only surrounding the topic of homosexuality but also interracial relations.[152] The linking of "lightning" with the simile "brilliant as a sword" can consequently be interpreted as having phallic connotations and as pointing to the knowledge of homosexuality, which, to use Cullen's phrasing, will "blaze the path of thunder." The knowledge gained from watching the scene of the black and the white boy in unison is in this utopian vision expected to blaze a trail—in Reimonenq's words, the "road to freedom"[153]—for a possible larger and powerful movement, metaphorically represented by the thunder that follows the lightning.

Particularly owing to this optimistic and powerful ending, Cullen's depiction of the gay couple seems reminiscent of Whitman's in "We Two Boys Together Clinging" (1867):

> We two boys together clinging,
> One the other never leaving,
> Up and down the roads going, North and South
> excursions making,
>
>   . . .
>
> thieving, threatening,
> Misers, menials, priests alarming. . . .[154]

This poem could be seen as a more militant treatment of the same-sex topic depicted in "Tableau," yet one without racial implications. Whitman was included in *Ioläus* with an excerpt of *Democratic Vistas* in which he outlined a vision of "threads of manly friendship, fond of loving, pure and sweet . . . [that have] deepest relations to general politics. I say Democracy infers such loving comradeship."[155] In "Tableau," Cullen turns Whitman's "dream" into reality, thereby interpreting his idea of "Democracy" along the lines of Carpenter, who saw the political implications of homosexual relationships as "bringing the Races of the world together."[156] The implication in "Tableau" is that gay men can advance race relations. Although Cullen actually deemed it significant to "keep a racial heart"[157] regarding the choice of male partners— an attitude that seems understandable in light of the pressures already burdening intraracial gay couples—he dared to follow his desire, opting for Duff as his partner. As the poem seems to indicate, gay men can like Cullen and Duff supersede the racial divide and form a strong union. This possibility of a happy ending for gay men and for members of all races constitutes an extraordinarily positive outlook by Cullen which, however, remains exceptional in his work.

Cullen's gay voice, ranging from somber depictions of same-sex love to the expression of hope for what Jean Wagner terms a "more brotherly future,"[158] manifests itself in poems in which paganism, death, but also courage and joy alternate. While pointing to Cullen's layering of racial and sexual themes and the validity of gay and racial readings of Cullen's poems, Reimonenq also suggests that Cullen "used race to blur the focus," race constituting a "poetic dodge," a cover for gay references.[159] Yet far from exclusively focusing on one theme, Cullen interwove religion, race, gay contemporary discourse, sexuality, and romantic literary form, thereby appealing to overlapping audiences: genteel critics, who applauded his employment of traditional poetic forms; a specifically black audience that undertook racial readings, finding in Cullen's poetry, as commented by Owen Dodson, all "dilemmas" `—"the hurt pride, the indignation, the satirical thrusts, the agony of being black in America";[160] and gay readers accustomed to the sounds of Cullen's gay voice and his references to a discourse known to an interracial community of gay men.

FOUR

Langston Hughes:
A "true 'people's poet'"

Publishing his first poems in the early years of the Harlem Renaissance, Langston Hughes quickly rose to prominence among the younger Renaissance writers, his popularity being matched only by Countée Cullen. Black critics frequently played the two authors off against each other, "praising the one and damning the other . . . the traditional romantic aesthete (Cullen) and the genuine 'New Negro' (Hughes)."[1] Contrasted with the "poet laureate" Cullen, Hughes was termed "poet lowrate" because he, as Skip Gates observes, "saw himself as a representative—qua poet—of the basic black man" and consequently focused on what might be termed "ordinary" Harlemites.[2] While some critics celebrated Hughes as a "true 'people's poet'" who deserved "the title of Proletarian Poet," particularly genteel black critics disapproved of his portrayal of working-class African Americans, labeling him a "Sewer Dweller" who had "gone off on the wrong track altogether."[3] Seemingly unperturbed, or perhaps even reaffirmed by criticism, Hughes insisted on his choice of subject matter, defiantly claiming that it was "the low-down folks, the so-called common element" who "furnish a wealth of colorful, distinctive material for any artist."[4] In 1943, Hughes expressed his conviction "that the function of the poet is to interpret not only his own people to the rest of the world but to themselves."[5] He intended to "interpret" particularly working-class African Americans who were usually excluded and without representative power, thereby aligning his cultural politics with his class and race politics and redefining the "burden of representation" for himself. Crucial to this redefinition was Hughes's distinct literary style. His choice of subject matter was emphasized by formal aspects, especially an adoption of blues forms and African American vernacular. Consequently, Hughes's language seems uncomplicated, as evident in, for instance, Nathan Huggins's reference to the "simple and unpretentious level"[6] of Hughes's works. Hughes fostered this image: His autobiography *The Big Sea* (1940) tellingly commences with the act of throwing books overboard on a sea journey, a symbolical distancing from intellectualism.[7] It therefore seems logical that he did not emulate consciously elitist modernists like Ezra Pound but followed writers like Carl Sandburg and Walt Whitman, who developed what might be termed a "democratic" free verse and clearly American brand of literary modernism.[8]

Hughes's redefinition of the representation of African Americans certainly contributed to his iconic status and to the fact that he, as Henry Louis Gates notes, "was elected popularly to serve as our 'representative negro.' "[9] Given this unique position, anything that might be regarded as blemishing Hughes's reputation is potentially controversial. Rumors about Hughes's alleged homosexuality circulated prior to the 1980s, yet only with Faith Berry's and Arnold Rampersad's biographies (1983/1988) does his sexuality appear to have become an openly discussed contentious issue.[10] In contrast to Cullen's case, no critics explicitly deny that Hughes's sexuality was at least ambiguous and that he had homosexual experiences. The Langston Hughes estate subjected *Looking for Langston* (1989), Isaac Julien's cinematic exploration of Hughes and gay black sexuality, to censorship. This instance, however, cannot be regarded as typical, as the estate had earlier given permission for the inclusion of some of Hughes's poems in gay anthologies.[11] A major impediment to an assessment of Hughes's sexual status is his successful shielding of his private life from public gaze. His correspondence evidences only scant references to sexual experiences, and he also excluded fellow Renaissance writers from his private life. Wallace Thurman, for instance, complained that Hughes was "such a mysterious person, so discreet in [his] reports of intimate matters" and "so damned impersonal and non confidential."[12] Richard Bruce Nugent, openly gay and a friend of Hughes's, also had no precise knowledge of Hughes's sexuality. His assessment varies from the characterization of Hughes as "intrinsically homosexual, but overtly not" to the conviction that he was "asexual."[13] The latter judgment is mirrored in Rampersad's assessment as well as in Carl Van Vechten's comment that Hughes "seemed to thrive without having sex."[14] A rare exception to this pattern of mystery and secrecy is Hughes's intimation of his first sexual same-sex experience to a friend. Rampersad briefly mentions this disclosure yet fails to give a date and also does not specify his source.[15]

Critics claiming Hughes's homosexuality challenge the assumption that he was "asexual." Criticizing the word choice as such, Seth Silberman suggests that " 'asexual' in a heterosexually-oriented world signifies 'asexually heterosexual.' "[16] Hilton Als goes much further in his critical comment, deploring that Hughes was "rendered pale and sexless through the (one hopes) quite witless machinations of biographers, critics, theorists."[17] In light of, for instance, Rampersad's research efforts, which included among many interviews with Hughes's friends and acquaintances conversations with Nugent, who was rather frank regarding sexual issues, this assessment seems unjustified. However, Reimonenq's suggestion that Hughes lived a "secret life silently in the confines of a very narrow, but well-constructed closet"[18] is helpful; there might have been a "closet" serving Hughes for hiding his transgressive desire. Some critics seem to imply that Hughes's sexual encounter with a crewman that he, as mentioned before, had confided to a friend, is sufficient to claim him to be gay. Berry notes Hughes's homosexual experience and reports on difficulties in his relationship with a woman, concluding that "At age thirty-one, he had lost his battle against homosexuality"[19]—a statement she fails to substantiate and in which she moreover evokes an image of same-sex desire as disease. Similar to Als, Reimonenq expresses disappointment in Rampersad's work: "[T]hough he documents Hughes's admission of a homosexual encounter with a seaman . . . Rampersad asserts that he could not find incontrovertible evidence that the writer was gay."[20] Compared to Reimonenq's implicit claim that Hughes's homosexual encounter "proves" his gay identity—a view that uncritically equates sexual practice with sexual identity—Rampersad's cautious approach may be more useful.[21]

In contrast to Cullen's case, there seem to be no indications that Hughes was a self-identified gay man. Considering that he was—perhaps on a sexual level—involved with women and at least on one occasion with a man, the possibility that he did not perceive himself to be included in any category such as homo- or heterosexuality seems given. Interestingly, Reimonenq and Berry seem to imply that Hughes's friendship with gay men indicates his own homosexuality.[22] While this constitutes a rather dubious claim, their observations are useful because they indicate that Hughes was presumably aware of contemporary models of same-sex love. One such model was offered by Cullen and Locke, who attempted to introduce Hughes into their gay "fraternity."[23] Fearing detection but also insecure about Hughes's sexual status, both were careful not to be too explicit in their letters to Hughes in which Locke, for instance, underlines his love of the "Hellenic view."[24] Although Cullen attempted to subtly unveil their gay connection, he believed he had failed in this respect, commenting that Hughes "was sympathetic but I do not believe that he fully understood the situation."[25] Cullen's conclusion appears to be the result of a strategy Hughes employed: He responded positively to Cullen and Locke's coded references, writing to Locke that he regarded him as "a sympathetic friend" and expressing enthusiasm for Whitman's " 'Song of the Open Road' and the poems in 'Calamus,' " thereby hinting at his familiarity with this type of gay discourse.[26] Yet he remained noncommittal when Locke and Cullen pressed him to unequivocally express his understanding of their campaign. Claiming that he was "stupid" and feigning ignorance of their motives, Hughes stated, for instance, in response to a poem Cullen sent him with the dedication "For L.H."—a symbol of Cullen's interest in Hughes—that "I don't know what to say about the 'For L.H.' but I appreciate it, and I like the poem."[27]

Hughes's motivation to at least partially participate in Cullen and Locke's gay discourse in spite of what appears to be his indifference to their advances might have stemmed from his intention not to antagonize them and particularly to retain Cullen's friendship. Hughes might also have wanted to curry favor with Locke, since he intended to enter Howard University, where Locke taught. In the long run, Hughes met neither of these potential objectives: His relationship with Cullen soured, and he never enrolled at Howard University. Why Hughes remained unresponsive to Locke and Cullen's campaign cannot be ascertained, but it seems as though he made a rule of not getting intimately involved with anyone within the Renaissance circle—male or female. Hughes furthermore might have had misgivings about Locke's brand of a men-loving identity and its accompanying discourse, as they were, apart from references to Whitman, largely elitist and based on a European cultural framework.

Hughes, who was equally familiar with alternative gay identities such as Nugent's, which was characterized by what was perceived as outrageous flamboyance, might not have found a model of same-sex love he felt comfortable with. Moreover, as pointed out earlier in this study, it must be noted that in the first decades of the twentieth century, different types of gay identities coexisted with an absence of any such identity despite an involvement in physical same-sex encounters. Against this background, unspecified claims that Hughes was gay seem inadequate and ignorant of historical circumstances, as the concept of a modern gay identity is thereby uncritically transferred to the 1920s.[28] Another difficulty with attempts at claiming Hughes's homosexuality is that heterosexist strategies are reversed: "Obstacles" in the perception of Hughes as a gay man—for instance, his displays of heterosexual interests—are smoothed over to facilitate a gay narrative without gaps.[29] As bell hooks summarizes, the "tantalizing gap between fact and possibility ... [makes] all attempts to document, in some exclusive way, Hughes's sexual practice a potential erasure."[30] The desire, as voiced by Reimonenq, to "settle definitely the question of the poet's sexuality"[31] and a demand for "wholeness" in the sense of a modern gay identity simply cannot be met.

In line with critics' differing assessments of Hughes's sexual status, attitudes toward potential gay readings of his texts vary decisively. Rampersad's comment that Hughes was a "sexual blank" whose libido represented more or less a "void" is, as Charles Nero suggests, problematic because he fails to consider the presence of homo-/heterosexual desire on Hughes's part and consequently neglects possible gay readings.[32] Interestingly, not all of those who claim Hughes to be homosexual establish a connection between his writing and his sexual orientation. Als seems to suggest that Hughes consciously excluded the issue of homosexuality from his work. According to Als, "none of Hughes' own works reveals the enormous tension under which he must have operated"—a tension that, he believes, derived from Hughes's burden of representation, his dependence on white patronage and, "his *terrible secret*," his homosexuality.[33] Similar to critics discussing Cullen's homosexuality, Als thereby seems to exclude the possibility of a link between same-sex desire and writing that is not negatively defined. As will be shown, this connection exists in Hughes's works of which many, as Reimonenq proposes, "invite gay readings."[34] By subordinating these readings to what looks like a biographical project, however, Reimonenq seems to regard Hughes's references to same-sex desire largely as further "evidence" completing his case of claiming Hughes as a gay man. Consequently, there is the danger that since Reimonenq apparently expects that it is possible to "elucidate the facts of Hughes's life" through explorations of Hughes's literary gay voice, the multiplicity of meanings contained in Hughes's works is reduced to the topic of homosexuality.[35]

According to hooks, "Hughes's open exploration of sexuality in his work indicates he was not afraid to address sexual issues,"[36] yet at least in his Renaissance works, explicit references to homosexuality are rare. This may be partly attributed to the very real threat of literary censorship. Considering his self-defined role as "interpreter" of the black masses, it seems unlikely that Hughes would have intentionally risked censorship, thereby valuing sexual over racial concerns. As Steven Tracy claims, Hughes sought acceptance "not only for himself, but for the black oral tradition."[37] It is therefore feasible that he abstained from sexual explicitness in his works to, as Tracy suggests, "clean up and 'legitimize' the blues,"[38] aiming at the inscription of black folk art and vernacular into mainstream culture. "In Hughes' work," as hooks emphasizes, "sexual passion is always mediated by issues of materiality, class position, poverty."[39] Hughes usually sets sexually transgressive topics like female prostitution in a material framework, avoiding a portrayal of sexual passion and giving economic reasons for what was generally perceived as "deviant" sexual behavior. This emphasis on materiality would not easily have been applicable to a portrayal of men-loving men. Nevertheless, there are several instances in Hughes's Renaissance writings in which, however ambiguously, same-sex desire is presented.

MULTIPLE MEANINGS, AMBIGUITY, AND STRATEGIES: HUGHES'S POETIC GAY VOICE

Particularly in his poetry, Hughes produces a multiplicity of meanings, works with an ambiguity of terms, and employs textual strategies, thereby opening up spaces also for gay readings. In the short "Poem [2]" (1925),[40] a speaker expresses grief for a lost friend. Exceptionally for Hughes's work, the poem carries a dedication—"To F.S."—that gains significance in light of the specification of the mourned friend as male. Writing "He went away from me," Hughes creates a male same-sex space in which the speaker's affection is underlined by the statement "I loved my friend" which frames the poem. This clarity and simplicity stand in contrast to the mystery engulfing Hughes's dedication "To F.S.," the identity of whom remains unclear.[41] Although it is uncertain whether his friend is dead, the speaker's mourning is evident. He does not indulge in his grief, however, stating: "There's nothing more to say."

Implying that the preceding expression of love explains everything, this statement constitutes a refusal to display further intimate emotions. In the fourth and fifth lines, the speaker comments on the poem's structure—"The poem ends, / Soft as it began"—emphasizing a point that might otherwise remain unrecognized: The poem's beginning and end, containing declarations of love, create a "soft" framework.[42] Although the speaker refuses to comment further, thereby perhaps retreating into an unemotional, "masculine" role, Hughes creates an all-male context in which admissions of love supersede a display of hardened masculinity. This space is also evoked in *Looking for Langston,* in which Julien presents the black male body as soft and vulnerable, thereby, as Henry Louis Gates points out, directing a "powerful assault on the well-policed arena of black masculinity."[43] Depicting a speaker who expresses love for another man in a situation of loss, Hughes could be said to employ a traditional gay literary strategy that, as indicated in Jessie Fauset's comment on the poem—"[Hughes] has feeling a-plenty and is not ashamed to show it"[44]—to some extent legitimizes the expression of love for a member of the same sex. Rampersad suggests that it would be "insensitive" to view this poem as "proof of [Hughes's] homosexual feeling," but gay readings nevertheless remain a possibility.[45]

Many of Hughes's poems are set in a heterosexual context, yet some of them constitute ungendered spaces that allow for a wide range of readings. Among other poems, Woods singles out "Desire" (1927), one of numerous poems by Hughes in which lovers are faced with the transitory nature of love.[46] As hooks asserts, in many poems Hughes shows himself to be a "sensual poet obsessed with desire," who speaks "about erotic longing, tormenting desire, unfulfillment, romantic abandonment, relationships between black men and women that don't work, that end in pain, bitterness, that leave folks overwhelmed by sorrow, deep in despair, longing for death."[47] In "Star Seeker" (1926),[48] unfulfilled desire can be detected on a metaphorical level. Employing an imagery reminiscent of the myth of Icarus and Daedalus, Hughes presents a speaker who has failed in his pursuit of a dream, a "flaming star," which leaves him with "scars." While his quest ends in pain as his aim "burned [his] hands," the speaker's attempt to pursue his dream seems positive, distinguishing him from the surrounding "dream-dead world." His aim is endowed with special qualities: A source of light that resembles "[w]ild beauty," it seems unattainable, desirable, and, despite or maybe because of its apparent danger, irresistible. As there are no concrete indications about what the "star" could be, various readings are feasible. Performing a racial reading, one might contend that the struggle for freedom from racist suppression left many with scars. The poem's imagery of flames and burning heat can however also be read as alluding to sexual desire. Given the status of same-sex love as the epitome of "forbidden" and potentially dangerous desire, the speaker's scars could also derive from the violent repression of transgressive desire.

The multiplicity of meaning surrounding the image of the dream resurfaces in various other poems, of which "The Dream Keeper" (1925)[49] seems particularly interesting. The poem's speaker invites all "dreamers" to bring their dreams for him to protect. The poem resembles Cullen's "For a Poet" (1925), in which a speaker carefully wraps his dreams in a "silken cloth," in that Hughes's speaker offers to wrap the dreams of others "[i]n a blue cloud-cloth."[50] The basic difference between the poems is that while Cullen's speaker seeks to protect his own dreams, the motives of Hughes's speaker are altruistic. Moreover, in Cullen's poem, dreams are taken into a grave, while the cloth in Hughes's poem is not to be buried. Instead, it acquires a skylike quality, promising freedom rather than death. The aim, protection "from the too-rough fingers / Of the world," is similar, however, to that in Cullen's poem which, as Amitai Avi-Ram argues, can be read as addressing transgressive desire.[51] Hughes also seems to invite this interpretation—particularly as his speaker encourages people to bring dreams he describes as "[h]eart melodies," thereby alluding to love and desire that need protection.

Ignoring the risks involved in the pursuit of their visions, many of Hughes's characters are adamant in their determination to break free from constraints. This spirit, underlined by a quadruple repetition of "we run," is evident in "Shadows" (1923),[52] in which people who seem confined to darkness are depicted as escaping the shadows, seeking light. Relating to what Woods describes as "a representation of openness and enforced closetry,"[53] this light–dark dichotomy seems applicable particularly to the issues of race and sexuality. "Shadows" can thus be read as describing the escape of African Americans from enforced confinement—for example, slavery or, more generally, racial oppression—into the "sun," or freedom. Reminiscent of depictions of "homosexuals" as "twilight men" in contemporary literature, "Shadows" can also be interpreted as depicting same-sex-interested people who seek to escape a life of darkness, desiring to literally "come out."[54]

Liberation is also a central issue in "Our Land" (1923).[55] A speaker declares that he and his ungendered lover deserve to live in a joyful land; toward the poem's end, he seems determined to emigrate. In contrast to his current environment in which "life is cold" and "birds are grey," the land he envisions features "sun," "fragrant water," "trees," and "chattering parrots," offering excitement as the senses of hearing, smell, taste, and vision are catered to. The difference between the present country and what could be described as the promised land is highlighted in the third stanza: "[W]e should have a land of joy, / Of love and joy and wine and song, / And not this land where joy is wrong." Again, a transference between the topics of race and sexuality seems possible. A racial interpretation in which Hughes, following a contemporary primitivist discourse, claims African Americans' higher capacity for and greater need of enjoyment—the term "joy," repeated thrice in the poem, occupying a central position—seems feasible. Following this reading, the speaker's exclamation "Oh, sweet away! / Ah, my beloved one, away!"

in the last couplet can be read as addressing either a single person or all African Americans, the "beloved" race, somewhat reminiscent of Marcus Garvey's "back to Africa" message. As joy and love are "wrong" in the present country, a gay reading seems equally valid. In this reading, the last couplet gains significance, as the "sweet" and "beloved one" could be the potentially male speaker's male lover.

Hughes presents another quest for joy in a poem of the same name. The "Joy"[56] the speaker refers to at first sight seems to be a woman's name: He searches for his lover "Joy" and eventually "found her" with the "butcher boy." "Joy," however, contains several subplots. It is feasible to read "Joy" not as a woman's name but as denoting happiness. Anne Borden suggests that the speaker is "dismayed and pleased" to find "Joy" with the butcher, as joy is thereby "demystified, found amidst the chaotic harmony of city streets and work."[57] To some extent, joy here seems democratized in a manner reminiscent of Whitman's ideal of democracy in which, as in "Song of Myself" (1855), characters such as a young "butcher-boy," "[b]lacksmiths," and a "negro" coexist happily.[58] However, Borden apparently fails to detect another level of meaning: The presumably male speaker finds joy "[i]n the arms of the butcher boy," thus with a man.[59] Hughes thereby establishes a gay link to Whitman's scenery pictured in "Song of Myself," which is not only "democratic" but, significantly for gay readings, also characterized by the presence of young men of various racial backgrounds who are linked by same-sex desire. Playing on the double meaning of the term *joy*, Hughes, as Woods points out, manages to "assert the joy of homosexual desire" while producing meaning on another level, creating a story about infidelity that also functions as a "decoy to inattentive homophobes."[60]

Similarly, in "To Beauty" (1926),[61] a poem replete with—for Hughes—unusual romantic imagery, Hughes seems to embed a sexually dissident tale within a heterosexual narrative. Only "fools" "worship / At the altar of Beauty," yet they are rewarded by the sensation of beauty's "loveliness and pain" and experience "a pleasure divine." Hughes's imagery, which seems reminiscent of Cullen's poetry, gives the adoration of beauty a sexual character: The admirers "drink Beauty's wine" and

> ... seek no other goddess
> Nor grapes
> Plucked from another's
> Vine.

Given the identification of beauty as a goddess, a male same-sex context seems excluded, yet a closer reading of Hughes's metaphors indicates a potential link to male same-sex desire. Hughes could well have been aware of the gay connotation of the phrase "to worship / At the altar," twice included in "To Beauty"—a slang expression for fellatio.[62] Reading "To Beauty" in this light, the female pronouns connected with Beauty become irrelevant. Hughes's depiction of the "drinking of Beauty's wine" can thus be viewed in a same-sex context—particularly as "Beauty" could in fact be the name of a beautiful man. This possibility is intriguing, considering that one of the protagonists in Nugent's homoerotic story "Smoke, Lilies and Jade,"[63] published one month after "To Beauty," bears this name. Hughes's phallic imagery produced with the alliteration "sharp, swift, silver swords"[64] is also noteworthy. What could be regarded as the poem's central statement can then be singled out: Hughes declares that "To worship / At the altar of Beauty / Is a pleasure divine"—an extraordinarily affirmative yet camouflaged depiction of same-sex desire. What Woods describes as Hughes's "sassy and incisive"[65] voice, is here certainly audible.

SAILORS AND THE WATERFRONT

Representations of sailors and sea journeys are crucial to an exploration of Hughes's gay literary voice. Prominent in his first volumes of poetry, several short stories from the 1920s, and in *The Big Sea*, they form a major theme, especially in Hughes's early works. Hughes's autobiographical narration of his experiences at sea conveys the impression that working onboard a ship constituted a formative experience and a clear break from his past. According to Hughes, "it wasn't only the books that I wanted to throw away, but everything unpleasant and miserable out of my past. . . . All those things I wanted to throw away. To be free of. To escape from. I wanted to be a man on my own, control my own life, and go my own way."[66] Becoming a "man on his own" entailed a sexual coming of age that Hughes presents in a heterosexual framework, stating that the crew, presumably including himself, "kept thinking about the girls."[67] Though he was only a mess boy, the fact that Hughes worked on a ship enhanced his masculine status. Sailors, as George Chauncey observes, were widely regarded as the "embodiment of the aggressive masculine ideal."[68] Their "manliness" appealed not only to women but also to same-sex-interested men, for whom they represented "trade," sought-after, "virile" sexual partners.[69] Hughes's experiences at sea certainly brought him the admiration of gay Renaissance figures: Cullen considered Hughes's seafaring "a glorious school in which to matriculate" and described him after his return from sea as "looking like a virile brown god."[70] Similarly, Nugent recounted that Hughes was "a made-to-order Hero for me. . . . he had done everything—all the things young men dream of but never quite get done—worked on ships, gone to exotic places. . . ."[71]

Central to the sexual image of sailors was that they were "seen as young and manly, unattached, and unconstrained by conventional morality."[72] Not being bound by wife and children increased their masculinity, as too close an involvement with and interest in women could be regarded as a sign of subordination and effeminacy.[73] Following Judith Butler's argument that gender is an ongoing performance, one could assert that Hughes narrates his performance of "manliness" in *The Big Sea*: "We had lived together six months . . . pal'd around together . . . worked together, played together, fought together, slept with the same women, drunk from the same bottles."[74] Hughes's depiction of camaraderie at sea fits Chauncey's account of New York's bachelor subculture, in which "solidarity . . . was expressed in the everyday ties built at work on the waterfront or in construction."[75] Among these men, masculinity was established through "[s]exual prowess with women," but, more significantly, it was "confirmed by other men and in relation to other men, not by women."[76] Drinking and gambling—elements present in *The Big Sea*—were distinct signifiers for "manliness" or, to borrow from Butler, "acts and gestures, articulated and enacted desires [creating] the illusion of an interior and organizing gender core."[77] It is significant, however, that Hughes in his narrative does not support straightforward misogyny and the violent suppression of women. Depicting the rape of an African girl, Hughes distances himself, displaying his unwillingness to share a concept of "manliness" that involves sexual violence.[78]

Considering the prominence of racial issues in Hughes's work, the absence of racial distinctions in his depiction of the tight-knit community of crew members is remarkable. In *The Big Sea*, Hughes's cabin mates Ramon and George are described as "colored" and "chocolate-colored,"[79] but the camaraderie Hughes describes is not based on race. The crew members figuring in Hughes's work form a transnational, interracial community including "Greeks, West Indian Negroes, Irish, Portuguese and Americans,"[80] in which race seems meaningless and, as is the case in most of his poems featuring sea-related themes, remains unmentioned. One racist incident, however, is briefly depicted in *The Big Sea*: Hughes recounts the refusal of an apparently white "Third Engineer" to eat with African customs officials.[81] The engineer's higher-ranking status constitutes a significant detail, as it underlines another feature of the sailors' camaraderie: Transcending race and background, they form what might be termed the ship's working class. The union of workers of all races, apparently impossible on land, is depicted as reality at sea—a vision fitting in with Hughes's interest in communism, which shaped particularly his poetry in the early 1930s but which, as Rampersad suggests, remained deliberately hidden in his autobiographies.[82]

As described by Hughes's narrator in the short story "The Little Virgin" (1927), a ship's crew is bound together by a "strange comradeship, a strict fraternity."[83] This queer bond linking crew members can be read as a reference to Whitman's "manly love of comrades."[84] Supportive of such a reading is a detail Hughes, maybe to camouflage the gay connection, excluded from the published version of his autobiography: While discarding all other books, Hughes held on to Whitman's *Leaves of Grass*. Whitman thus seems to replace or join Saint Christopher, protecting Hughes and the rest of the "manly" crew of potentially men-loving men during their trip. As Nero suggests, this journey could, particularly in light of Hughes's homosexual encounter during his maritime travels, be viewed as what Jacob Stockinger describes as an "external itinerary that corresponds to an internal journey of self-discovery."[85]

For gay readings of Hughes's poem "Long Trip" (1926),[86] the vision of a crew as an all-male camaraderie is of central significance. As its title indicates, the poem is on one level about a long sea journey. A closer scrutiny of imagery and word choice reveals another level, as Hughes's indulgence in sounds, effected by the repeated employment of alliterations, gives the poem an almost sensuous character. The sea is twice described as a "wilderness of water," and the sailors "dip and dive, / Rise and roll, / Hide and are hidden." This sequence on the surface describes the ship's movements but could also point to sailors' movements. The expressions "dip and dive" and "Rise and roll" have sexual connotations—the latter terms, for instance, indicate arousal and, as employed in contemporary blues songs, motions of intercourse.[87] As ships seem to be almost exclusively male environments in Hughes's maritime-themed pieces, these sexual acts are set in a same-sex context. According to the law of the land, same-sex affairs were outlawed, yet as Hughes seems to suggest, the sea constitutes a space where such laws do not apply. The sea's "wilderness" and what Borden describes as Hughes's juxtaposition of "seemingly binary images"[88]—the repeated reference to the "desert of waves"—indicate that the sea, as a space in which binaries are no longer stable, is uncontrollable. Just like the desert, the epitome of dryness, is no longer antithetical to water, the dichotomy of normal–deviant sexuality could be said to be disrupted. Moreover, sexual encounters between sailors appear to remain secret acts of sexual transgression as the crew members "Hide and are hidden" by the sea.

The sea and "exotic" African destinations serve as the backdrop against which Hughes describes attractive women but predominantly seductive male bodies. Regarding his presentation of women, Hughes's short stories "Bodies in the Moonlight" (1927) and "Luani of the Jungles" (1928), described by Chidi Ikonné as "reveal[ing] a sacrifice of realities on the altar of masturbatory exoticism," seem exceptional.[89] Hughes's emphasis on color and bodily features, epitomized by his description of the two stories' female protagonists as "delicate and lovely as a jungle flower" and as "dark and wild, exotic and strange,"[90] conveys the impression that these women are irresistible creatures who cast a spell over men. Hughes's sexual presentation of women in these short stories seems extraordinary. Woods suggests that attractive men and boys "appear among at least as many, if not more, beautiful women"[91] in Hughes's poetry. However, reading Hughes's work, it seems that particularly in his poems, women are often assigned the role of victims of male abuse, serve to reaffirm male characters' masculinity, and, if portrayed as attractive, as is the case in "When Sue Wears Red" (1923), are featured less as objects of desire than of distant admiration.[92]

Interestingly, a close reading of "Bodies in the Moonlight," in which two sailors, Porto Rico and the narrator, pursue the African girl Nunuma, reveals that Hughes's focus on female attractiveness and thus on a heterosexual plot, seems undermined by the sailors' relationship. Wanting Nunuma for himself, Porto Rico attacks the other sailor, yet eventually both men are reunited on-board their ship. Women thus remain but an interlude for them. Crucial to the story's subtext of same-sex desire is the narrator's equivocal assertion that "Porto Rico and I are in love."[93] While the record is set "straight" through the qualifying statement "Yea, and with the same girl,"[94] the possibility of reading the statement as affirming same-sex love remains valid.

The central position Hughes assigns to male sexual attractiveness is evident in his short story "The Young Glory of Him" (1927),[95] in which the young daughter of two missionaries bound for Africa has an affair with a sailor and commits suicide on realizing that he does not love her. The narrator's reading from the girl's diary could constitute a textual strategy, allowing Hughes to praise a man's beauty—the sailor is described as "look[ing] like a blond Greek god"[96]—within a heterosexual context. Given the fascination of women and men with sailors, the statement "I always dreamed of being loved by a sailor," apparently read from the diary, has sexually dissident potential. While these comments are directly linked to the girl's diary, her perspective gets confused with that of the presumably male narrator when Hughes, without clarifying the perspective, affectionately writes that the sailor "had lost his cap and his blond hair was tousled. His blue eyes sparkled and his boy's face flushed with the joy of wine."[97] The story's overall heterosexual perspective is thereby questioned.

Hughes does not restrict himself to a tactic of ambiguity but also comments on male bodies from a clearly male perspective. In *The Big Sea*, he describes his friend George as lying "stark naked"[98] on his bed—a bodily position and nakedness suggesting availability. Nudity resurfaces in a scene featuring "a host of naked Africans—our extra helpers—bathing nude beneath a salt-water hose every evening on the afterdeck in plain sight of everybody."[99] In both instances, Hughes gives no indication of a personal interest in the men's nakedness, in the latter case adding humorously that the Africans, out of respect for white missionaries onboard, "hid their sex between their legs, evidently not realizing it then stuck out behind."[100] This amused authorial distance vanishes in another scene: Hughes describes his fascination with the sight of a "dozen black Kru boys,"[101] who, swimming in the ocean, tie together logs of wood. Describing their work as "beautiful and dangerous," Hughes appears intrigued by this combination of pleasure and risk.[102] The scene's sexual overtones are evident: The phallic logs the boys handle and the "tossing waves" and "great rolling logs" seem suggestive of intercourse.[103] While such a depiction could, perhaps because of its lack of explicitness regarding bodies, presumably pass most readers by, an audience aware of this classic feature of homoerotic writing would recognize this instance of same-sex attraction.

Hughes's sailors are predominantly embodiments of images of sailors as figuring in the gay and heterosexual imagination—strong men living together outside society's restraints. The protagonist of "Young Sailor" (1926)[104] represents a good example of this attractive freedom:

> He carries
> His own strength
> And his own laughter,
> His own today
> And his own hereafter.

This fusion of physical strength and a capacity for enjoyment is, as Woods puts it, "irresistible"[105] for women and men. The poem's protagonist, who refuses to settle, rejects marks of respectability that are defined by others and is, as emphasized by repetition, in control of his "own" destiny. A similar rejection of morality is evident in "Boy" (1928),[106] in which Hughes's speaker describes a young man who has "a way with women / Like a sailor man." Having fleeting affairs with women, he brings joy like an angel but at the same time is evil, in that he is unfaithful. The boy resembles the protagonist of "Young Sailor," yet in "Boy" bodily details are given:

> He was straight and slender
> And solid with strength
> And lovely as a young tree
> All his virile length.

He seems to be the incarnation of everything "manly," a human phallus whose sexual energy cannot be tamed. In line with the depiction of his prowess, he is presented not only as irresistible but, like Hughes's sailors, as unable to adhere to general moral and particularly Christian standards. Similar to Cullen's speakers in "For One Who Gayly Sowed His Oats" and "Ultimatum," Hughes's speaker would, as he announces in direct speech, " 'rather be a sinner, . . . and go to hell' " than subject himself to rules.[107] Against the backdrop of the poem's overall heterosexual context, which might be underlined by the depiction of the boy as "straight," the sin is heterosexual promiscuity. However, given sailors' casual sexual transgressions and their iconic status in women and men's sexual imagination, Hughes seems able to give veiled indications of same-sex desire while operating within a heterosexual framework.[108]

In "Port Town" (1926),[109] Hughes plays on sailors' transgressive sexuality without the cover of a heterosexual framework. Refraining from specifying the speaker's gender, Hughes portrays a scene that he describes in *The Big Sea* as typical of a ship's arrival: Sailors go ashore thirsting for alcohol and hungry for sex.[110] In "Port Town," they are immediately approached:

Hello, sailor boy,
In from the sea!
Hello, sailor,
Come with me!

Woods notes that the poem is "safe in the complacent assumption that it is spoken by a woman, but daring in the possibility that it is not."[111] Presuming that competition among same-sex-interested men and female prostitutes for sailors was familiar to Hughes's contemporaries—it was, for instance, featured in caricatures—one can assume that Hughes deliberately played on this ambiguity.[112] Intriguingly, the poem can also be read from Hughes's personal perspective: He vies for the attention of sailors—a reading he seems to invite, because he allows for a linking of the author with the poem's content, as it is written in uninterrupted direct speech.

A play on sexual ambiguity seems similarly evident in "Water-Front Streets" (1926),[113] which again focuses on sailors in ports. In this poem, the environment of the port is unattractive, yet similar to the speaker in "Our Land," the "lads" embark on a trip "[t]o where the spring is wondrous rare / And life is gay." The destination is not specified but represents what Woods describes as one of Hughes's "distinctly un-American"[114] dreams: Following the metaphor of spring, it can be any land allowing for freedom, color, and liveliness. Considering the multiple meanings of the term *gay*, Hughes might have employed it not only to denote happiness and joy—the latter being another ambiguous term in his poetry—but also to indicate the destination's sexually transgressive character.[115]

"Water-Front Streets" is replete with dream elements: "[D]ream ships" are manned by sailors "[w]ho carry beauties in their hearts / And dreams, like me." It is conceivable that the ships' destinations make them "dream ships," or that they are but figments of the speaker's imagination. There is also a third possibility: The ship might be freighted not only with goods but also with "dreams"—strong and beautiful sailors, who additionally carry their own dreams, thereby doubling the ship's dreamy freight.[116] Again, Hughes leaves scope for various interpretations. In light of sailors' potential sexual transgressions and the speaker's presumably male perspective, the sailors could be dream objects of men-loving men. In this context, Hughes's finishing touch to the poem, the addition of "like me" after mentioning "beauties" and "dreams" at the poem's end, is intriguing. The speaker not only shares the sailors' "gay" memories and dreams but also, as Woods suggests, "identifies himself as the possible subject of an absent sailor's dream."[117]

Contrasting virility, and at the same time allowing for slight gaps in his "manly" narrative, Hughes at several points in his maritime tales introduces instances of sexual ambiguity in which masculinity is either doubtful or absent. He thereby often strongly hints at gender inversion, a mark that was generally regarded as characteristic of "homosexuals." In *The Big Sea*, Hughes's roommate Ramon seems to lack all signifiers of "manliness": "He didn't gamble. I saw him drunk only once. He seldom drew any money, and when he did he spent it on sweets—seldom on a woman."[118] Moreover, Ramon "didn't care much for women" but "preferred silk stockings."[119] Hughes's remarks seem nonjudgmental, yet they raise questions about Ramon's masculine status and, implicitly, his sexuality.

A similar lack of manliness is depicted in "The Little Virgin," in which Hughes's fictional treatment of the protagonist resembles Herman Melville's to the extent that Melville, as Georges-Michel Sarotte observes, shows that "on board ship effeminacy was treated with contempt."[120] As in Melville's novel *White Jacket*, the sailor in Hughes's story is given an insulting nickname by the crew—"Little Virgin"—which underlines his "inferior" sexual status.[121] Moreover, similar to Melville's *Redburn*, Hughes's "unmanly" sailor is persecuted by other sailors who address him as "pink angel" and ridicule him by calling him "Mama's nice baby" in a "falsetto" voice.[122] These indicators are as strong as Ramon's preference for silk stockings: The "Little Virgin" is, as suggested by his descriptions as baby and angel, to some extent genderless, but, more importantly, the term "pink" and the "falsetto" voice directed at him suggest his lack of masculinity. Although one crew member is willing to introduce "Little Virgin" to sailors' "manly virtues,"[123] these attempts at "correcting" or fostering his masculinity fail dramatically, as the two men get into a fight over the treatment of women. Consequently, "Little Virgin" falls ill and needs to be hospitalized. Hughes's narrator again withholds any judgment, and it seems that as in *The Big Sea*, a certain critique of a masculinity that involves cruelty and the violent subordination of women is implied. The conclusion, however, seems clear: The effeminate man is not fit to be part of a ship's "manly" crew.

Sexual ambiguity is alluded to differently in the case of George in *The Big Sea*. Before joining the crew, George worked as a valet to a female impersonator. To some extent, this association stains his "masculine" image and, given female impersonators' public image as "fairy"-like, also his sexuality. Moreover, he is described as "talking and laughing and gaily waving his various appendages around."[124] As George's gestures could be viewed as flamboyant behavior, suiting a female impersonator, this depiction could be read in a gay context. Hughes retracts immediately, however, by explicitly linking him to heterosexuality: "George was talking about women, of course."[125] It must be recognized here that Hughes's autobiography, which Rampersad describes as a "tour de force of subterfuge,"[126] can be regarded as a meticulous rewriting of his life. Claiming heterosexuality for George consequently seems necessary in light of Hughes's declaration that "George and I became pretty good pals."[127] Hughes nevertheless continues his play on ambiguity in another scene which involves himself. Calling at Horta, "Some of the boys made straight for women, some for the wine shops. It depended on your temperament which you sought first."[128] According to Hughes's account, he and George bought cognac. It thus seems as if they indeed followed their "temperament"—a term Locke employed in his correspondence as an equivalent to "sexual orientation"—spending the night together in what is depicted as an almost romantic, but, because of the marker of alcohol, still "manly" scene.[129]

While Hughes in the last example allows for a measure of sexual ambiguity about his own person, he seems careful to present his seafaring experiences in an overall "manly," heterosexual framework. Significantly, he omits same-sex incidents from his narratives. During his sea journeys, black boys were openly sodomized onboard one ship—an incident which, according to Rampersad, caused Hughes to feel "greater disgust" than the aforementioned heterosexual rape scene.[130] The other instance missing in *The Big Sea* is Hughes's first physical same-sex encounter experienced during his trip to Africa. Hughes excludes explicitly homosexual incidents from his autobiography, but by depicting an all-male camaraderie at sea in various poems and *The Big Sea*, he constructs a framework for same-sex experiences, allowing for instances of sexual ambiguity which do not directly endanger his "manly" performance and distinguish "comradely love" from effeminacy.

REPRESENTING "THE HOMOSEXUAL"

Few of the characters in Hughes's Renaissance works and his autobiography are explicitly depicted as "homosexual." There are nonetheless numerous allusions to characters' transgressive sexualities—most of them presented in the context of gender inversion. Apart from the aforementioned maritime depictions, Hughes casually mentions a male soprano, Harlem's drag balls, and the "large, dark, masculine" blues singer Gladys Bentley in his autobiography.[131] To this enumeration can be added an "EFFEMINATE YOUTH" and a "MASCULINE LADY" who speaks in a *"bass voice"* in his play *Little Ham* (1935), which is set in the 1920s, and an effeminate man, a female "masculine" teacher with a "deep, mannish kind of voice," and a "long-fingered, sissyfied" pianist in his novel *Not Without Laughter* (1931).[132]

Against the backdrop of these allusions to homosexuality, Borden's assertion that Hughes "resists genderracial stereotypes" and "promotes dialogue on taboo genderracial issues"[133] needs to be reassessed. Several of Hughes's poems fit Borden's suggestion about "genderracial resistance" regarding representations of women—for instance, "Hard Daddy" (1927), in which a female speaker is intent on violent revenge for her lover's ignorance, or "Lover's Return" (1928), in which a woman refuses to welcome a former lover who fell ill, following the devil's voice: *"Damn a lover / Come home to die!"*[134] Portraying these female speakers, Hughes challenges the stereotype of women as docile and enduring, yet it can already at this stage be argued that Hughes does not live up to the transgressive image some scholars construct for him. Tracy observes that Hughes "classified the blues as masculine or feminine in theme," thereby restricting female blues to the topic of love while allowing men to sing an "economic blues."[135] Hughes thus does not break down the male–female dichotomy but apparently reaffirms it. Moreover, as for instance in "Suicide" (1926), "Lament over Love" (1926), and "Midwinter Blues" (1926), he presents numerous desperate women weary of life after the separation from their lovers—a representation through which, as hooks points out, his female characters become "synonymous with sexual vulnerability."[136] As in his depictions of female prostitutes who, as in "Young Prostitute" (1923) and "Ruby Brown" (1926), are presented less as immoral than as victims of economic pressure, Hughes's representations of vulnerable women seem to shift emphasis in genderracial stereotypes rather than transcend them.[137]

Regarding Hughes's representation of homosexuality, Borden seems to ignore the aforementioned examples of effeminate men and masculine women, merely concentrating on two later works—"Café: 3 a.m." (1951) and "Blessed Assurance" (1963).[138] She suggests that "Café: 3 a.m." advocates "greater understanding of gays and lesbians."[139] This seems to be the case, as Hughes here emphasizes the cruelty manifest in the "weary sadistic eyes" of police troops looking for "fairies" and "Lesbians," thereby questioning the perception of gay men and lesbians as "[d]egenerates." By asking "Police lady or Lesbian / Over there?" Hughes moreover blurs the distinction between law enforcer and outlaw, righteousness and deviance, suggesting that the woman in question could be both.[140] In the short story "Blessed Assurance," Hughes depicts what looks like an essentially comic scene in which Delmar, "a brilliant queer" who is depicted as effeminate, sings an anthem in a high-pitched voice that causes the "Minister of Music" to faint and infuriates his embarrassed father.[141] In Hughes's listing of stereotypical negative reactions displayed by Delmar's father in the face of his son's "queerness"—his belief in God is shaken, he seeks possible genetic reasons, and he disapproves of his son's "unmanly" good behavior and fashion sense—satire, which also encompasses black families' "best foot forward"[142] attitudes, cannot be overlooked. Nero emphasizes that Rampersad, according to whom the story "aims at satire all around," again misses Hughes's gay voice, as he fails to notice that a critique of homophobia and traditional gender roles is evident beneath the story's comic surface.[143] As Borden points out, Hughes "works to move homosexuality out of the realm of the dangerous and deviant in our minds"[144] by portraying a young gay man as popular and successful. Moreover, he questions a traditionally defined masculinity, suggesting that personal success does not depend on performances of stereotypical gender rituals—masculinity as "proven" by, for instance, "juvenile delinquency"[145]—but can be enhanced by crossing into the sphere of the "other" gender. In "Café: 3 a.m." and "Blessed Assurance," Hughes includes stereotypical images of gender inversion and employs terms such as "fairies" and "queer," yet he implicitly questions them.

Hughes's Renaissance works, in contrast, paint a different picture of homosexuality, as they largely feature gender inversion outside a satirical or critical framework. In *Little Ham*, Hughes clearly does not "[resist] stereotypes of gay identity,"[146] as Borden suggests regarding "Café: 3 a.m." Instead, he presents an effeminate male character, a female impersonator, as a ridiculous coward who faints when hearing gunshot. This portrayal not only reiterates clichés about "homosexuals" but furthermore deprecates femaleness and women through the establishment of a link between effeminacy/femininity, weakness, and cowardice.[147]

In contrast to his generally nonjudgmental stance toward "deviant" behavior like gambling or drinking, it seems that Hughes in some of his works does not refrain from value judgments when alluding to homosexuality. This is overlooked by critics who, if mentioning the topic of homosexuality at all, usually regard it as being located on the same level as other "low-life" subjects in Hughes's works.[148] In *Not Without Laughter*, Hughes makes an obvious distinction between the "homosexual" approaching the young male protagonist Sandy and those who are involved in other "immoral" activities. These distinct portrayals seem based on the differentiation between "unmanly" and "manly," or "sick" and "healthy" behavior. Describing pimps, bootleggers, and young men who fight, Hughes's narrator presents these black people who "ceased to struggle against the boundaries between good and bad . . . and surrendered amiably to immorality"[149] in a favorable light. Stating that their behavior was linked to either "what they wanted to, or what they had to do,"[150] Hughes indicates that they enjoy their state of "sinfulness," but that living circumstances—for example, unemployment and racial discrimination—also shape their lives. This material and racial framework cannot easily be applied to the topic of homosexuality, and this clearly was not Hughes's intention. Over two pages in *Not Without Laughter*, Hughes displays disapproval of effeminacy and same-sex desire, as he depicts a black youth's negative experience with a man who, reminiscent of some contemporary news stories, is presented as a child molester. Significantly, he has all the signifiers of a fairy. Describing him as "a small yellow man with a womanish kind of voice," who "smelled of perfume" and whose face is "powdered with white talcum," Hughes depicts this aggressor as the epitome of disgust and what Roger Rosenblatt terms "predatory desperation."[151] Hughes indicates that he portrays a "typical" brand of sexual "deviant": The youth Sandy states that "he heard the men talk about queer fellows who stopped boys in the streets and tried to coax them to their rooms."[152] Sandy's pursuer attempts to lure him with "swell French pictures . . . [of] naked women," thereby feigning heterosexual interests, and furthermore offers alcohol. He seems symbolic of all those "queer" types of men and women featured in contemporary newspaper articles, who "openly bag for normal people who may be corrupted."[153] Though unsure about the man's motivation, even Sandy is "wise"[154] to the ap-

parent "threat" his pursuer poses; the fairy cannot fool even a child—a fact
that adds intellectual inferiority to his "perverse" character. In short, Hughes
pictures the homosexual "deviant" as effeminate and degenerate.

Hughes's allusions to lesbianism are also presented in a negative and
stereotypical, albeit less explicit, context. References to lesbianism in the context of Hughes's Renaissance years are veiled in *The Big Sea* but could have
been identified by contemporary readers. Referring to his work as a guard in
a Paris club, Hughes explains his fear of possible fights he would have to me-
diate by his having seen a dispute "between ladies, who shattered champagne
glasses on the edge of the table, then slashed at each other with the jagged
stems."[155] Rampersad reads this scene as a prostitutes' quarrel over men, yet
the scene is reminiscent of contemporary perceptions of lesbians as morbid
and violent.[156] This interpretation gains credence in light of the depiction of
the club's female owner and her "friend," a tall woman "with large green circles painted on her eyes, who often came to the club in a white riding habit,
white boots and hat, carrying a black whip."[157] Rampersad points out that
this woman was the owner's lover—a fact Hughes hints at by indicating that
"madame herself would fight if the girl were insulted by any of the guests."[158]
While Hughes does not exactly describe "madame's" partner as having masculine features, her physical appearance marks her as a freak.

Several interconnecting motives behind Hughes's stereotypical and often
deprecating representations of lesbians and, more frequently, gay men seem
plausible. Significantly, Hughes published many of his more negatively stereotypical portrayals of sexual "deviance" toward the end of the Harlem Renaissance. As Rampersad points out, in the early 1930s Hughes "was altering
his aesthetic to accommodate social reality"—a transformation that led to
his "becoming at least three different writers—radical . . . ; commercial . . . ;
and genteel, if also racial."[159] Creating work to suit these categories, it is possible that Hughes allowed stereotypes to enter his texts. Darwin Turner suggests that with the farcical *Little Ham*, which, similar to stories such as
"Luani of the Jungles," must be regarded as somewhat exceptional, Hughes
aimed at the "commercial exploitation of Harlem's exoticism" and "catered
to the predictable taste of Broadway audiences."[160] According to Turner,
Hughes intentionally depicted stereotypes—not only effeminate gay men but
also gamblers and gangsters—to entertain white audiences.[161] This possibility
is feasible, yet considering that works written in what appears to be a more
serious tone, such as *Not Without Laughter*, also feature stereotypes of
transgressive sexuality, it seems only partially applicable in this context. Another, perhaps more significant reason can be seen in Hughes's self-styled
role as "interpreter of the black masses." As described by critics, Hughes was
intent to write "[l]iterature in which the masses of black people would find
their life experiences reflected and illuminated," and he "express[ed] the preoccupations and attitudes of the people, *in their own language*."[162] Given that
the effeminate gay man and the butch, violent lesbian constituted the sexu-

ally transgressive figures known to the public, it seems to some extent logical that Hughes reflects these images in his work.

As evident in *Not Without Laughter*, Hughes also seems willing to affirm particularly negative stereotypes by presenting a child molester who features all stereotypical attributes perceived by the public as "signs" of homosexuality. A similar argument can be made regarding his depiction of Harlem's drag balls in *The Big Sea*. While most newspaper reports on masked balls seem based on a general rejection of cross-dressing men and women, in many of them appreciative comments, describing costumes as "gorgeous"[163] and participants as fascinating curiosities, can be found. Hughes settles for a different path, as he emphasizes his personal distance from any such spectacle, refusing to indicate interest in or fascination with these women and particularly these men, whose cross-dressing abilities he denounces: "[C]lose up, most of them look as if they need a shave, and some of their evening gowns, cut too low, show hair on the chest."[164] These negative, stereotypical portrayals of gay men and lesbians to some extent seem to affirm Hughes's overall "manly" and heterosexual narratives.

One might thus conclude that Hughes displaced social stigmata connected with homosexuality onto one particular group of gay men and lesbians in his literary works—the fairies and "mannish" women—thereby differentiating between strength and weakness and, in more extreme cases, beauty and ugliness.[165] He thus seems to create two camps of men linked by transgressive sexual desire—"manly" comrades detectable by uncovering textual strategies and Whitmanesque codes and by investigating textual and sexual ambiguities; and "pansies" to be, as described in the *Inter-State Tattler*, "spot[ted] . . . on parade."[166] In light of this portrayal of homosexuality, Reimonenq's claim that Hughes was a gay man and writer "whose complex achievement includes battling oppression through his veiled homosexual expressivity"[167] seems questionable. Hughes's literary gay voice appears to have changed over the years, yet it seems that critics, presuming the existence of a gay identity for Hughes, falsely claim his all-encompassing tolerance and empathy for gay men and lesbians, thereby creating an image incompatible with Hughes's life and work.

FIVE

Claude McKay:
"*enfant terrible* of the Negro Renaissance"

According to Steven Watson, Claude McKay was "perhaps the purest example of the dual identity so common among the New Negroes: Jamaican and American, homosexual and heterosexual, Harlemite and Greenwich Villager, revolutionary and decadent, servant and celebrity."[1] Even "dual identity" may be too narrow a term to encompass what seem to be McKay's and his writings' frequently contradictory characteristics. Born and raised in Jamaica, McKay arrived in New York in 1912 and left the city after the publication of his poetry volume *Harlem Shadows* (1922), spending most of the Harlem Renaissance years in Europe and North Africa. *Harlem Shadows* was acclaimed for its formal excellence and spirit of defiance and prompted Langston Hughes's retrospective comment that "McKay might be termed the first of the New Negroes. . . ."[2] McKay's subsequent publications stirred controversy: The Niggeratti praised particularly his sexually explicit novels *Home to Harlem* (1928) and *Banjo* (1929), which rekindled the debate about artistic representations of African Americans sparked by Carl Van Vechten's *Nigger Heaven* (1926).[3] James Weldon Johnson and Walter White demonstrated their appreciation of McKay's work and regularly attempted to persuade McKay to return to Harlem, but others were less sure whether he should be part of the Renaissance. Writer and critic George Schuyler, for instance, expressed relief that McKay was "reputed to be independent of the [Renaissance writers'] group."[4] Sentiment was also against McKay within segments of the African American community. As Harold Jackman informed McKay, reactions to *Home to Harlem* were harsh: "People have said that you made it up and it is a shame . . . and, after all you have been away from here so many years . . . and . . . what right have you a West Indian (no, I think she said <u>monkey chaser</u>) got writing about Harlem."[5]

McKay's position within the Harlem Renaissance is clearly a matter of debate. In this context, P. S. Chauhan's assessment that McKay "was *for the*

Harlem Renaissance, but certainly not *of* it"⁶ merits consideration. Born in 1889, McKay was older than writers such as Hughes and Cullen; moreover, his Jamaican background set him apart from the American-defined movement.⁷ Probably more importantly, while McKay was supportive of the general notion of a renaissance in black art and literature, his politics of representation clashed with those of genteel African American critics. Similar to Hughes, McKay advocated a focus on the black working class.⁸ The only black writer associated with the radical environment around the *Liberator*, McKay regarded himself as a "Negro radical" whose "birthright" and task was "to educate the black worker, . . . [and] to interpret him to the uninformed white radical."⁹ He defined the black artist's duty as "giv[ing] back to the Negro race its heritage" and "help[ing] the . . . race, corrupted by civilization, to see that it has something finer than the thing it hankers after in itself."¹⁰ When McKay made these last statements, he had already passed two distinct creative phases: He had published poetry written largely in the Jamaican vernacular and subsequently, as evident in *Harlem Shadows*, turned to sonnet poetry.¹¹ His interest in "common" as opposed to middle-class blacks is displayed in his Jamaican poetry, but, indicating the validity of his acknowledgement that "[p]oetry is too limited a range for all I've got to do,"¹² it seems only fully developed in his fiction.

Residing outside the geographical boundaries of Harlem, McKay was allowed a measure of private and creative space unavailable to other Renaissance writers. Using Renaissance networks only through mediators like Walter White and black bibliophile Arthur Schomburg, he attempted to steer clear of what he termed the "sea of shit"¹³—quarrels in black American elitist circles about issues such as artistic representation. However, McKay did not stay away from Harlem to avoid conflict. He displayed disregard for respectability, barely concealing sexual relationships not only with black and white but also with female and male partners in foreign countries as well as within the United States.¹⁴ McKay, whom Alain Locke retrospectively described as "the *enfant terrible* of the Negro Renaissance,"¹⁵ headed for a confrontation with the black American elite, creating prose works at odds with the black bourgeoisie's philosophy of "racial uplift." Joining the primitivist discourse popular with white contemporaries in which blacks were regarded as "noble savages," he placed emphasis on sexuality, including the topic of homosexuality, particularly in his novels.

The only stricture McKay apparently recognized regarding his literary sexual dissidence was censorship. Although he deliberately shocked African American readers with unapologetic portrayals of black "low life," he would not usually risk rejection by publishers. In contrast to the Niggeratti, whose opposition to the Renaissance was epitomized by their privately organized publication of *Fire!!*, he remained conservative in his choice of publishers.¹⁶ Opting to publish with Harper & Brothers, McKay seemed intent on avoiding official censorship, repeatedly emphasizing that he was "quite willing to cut out anything that is thought obscene"—an attitude that can also be linked to his constant lack of funds.[17] McKay's correspondence indicates his awareness that an emphasis on sexuality could provoke a ban of his novels. Although stating that his characters were not "more sexy than the characters of white modern authors," he admitted that he had included "so many brothel scenes, which is unusual in literature."[18] McKay's publishers were indeed "somewhat disturbed by certain passages" and believed that "[t]here are a great many passages which, as they stand, are certainly not within the law" and consequently needed "considerable expurgation."[19]

In light of the indignation McKay's novels caused among African Americans, it might come as a surprise that they, as evident in the case of McKay's first novel "Color Scheme," which was never published, apparently passed several stages of censorship before publication. First, as McKay informed Schomburg, he was "careful . . . to use fine language and that covers up many an unpleasant scene and word."[20] In a second stage, he consulted white intellectual Max Eastman, who "put his finger . . . on every point that he thought objectionable and impossible for the American market—and there were many!"[21] McKay seems to have heeded Eastman's advice, but even then, his publishers interfered, declaring that "discreet editing"[22] would be undertaken. His sensitivity regarding censorship apparently increased after the publication of his first novel, as is evident in his protest against the toning down of the language employed in *Banjo*.[23] McKay's novel "Romance in Marseilles" (1930),[24] which contains sympathetic depictions of male same-sex relationships, may provide clues regarding the extent to which his representation of homosexuality was subject to censorship. Wayne Cooper points out that the publishers' literary editors suggested only few alterations. Whether these proposed changes concerned the topic of homosexuality remains unclear, but it is noteworthy that McKay refused to accept them.[25] His at least initially very pragmatic stance toward censorship probably shaped McKay's literary gay voice, yet he obviously did not always succumb to pressure.

Before McKay's gay voice is explored, his identity as what has been described variously as a "bisexual," "homosexual," "sexually ambiguous," and "gay" man must be discussed. While Watson carefully refers to McKay as "homosexual and heterosexual," acknowledging that he withstood a clear-cut hetero-/homosexual binary, other critics choose to ignore McKay's interest in women or simplify issues, describing him as "gay."[26] Cooper suggests that McKay was homosexual, arriving at this conclusion by comparing the number or "significance" of McKay's relationships with men and women and by putting forward a Freudian analysis of McKay's relationship with his parents. He concedes, however, that "McKay may not have chosen to identify himself as explicitly homosexual."[27] An indication of McKay's attitude toward the term *homosexuality* is given in a 1938 letter by Charles Ford, the coauthor of *The Young and Evil* (1933), a novel that depicts flamboyant gay men. Responding to a previous letter by McKay, Ford expressed disappointment in McKay, who appears to have made a "charge of homosexuality, with moral implications"[28] against him. This wording implies that the term *homosexuality*, usually employed in the context of degeneracy and disease in contemporary discourses, was not one McKay deemed appropriate for himself.[29] Tyrone Tillery chooses an alternative path: Apparently disappointed to have "evidence" of McKay's relationships with men, he concedes that "it must be admitted that McKay himself was bisexual."[30] Tillery thereby apparently attempts to redeem McKay from the "charge" of homosexuality, since labeling him bisexual implies some "normal" heterosexual interest. Nevertheless, one might conclude that from today's perspective, the term *bisexual* best describes McKay.

In his autobiography *A Long Way from Home* (1937), McKay emphasizes that "sex was never much of a problem to me," a statement on which he elaborates to such an extent as to almost arouse suspicion about what he might be attempting to cover up, were it not for his pitting of his "natural" black sexuality against an "unnatural" white sexuality.[31] McKay's understanding of his sexuality along primitivist lines as "wholesome" may have been profoundly influenced by English folklorist Walter Jekyll, who, like Edward Carpenter, turned his back on "civilization," rejecting comfortable city life for the countryside.[32] Cooper suggests that Jekyll introduced McKay to a cultural concept of male same-sex relationships—they read, among other writers, Oscar Wilde, Carpenter, and Walt Whitman—and perhaps also to the physical side of homosexuality, their relationship thus mirroring the classic Greek homosexual scenario of an older educated man's relationship with his student.[33] While Tillery refutes this suggestion, McKay's autobiography *My Green Hills of Jamaica* seems to contain some clues.[34] Describing his relationship with Jekyll, McKay comments that "[w]e liked each other immediately."[35] He was apparently strongly attracted to Jekyll, even "run[ning] away from home to be near him."[36] McKay stayed in Kingston, from where he could more easily reach Jekyll's retreat in the mountains, and began training to join the constabulary. Among his colleagues, he recounts, he "had kept a very close mouth about the relationship between Mr. Jekyll and myself. When I had gone up to Kingston for the week-end, the boys always thought that I had gone to see friends or girls."[37] McKay places this sentence in the context of his intent to keep his poetic achievements secret, yet this excerpt can be read as an attempt to distract from a possibly homosexual bond that crossed boundaries of race and class. Their close relationship ended when Jekyll provided tuition fees for McKay to study in the United States. It was the first of many similar relationships McKay formed with powerful and affluent men like, for instance, Eastman—bonds that were located on various points of what Eve Sedgwick describes as a male "homosocial continuum," spanning from men-promoting men to men-loving men.[38]

Like many other same-sex interested black writers, McKay was connected to Locke's gay network. He did not need an introduction to same-sex love, however—his correspondence with Locke indicates that they communicated as equals.[39] Yet their different politics set the two men apart: While Locke by and large did not cross class boundaries, McKay, in Michel Fabre's words, a "man of simple tastes," consciously sought contact with working-class men while also pursuing affairs with intellectuals.[40] In this context, McKay's friendship with a white New York pickpocket named "Michael," introduced in *A Long Way from Home*, is of interest: Michael "did his tricks most of the time in the subways and parks. He got at his victims while they were asleep in the park or by getting friendly with them."[41] The locations mentioned are also gay men's cruising spaces. Moreover, Michael's "getting friendly" with men opens up the possibility of the presence of same-sex attraction at least on the part of the potential victims. McKay describes his friendship with Michael as one of his "little eccentricities" and does not reveal Michael's real identity to his friends, who, however, "were aware that our relationship was not a literary one."[42] This statement offers manifold possibilities for interpretation, particularly as McKay stresses that "Michael was profoundly sentimental about friendship."[43] In whatever way one reads such passages in McKay's autobiographies, the impression is that he intentionally leaves gaps allowing for gay readings in his otherwise "straight" narratives.

McKay's fictional focus on working-class culture needs to be understood as part of his social politics but particularly his sexual politics, which he seems to have shared with other same-sex-interested men—a belief in what was perceived as the "manliness" of the lower classes allegedly absent in middle- or upper-class men. In this context, McKay's rejection of Locke as an elitist who lacked "manliness" is of significance. Repeatedly emphasizing Locke's alleged "artificiality" and weakness, McKay linked these attributes to his educational background, arguing that they derived from a "kink in Dr. Locke's artistic outlook, perhaps due to its effete European academic quality."[44] This linking of intellectualism, whiteness in the form of a European education, and "effeteness" hints at McKay's alignment with primitivist notions—the distinction between "weakness" and "strength" in reference to a racial binary defined as white–nonwhite. Furthermore, McKay's differentiation within the category of whiteness between America and Europe is noteworthy. This distinction resurfaces in his discussion of Ernest Hemingway's writings, to which he ascribed "the hard-boiled contempt for and disgust with sissyness expressed among all classes of Americans. Now this quality is distinctly and definitely American—a conventionalized rough attitude which is altogether un-European."[45] Although McKay did not consider himself "American," he clearly embraced the culture's purported emphasis on virility.[46]

McKay's remark on Hemingway offers an insight into what could be described as his "manly" literary project—the lifting of literature out of a sphere he perceived to be "sissy." In *A Long Way from Home*, McKay underlines this point through Michael, who had received books from McKay: "I guess when the gang sees me with these [books] here, . . . they'll be thinking that I'm turning queer."[47] McKay was not unique in linking class, intellectualism, and "queerness," yet his case is interesting, as this view apparently influenced his writing substantially.[48] Though he positioned his work in the context of American literature, his particular concern was with the production of "black" literature. He obviously believed that the creation of literature, as one of many other spheres of black life, was "unmanly" because black writers, faced with discrimination in the white-dominated field of literature, "[indulged] in whining and self-pity."[49] Furthermore, he claimed that minority artists like black writers "are made impotent by the fears and misgivings of minorities and by the harsh judgment of majority opinion, and thus we become emasculate in ideas and the expression of them."[50] McKay sought to reverse this "emasculation" and, as the critical reception of his work indicates, appears to have completed his mission successfully: His sonnets were claimed to display "virile and unabashed hatred," and Wallace Thurman pointed out that "[t]here is no impotent whining" in McKay's work.[51] McKay also convinced contemporaries of his own masculinity. Described by people aware of his same-sex interests as "somewhat dandified,"[52] he was never regarded as effeminate. Revealing the close connection between effeminacy and homosexuality in public perception, Cooper mentions that friends of McKay's remembered him as "openly homosexual but not at all effeminate," and one of his female sexual partners stated that "McKay was bisexual, although he had none of the mannerisms of most homosexuals."[53] Considering this "achievement" of masculinity on a personal and literary level, it is of central significance to explore how this vision of virility, which, as will be seen, seems almost absent in McKay's nonfiction, interacts with his gay literary voice.

RESPECTING THE FORM: McKAY'S GAY POETIC RENAISSANCE VOICE

Underlining the distinctiveness of McKay's creative phases, his poetic works created during the Harlem Renaissance do not evidence the emphasis on race and masculinity that his later fiction would.[54] Moreover, in contrast to his employment of black vernacular in his fictional work, McKay's Renaissance poetry is characterized by formal restraint. Many of his poems are presented in sonnet form, and he usually strictly adheres to rhyme patterns. Like Cullen and Hughes, and befitting his own sexually "open" lifestyle, McKay seems to invite multiple readings in his love poetry, in which he frequently refrains from stating the gender of those addressed or described.[55]

Looking back at a deceased person's strenuous and bitter life in "Rest in Peace" (1922),[56] the poem's speaker in the last lines exclaims: "Farewell, oh, fare you well! my friend and / lover." Suggesting that McKay here "mentioned . . . one of his homosexual relationships in verse,"[57] Cooper links this commemorative poem with same-sex desire but does not give a reference to any biographical material that might establish a link to one of McKay's male lovers. Cooper bases his argument for the poem's homosexual content on the terms "friend" and "lover," stressing that McKay states them "explicitly,"[58] yet these terms can also be viewed in a heterosexual context. This is not to argue, however, against the validity of a gay reading in which the combination of "friend" and "lover" can be read as referring to a "beloved comrade" in a Whitmanesque sense.

Some of McKay's poems give prominence to seemingly insurmountable obstacles between lovers. In "The Barrier" (1922) and the first section of "One Year After" (1922), lovers are separated by an invisible yet ever-present barrier which obstructs their love, leading to frustration and pain.[59] Race, the crucial impediment to love, is mentioned only toward the poems' end. In "One Year After," the speaker concludes that he was "faithless to [his] race" and in "The Barrier" the obstacle is named explicitly in the final two lines: "For there's the barrier of race, / You're fair and I am dark." Prior to these denouements, one is, as Gregory Woods suggests, "free to perform a gay reading"—a valid proposition, as the reference to "illicit wine" and a beloved person that may not even be looked at could well describe any kind of potentially physical, outlawed love.[60] McKay thus leaves space for dissident readings, transferring the "necessary" racial conclusion, the only one that would have been deemed acceptable, to the end.[61] It is also feasible to read the poems as complete mergers of the topics of homophobia and racism: The "impossible" couple is maybe not only interracial but also gay—a combination which, as same-sex-identified African American bohemian Alexander Gumby wrote in his sonnet "To . . . . You," constitutes a "social sin."[62]

In "Courage" (1922), race and same-sex love again both seem possible themes.[63] The poem's speaker addresses an ungendered person in whose "lustrous-warm eyes" he recognizes a "dreamy tale" that he apparently shares. It seems that this dream, which remains unspecified, needs to be concealed by the addressed person, who leads a "guarded life" in a hostile and barren environment which could be interpreted as racially oppressive. The speaker encourages the addressed person to show resistance in the face of this stifling environment. His promise that they will eventually "drink [their] share of ardent love and life," and his addressing of the person with "O lonely heart" also allows for a reading of the poem in the context of sexual oppression. It could thus be said that in "Courage," two men are determined to realize their shared vision of a haven for men-loving men, as outlined in Whitman's *Democratic Vistas*.[64] Like McKay's most popular poem "If We Must Die" (1919), "Courage" can thus be read as referring to the fight against a homophobic environment that oppresses men-loving men. Yet in contrast to the former poem, in which an "open grave" awaits those fighting for freedom, the speaker in "Courage" assures the addressed person that success will be their reward: Those who share a vision of men-loving men form "serried files in all the lands" and eventually fulfill their love-affirming dream.[65]

An awareness of the dominant view of men-loving men as deviant, degenerate, and diseased could be said to have informed McKay's poem "I Know My Soul" (1922),[66] which can be read as starting with an expression of frustration in the face of non-normative sexuality. The poem's speaker is described as taking his "soul out of its secret place," observing it closely to find out why "[t]his awful key to my infinity / Conspires to rob me of sweet joy and grace." Amitai Avi-Ram suggests two different readings of the term *soul*. It could be said to refer to a person's soul in a religious sense, but a sexual reading of "soul" that would correspond to its description as a "twitching body quivering in space" is also possible. Following this reading, "soul" could be regarded as a circumlocution for "penis," through which infinity can be attained in the form of reproduction.[67] It seems that the speaker is burdened by sexual problems that keep him from happiness; while recognizing that he can achieve the acknowledged aim of infinity only through his "soul," he seems unable to relate to it positively, viewing it as a distant and almost hostile object. The "sweet joy and grace" can thus be read as what dominant society defines as happiness and respectability achieved through reproduction and, implicitly, heterosexuality. The speaker's inability to follow this ritualized pattern seems to lead him to regard his sexuality with frustration. Almost halfway through the sonnet, however, a shift in the speaker's attitude is discernible. He appears satisfied that his exploration has yielded a result and now seems able to "comprehend" or come to terms with his sexuality, realizing that he does not fit into the pattern of reproductive and/or heterosexual relationships. He therefore ceases to deplore his inability to "control" his sexuality, which remains a "sign [that] may not be fully read."

The second section of "One Year After"[68] may be read as depicting the consequences of not only an acceptance but also an espousal of the powerful force that transgressive sexuality in a racial and/or homosexual context constitutes. This force remains unspecified, yet it keeps the speaker, who "shun[s] all signs of anchorage," from settling down. Instead of opting for safety and respectability, he follows his desire, thereby treading on "risky ways," as his joyful lifestyle "exceeds the bound of laws." Standing outside a "respectable" framework, he refuses to follow normative patterns and becomes an outlaw—a description which fits McKay, who characterized himself as "a truant by nature"[69] and who furthermore stood outside the law, owing to his interracial and same-sex affairs. As in "I Know My Soul," difference and an outsider position are accepted if not embraced as the speaker submits to "beauty-burning bodies" that could be interpreted as white and/or male, giving way to the "passion boldly rising in [his] breast."

Desire and passion also play a central role in the sonnet "Honeymoon."[70] Sexual acts are clearly alluded to in this poem, which describes the joyful days two people experience together. The poem's speaker not only wishes to kiss the other, ungendered person but also wants to be "drunken with [his/her] passion's wine." While this sexual encounter might be of a heterosexual character, it could also involve two men. In this latter reading, the poem describes a male oral same-sex scene. Supporting this interpretation, it seems that the "honeymoon" the lovers enjoy is not an actual trip as would usually follow a wedding. These two male lovers, for whom such a ritual is impossible, instead celebrate their union by embarking on a sex trip spanning several "uplifted days." The validity of a gay reading seems affirmed particularly in the poem's last lines, in which their trip is likened to a "heaving ocean / Whereon [they] drift foam-sprinkled, shot with zest"—a post-coital scene which provides a link to Whitman's "Song of Myself" (1855) where young men swim together and "do not think whom they souse with spray."[71]

While, as Alden Reimonenq suggests, further poems and further gay readings could be discussed, the poems selected suffice to indicate that McKay's poetic gay voice seems characterized by what Gregory Woods describes as "discretion."[72] Many of these poems display an affirmative view of same-sex relationships, but it seems that McKay's adherence to classic poetic forms restricted his range of expression. "Form," Nathan Huggins observes, "forced [McKay] into strange syntax," and it seems that it also had an effect on the gay dimension of his poetic works, which, as Woods points out, "give an impression of [a voice] stifled and held back"—a statement that certainly does not apply to McKay's fiction.[73]

RACE, MASCULINITY, AND SEXUALITY

With his fictional work, McKay can be said to have joined a primitivist discourse popular during the 1920s that pitted "Western culture" against notions of "innocence," "purity," "wholesomeness," and "strength" which were defined as nonwhite. If given a negative spin, this discourse could serve to interpret the "primitive" subject as "uncivilized" and "underdeveloped," but its participants could also idealize him or her as "untainted" by civilization.[74] The focus in this section is on *Home to Harlem* and *Banjo*, in which black protagonists, though living in a world defined by "white" values, enjoy their lives because of what is presented as a specifically "black" vitality which apparently immunizes them against the "corrupting" influences of a "civilization" McKay defines as Western, white, materialistic, Christian, and inherently racist. Black genteel critics viewed McKay's novels with dismay, accusing him of copying Van Vechten and pandering to "white" tastes. Considering McKay's perennial financial problems and his awareness that primitivist "exotic" portrayals of black people were marketable, this possibility must be entertained. However, as Tracy McCabe points out, primitivism can be "a sort of double-voiced discourse": While "a text can be read as at one level simply catering to . . . a white audience who holds power," it can also be viewed as "a more complicated discursive act that is actually aimed at serving a disempowered position or voice."[75] By competing within the field of literary primitivism, "an ideologically complex site on which cultural struggles for power are waged,"[76] McKay attacks racial hierarchies, offering representations of "blackness" that constitute alternatives to those created by white writers in spite of sharing their premise of viewing black people as the "other" of a white-defined civilization.

Timothy Chin observes that McKay's participation in a primitivist discourse implies his adherence to a strict racial binary.[77] McKay's use of essentialist categories requires some elaboration, however. Juda Bennett asserts that although employing an essentialist discourse, McKay satirically undermines essentialist binaries, as he, for instance, plays with the subject "color" as a metonym for race, breaking it up into endless nuances, thereby suggesting the "parity" of colors.[78] Bennett cites a song contained in *Home to Harlem* that focuses on a "[b]rown gal" and her jealousy of a "yaller," thus light-brown-complexioned woman, concluding: " 'White,' 'green,' or 'red' in place of 'yaller' might have likewise touched the same deep-sounding, primitive chord."[79] Rather than refuting McKay's persistent use of binaries, the example chosen by Bennett seems to underline this practice. While McKay seems willing to exchange colors, this is only the case within the group of colors opposing the "[b]rown gal" who attempts to convince her lover of a "yaller" girl's inferiority. The binary brown–"yaller" mirrors that of black–white, and the variations of the term "yaller" by no means challenge this binary, as the oppositionality to the term "brown" remains stable. Colors might, as Bennett points out, be shown to be constructions, but this seems to be the case only within the binary of black–white.[80]

Binaries clearly remain stable in McKay's juxtaposition of blacks and whites. In some rare instances, white characters are portrayed positively, as is the case with Crosby, a white student featured in *Banjo*. His description as "too fine a type," however, prompts suspicion and disbelief, expressed by the black character Ray, who seems unable to fathom the combination of whiteness and decency, thereby pointing to the general "evil" whites represent.[81] In some instances, McKay's characters discuss the uselessness of the category race, concluding: "In the can with race!"[82] However, this comment does not, as might be presumed, point to a shared humanity but is employed in the context of a generalizing, negative statement about women. In another scene, Banjo supports a starving white boy and is described as "color-blind"; but it is significant that like the other black characters, he essentially remains color-conscious, as is evident in his comment that he could never "love white moh'n colored," to which he adds: "White folks smell like laundry soap."[83]

Similar to white primitivist writers, McKay highlights the issue of "vitality," presenting people of color as more "alive." Sexuality serves as a metaphor for what McKay portrays as the fundamental difference between vitality and weakness.[84] The intertwining of sexuality and race is manifest in the settings of *Home to Harlem* and *Banjo*, which indicate McKay's deviation from a typical characteristic of traditional white representations of blacks as "noble savages": Locating his protagonists in cities, McKay modernizes the primitivist tale of blackness, introducing urban black heroes.[85] McKay sexualizes Harlem and Marseilles, yet Harlem appears in a more positive light. Based on the quest of protagonist Jake to find Felice, with whom he had a one-night affair—a goal that does not preclude his pursuit of numerous other sexual encounters—*Home to Harlem* is a celebration of Harlem's vibrant sexual life. All spaces, including cabarets, speakeasies, and even the streets, offer ample opportunities for sex, which at least at the outset of the novel seems joyful, embedded in a colorful atmosphere that resounds with music and laughter.[86] Marseilles, the city in which *Banjo* is set, by contrast is characterized by "an atmosphere of prostitution and perversion."[87] The city is depicted as a crime-ridden place where sex has degenerated into a commodity and where those in pursuit of sex are in constant danger of being robbed, humiliated, or killed. Harlem, in contrast, is portrayed as a nurturing environment which offers delicious-looking women—"low-brown, high-brown, nut-brown, lemon, maroon, olive, mauve, gold"[88]—who seem ready to be consumed.

Marseilles would appear devoid of humanity were it not for the Pan-African community of black sailors and beach boys, whose "presence had brought a keen zest to the [port area] that made it in a way beautiful."[89] Banjo, the beach boys' charismatic leader, embodies the vitality this group injects. In contrast to professional performers, he offers "authentic" entertainment and refuses to play his banjo for money, thereby rejecting what is presented as a materialistic society. His music signifies creativity and, moreover, seems to reflect the essence of blackness: "Rough rhythm of darkly-carnal life. . . . Shake that thing! Sweet dancing thing of primitive joy, perverse pleasure, prostitute ways, many-colored variations of the rhythm, savage, barbaric, refined. . . ."[90] This sexualization of blackness is exercised against the backdrop of "white" impotence and lack of sexual desire. While Jake and Banjo could be described as personifications of phalli—Banjo is addressed as a "strutting cock," and a contemporary critic described Jake as "[t]all, muscular and highly charged with sex-appeal"—McKay's white characters are usually linked to sexual dysfunction or a complete absence of sex.[91] White characters apparently never have sex in *Home to Harlem* and *Banjo*. In McKay's novel *Banana Bottom* (1933), which is set in a Jamaican village, the lives of the white Reverend Craig and his wife are characterized by sexual repression, the product of their union being a disabled child.[92] What Chin calls the "premise" of *Banana Bottom*, the "potentially degenerating effects of an overcivilized, sexually repressed, Western (European) civilization that privileges intellect over instinct, reason over emotions,"[93] clearly comes to the fore.

Ray, a Haitian intellectual and aspiring writer who figures prominently in *Home to Harlem* and *Banjo*, seems to embody the emasculating consequences of blacks' contacts with "white civilization." His acquisition of "white" knowledge at college sets him apart, sexually and otherwise, from what seem to be the "average," uneducated black characters in McKay's novels, rendering him, as Huggins suggests, "impotent by thought."[94] Jake's intimation to a brothel-keeper that Ray "ain't regular"[95] seems appropriate, as Ray, though feeling faint impulses that seem linked to his "primitive" core, cannot respond with "regular" actions. When asked to dance by a prostitute, he thus senses "some strange thing [that] seemed to hold him back from taking the girl in his arms."[96] Several situations in *Home to Harlem* and *Banjo* offer Ray the opportunity to engage in sexual relationships, but what he describes as the "used-up hussy of white morality" implanted in him through education apparently bars him from sexual fulfillment, making him "a misfit," an educated, "unmanly," and impotent black man.[97] Jake's additional assessment of Ray as "awful queer,"[98] presented in the context of what looks like Ray's heterosexual impotence, could be read as alluding to his potential same-sex interest. Ray is clearly able to feel heterosexual desire, however, and it seems that queerness is here linked with intellectualism in a way reminiscent of *A Long Way from Home*.[99] Next to Ray, several other black male characters—for instance, "Negroes doing clerical work wearing glasses that made them sissy-eyed"—appear to lack masculinity because of their exposure to "civilization."[100] The link between intellect, impotence, and "effeminate" weakness is thus clearly established.

Befitting his "manly" literary project, McKay forcibly attempts to achieve harmony between Ray's intellect and the "primitive" essence that appears to still exist within him. Ray embarks on a vagabondage with Banjo, determined to "bring intellect to the aid of instinct."[101] He gains deeper insights into his own "blackness" and positive aspects of the black masses who, as he learns, harbor the essence of black primitive life, yet sex remains "alien to his nature."[102] Consequently, the conclusion to be drawn from Ray's struggle is that it is impossible for whites to develop a "natural" sexuality. Their "whiteness," and by extension their deeply ingrained "civilized" values and morals, are responsible for the extinction of "natural" impulses. Unlike Ray, they cannot even refer to some inner "black"—for example, "natural" or "wholesome"— core that would enable them to at least become aware of their sexual inadequacy. Though accused by black critics like Schuyler of affirming the prejudice "that the Negro is still constitutionally unmoral and hyper-sexual,"[103] McKay here argues against this stereotype by defining his own sexual norms according to which blacks possess or maybe even represent not an excessive, but a normal, "natural" sexuality. According to Ray, "white people had developed sex complexes that Negroes had not."[104] McKay thus inverts the binary of norm–deviation, thereby, to borrow from Jonathan Dollimore, transgressively reinscribing black sexuality at the expense of whites, who are identified as "deviants."[105]

As the "other" of white sexuality, in McKay's novels black "wholesome" sexuality is under assault by "civilization" and its harbingers, white people.

As Ray points out, there is a "war joined between civilization and sex."[106] The impression conveyed is that the Pan-African community in Harlem and particularly in Marseilles, where the beach boys represent a minority at the mercy of white authorities, is surrounded by whites, who increasingly exert pressure on sexuality and, by extension, on black identity. On the one hand, McKay suggests that this encroachment poses no serious threat, owing to blacks' display of resistance. Ray thus concludes that "this primitive child, . . . big-laughing black boy of the world, did not go down and disappear under the serried crush of trampling white feet. . . . Before the grim, pale rider-down of souls he went his careless way with a primitive hoofing and a grin."[107] On the other hand, as indicated in Jake's comment that "Wese too close and thick in Harlem. Need some moh fresh air between us," the tension within the black community is rising, and, apparently as a consequence, intraracial conflicts and violence occur.[108] Ray also acknowledges the threat "civilization" poses, realizing that "[t]he hand of progress was robbing his people of many primitive and beautiful qualities."[109] His own predicament—the apparent mutilation of his masculinity and sexual potency through "white" education—serves as a strong reminder of blacks' vulnerability.

What Ray refers to as the "fundamental, unconscious cause of the antagonism between white and black" is that "the white man considered sex a nasty, irritating thing, while a Negro accepted it with primitive joy."[110] Whites' unease translates into what McKay depicts as the repression and materialistic corruption of black sexuality. An attempt to suppress black sexuality is presented in *Home to Harlem*: A group of young white men join a buffet flat, participate in the entertainment, and eventually "[unmask] as the Vice Squad."[111] Underlining the gap between black and white, their participation in the party is depicted as but a performance of vitality. Whites may be able to study and copy "blackness," but they cannot live it. Black vitality and, by extension, sexuality, are viewed as a crime by the undercover agents, who "killed"[112] the party with the force of white-defined laws. The term "Vice Squad" indicates a close link between morality and law enforcement. Black entertainment is believed to be immoral—particularly since it entails free and apparently unrestrained sexuality. In *Home to Harlem*, one gay-themed song mentioning a "bulldycking [sic] woman and a faggotty man" is banned by the police, and music generally seems to inspire black dancers to moves that are of a clearly sexual character, dancing constituting a "gorgeous sublimation of the primitive African sex feeling."[113]

The sexually repressive role of Christianity is depicted in *Banana Bottom*. The young black man Herald Newton, who lives in a Christianized Jamaican village, plans to get married and is about to succeed the white Reverend Craig in his office when he "suddenly turned crazy and defiled himself with a nanny goat."[114] Attempting to suppress sexual urges by repeating parts of his sermon, he breaks down under the pressure. Instead of finding a "natural" outlet with a woman—an act judged a sin if consummated outside marriage—his sexual desire is "perverted." Involuntary sexual "perversion" is thus presented as the factual result of repressed sexuality.[115]

Distinct from this group that shares a moralist view are whites that McKay portrays as actively involved in the sphere of black sexuality. Miscegenation represents one important strand of what is depicted as white interference. Barbara Griffin contends that "[t]here is no doubt that McKay was advocating miscegenation and not racial distinctiveness"[116] in his works, yet a closer look at McKay's novels suggests a different picture: Miscegenation is presented as a threatening phenomenon, undermining black "strength" and "wholesomeness." While not elaborating on white men's roles in miscegenation in his fictional work, in *A Long Way from Home* McKay expresses disgust with white "faddists," whom he perceives as "white lice crawling on black bodies."[117] In McKay's fiction, strong emphasis is placed on black women's role in miscegenation. In *Banjo*, Ray claims that women "[worship] the active success of man" and that the black woman, given whites' economic dominance, "give[s] herself to the white man because he stands for power and property."[118] While Ray concedes that some black women possess "race feeling" that keeps them from engaging in sexual relations with whites, this is portrayed as exceptional.[119] Heather Hathaway's description of McKay's portrayal of women's central role in miscegenation as a "feminization of assimilation"[120] thus seems accurate.

McKay's critique of miscegenation does not leave black men unscathed. Ray, for instance, claims that because of their racial inferiority complexes, black men in Europe tend to marry white women, who are "inferior to [black men] in brains and physique. The energy of such a Negro is lost to his race and goes to build up some decaying white family."[121] Whiteness is here equated with degeneracy but is simultaneously deemed dominant over black genetic material. Congo Rose, a mulatto blues singer portrayed in *Home to Harlem*, serves as an example of the powerful influence of white genes. She displays a master–slave attitude, treating the novel's protagonist Jake like "her big, good slave."[122] Additionally, her sexuality seems to have been "corrupted," as she displays masochistic tendencies. Both of these "perverse" traits are clearly linked to her "high-yaller" complexion and thereby to her partially white parentage.[123] Against this rejection of miscegenation, the defense of the issue in *Banjo*, where Ray claims that it "produces splendid and interesting types,"[124] appears like a token gesture. Already at the end of this argument, Ray expresses horror at the thought of the assimilation of blacks into white dominant society, worrying about the "identity of the black race in the Western World."[125]

A further variety of the "corruption" of black sexuality in McKay's work is presented as rooted in capitalism. Owing to the unequal distribution of economic power, blacks are forced to satisfy whites' desires in order to survive. Given the "perverse" nature of these desires, blacks' struggle for survival entails corruption, as McKay's depiction of a group of white occultists in *Banjo* indicates. The group's leader has "a penchant for exotic sins"—clearly a circumlocution for "perverse" desires because his group is rumored to indulge in "celebrations of occult rites and barbaric saturnalia with the tempo of nocturnal festivities regulated by the crack of whips."[126] The occultists' wealth allows them to spice up their rites by buying a "splendid"[127] African man who, as might be expected, will become their sex slave. The "corruption" or "perversion" of black or nonwhite sexuality is thus clearly linked to whites' economic power—a fact further emphasized in the depiction of the group's stay in Marseilles. After observing male and female prostitutes, the occultists insist on visiting the Blue Cinema, a sex theater, to watch a film Ray describes as inhumane. Only the presence of the group's female member averts the staging of a planned live sex performance by Chinese men. Significantly, this "very flourishing business"[128] is presented as existing purely because of white demand. Establishments like the Blue Cinema seem necessary for whites who, unable to experience sex themselves, constantly seek out sexual novelties to collect and observe. Sex, depicted by McKay as a celebration of vitality for blacks, is thus perverted into a silent and emotionless freak show for white customers.

Ray points out that the Chinese performers are one of many minority groups such as Arabs and blacks who are "hired to perform like monkeys"[129] in Marseilles' sex shows. Griffin views McKay's employment of animal imagery in reference to blacks as a "manifestation of his underlying contempt for Harlem,"[130] yet in the context of the discussion of whites' "corruption" of blacks and other ethnic minorities, McKay seems to employ this imagery transgressively as part of a strategy of admitting to ethnic sexual "corruption" while blaming the racial "other." While whites are described as "monkeys," blacks and other minorities are transformed into monkeys only through corruption.[131] McKay inverts the practice of white racist writers who depict particularly blacks as junglelike, nonhuman creatures, thereby claiming blacks' humanity. Apart from ethnic performers who seem to be victims of a capitalist regime, McKay depicts black men who enter the "white" business of sex on an exploitative level as "gigolos"[132] and pimps, attracted by the prospect of financial rewards. He is careful, however, to emphasize some of these black imitators' original purity, stressing that they were "created by the conquests of civilization."[133] In *Banjo*, the occultists' leader admits that whites actively and intentionally corrupt, stating that they "teach"[134] blacks sexual "perversion." In this context, blacks' ability to adapt and learn quickly, usually regarded as an asset, has distinctly negative consequences: They overachieve, "beating [whites] at their game."[135]

As hinted at in the case of the predominantly male group of occultists whose rituals, which involve an African man, could imply homosexual activities, the allegedly perverse sexuality of whites is not limited to the field of heterosexuality. In *A Long Way from Home*, McKay relates that he was offered work in "a special *bains de vapeur*" in France.[136] While he gives no details, a same-sex context is obvious, as steam baths were known meeting places for same-sex-interested men. Moreover, McKay's explanation—"I felt that if I sacrificed [my individual morale] to make a little extra money, I would become personally obscene"—supports this impression.[137] He thus resisted the lure of money, apparently denying white men the satisfaction of "perverse" desire.

The protagonist in McKay's unpublished poem "Boy Prostitute,"[138] in contrast, does not display what is presented as McKay's strength of character. Race is not mentioned, but the poem still fits into the context of "civilization" and its "corrupting" influences: Living "in this full inventive-wonder age" and lacking the "wisdom of the worldly-wise," the protagonist seems to be a naïve young man at the mercy of the forces of modern "civilization." The boy's beauty is outstanding, yet his physical qualities, which would have been admired in former ages in which "[h]e might have stirred the mighty Angelo," seem wasted. McKay makes a similar claim in his poem "Alfonso, Dressing To Wait At Table, Sings" (1922): The protagonist, a "handsome bronze-hued lad," has to serve "importunate palefaces" who seem unable to appreciate his physical excellence.[139] This service to whites could already be regarded as a kind of prostitution, yet only the protagonist of "Boy Prostitute" gives away his body to please "a whim perverse."[140] Inexperienced and vulnerable, the boy thus "gains his first sensation of disease," presumably syphilis. Considering the severe physical consequences of syphilis, his beauty, symbolizing his sexual purity, seems bound for destruction. It might be assumed that McKay here links disease with "civilization"/whiteness and homosexuality, thereby establishing a connection which, as discussed earlier, was made during the Harlem Renaissance and was to be emphasized by the black nationalist movement of the 1960s. However, a close reading of *Home to Harlem* suggests that disease—for example, syphilis—is here linked only with whiteness as it pervades homosexual and heterosexual relationships. Jake falls ill with syphilis—a contamination clearly linked to his heterosexual promiscuity—and is attended to by Ray, who attempts to convince him of the necessity of safe sex because of whites' "corruption" and "perversion" of sex through syphilis.[141] Instead of claiming homosexuality as a distinct form of "white perversion," infiltrating and contaminating black communities, McKay emphasizes whites' "corruption" of sex in general.

PORTRAYING HOMOSEXUALITY

Emphasizing McKay's strict adherence to a racial binary that also distinguishes between "natural" and "unnatural" sexuality, Chin argues that McKay "marginalize[s] gay and lesbian sexualities" by inextricably linking them to whiteness, thereby prefiguring the emphasis placed in black nationalist discourses on "homosexuality and the homosexual as products of foreign 'contamination.' "[142] Yet rather than constituting a "white" phenomenon, homosexuality is presented by McKay as an inherent aspect of black sexuality. "Pansies," effeminate gay men who repeatedly feature in McKay's works, are, for instance, not generally linked to whiteness. They clearly represent a deviation from normative heterosexuality—a fact that invalidates Chin's claims regarding McKay's alleged heterosexualization of black sexuality.[143] In McKay's novels, black and white pansies are marked by effeminacy and share numerous characteristics with women. The depiction of a "doll baby,"[144] an effeminate African American cabaret dancer, shows that these men appropriate women's "feminine" signifiers: "The boy was made up with high-brown powder, his eyebrows were elongated and blackened up, his lips streaked with the dark rouge so popular in Harlem, and his carefully-straightened hair lay plastered and glossy under Madame Walker's absinthe-colored salve 'for milady of fashion and color.' "[145] Interestingly, pansies do not merely copy femininity: In *Home to Harlem,* some women are described as "painted like dark pansies."[146] While a reading of "pansies" as a variety of flowers is possible, McKay's repeated use of the term to describe effeminate men could imply that these are not imitators but originators of "feminine" style—an inversion underlining their position in the "feminine" sphere. In "Harlem Glory," a novel written after the Harlem Renaissance but of interest in this context, McKay mentions a female impersonator who parodies "congenitally effeminate female impersonators."[147] Starting off from the premise that some men are pansies because of their genetic makeup, these men could certainly originate feminine/effeminate style such as the use of cosmetics.

McKay's pansies and women share the same working environment—cabarets in Harlem and "wide-open holes in the wall"[148] in Marseilles' "Boody Lane." They are portrayed as weak, dependent, and in need of protection, which, since most pansies and women work as prostitutes, is offered by pimps who exploit them. Pansies target the same "manly" customers as women: In McKay's novel "Romance in Marseilles," "the little brothers steal business away from [female prostitutes]."[149] The inappropriateness of an unqualified transference of the concepts of hetero- and homosexuality into McKay's real and literary world becomes obvious here, as the logic underlying his portrayal of effeminate gay men's relationships with "manly" men derives from a different set of assumptions. McKay's effeminate gay characters are "painted boys,"[150] located on a male continuum, but they are also presented as quasi-female. Their sexual contacts with men could thus be said to largely stay within what would today be termed a "heterosexual" framework, as these sexual partners cover the masculine–feminine dichotomy, which seems to be of greater significance for McKay than the binary male–female. The position of pansies and their partners within the dichotomy of masculinity–femininity, which is in the case of pansies modified into masculinity–effeminacy, seems all-important.

Casual sexual involvement with pansies seems socially acceptable: In a cabaret scene in *Home to Harlem,* "dark dandies were loving up their pansies."[151] The couples do not encounter hostile reactions because they apparently do not challenge the structure of sexual relations existing in McKay's Harlem. The development of the above-described scene is revealing: When an attractive female singer dances "a jagging jig," the dandies' attention swings away from their effeminate companions toward the singer—a reaction noticed by the "pansies," who "stared and tightened their grip on their dandies."[152] It remains unclear whether the dandies would prefer sex with a woman or whether the singer's momentary sex appeal catches their attention, but the scene illustrates that their focus is not on male-male love but on sex with someone feminine/effeminate. Even the "manly" Jake seems to have sexual contact with pansies: Frustrated because of his unsatisfactory relationship with the cabaret singer Rose, he starts frequenting a speakeasy where he "[luxuriates] with charmingly painted pansies among the colored cushions and under the soft, shaded lights."[153] This depiction bears striking resemblance to the aforementioned scene in which dandies were "luxuriating under the little colored lights" with their effeminate partners.[154] For Jake, and presumably for other men, sexual contact with pansies seems to constitute an alternative to heterosexual sex which does not diminish their masculinity.

Effeminate gay men are cast in a different light in *Banjo*—none of the black male characters even gets close to white pansies. More than in *Home to Harlem*, McKay seems inclined to delve into negative stereotypes: He depicts white pansies' "queer gestures and queerer screams" and describes their movements as "smirking" and "minc[ing]."[155] Although McKay does not explicitly mark "a group of pale touting youths" mentioned in *Banjo* as "pansies," they seem unmanly and are furthermore linked to "deviance" in an extremely negative context, as they are advertised by their pimp as willing to "[s]teal, murder, love in all ways, lie, and spy."[156] This distinct portrayal may be linked to the two novels' different settings: In Harlem, black effeminate gay men are part of a "natural" black sexuality, while in Marseilles, white pansies' sexuality seems just as "unnatural" and uncomfortable as that of other white men. Their exaggerated and criminal behavior thus fits the commercialized bad show that sex in Boody Lane seems to be.

In "Romance in Marseilles," in contrast, the white effeminate gay man Petit Frère and his "manly" companion Big Blonde are portrayed rather sympathetically.[157] However, it must be noted that the depiction of the effeminate man as somewhat "freakish"—he is described as "fascinating with his pale prettiness and challenging deep dark-ringed eyes and insolent mouth"—contrasts with the description of the butch Big Blonde as a "big firm-footed broad-shouldered man, splendidly built."[158] Yet Big Blonde's "haunting eyes of a lost child"[159] equally mark him as "queer." Distinguishing the portrayal of gay men in "Romance in Marseilles" from that in *Home to Harlem* and perhaps indicative of McKay's attempt to evoke a picture of gay men and homosexuality as oppressed, the presence of a pansy among "normal" men is described as an exception. The café Petit Frère and Big Blonde frequent is thus described as an atypical hangout for the latter's "manly" friends. It constitutes a "retreat"[160] in which Big Blonde enjoys spending time alone with Petit Frère in an apparently "gay-friendly" atmosphere dominated by the presence of men who can easily be linked to same-sex desire: men "of middle-class respectability" who go "slumming" with "lads"; "fine and handsome sailors"; and a soldier sitting alone at a table, maybe waiting to be picked up.[161] In the company of his friends, Big Blonde's self-consciousness about the presence of his effeminate male partner is obvious. He would prefer not to be seen with him and "didn't want to impose Petit Frère upon them"[162]—an attitude which seems linked to his awareness of a generally homophobic environment. Readers learn that Big Blonde once "broke up the furniture in [a] saloon . . . because a boy companion of his was insulted there."[163] The presence of anti-gay sentiments seems furthermore confirmed by the introduction of an old white woman who, provoked by Petit Frère's dismissive attitude toward her, abuses him verbally and eventually physically: She "took a paper full of filth from her basket and slapped it in Petit Frère's face," screaming "There! That is your life."[164] McKay contrasts this display of homophobia with what seems to be blacks' relaxed attitude toward homosexuality. Big Blonde's black friends tolerate his partner, making playful rather than abusive comments. They apparently accept their friend's involvement in a "queer" relationship.[165] McKay ends the scene almost with a plea as Big Blonde, frustrated and "crying softly,"[166] seems to despair because of the cruelty men like himself and Petit Frère have to endure.

While reaffirming the effeminate stereotype of gay men, McKay's overall portrayal of pansies seems, apart from exceptions in *Banjo*, rather tolerant, as they appear to be an accepted part of reality or, as seems to be indicated in "Romance in Marseilles," deserve to be. By placing the majority of "homosexuals" he depicts in a feminine/effeminate sphere, McKay legitimizes their existence and simultaneously naturalizes them. This naturalization could be viewed in the context of the link between homosexuality and congenitality that McKay evokes in "Harlem Glory." Like sexologists who distinguished between congenital and acquired homosexuality—"inversion" and "perversion"—McKay might have categorized pansies as reacting to "naturally" inverted impulses, while, for instance, the white men requiring service in the bathhouses in *A Long Way from Home* are presented as following "perverse" sexual desire. What Jeffrey Weeks describes as sexologists' implied assumption "that homosexual behaviour was only acceptable if it was involuntary and could not be suppressed"[167] is thus apparently also recognizable in McKay's portrayal of men who are openly attracted to members of their own sex.

The concept of "inversion" does not apply to Billy Biasse, another "type" of homosexual male McKay depicts in *Home to Harlem*. A link to a congenital source could still be implied, however, as Billy's same-sex interest seems involuntary and thus "natural." Superseding the category of effeminacy in his portrayal of gay men, McKay portrays Billy as a "wolf" who displays a strong and aggressive masculinity and "eats his own kind"[168]—his sexual relations are exclusively with men. Big Blonde could also be counted among "wolves," yet his emotional, "unmanly" outpouring to some extent disqualifies him. There is no precise description of what kind of men Billy desires, yet there are indications within the text: Billy is depicted as sharing a table with an effeminate man, and he is generally in close contact with pansies. This is significant against the backdrop of his wholesale rejection of women, from which it would follow that were he not sexually interested in pansies, he would reject their physical closeness, as they appear almost female.[169] This impression is supported by Chauncey, who observes more generally for 1920s gay New York: "Wolves generally did not seek sexual encounters with other 'men,' in which they might have been forced into sexual roles that would have compromised their own masculine identification, but only with punks or fairies, males ascribed lower status because of their youth or effeminacy."[170] Most male characters get along well with Billy and Big Blonde, who, like pansies or fairies, do not threaten their masculine identity. Additionally, quarrels about women that frequently lead to conflicts between men cannot occur with butch gay men: "Their intimate interests never clashed."[171] Like the wolves Chauncey discusses, Billy is regarded as somewhat "*different* from other 'normal' men."[172] The character Zeddy, for instance, responds to some teasing remarks Billy makes by asking: "Ain't it better than being a wolf?"[173] Billy's exclusive interest in sexual relationships with effeminate men is regarded as "queer," yet not in the sense of "gay," but rather as "strange"—an indication of what Chauncey describes as "the degree to which gender status superseded homosexual interest as the basis of sexual classification in working-class culture."[174] Some stereotypical assumptions surrounding "the homosexual" as depicted in contemporary literature, however, seem evident in *Home to Harlem* where the dismissive term "lonesome wolf,"[175] reflecting the image of "the homosexual" as a tragic figure whose "affliction" condemns him to loneliness, is uttered every time Billy reprimands others for their alleged lack of masculinity. Yet Billy, to a far greater extent than Big Blonde, displays self-confidence, retorting, "yours truly lone Wolf ain't nevah lonesome," and asserting: "Ise the happiest, well-feddest wolf in Harlem."[176]

Chauncey's sociohistoric findings on 1920s gay men seem reflected in *Home to Harlem*—a fact supporting Locke's description of the novel as a "bare-faced peace [*sic*] of realism about the lowest of city made types."[177] McKay defended his choice of milieu and language along similar lines, stating that he "had written only what he had seen."[178] His presentation of homosexuality constitutes a rather positive picture of "realism," however: Effeminate gay men in the form of pansies are inscribed into "real" life, and particularly wolves are portrayed sympathetically. While the latter variety of "homosexual" might have been generally known, it did not usually feature in literary works.[179] The portrayal of Billy thus constitutes a transgressive literary representation, as McKay inverts the cliché, creating a new literary type —the butch gay man. While still representing an excessive and queer image of homosexuality, McKay reinscribes some gay men, who would usually be regarded as the "other" of manliness owing to their same-sex interest, into the policed realm of masculinity, thereby adding another homosexual level to the feminine–masculine binary that governs his explicit presentation of male same-sex interests.

Lesbianism figures as a minor feature in McKay's fictional works. Generally, McKay portrays female characters as operating on their own, perceiving other women as competition. McKay's depiction of two West Indian women fighting naked in a backyard over a man is the most explicit but not the only depiction of such a scenario.[180] Susy, hostess of numerous parties in *Home to Harlem*, exemplifies the egoistic tendency of most of McKay's female characters: She starts organizing parties with a female friend, who, because of her physical unsightliness, does not count as competition.[181] Susy does not invite other women to her parties because, "[l]ike so many of her sex, she had a congenital contempt for women."[182] While McKay seems to indicate that men can be bound closely to each other because of congenital factors, he portrays women's dislike of members of their own sex as "naturally" given. Lesbians, women who prefer women as partners to men, consequently must be "unnatural."

McKay's presentation of lesbianism in *Home to Harlem* contains both a defense and a dismissal of women-loving women. Jake, the sexually "wholesome" Harlemite, believes that lesbians are "bulldykers" and "all ugly womens," while Ray to some extent defends lesbianism.[183] However, he only makes the qualifying statement that "[n]ot all [lesbians are ugly]," thereby implicitly confirming the existence of "ugly" lesbians. This latter stereotype of the lesbian as unattractive, which seems mainly based on the perception of lesbians as butch, is reiterated in *A Long Way from Home*, in which McKay describes the "companion" of his female sponsor Louise Bryant as an "ugly-mugged woman" who was like "an apparition of a male impersonator, who was never off the stage."[184] By his mention of the woman's nickname, "Sappho-manqué,"[185] a lesbian context is established. Interestingly, McKay suggests that had Bryant chosen one of the "many attractive women in the world,"[186] he would not have objected to their "companionship." As indicated by Lillian Faderman, this distinction was not unique:

> If a woman dressed like a man, it was assumed that she behaved as a man sexually. If she dressed in clothes suitable to her sex, it might be assumed that she was not sexually aggressive, and two unaggressive females together would do nothing to violate men's presumptive property rights to women's bodies. . . . As long as they appeared feminine, their sexual behavior would be viewed as an activity in which women indulged when men were unavailable or as an apprenticeship or appetite-whetter to heterosexual sex.[187]

In *Home to Harlem*, this distinction between same-sex-interested women is evident in the sense that McKay here discusses the opposite of a "Sappho-manqué"—the "real" Sappho. Ray describes Sappho as a "wonderful woman" and criticizes the use of her name in a novel by Alfonse Daudet in which she is a "sporting woman" who has female lovers.[188] It remains unclear whether Ray objects to the employment of her name because of Sappho's clear identi-fication with female lovers or whether he rejects its use in an apparently "trivial" novel. Significantly, her attractiveness, on which Ray's defense seems based, is presented in the context of the heterosexual version of the Sappho epic according to which Sappho in the end renounces lesbianism for the fer-ryman Phaeon. Thus even the less "manly" Ray only partially defends les-bians, insisting on the femininity, clear subjugation, and availability of same-sex-interested women to men. What is perceived as particularly threatening about lesbians is their sexual independence. Even lesbians who depend on heterosexual sex as a source of income, such as La Fleur, a prostitute de-picted in "Romance in Marseilles," do not fully subject themselves to male power. When La Fleur finds a client, her "girl friend" and pimp—in itself a usurpation of a male-defined position—demands, "Save the sugar," a re-minder not to give the best away to a man.[189] This seems unnecessary accord-ing to La Fleur, however: "That goes without saying. . . ."[190]

In tune with his linking of "perversion" with whiteness, McKay chooses white women for his most negative depiction of lesbians. In the short story "Highball" (1932), black pianist Nation's unsympathetic white wife Myra or-ganizes parties behind his back with her white female companion Dinah. While McKay does not explicitly describe Myra and Dinah as a lesbian cou-ple, what James Giles describes as a "subtly developed implication of lesbian-ism" is evident: The two women are "everlastingly embracing and kissing each other"; Myra "put [Dinah's] hands up to her breast and squeezed Di-nah's pretty hands"; and it seems to Nation that "Myra was more affection-ate towards Dinah than she was towards him."[191] Giles suggests that Myra's "lesbianism constitutes a shield against Nation's sexuality,"[192] implying an extension of her race prejudice to the field of sexuality. Myra chose Nation as her husband, opting for a successful pianist toward whom she, despite her physical unattractiveness, could feel superior due to her whiteness. This un-equal relationship does not seem to expose her to Nation's sexuality: Given her husband's busy schedule, she is free to pursue her relationship with Dinah while enjoying her husband's financial support. Myra, described as "a rather coarse-fleshed woman, with freckled hands, beet-colored elbows, dull-blue eyes, and lumpy hair of the color of varnish,"[193] fits McKay's stereotype of the lesbian as the unsightly "other" of femininity; Dinah's looks, in contrast, are reminiscent of a vampire: "Dinah was tall and black-haired, sharp-featured and snub-nosed. Her arms were uncommonly long. Her nails were mani-cured to sharp and exceedingly long points. Her lips were carmine—exces-sively rouged. And she affected black dresses with a touch of red, black velvet slippers and purple stockings."[194] Dinah exceeds "feminine" looks, and the colors identified with her are reminiscent of the figure of the devil; she is the lesbian from hell who "slim, lizard-like, crept after [Myra],"[195] a vampire whose black dress seems blotted with blood. While the combination of what seems to be vampirism and lesbianism may be reminiscent of J. Sheridan Le Fanu's story "Carmilla" (1872), the setting is clearly different in "Highball," as Dinah and Myra are neither young nor beautiful. Moreover, Myra can hardly be viewed as a "victim," as she responds favorably and actively to Dinah's advances.[196]

McKay's portrayals of lesbians are clearly negative. Although he opens up space for the existence of women-loving women outside a stereotypical framework of degeneracy, he immediately sets up new boundaries, as his legitimization depends on a differentiation between "feminine" women available for heterosexual relationships and butch women who enter the sphere of masculinity and compete for men's objects of desire. While McKay's male gay characters are allowed to occupy both segments of the feminine–masculine binary, lesbians, if they are to be viewed outside a negative context, are confined to a "feminine" sphere, forced to at least display what could be described as "bisexual" interests, thereby acknowledging their dependence on men.

DEFINING MASCULINITY

As McKay chose the sphere of sexuality to challenge the existing racial hierarchy, pitting black male "wholesome" potency and masculinity against white impotence and "perversion," his portrayal of threatening, sexually independent lesbians and of female characters as "objects of sexual gratification"[197] seems predictable. Almost all female characters in *Banjo* and *Home to Harlem* are presented within a sexual framework, most of them as prostitutes. Black masculinity is not, however, exclusively defined through the sexual subjugation of women. This may be due to the wide availability of sex, which makes it the lowest of "manly" achievements—albeit one beyond the reach of white men and "contaminated" blacks like Ray. In McKay's prose, black men nevertheless need to perpetually act out "manly" rituals that involve women or femininity as a foil against which to assert maleness to be accepted by other men.[198] Among what could, to borrow Judith Butler's phrasing, be termed the fundamental "performances" of maleness in McKay's novels is the display of aloofness despite the existence of sexual desire for women.[199] While men might behave less roughly when alone with women, it seems essential that when in the company of men, they downplay emotions and sexual desire in largely verbal performances by statements such as: "I ain't gwina bury mah head under no woman's skirt and let her cackle ovah me."[200] Repetitions of such usually misogynist statements seem necessary to ensure a masculine status. As is the case in works by other male writers, in

McKay's novels the subjugation of women becomes what Cora Kaplan in a different context describes as "the premise and occasion of the masculine."[201]

Male characters' dismissive attitudes toward women do not usually imply physical violence. Jake, for instance, explains: "Mah mother useter tell me, 'Nevah hit no woman.' "[202] While Jake does not represent the "average" Harlemite—he is somewhat more sophisticated and sensitive—it still seems as if unprovoked violence against women seems generally inappropriate, as men's physical dominance over apparently "naturally" weaker women is not contested anyway.[203] Jake is therefore disgusted by Rose's masochist desire to be beaten. When he eventually loses his temper and hits her, she confesses to a friend that she had "almost thought he was getting sissy,"[204] as he had not hit her earlier despite her constant provocations. She now concludes that "he's a *ma-an* all right."[205] Jake regrets his action, however, as violence does not fit his "wholesome" definition of masculinity—but possibly also because Rose, a woman, attempted to define and police his masculinity through an act of "perverse" empowerment.[206]

Economic power does not constitute an essential part of black masculinity in McKay's fictional works, which include the depiction of sweetmen, who live off women's money. As indicated earlier in this study, men could prove their masculine status and earn their friends' respect in this way.[207] An example from *Home to Harlem* indicates the pitfalls of the sweetman business. As visible in the case of Zeddy, the domination of a woman in a sweetman relationship requires special skills. Since Zeddy lacks these, his social uplift, manifest in the "fancy-colored silk shirts" provided by his lover, is of short duration because he cannot balance power relations to his advantage.[208] Other manifestations of masculinity are not wholly dismissed, however, as is evident in the case of Jake, who asserts that "[he had] never been a sweetman yet. Never lived off no womens and never will."[209] But Jake may be exceptional in that his personal definition of masculinity does not allow for a financial dependence on women.

Exercising what Hathaway, borrowing from Werner Sollors, describes as a "'contrastive identification' of women as the complete opposite of men,"[210] McKay also conveys the significance of a spatial separation of the sexes. Jake reprimands Ray for giving a woman his address "Because you nevah know when they might bust in on you. . . . Them's all right, them womens . . . in their own parlors."[211] In *Home to Harlem*, Ray points out that "[r]eal men" do not sit in a saloon, particularly not in the saloon's "family room," an area designated for prostitutes and their clients; for men to be there would be "sissified."[212] The space of the family room—an intriguing name, as such—shows that men are supposed to quickly enter or penetrate the "feminine" sphere as clients, with the sole objective of satisfying sexual desire. As the narrator points out, a man's real place is at the bar: "We will leave our women companions and choice wines at the table to snatch a moment of exclusive sex solidarity over a thimble of gin at the bar."[213]

Except in the case of Jake, McKay does not clarify whether his male characters consciously perform masculinity. Jake's masculine status is never seriously questioned, yet he himself questions masculinity as defined along lines of potent promiscuity: "It gave him a little cocky pleasure to brag of his conquests to the fellows around the bar. But after all the swilling and boasting, it would be thousand times nicer to have a little brown woman of his own to whom he could go home and be his simple self with."[214] Jake seems weary of women and men who demand of him a performance as a "prancing he-man" or, as could be said, a constant performance of masculinity by means of what Butler describes as a "*stylized repetition of acts.*"[215] Yet while McKay allows for Jake's individual definition of masculinity which results in his transformation into a family man, this model is by no means advertised as an ideal. As evident in *Banjo*, marriage tames Jake, effecting his transformation from "a wild stallion" to a "draft horse"—a change he apparently accepts.[216] Marriage remains just one option, as evident in *Banjo*, whose protagonist Banjo leads a happy existence having only casual sexual relationships. Moreover, though redefining "masculinity" for himself, Jake nevertheless seems to hold on to his generally dismissive view of women.

What links all "manly" black characters—with the exception of Billy—is that they are sexually attracted to women. Because of the corruption of sexuality by whites, however, their sexual desire is set in an environment where joyful sex remains a rarity. At this point, an interesting argument in McKay's dissociation of men from women comes to the fore: While "civilization" is identified as the source of the "corruption" of sex, it seems as if McKay places guilt on women's shoulders by inextricably linking them to civilization. He presents women, particularly in the figure of the prostitute, as closely connected to capitalism. Apparently, as Hathaway points out, "us[ing] their sexuality to control situations to their own advantage,"[217] McKay's female characters live off men's sexual desire. The prostitutes in Marseilles are thus "always after the beach boys, whenever the boys had some paying business in hand,"[218] but immediately lose interest when their money runs out. Depicted as cynically exploiting men's sexual urges, women function as material signifiers, a good example being the term " 'leetah girls,' " used for prostitutes in *Banjo*, whose name derives from the fact that "their short-term value was fixed at about the price of a liter of cheap red wine."[219]

Among the female characters McKay portrays, black women assume a more positive role. Far from being equated with cheapness, they are frequently described as delicacies. Moreover, unlike their white counterparts, they do not feed on black men—at least not to the same extent. Felice, for instance, loves Jake and returns the money he paid for her sexual services, and Rose, though "perverted," also does not get involved with Jake for financial gain. White women in Marseilles seem generally incapable of such generosity and affection.[220] These subtleties are overshadowed, however, by numerous generalizations that blur racial differences, presenting the argument that "[w]oman is woman all over the world, no matter what her color is."[221] McKay conveys the impression that women lack the resilience to resist the forces of capitalism and are consequently absorbed, owing to what he depicts as their inherent passivity.[222] They are portrayed, however, not as victims of an overwhelming "civilization" but as "the real controlling force of life" and as fundamentally evil.[223] Ray's comment that "society is feminine" inextricably ·links women with "civilization," with all negative implications: Heterosexuality and, implicitly, women are, as Hathaway points out, equated "with the evils of white 'civilization,' capitalism and colonization."[224] This link gains importance against the backdrop of male protagonists' desire for women, which is portrayed as "natural" and necessary. Women's reproductive function is important: "[T]here ain't no life anywhere without them."[225] Men are thus presented as "victims of sex," at the mercy of women who not only exploit them but who also represent what Giles describes as "obstacles to true male comradeship": The "common, commercial flesh of women" is viewed as the trigger for clashes among men in an interracial but also in an all-black context.[226]

MALE CAMARADERIE

As a counterweight against the menacing nature of heterosexual relationships, McKay positions black male camaraderie as a central issue in *Home to Harlem* and *Banjo*. This vision of intimate male bonding is also evident in McKay's constabulary theme, which surfaces in his Jamaican poetry (*Songs of Jamaica* [1912] and *Constab Ballads* [1912]), in the short story "When I Pounded the Pavement" (1932),[227] and in *My Green Hills of Jamaica*. Significantly, the all-male intimacy McKay depicts against the background of constabulary life is distinct from that in *Home to Harlem* and *Banjo*: Here, blackness and masculinity appear to be of no significance. Nevertheless, joining the police force in McKay's short story and his autobiography constitutes a delimitation from women and heterosexual relationships. As McKay recalls, the friend with whom he joined the constabulary "had been kept a long time by the most beautiful prostitute in the city" but was then "fed up."[228] The impression conveyed is that he had been dominated financially and sexually. The decision to join the police force can be seen as a sign of self-determination and, following Sedgwick's observation that men could perceive the "exclusion of women from their intimate lives as virilizing them,"[229] as a decision for an active and "manly" existence. The constabulary itself thus constitutes an exclusively male world from which heterosexual relationships are barred or in which heterosexual desire might even be absent.

Male camaraderie already figures prominently before the constabulary theme is fully introduced. Paralleling McKay's story line in *My Green Hills of Jamaica*, the narrator in "When I Pounded the Pavement" recounts that he "joined the constabulary under the impulse of a strong adolescent friendship."[230] The environment of the constabulary seems to encourage male–male intimacy. The narrator's description of the police compound as "a big depot of men"[231] seems to hint at the location's potentially homoerotic atmosphere: The term "depot" can be read as describing a place where recruits assemble for their training but can also mean a "warehouse" of male bodies. McKay's narrator can thus choose from a wide variety of men "from bush and small town,"[232] while himself becoming part of a fresh supply of men others can select from. In this reading, the constabulary represents the ultimate cruising ground, sheltered from a dominant heterosexual and potentially homophobic society and allowing for a never-ending provision of young men.

Within this setting, two types of camaraderies can be identified. On the one hand, there is a general bond linking recruits, who do "everything in common, drilling, eating, bathing, dressing, sleeping."[233] This intense homosocial bonding has homoerotic potential and seems reminiscent of Whitman's vision of "fervid comradeship" among men; however, in contrast to Whitman's depiction of vagabonding comrades, this camaraderie is supervised and confined to the constabulary compound.[234] On the other hand, as also evident in McKay's early poetry, intimate bonds between two men feature prominently. Given this study's focus on the Harlem Renaissance, McKay's Jamaican poetry is not explored in detail here, yet it is worth noting that it features a depiction of an intimate relationship between a speaker and a character called Bennie in three poems that span both of McKay's early poetry volumes, giving the impression that McKay is relating a love story in episodes.[235] With these poems, particularly with "Bennie's Departure," which describes the speaker's mourning for a friend who has been transferred, McKay presents pieces that, as described by Cooper, "bordered upon a passionate declaration of homosexual love."[236] In stark contrast to his later work, male camaraderie here involves same-sex passion and men's emotional outbursts in poems that can be described as sentimental.

Indicative of McKay's ability to transform his style of writing and ideological outlook over time, sentimentality is absent from "When I Pounded the Pavement." The story nevertheless contains a detailed depiction of intimate male bonding between the narrator and his friend. According to the narrator, acquaintances "extended to ripe comradeship in the barracks."[237] An intensification of the two men's relationship—possibly, as the term "ripe" might indicate, on a sexual level—is evident: During their police training, they spend day and night together, relishing the unprecedented opportunity for intimacy, as they had not conceived "of anything so realistically romantic"[238] occurring in their lives. When instructed to work in the same office, which implies their exemption from lectures and drill, they begin to lead a life separate from their colleagues. As the narrator recounts, he "had always been absent conspicuously with [his] friend"[239]—an absence that may be read as offering the two men the opportunity to be intimate while everyone else is occupied. This possibility might also have been entertained by others, who, as the term "conspicuously" indicates, find their absence noteworthy, if not suspicious. The two men's romantic alliance deteriorates when they are eventually forced to go on the beat and the narrator's friend arrests a prostitute he used to visit before joining the police force. This hypocritical act seems unacceptable for the narrator and destroys "[t]he last thread of feeling attaching [him] to the place"—and, as might be added, borrowing from Whitman's terminology of "comradely love," the "threads of manly friendship" that linked the two men.[240] McKay thus depicts the constabulary as both affirmative and stifling: On the one hand, it constitutes a legitimate same-sex space allowing for intimate contacts; on the other, the very nature of police work seems life- and love-destroying, and, as evident in "Bennie's Departure," transfers can cruelly terminate intimate relationships.

McKay's protagonists in *Home to Harlem* and *Banjo* create an explicitly black-defined homosocial haven. Black men in Harlem form a large community subdivided into circles of friendship; the beach boys in Marseilles forge a more tight-knit camaraderie that still leaves enough space for each of them to follow individual paths. Women are generally excluded from male bonds. Latnah, Banjo's sexual partner, is a notable exception, yet while she is considered a "pal," her gender and different ethnic background—she appears to be of Arab-Asian origin—set her apart.[241] The beach boys spend much of their time together eating, stealing, and, at the end of the day, "flopp[ing] together in a room."[242] Their lives are clearly male-defined, evolving around the port of Marseilles that, similar to the police compound in McKay's constabulary-themed works, attracts a steady flow of young black men. In a way, the group of the beach boys seems self-sufficient, leadership being provided by Banjo with Ray contributing expertise in coping with French bureaucracy.

The black community in *Home to Harlem* is much larger and men seem less dependent on each other. Jake moves within a circle of black male friends who treat each other roughly. His relationship with Ray, however, stands out: theirs is a "big friendship," and Ray has the privilege to be affectionately called "chappie."[243] Forced to part because Ray accepts a job on a freighter, they become almost sentimental: Jake declares "I likes you" and "looked into Ray's eyes with frank savage affection"—a clear and apparently "unmanly" display of emotions for which Billy immediately reprimands him.[244] The scene of their short reunion in *Banjo* is couched in even more intimate terms. Whereas their physical intimacy at the time of their farewell was restricted to "Jake grip[ping] Ray's shoulder," they "embraced and kissed" at their unexpected meeting in Marseilles.[245] Jake's relationship with Felice has at this point superseded his friendship with Ray, yet the spirit of vagabondage—or, as one might say, his desire for intimate male bonding—is still alive within him. Moreover, although Jake's heterosexual desire dominates, his homosocial bond with Ray is imprinted on his life: Symbolic of their friendship, Jake's son is named Ray.[246]

In the beach boys' everyday life, physical aspects of their camaraderie, and particularly McKay's depiction of their bathing together, are of interest. While the bathing scene depicted in *Banjo* focuses on Latnah, it nonetheless can be viewed in terms of male bonding as it is mentioned that "The beach boys often bathed down the docks. . . ."[247] On this occasion, and generally "when they had the extreme end of the breakwater to themselves, they went in naked."[248] As a precautionary measure, one of the beach boys, Dengel, is asked "to keep watch."[249] The necessity for a guard can be read as deriving from the fact that bathing naked, an activity presented as cleansing and "natural," is illegal in "civilized" France. It is also possible to detect space for homoeroticism: Maybe not only the men's nudity but also their intimacy within the water is deemed illicit.

Emphasizing the beach boys' resistance in the face of civilization by unveiling their bodies, McKay provides a link between their camaraderie and memories of Jamaica he depicts in his sonnets "Sukee River" (1920) and "Home Thoughts" (1922).[250] Black male nudity constitutes part of the speaker's reminiscing about his youth spent near "Sukee River" as he wonders "What naked lad doth linger long by thee."[251] While McKay in this poem paints a picture of youthful enjoyment in which the boy's naked body might be read as mainly illustrating the Edenic situation, "Home Thoughts" clearly has homoerotic potential. The poem's speaker feels compelled to reflect on what appear to be childhood memories of school friends in a tropical setting. The scenery, featuring fresh water, bananas, and mangoes, evokes deliciousness, but the true delicacies that can satisfy bodily needs appear to be boys, whose physical activities are described in an admiring tone.[252] Starting off with an alliteration, the speaker visualizes "dexterous Davie" who climbs trees to harvest mangoes before turning to Cyril who carries bananas, and finally, as a climax, he introduces the talented diver Georgie who is "Throwing his scanty clothes off for a swim." Rounding off this all-male Edenic existence, schoolboys watching the river but possibly also the talented and beautiful boys performing their tasks are introduced. As indicated by the poem's framework of two gasped exclamations—"Oh something's happening there this very minute!"—but also by the fact that the speaker "quiveringly" thinks about the boys' activities, this vision arouses the speaker emotionally but possibly also sexually.

In *Home to Harlem* and *Banjo*, homoeroticism surfaces in reference to Ray, who is portrayed as a stranger to black male camaraderie but who joins in enthusiastically, praising the "surprising and warm contacts with the men of his own race."[253] In *Home to Harlem*, Ray admires Jake in his sleep, describing him as "so happy and sweet and handsome,"[254] but only *Banjo* features a scene revealing the eroticism of black male bodies. Observing the docks in Marseilles, Ray envisions "Sweat dripping bodies of black men naked under the equatorial sun" and, taking drugs, he desires to indulge in a fantasy of poetically described "Salty-warm blue bays where black boys dive down deep into the deep waters. . . ."[255] Noteworthy about the latter example is that heterosexual desire cannot be shut out, for the vision forcing itself on Ray is of "the fascinating forms of Harlem" and the "voluptuous caressing motion of feminine folds"; homo-and heterosexual desire thus co-exist.[256]

Featuring heterosexual desire in a less compulsive manner, bisexual interests are also depicted in McKay's short story "The Prince of Porto Rico" (1932).[257] The "Prince," the story's protagonist, works in a barber shop and is characterized by his beauty as he is "the handsomest and most elegant" of all surrounding men.[258] Already his work environment is described as erotically charged: "Pink cream smeared all over chocolate skin. Sugar-brown experts bending over chocolate lads, luxuriating under the process. . . ."[259] While McKay heterosexualizes the scene, mentioning that the customers prepare for their "chippies,"its homoeroticism is undeniable, particularly as the "bending" of the male employees—"experts" in their profession but maybe also in the art of love—over their male customers could be read in a sexual context.[260] While the story's focus is on the Prince's affair with a "grass widow" whose envious husband eventually kills him, he also displays a certain aloofness concerning women. As pointed out before, this would be a typical characteristic of McKay's "manly" characters, but the Prince goes further, describing his emotional and potentially sexual interests in a reply to his female lover: "Oh, I love a lot. . . . I love the girls. I love the boys. I love to love."[261] He is obviously not exclusively interested in women, and his sexual orientation that, from today's perspective, could be described as bisexual, is apparently answered favorably by men and women: "Women ran after him" and "Men also liked the Prince."[262] In *Home to Harlem,* Jake provokes even stronger reactions as desire enters the scene: "[T]here was something so naturally beautiful about his presence that everybody liked and desired him. Buddies, on the slightest provocation, were ready to fight for him, and the girls liked to make an argument around him."[263]

Sedgwick suggests that desire linking men in homosocial bonds can be viewed as any kind of "social force, [or] glue, even when its manifestation is hostility or hatred."[264] In McKay's portrayal of male bonding, misogyny and the delimitation from "corrupting" forces of a white-defined "civilization" can be said to provide this glue. However, as Ray's homoerotic dream visions and "The Prince of Porto Rico" indicate, men are also linked by same-sex desire, pointing to what Sedgwick describes as the "potential unbrokenness of a continuum between homosocial and homosexual."[265] Since both Jake and the Prince are identified as examples of a lifestyle and masculinity other men wish to emulate, McKay's opening up of the possibility of sexual interests in these characters for non-effeminate men looks like a deviation from his insistence on the adherence to the femininity–masculinity binary. Significantly, however, while "manly" men like Jake develop strong bonds with other men, sexual contacts between them remain absent, constituting but haunting possibilities for gay readings.[266] This is particularly the case in *Banjo:* As soon as the more general camaraderie between the beach boys disintegrates as the group disperses, there is room for intimate friendship between two men. Whereas *Home to Harlem* ends in heterosexual happiness, *Banjo* ends in male homosocial happiness between Ray and Banjo. They decide to embark on what George Kent describes as "a romantic vagabondage" which seems to fulfill Whitman's vision of loving comrades. Kent characterizes Ray and Banjo's relationship as "a kind of chaste homosexual relationship,"[267] thereby acknowledging the presence of men-loving men while at the same time denying the possibility of sexual contacts—without any textual reference. Yet same-sex contacts could constitute one of the things on Banjo's mind when he concludes that "Theah's a lotta things befoh us we'll have to make together"—particularly since women are on Banjo's insistence excluded from their future plans.[268] The absence of an Eve from their "Edenic existence" is thus not, as Kent suggests, "the price" they have to pay for their close relationship but the necessary precondition for the celebration of an all-male camaraderie.[269]

Cooper and Chin claim that McKay "did not seriously challenge the rule that [homosexuality was] not to be discussed openly in creative literature" and that his novels do not "contain any overt homosexual characters."[270] While McKay's gay poetic voice may, apart from instances in his Jamaican poetry, be described as reticent, these claims do not do justice to his fictional work, in which various homosexualities—some of them presented explicitly, others detectable for attentive readers—are explored. McKay's presentation of homosexuality, in which he reinscribes male same-sex love into the sphere of "natural" sexuality, appears to be but a sub-agenda included in his overall project of creating "manly" black literature which implies a challenging of racial hierarchies. It seems that in order to avoid an "unmanly" narrative, McKay's presentation of intimate male camaraderie remains non-sexual. Furthermore, not wanting to jeopardize his project through censorship, McKay could presumably not afford to be more explicit in his portrayal of homosexuality. As indicated in his largely dismissive portrayal of lesbians that is symbolic of his overall negative depiction of women, McKay's variety of primitivism seems to be one which in McCabe's words "drag[s] in ideologies of difference that reinscribe hierarchies in other sites"[271] in the process of opposing racial stratifications. The central hierarchies in McKay's case are those of race and gender. The latter hierarchy governs his portrayal of homo-/sexuality and indicates his absolute reliance on binaries. While challenging the positioning of groups within binaries, he never transcends these structures, thereby mirroring what Kobena Mercer describes as the "racist stigmatization of blacks"[272] by whites. The "other"—in McKay's case whites—is pictured as inferior and, given McKay's emphasis on sexuality, as impotent and "perverse." It can be concluded that McKay's focus as displayed in his fiction remains almost fully on the issue of black masculinity, an emphasis that links him to the 1960s black nationalist movement for whom, as hooks points out, issues of race and masculinity were equally central: "It was a case of 'will the real man please stand up.' And when he stood up, he was, in the eyes of the black power movement, a black male."[273] This could also be said to hold true for McKay—albeit with the significant difference that his "real" black male would not have to be heterosexual.

SIX

Richard Bruce Nugent:
The Quest for Beauty

Richard Bruce Nugent is generally given credit as "an invaluable source of information"[1] on the Harlem Renaissance, but apart from brief comments, his creative work and role as an artist and writer in his own right have to date been largely neglected. This was somewhat different during the Harlem Renaissance, when, as Nugent remembered, "even Du Bois"[2] counted him among the Talented Tenth. Living with Wallace Thurman at "Niggeratti Manor," the center of the self-consciously transgressive younger Renaissance writers, Nugent was closely involved in the publication of *Fire!!*, to which he contributed the openly homoerotic story "Smoke, Lilies and Jade."[3] Few of Nugent's drawings, short stories, and poems came into print during the Renaissance, but he was represented in the period's hallmark publication *The New Negro* with his short story "Sahdji."[4]

Nugent is in many ways distinguishable from other Renaissance figures. It seems that Harlem was not large enough to contain Nugent, who, already in a geographical sense, transgressed its boundaries, spending "half the time"[5] in Greenwich Village even at the height of the Renaissance. One of the few Renaissance artists to establish close contact with the contemporary white avant-garde—particularly with those willing to transgress sexual boundaries—Nugent counted Parker Tyler, for instance, among his closer acquaintances.[6] In light of this physical crossing of boundaries, it is not surprising that Nugent's artistic inspiration also transcended racial categories. While this is certainly also true of other Renaissance writers, Nugent is exceptional, as his work incorporates references to African motifs and simultaneously manifests the influence of white artists like Aubrey Beardsley and Erté, "decadent" authors like Joris-Karl Huysmans, and, particularly regarding formal aspects such as the application of a stream-of-consciousness technique, modern white writers.[7]

As these interracial affiliations indicate, Nugent, perhaps more than any other author discussed in this book, refused to bear the black artist's "burden of representation." Yet his stance toward the black leadership's aspirations seems indifferent rather than rebellious. While his contribution to *Fire!!* indicates his involvement in a violent reaction against the task of representation, his other writings, as will be seen, transcend this context. Nugent described his motives for joining in Renaissance activities as largely personal. For instance, he accompanied Hughes to poetry readings not for any "cause"—for example, the advancement of interracial relationships or the "uplift" of African Americans—but "because Langston asked [him] to do it."[8] Being a "better follower than a leader,"[9] it seems that Nugent, when near productive friends like Thurman and Hughes, could not but join in. One crucial factor distinguishing Nugent from other Renaissance figures was, as Thomas Wirth points out, that he "refused to pursue a 'career.' "[10] Despite Nugent's elite Washingtonian family background, this refusal cannot be linked to financial well-being, as his family's high social ranking derived from the fact that it was old and respected as well as distinct because of family members' light complexion rather than from wealth. Where other writers consciously sought publishing opportunities, Nugent responded to requests for contributions. Moreover, while most Renaissance writers and artists concentrated on one field, Nugent wrote, drew, danced, and acted.[11] Born in 1906, he was the youngest member of the Niggeratti—a fact which seems to have influenced his lifestyle. He felt free to behave like the group's "clown," opting for the role of the "flamboyant one"—a position acknowledged by various scholars who refer to him as the "ultimate bohemian."[12] Nugent was famous, or rather notorious, for turning up without the attire deemed appropriate: Where Cullen met with approval for his perfect suits, Nugent would cause excitement, being unwashed and wearing neither shoes nor a necktie. Carl Van Vechten, for instance, gave an account of Nugent attending a party "with his usual open chest and uncovered ankles. I suppose soon he will be going without trousers."[13]

Nugent's working methods can also be described as "bohemian." He recalled writing on "paper bags and toilet paper and things like that," which sometimes, as happened with the first version of "Smoke, Lilies and Jade," were accidentally believed to be "trash" and consequently discarded.[14] Characteristically, Hughes had to retrieve Nugent's poem "Shadow"—subsequenly published in *Opportunity*—from a waste bin.[15] Another example of the rather incidental nature of Nugent's literary career is his story "Sahdji." Approached for a contribution to be included in *The New Negro*, Nugent presented a drawing to Locke, who then suggested that Nugent write an additional story. Locke eventually chose only the story, leading Nugent, who previously did not consider himself a writer, to the field of literature.[16] Nugent appears to have favored drawing over writing, yet also in this field, he apparently did not aim at wealth and fame. He often lost, destroyed, and gave away drawings—a fact that complicates an assessment of his creative work, as a substantial part remains irretrievable.[17] Bohemianism was clearly central to Nugent's self-representation: A closer examination of his creative processes and artistic life reveals that these were not as simple and casual as Nugent suggests. While he claimed to have written "Smoke, Lilies and Jade," for instance, with "no plan, no anything," this attitude seems to have changed with growing experience, giving way to a concentrated effort: "Cutting, moulding, adding, throwing away, building. Giving this thing parts of your very self. . . ."[18] Moreover, Nugent repeatedly joined literary and artistic competitions, even applying for a scholarship with the Guggenheim Memorial Foundation, as "[his] heart and ambitions [were] set on a year or so of serious study of the Theatre abroad."[19] Nearly all these efforts failed, however.

The feature of Nugent's lifestyle that distinguished him most clearly from other Renaissance figures was his openly displayed same-sex interest, which, in his own assessment, brought him the admiration of more closeted figures like Thurman and Hughes.[20] Like many other young gay men involved in the Renaissance, Nugent corresponded with Locke, discussing art and personal matters regarding same-sex relationships. In contrast to most other correspondents, however, Nugent was aware of his homosexual interests and apparently felt at ease with his sexual identity. While others used the coded discourse of "friendship," Nugent's letters were more explicit: In a 1929 letter, for instance, he referred to his perspective as that of a "homo- or duosexual's."[21] As Nugent recounted in an interview, the formation of his gay identity was largely informed by Richard von Krafft-Ebing's *Psychopathia Sexualis* (1892), a book-length accumulation of case studies of so-called pathological forms of sexuality, which he read at age 13.[22] Nugent's personal experience seems reflected in his fictional persona Stuartt in "Gentleman Jigger," who "had the time to discover Kraft Ebbing [*sic*] and the regretable [*sic*] similarity between the symptoms uncovered in one-hundred-and-twebty-seven [*sic*] cases and himself."[23] While this expression of regret may be viewed as mainly ironic, any such emotion would seem understandable, as most men described in *Psychopathia* apparently contacted Krafft-Ebing in a state of desperation, desiring to be "cured"—a task Krafft-Ebing accepted, recommending therapies and sexual contact with women. Also owing to the support offered by his parents, whom Nugent described as "freaks" because they belonged to Washington's bohemian community, Nugent developed what one could, from today's perspective, term a positive "queer" identity.[24] Nugent's mother, who accepted that her son was "peculiar," made only one stipulation: He was not to "disgrace the family name"—a condition Nugent formally fulfilled by almost never giving his full name in publications.[25]

While Nugent retrospectively accepted the term *gay* to describe his sexual orientation, his statement that he was "homosexual" or "duosexual" indicates a potentially more ambiguous sexuality. It seems that in 1929, Nugent did not exclude the possibility of being sexually interested in women. However, as he stressed in interviews, he only once had sexual contact with a woman. His display of bisexual interests—bisexuality is also featured in "Smoke, Lilies and Jade"—might, as Wirth suggests, be viewed as part of his play on sexual ambiguity.[26] It could also be seen against the background of the rather popular status of bisexuality: It seems that bisexual "experimentation," rather than homosexuality, was at least in artistic circles fashionable and accepted during the 1920s.[27] However, this possibility would contradict Nugent's otherwise open transgressions of social and moral norms. Nugent married in 1952 yet always seems to have preferred sexual contacts with men. His relationship with his wife, based on his openness about his same-sex desire, remained platonic.[28] Refusing to move into "what they call the closet," Nugent openly embraced what he termed the "under-/anti-social-/homosexual world"—an espousal he could to some extent afford, as his privileged social position allowed him a measure of freedom.[29] Yet even Nugent once only narrowly escaped incarceration after a "lover's [*sic*] quarrel"[30] with a sailor. Moreover, he was aware of the social ostracism that could follow public exposure, as happened to one of his gay friends.[31] These experiences seem to have left him unimpressed, however. Despite predominantly negative legal, medical, religious, and public discourses on homosexuality, Nugent rejected any notion of shame, pursuing his individual path as a bohemian, queer artist, who, when asked to leave Washington because of his open pursuit of same-sex affairs, moved to New York.[32]

The fact that Nugent's self-identification as a gay man was inextricably linked to his existence as an artist is of high significance for an assessment of his literary sexual dissidence. The conclusion of Nugent's fictional persona Stuartt after discovering his transgressive sexuality is that "[h]e would become an artist. All artists were strange or expected to be."[33] This conflation of same-sex interest and an artist's identity is also evident in the aforementioned letter to Locke: Nugent complained of depression that could be viewed "from the angle of a homo- or duosexual's juxtaposition to life or an artist's. Doubly hard and fascinating when regarded from the angle of both rolled into one."[34] Unsurprisingly, the theme of men-loving men is a recurrent feature in Nugent's works, which, as Eric Garber claims, are only small in number, representing but a "modest literary output."[35] Garber's assessment is flawed, however, as Nugent's published works comprise only a small segment of his overall creative efforts. Nugent's surviving texts and drawings prove that his creative activities were intense and manifold. In a letter to Locke, Nugent mentioned, for instance, an outline for a "chanted dance or a chanted Ballet," the story "The Geisha House Man," and "another something" on intraracial color prejudices.[36] Some of his works seem to have been on the verge of publication. One of Nugent's literary ventures—a "book" which may have been the fictionalized autobiographical account "Gentleman Jigger," the novel "Geisha Man" or, as Wirth suggests, a privately printed edition of the story "Beyond Where the Star Stood Still"—was, for instance, claimed to be a "jewel" by Georgia Douglas Johnson, who inquired about its prospective sales price, yet no publication followed.[37] In another case, Nugent intimated to Johnson that the publishers Boni & Liveright and Knopf had expressed interest in his "novellett" [sic] "Smoke, Lilies and Jade."[38] Despite Nugent's optimistic assessment, this prospect did not materialize.

As Wirth points out, Nugent's meager publishing record was linked to the fact that his work "profoundly subverted sexual, racial, and religious norms."[39] Presenting men-loving men explicitly, his writing was—certainly according to contemporary censorship laws—presumably not considered fit to print. Nugent consciously or unconsciously circumvented censorship with his cover design for the March 1926 edition of *Opportunity*: At first sight, an African man, flanked by a palm tree with coconuts, is visible, but at a closer look, he appears to be in drag, positioned next to a gigantic phallus.[40] However, Nugent did not succeed in publishing many of his literary works in which his gay voice is usually unmistakably audible.

RACE AND COLOR

Against the backdrop of Nugent's light complexion and his interracial contacts, the role that the topics "race" and "color"—of such central significance in Claude McKay's work—play in Nugent's representation of same-sex desire merits an exploration. Nugent was frequently involved in African American community activities, engaging in, for instance, the formation of the Harlem Cultural Council in the late 1960s. As Nugent stated in an interview, he was never "in the closet about [his] race."[41] Because, as he commented, "Anything was preferable to being Negro in those days," he nevertheless had no qualms about occasionally passing as "this, that, or other."[42] Befitting his sexual behavior, Nugent was "racially" outrageous, recounting his "passing" experiences with pleasure, thereby frankly discussing an issue usually shrouded in secrecy, fear, and shame.[43] He had to confront his personal color prejudices, however—he apologized to Thurman after their first meeting, from which he had left abruptly, unable to face Thurman's dark complexion.[44] While Nugent's work certainly deals with issues of "race"— his "Drawings for Mulattoes"[45] series and pieces like "Sahdji" illustrate this point—they are not dominant. This refusal to focus on the creation of positive representations of "black" life called for by Renaissance leaders caused disappointment. Nugent recalled that Du Bois, implying the absence of homosexuality among African Americans, asked Nugent after the publication of "Smoke, Lilies and Jade": "Why don't you write more about Negroes?" Nugent responded: "I write about myself, and I'm a Negro, aren't I?"[46] Like Cullen, Nugent did not regard his racial origin as a defining factor for his creative work. Yet in contrast to the "poet laureate," he produced works in which explicitly described same-sex desire frequently occupies a central position.

Among Nugent's surviving works from the Renaissance period, one story and two poems are presented in a "racial" context. In "Sahdji," Nugent chooses an "exotic" African setting: The "young buck" Numbo is in love with the chieftain's son Mrabo, who in turn loves Sahdji, one of his father's wives.[47] Intent on helping Mrabo, Numbo murders the chieftain, thereby causing misery, because Mrabo is distraught when Sahdji opts for ritual suicide at the site of her husband's grave. The story's setting is "racial," yet the underlying same-sex attraction between Numbo and Mrabo, serving as a trigger to the plot, is not linked to signifiers of blackness, which are employed only to describe the female protagonist's "beautiful dark body" and "overfull sensuous lips."[48] In the poems "Bastard Song"[49] and "Shadow," in contrast, race is of central importance. Fitting Nugent's belief that "poets can say what prose writers can't, just by not saying it, by implying it, by inferring it,"[50] the two poems' racial narratives appear to contain a same-sex subtext. Already, the title of "Bastard Song" hints at the mixed racial background of the speaker, who addresses an ungendered "pale white"[51] person with a love poem. A veiled indication of the poem's interracial theme and its same-sex context is given by Nugent's dedication "for H.F.," presumably Hank Fisher, a white lover of Nugent's around 1930. In the first of the poem's two stanzas, the speaker seeks to justify his identity and thereby give validity to his love, metaphorically defining himself as "dusk," which is "just as true a thing as either night or day."[52] Yet there seems to be no hope for a loving relationship, the factor of "whiteness" being identified as a destructive force that drenches life, dreams, and love out of the speaker's lover. Apart from the dedication, the potential for gay readings lies, as is the case in Hughes's poems, in the undefined nature of the speaker's "dreams."[53] Issues of race and color are the poem's obvious focus, yet especially in the second stanza it is possible to read "whiteness" as denoting purity, virginity, or heterosexual "cleanliness." The preservation of these attributes keeps the addressee from following dream visions and leads him/her to "refuse to live"[54] and give way to his/her desires. This opens up the intriguing possibility of reading the speaker's intermediary status—"neither true the one nor really true the other, / . . . I must be the third"[55]—as referring to what was termed the "third" or "intermediary sex," gay men and lesbians, whose sexual identity was believed to defy the male–female binary.[56]

The "dark" and "Black" speaker in "Shadow" sees himself as a lonely outsider, placed against a white background "on the face of the moon."[57] He seems characterized by blackness and defines his identity negatively, describing himself as a "shadow," a "silhouette," "lacking color / Or vivid brightness." Since he represents but an outline and a shape, there seems to be no content or life to him, because he regards his defining attribute, blackness, not as a color but as a taint. Apparently representing a minority that cannot blend in, the speaker is exposed to the potentially hostile gaze of others. As Gregory Woods points out in reference to Renaissance writers' gay poetic voices, "[i]t is often possible to read a particular poem as referring (in images such as that of the social outcast) to either racial or sexual oppression."[58] This seems to be the case in "Shadow," which, though "considered a race poem" by contemporary readers, Nugent thought of as a "soul-searching poem of another kind of loneliness."[59] It seems fitting that in performing a gay reading, the speaker describes himself as "not understood," thereby referring to the intolerance expressed in contemporary newspaper articles that asked "Are Pansies People?"[60] Forced to lead a shadow existence, unable to voice and act on desire, sexual "deviants" cannot escape exposure and thus seem condemned to solitude, surrounded by a heterosexist society.

In his presentation of racially defined characters in the context of same-sex attraction, Nugent usually does not link protagonists of the same color, the briefly outlined attraction between Numbo and Mrabo constituting an exception. Interestingly, Isaac Julien transformed Nugent's "Smoke, Lilies and Jade" into a cinematic tale of homoerotic blackness. Manthia Diawara remarks that in Julien's film *Looking for Langston* (1989) "black men [look] at black men as objects of desire."[61] Nugent's story, however, which focuses on a sexually charged street encounter between the racially unidentified Alex and the Latin "Beauty," contains the explicit definition of Beauty's body as "white."[62] A racial context for Alex can be constructed only by taking into account his enumeration of Harlem Renaissance figures Hughes and Cullen as his acquaintances, yet it must be considered that he also lists writers such as [H. L.] Mencken and [James Branch] Cabell, who blur the racial focus.[63] Nugent, who personally preferred Italian or Latin sexual partners, clearly did not intend to portray same-sex love as bound by racial categories.[64]

While McKay's representation of homosocial/-sexual male bonding is based on blackness, Nugent's all-male lovers and his rarer portrayals of heterosexual relationships are usually set in a racially undefined or multiracial context. The choice of a mythical time frame and background in the form of a biblical setting for a group of five stories allowed Nugent to avoid references to a "race problematic." Two of these stories—"Tunic with a Thousand Pleats" and "The Now Discordant Song of Bells"[65]—focus on the sexual attraction of color contrasts, thereby presenting the sensitive topic of miscegenation without addressing it as a contested issue. In "Tunic," the light-skinned Shela prepares for the games, where she intends to meet her black lover Simon, who, however, fails to turn up. Attending the event with another man, Shela recognizes Simon as he walks behind Jesus, carrying his cross. Her attempts to attract Simon's attention fail, and she is infuriated when Simon, "suffer[ing] for Jesus,"[66] leaves her. In "Bells," Herod's white catamite Carus, who leads a decadent lifestyle and exercises pagan rituals, falls in love with Caspar, the black member of the Magi. Intent on winning his love, he attaches himself to Caspar, yet at Caspar's insistence their relationship remains chaste.

In both stories, Nugent presents male blackness as the focus of white desire. Shela is infatuated with Simon's curls, adoring "his blackness [which was] a strangeness beautiful like his speech" and "his cheek, so dark as the night." Carus loves Caspar's "exotic beauty," "desiring to see the full lips move more."[67] Simon's and Caspar's racial identity appears to be all-defining, as not only their bodies but even their voices seem black, triggering sexual desire in their observers. While Simon is absent for most of the story and Shela only recalls her desire for him, Carus's active gaze on Caspar is emphasized. In a reflection on this sensual perspective, a description is included of how "Caspar moved sensuously in the brilliant sun," "his beautiful black body bare and a linen cloth of great whiteness thrown across his loins."[68] Without doubt, Carus would like to replace this cloth with his own body. Desire for contact of white and black flesh is made explicit in another scene in which Carus "had desire to note the contrast his hand would offer on Caspar's"—a scene paralleling one in "Tunic" in which Shela muses: "I like to see his hand on my arm—I am made so white."[69] Both Shela and Carus view their partner as the "exotic other," yet because of Nugent's choice of a biblical setting, their gaze and desire is not that of a colonizer or a 1920s "Negrotarian," fascinated by the alleged "earthiness" of African Americans, since whiteness is not linked to superiority. A partial exception can be found in "Tunic," in which one female character describes Simon as "almost as dark as one of Pilate's Nubian slaves"[70]—a comment which links blackness to social inferiority. Shela, however, insists that her color does not make her superior but that it requires the foil of blackness to achieve beauty.[71] In "Bells," Carus's desire for Caspar is described as the wish to "possess this rarity"[72]—an indication of Carus's intention to "acquire" and eventually consume Caspar's body. Yet in contrast to the "virgin youths"[73] whom Carus seems to devour sexually at the beginning of the story, Caspar can, because of his religiousness which allows only for "brotherly"—that is, nonsexual—love, apparently not be "corrupted." Maturing, Carus's "fondness for Caspar became even love"—a process which indicates that Carus's longing for the possession of Caspar was motivated by a fusion of decadent desire and exaggerated wealth resembling that of Huysmans' protagonist Des Esseintes in *Against Nature*, and not by a spirit of racial superiority.[74]

"Race" seems reduced to a matter of aesthetic contrast in both stories. Blackness—not in a cultural context but merely in regard to color—thus provides the perfect foil to whiteness, effecting homo- and heterosexual desire. Reading the issue of race as one of color, it is possible to identify it as one of numerous "aesthetic" color combinations with which Nugent literally paints his written work. "[T]aking colours from all palettes,"[75] Nugent seems to adhere to Théophile Gautier's definition of decadent style. In the Bible story "Beyond Where the Star Stood Still," the beautiful Magi represent three shades of complexion and are set in an environment that interacts with their own color: The "black man" Caspar rides on a "great white camel," "saffron" Melchior wears a robe of "bright blue wool," and the "pale tan" Balthasar's "robes were royal and red."[76] This multitude of contrasting colors is also evident in many other prose pieces by Nugent, who thereby creates a dazzling multicolored background for plots, extending, to use Holbrook Jackson's phrase, readers' "boundaries of sensation"[77] by including a visual level within the textual narrative. While race thus plays a role in Nugent's depiction of same-sex and heterosexual desire, it is largely stripped of a cultural context and thereby integrated into the color play visible in his work.

BEAUTY, BODIES, SENSUALITY, AND LOVE

In light of Nugent's focus on the creation of aesthetically pleasing work, it seems appropriate that he creates characters whose beauty is celebrated. This is the case in the Bible story "Tree with Kerioth-Fruit," which centers on Jesus and the disciples and portrays Judas not as a traitor but, similar to Cullen's poem "Judas Iscariot," as Jesus' closest friend. Remarkably, the word "beauty," describing men, appears eight times on the story's first two pages alone.[78] Nugent thereby transgressed sexual conventions in the literary field because, as he emphasized in an interview, "you didn't call a man beautiful"[79]—this judgment was set aside exclusively for female bodies. While without doubt focusing on male attractiveness, Nugent does not exclude female bodies from his definition of beauty. Many of his drawings feature female figures with well-formed breasts in transparent dresses, and in a short literary sketch of well-known actress Rose McClendon, a close friend of Nugent's, variations of the word "beauty" are almost as numerous as in "Kerioth-Fruit."[80] Sexual contacts with women feature only rarely in Nugent's work, yet women are nevertheless presented as sensual and capable of attracting men's attention through physical qualities. Even in the explicitly homoerotic "Smoke, Lilies and Jade," female beauty is portrayed alongside male beauty in the form of Melva, whose depiction—"two well turned legs curving gracefully from slender ankles . . . past the narrow rounded hips to the tiny waist . . . the fragile firm breasts"—is clearly sensual.[81] Yet in most of Nugent's stories, a desirous gaze is directed at male bodies—either because women look at men or, as is the case more often, because only male characters are depicted.

When it comes to the depiction of not only beauty but also attractive male bodies and sensuality, Nugent's stories are best separated into the largely unspecified depictions of male beauty in the Bible stories and the detailed, sensual representations in "Smoke, Lilies and Jade" and "Geisha Man." In his Bible stories, Nugent pays much attention to the opulence surrounding his beautiful male characters. Although the reader can catch glimpses of bodily beauty—Caspar's "slender body," Carus's "long green eyes," and Balthasar's "beautiful thin lips"—bodies seem to serve only as attractive details of a colorful work of art.[82] They thus remain on the level of luxurious objects such as jewelry and perfumes. Particularly the bodies of the Magi seem to exist only to allow for a detailed description of garments and precious stones.[83] Nevertheless, male beauty stands out as an attractive power in "Bells," in which Carus, as mentioned before, falls in love with Caspar.

Beauty unites a larger group of men in "Kerioth-Fruit." Jesus' disciples are depicted as gathering around him not so much because of his religious teaching, which is presented as poetry rather than religion, but because of his physical virtues.[84] John is the first to be attracted to Jesus, whose beautiful body and voice trigger a "pleasant tremor vibrating his young knees."[85] Overcoming an initial feeling of jealousy, John's close friend Simon seems equally overwhelmed when he meets Jesus: He becomes "impetuous in his affection," believing that Jesus "liveth completely in the physical beauty he hath inherited."[86] Proving irresistible, Jesus eventually attracts all disciples "in such a way,"[87] convincing yet another male couple—Philip and Nathaniel—to join him. Not only Jesus but the disciples themselves represent beauty, with John, as acknowledged by Jesus, who had "never . . . seen such beauty as was John's,"[88] standing out. Jesus thereby reciprocates John's passion and physical reaction, as John's beauty "excited him strangely and left him embarrassed for words."[89] This seems to be a case of love and desire at first sight.

The term "beauty" disappears after the story's introductory pages and is superseded by another word—"love." The all-male ties, initially established on the basis of beauty, have evolved into bonds of love. Not only are the disciples in at least one case in love with each other, but they also "loved"[90] Jesus. Similar to Cullen's interpretation with homoerotic implications of Judas as Jesus' intimate friend, Nugent's Judas is closest to Jesus "because he loved him."[91] A narcissistic element in their love is evident, as they, who are "as twins, so alike in thought and desire . . . [a]nd in appearance also,"[92] seem infatuated with their own reflection. Portraying both John's and Judas's bond with Jesus as particularly intimate, Nugent gives the story an interesting twist by introducing jealousy as Judas's response to the "affection bestowed on John"[93] by Jesus. Nugent could have constructed a narrative resembling that outlined in Edward Prime Stevenson's *The Intersexes* (1908) in which Stevenson proposed the possibility that "the treason of Judas was the madness of a jealous homosexual passion, on the part of the betrayer."[94] Instead of opting for this kind of plot that links same-sex desire with crime and mental instability in a way reminiscent of contemporary discourses on homosexuality, Nugent portrays male same-sex desire as a positive force. Judas overcomes what could be described as petty feelings, giving way only to his grand emotion of love, which is combined with a sense of responsibility for the fulfillment of his "duty of love."[95] Only because of the strength of Judas's same-sex love could Jesus become Christ, the religious savior of humankind.

Wirth rightly refers to an "open, uncoded conflation of homosexuality with the gospels" in the context of Nugent's Bible stories, yet while presenting male same-sex love as constituting the basis for Christianity certainly "challenge[s] both homophobia and shallow piety," Nugent's sexual dissidence seems somewhat limited—an impression that is linked to his presentation of same-sex contacts.[96] Physical contact in a male same-sex context seems largely restricted to nonsexual instances, and gay sex is in some cases explicitly rejected. In "Kerioth-Fruit," Simon initially mocks John's affection for Jesus, stating that "[o]ne would think thou wert enamored of this stranger," to which John replies that he has "never indulged in the Greek refinement. 'Tis not according to the laws of Moses, nor truly to my desire."[97] Nugent thereby not only apparently accepts and reiterates the negative representation of homosexuality in Judeo-Christian belief but additionally strengthens the argument by attributing a dislike of same-sex activities to the most attractive of all disciples. Furthermore, Nugent seems to explicitly desexualize John and his relationship with Jesus, who loves him "as a mother loves her first-born child."[98] Jesus' statement "I preach only brotherly love. I do no wrong"[99] also seems to refer to the nature of love that links men or, in this case, particularly the disciples and himself. He thereby attempts to defend himself against the Pharisees' claim that he was a "mountebank,"[100] yet readers seem invited to read Jesus' comment as a reference to a distinction between physical same-sex love and platonic or "comradely" love, a possible defense against accusations of his moral "corruption" of young men. In "Bells," Carus is apparently sexually involved with male dancers, priests, and young men in a pagan ritual, but this singular occurrence of sexual same-sex contact in Nugent's Bible stories is embedded in a tale which centers on Carus's maturation from youthful debauchery to wisdom. Similar to "Kerioth-Fruit," a rejection of homosexual sex is highlighted in the portrayal of Caspar's rejection of Carus's admission of love and desire through his insistence that while he loves Carus, he does so only "[a]s a brother. Nothing can alter that."[101] There is clearly no hope for the establishment of a sexual relationship.

Exploring these narratives more closely, it is possible, however, to view Nugent's representation of gay sex in his Bible stories in a different context. Wirth suggests that the tension between the disciples' chaste love, the antisexual/antihomosexual teachings of the church, and the stories' strong undertones of homoerotic desire are essential for the development of Nugent's narratives.[102] Moreover, what seem to be deliberate gaps can be detected within the stories. Philip and Nathaniel's relationship in "Kerioth-Fruit" is far more intimate than that of other disciples, as they "when together were blind to else."[103] It is clearly stated that Philip "loved"[104] Nathaniel, and Nathaniel's jealousy of Jesus is intense. This does not point to a sexual component in their relationship, but it is evident that they are what Simon before mockingly described as "enamored" of each other, and at no point in the story is this love condemned. In spite of the negative ending of "Bells"—Caspar asks the matured Carus to leave and assume responsibility as a teacher and friend to Simon of Cyrene—Nugent here also leaves scope for dissidence. Reading the story as based on a parallel centering on the topic of supreme sacrifice, Caspar's moral superiority is questioned. Nugent frames his story by two sacrifices in the name of love: Carus demands the ultimate sacrifice of his cat Sextabius—death—and kills him, and Caspar seems to ask for the death of Carus's emotions when enforcing their separation. Carus's slaying of his cat is depicted as a decadent, cruel gesture. Given the story's parallel narrative structure, the same conclusion can be drawn from Caspar's action, which can thus no longer be considered a virtuous, moral rejection of physical same-sex love. The text contains further indicators pointing to a fundamental questioning of Caspar's wisdom and virtuousness. Although "Bells" describes Carus's maturation, his development away from a "decadent" indulgence in physical same-sex acts to chastity does not seem to form part of this process of growth. The fact that Carus, when matured, still desires Caspar—now in the context of love and not "decadent" lust—constitutes an argument against branding same-sex desire decadent and immature and exposes the enforced nature of Caspar's sexual abstinence. As Wirth notes, "In the end, the formerly decadent youth [Carus] surpasses the gentle and restrained Caspar in profundity."[105] Carus, who has grown "so gentle and wise in religious meaning," has the last word on the contested question whether the statement "God is love" can be inverted.[106] His parting words—"So also is Love God"[107]—remain unchallenged. By making love, Carus seems to say, one can become God or please God, and this seems to be the final verdict. The pupil appears to possess more wisdom than his teacher, whose restrictive understanding of religion and morality stands in the way of his consummation and enjoyment of a sexual relationship.

In "Geisha Man" and "Smoke, Lilies and Jade," Nugent displays a sexually transgressive content that includes sexual contacts among men. Already in terms of form, these two pieces reflect their challenging content: "Geisha Man" is broken up by ellipses and the insertion of songs and poems; "Smoke, Lilies and Jade" is written in an elliptical stream-of-consciousness style. As Michael Cobb observes for the latter story: "[T]he queer violation occurs . . . at the level of the sentence, the ellipses . . . serv[ing] to describe the grammar necessary for the production of such a shocking, queer text."[108] Form and content form a rough and challenging, transgressive entity. Kondo, the young Japanese American protagonist of "Geisha Man," seems sexually obsessed with the figure of his absent American father. The story's focus is on his erotic encounters with various men, ending in his reunion with his lover and father Gale, which eventually leads to frustration and Kondo's suicide. From the outset, the reader is introduced into a sensual atmosphere in which beautiful bodies rather than attractive people are focused on. Reminiscent of Nugent's unpublished autobiographical fragment "I Am Twenty Five," in which he declares "Bodies. I worship bodies," "Geisha Man" contains the rhetorical question: "Is it wrong to love bodies?"[109] Kondo's joyful encounters with male bodies suggest that loving bodies is a satisfying undertaking and that a rejection of moral norms remains unpunished. An overriding of questions of morality is also evident in "Smoke, Lilies and Jade," yet these moral issues concern less the field of sexuality than the protagonist Alex's espousal of a bohemian lifestyle. While his consciousness seems pierced with moral criticism, he never seriously questions his actions. Acknowledging yet transgressing society's norms and values, Kondo and Alex are thus able to embark on their explorations of bodies.

A visual level seems to be of particular significance in Kondo's pursuit of men. He desires to be covered "with the sight of bodies" and seems irresistibly drawn to bodies that "pierce [his] vision" as if he were a preying bird.[110] Wandering the streets at night, Kondo is in search of a sexual partner, desiring bodies. Beauty constitutes the essential element in Kondo's cruising. While beautiful bodies are given short shrift in the Bible stories, the reverse is true in "Geisha Man." Kondo gazes through men's clothes, catching glimpses of "contours showing through [a man's] trousers" and the "warm movement of his thigh suggested beneath his clothing."[111] In "Gentleman Jigger," the protagonist Stuartt similarly admires an Italian gangster's "compact figure so slender, yet showing hard contours beneath its dark grey 'sharkskin' suit."[112] This emphasis on visual perceptions of male beauty is similarly present in "Smoke, Lilies and Jade." In a dream, Alex envisions his lover Adrian, whom he appropriately calls Beauty, naked: "[He] saw two strong white legs . . . his eyes wandered . . . on past the muscular hocks to the firm white thighs . . . the rounded buttocks. . . ."[113] By depicting gay men's experiences on a visual level and furthermore introducing other senses, Nugent, as Wirth observes, invites the reader "to share the protagonist's (largely homosexual) erotic sensibilities."[114] Alex and Kondo love their partners' breaths, which seem to have a "masculine" quality, smelling of "warm tobacco and wool."[115] More significant are men's touches that are both caressing and aggressive—similar to men's bodies that, though "soft . . . soft . . . soft," are endowed with "hard muscles."[116] Like Kondo, Alex enjoys touching his lover's "soft" hair, and Beauty at one point asks him to scratch his head, which leads to a scene that radiates care and intimacy, with "Beauty's head in [Alex's] lap."[117] Aggressive manifestations of same-sex desire are equally present: When Beauty kisses Alex, his "lips pressed hard against his teeth."[118] Lust evidently constitutes part of their relationship. Fitting the central position assigned to the encounter of male bodies in "Geisha Man," more space is in this story devoted to the depiction of desire than in "Smoke, Lilies and Jade." Adam is "Pressing hard with his lips and leaning on [Kondo]," the leg muscles of Kondo's dancing partner at a ball are described as "darting" into his clothing, and, as a sign of sexual interest as well as a display of possession and domination, Kondo's sexual partners cross their legs over his.[119]

In "Geisha Man," same-sex relationships are frequently linked to a sensation of pain. Kondo receives a blow "full in the face" from his lover Don for kissing another man and remembers how Gale's fist "had left a taste of blood on [his] lips."[120] While these acts are indicative of jealousy rather than desire, sadomasochistic undercurrents can be detected in Kondo's relationships. Sexually aroused during his first meeting with Kondo, Don wants to "hurt you . . . . and myself."[121] Kondo experiences a mixture of pain and pleasure when Gale "bit [his] lip. Once. Softly. Then again and again till [he] whimpered. He kissed the hurt tenderly."[122] Pleasure is experienced by Gale, the perpetrator of pain, and the recipient Kondo, who in a masochistic fantasy imagines how one should

> Allow [Gale's] hands to grip one so forcibly as to hurt and make one wince into a proffering attitude, until his chest presses like a wall . . . to feel the cording of hard muscles under a soft skin press against one until it hurts. One should allow oneself to be hurt by Gale.[123]

By letting his protagonist, whose relationship with Gale crosses moral boundaries owing to its same-sex context and incestuous nature, voice these sadomasochist desires, Nugent widens his challenge and transgression of sexual norms, transcending the issue of sexual orientation per se.

Boundaries of a sexual or moral nature seem insignificant in these two stories, yet explicitly mentioned or described sexual contacts remain absent. In this context it is noteworthy that while Nugent enjoyed sexual affairs with men, he described himself as "sensual rather than sexual"—an evaluation that seems reflected in his texts.[124] Countering descriptions of "Smoke, Lilies and Jade" as "vaguely pornographic," Wirth argues that Nugent's works can more appropriately be termed erotic in that they depict beauty rather than effect sexual stimulation.[125] Focusing on sensuality through his detailed depiction of desirous looks and touches, Nugent seems to assign sex a subordinate position in his work. This appears to be the case in both "Smoke, Lilies and Jade" and "Geisha Man." Arriving at Alex's flat after their street encounter, Alex and Beauty undress and, given the circumstances—nakedness and attractive bodies—there is little doubt that sex will take place. However, sex is represented only by ellipses: They "talked and . . . slept. . . ."[126] A similar gap is evident in "Geisha Man," where Kondo's long-desired reunion with Gale quickly leads both men to the bedroom. Sexual activities are not depicted yet are clearly implied: "For a long time afterwards we lay in each others arms, whispering and kissing."[127] This absence of explicit representations of sex and employment of meaningful gaps perhaps must also be seen in the context of censorship. As outlined earlier, Nugent apparently intended to publish his works, and while depictions of same-sex relationships can already be seen as clearly offending censorship laws, explicit sex scenes would have constituted obvious, insurmountable obstacles to publication.

Nugent depicts casual sexual contacts that lack empathy as distinctly unattractive. Attending a gay party in "Geisha Man," Kondo is disgusted by the sight of men's public caresses. While Nugent portrays sexual encounters occurring in the privacy of protagonists' homes as celebrations of male beauty and same-sex desire, the sexual contacts at the party are presented as "the mere pressing of lips. The mere rubbing of bodies. The tasting of bad breaths.

All before the eyes of others."[128] The sexual experiences of Nugent's protagonists are distinct from these "cold" male–male encounters that are characterized by a lack of emotion. As Shawn Ruff comments in reference to "Smoke,
Lilies and Jade," Beauty "becomes the succulent subject of not only Alex's
desire but his love."[129] As soon as this combination of feelings occurs in Nugent's works, sensuality enters the scene. Significantly, Nugent's protagonists'
feelings of love and desire do not seem to be linked to monogamy. On the
contrary: As affirmed in both "Smoke, Lilies and Jade" and "Geisha Man," it
is possible to love more than one person, and it is also possible to fall in love
or be infatuated repeatedly.[130]

SEXUALITIES AND THE CLOSET

Despite offering conflicting representations of same-sex desire and love or, as
might be said, critical, nonidealizing images of homosexuality, Nugent gives
a sympathetic portrayal of men-loving men. Nugent declared that he "probably wouldn't talk about homosexual things . . . [and say] that's my cause,"[131]
yet the fact that many of his writings challenge dominant representations of
"homosexuals" means that his work has political implications. While refusing to participate specifically and exclusively in the circulation of positive images of African Americans, Nugent creates positive images of men-loving
men who are beautiful, intelligent, often joyful, and usually confident in their
sexuality. Nugent thereby consciously or unconsciously challenges the views
of most contemporary artists who, as Byrne Fone points out, presented gay
men as "lonely, self-absorbed, isolated, and incapable of love."[132]

Nugent believed he had "a great deal of Huysmans in [him],"[133] yet regarding the representation of homosexuality, Nugent's works are distinct
from those of decadent artists, who usually refrained from explicit representations of homosexuality while employing numerous "signs" which seem to
hint at same-sex passion without naming it. Nugent, in contrast, consciously
incorporates these signs or "codes" for instance in the form of a street encounter between men, and adds explicit representations of same-sex love as
evident in "Smoke, Lilies and Jade."[134] Moreover, while decadent writers
dared to hint at sexual transgression, they created images that in their essence
did not deviate from those of other contemporary authors. Edmund Wilson
points out that the decadent school of writing "derived its principal force
from its constant conviction of sin"[135]—a realm to which same-sex love was
assigned. Although sex is a sensitive area in Nugent's writing, gay sex seems
in no way connected to "shame, remorse, disgust, and the occasional bout of
syphilis"[136] which Ellis Hanson names as typical representations of sex in
decadent literature. Where Huysmans portrays Des Esseintes' apparently homosexual experience with a young man as what Alan Sinfield describes as the
"ultimate debauchery,"[137] Nugent depicts sexually charged encounters of two
men as celebrations of beauty and desire.

Presenting same-sex-interested men as positive characters and depicting various sexualities, Nugent challenges the boundaries drawn around sexuality by gender norms. While most of his female characters appear in a clearly heterosexual context—exceptions being "[g]irls dressed as boys" at a masked ball and a "Sappho"—his representations of male sexuality include heterosexual, homosexual, and bisexual characters. In light of this portrayal of multifaceted sexualities, Garber's statement that "Smoke, Lilies and Jade" constitutes a "defense of homosexual love"[138] is noteworthy in that it implies an exclusive focus on same-sex love which, considering the protagonist's sexual and emotional involvement with both Melva and Beauty, is not given. Nugent's positive portrayal of same-sex love in the story could be said to implicitly represent a "defense" against stereotypical notions, yet same-sex interest, though crucial, seems to be just one transgressive issue among others such as bisexual polygamy and "decadent" idleness. It seems that critics, impressed by Nugent's story because of its singular status as a published openly homoerotic 1920s fictional work by an African American writer, have generally failed to undertake close readings of the story. Contrary to David Levering Lewis' suggestion, "Smoke, Lilies and Jade" does not end in "pederasty and androgyny, Beauty metamorphosing into Melva . . . and Melva into Beauty."[139] Instead, Alex seems torn because he loves both Melva and Beauty—a significant point. Garber implies that the conflict within the story centers on a "confusion about [Alex's] sexuality," and Seth Silberman suggests that Alex is involved in a "search to name his sexual identity," yet sexuality or sexual identity is not an issue in this context.[140] Cobb correctly concludes that "Alex struggles not with the acceptance of his sexuality"[141] but also emphasizes the gender of Alex's lovers. It seems, however, that Alex's "concerns" are not "about loving both a man and a woman"[142] but about the fact that he is in love with two people. The number—not the gender—of his lovers is troubling Alex, who solves his problem by concluding: "[O]ne *can* love two at the same time."[143] Against all expectations of critics, Nugent in "Smoke, Lilies and Jade" presents neither homosexuality, heterosexuality, nor bisexuality as areas of conflict.

There seems to be confusion about sexuality in "Geisha Man"—but only regarding what turns out to be a heterosexual character. In light of the story's ending—the gay character Kondo commits suicide—one might assume that he, like gay characters featured in the works of contemporary authors, is characterized by despair because of his "affliction" with homosexuality. Yet Kondo, like other same-sex-interested or gay-identified male characters in Nugent's works, seems confident in his sexuality. He ends his life in a dramatic gesture not because of despair about his own sexuality but because of frustrated love. His suicide is linked to sexuality, however, insofar as his partner Gale does not reciprocate his love and desire because, as Kondo has to recognize, "God made Gale normal."[144] Narrated from Kondo's perspective, "Geisha Man" thus posits heterosexuality, which, as indicated in Gale's initial sexual interest in Kondo, is not a thoroughly stable sexual identity, as the problematic issue.

Gale's heterosexuality implies his lack of desire for Kondo, yet it is not equated with homophobia. Kondo nevertheless fears what is presented as a likely link between heterosexuality and the dislike of gay men, dreading the thought of noting "some little gesture of disgust or boredom"[145] in Gale. As portrayed in "Geisha Man," gay men have to endure restrictions placed on them by a society hostile toward non-normative sexuality. Like the speaker in "Shadow," the same-sex interested men presented in "Geisha Man" seem to abhor light because it threatens to expose their "deviant" sexuality to the gaze of potentially hostile onlookers. Against this background, it is noteworthy that daytime activities are described neither in "Geisha Man" nor in "Smoke, Lilies and Jade." Kondo's and Alex's lives center on the night, when they start cruising, attend parties, or visit cafés. To some extent, gay men seem to appropriate the night for their purposes. Wandering the streets at night, Kondo reports that "[o]n the dusk-hidden benches youths sat in couples. Arms around each other."[146] These couples need the cover of darkness, yet when protected from light, they are unafraid to express their love and desire. These are certainly not unhappy and desperate same-sex-interested men as represented in, for instance, André Tellier's novel *Twilight Men* (1931).[147] In Nugent's work, nighttime is the occasion for beautiful men, not frustrated creatures, to cruise the streets.

While offering protection, darkness also entails negative aspects. First of all, it covers up beauty. While Kondo can discern men's beauty at night, it is clear that splendor cannot be met in the dark, since it would draw potentially dangerous attention. When Kondo prepares for a masked ball and tries on a gown made out of hundreds of shining silver poppies which "trailed in a silver moon a yard behind [him]" and in which he feels precious and "happy," it becomes evident that gay men are usually deprived of the pleasure of displaying flamboyance because they need to remain inconspicuous, able to blend into the night.[148] Furthermore, the night cannot completely fulfill its protective function, since what Kondo describes as "[l]ittle circles of light [prying] into the secrets of the couples on benches"[149]—presumably guards with flashlights—illuminate the night and thereby the cruising grounds of same-sex-interested men. Moreover, the night remains a contested space in which heterosexuals also seek cover. As Nugent's mentioning of "snickers and innuendoes of passing couples of men and women"[150] indicates, the daytime balance of power seems to be transferred to the night, as heterosexuals display contempt toward sexual "deviants." Nevertheless, somewhat reminiscent of Cullen's poem "Tableau" in which a young male couple ignores the stares and comments of onlookers, the gay couples in Nugent's story are defiant and "oblivious"[151] to the hostility they encounter.

The predicament Nugent's young male characters face—having to hide in the shadows while openly displaying same-sex affection within that space—

points to the key role openness and being closeted play in "Geisha Man." Acknowledging the young men's defiance, Kondo wonders by what their open displays of affection are motivated: "Courage. Or was it lack of shame?"[152] The same issue emerges in the aforementioned party scene in which Kondo seems disgusted by the sight of men openly engaging in physical contact with various partners. Nugent's protagonists prefer privacy to public exposure, deeming public displays of intimacy exhibitionist. The rejection of this kind of openness is not necessarily restricted to homosexual affairs, however, and therefore cannot be equated with a demand for being closeted, which Nugent, as stated in an interview, deemed "unsavoury."[153] As Kondo puts it, his concerns are more about "refinement."[154] At some points in "Geisha Man," however, it becomes impossible to differentiate between the desire for "refined" privacy and what Nugent presents as an enforced retreat. When Don kisses Kondo in the dark, the latter reacts negatively: "Don't. Someone might come. And besides, we're nearly home."[155] The safety of a private home is presented as the appropriate space for male–male intimacy, yet it remains unclear whether this is due to fear of exposure or a desire for privacy. According to Nugent's portrayal, men-loving men live in a world in which only spaces such as private homes or privately organized parties and masked balls, as depicted in "Geisha Man," guarantee safety. As evident in "Smoke, Lilies and Jade," in which Alex takes Beauty to a popular café, artists' meeting places can also be counted among "safe havens" where tolerance is exercised.

Although they accept restrictions, Nugent's men-loving male characters express a desire for openness, which, however, remains unfulfilled. Kondo believes that "It's all right to let the world know a man cares for another man."[156] For this reason, he regards the young men on the benches not simply as exhibitionist but also as brave. While Alex in "Smoke, Lilies and Jade" finds his visit to a café with Beauty a liberating experience, because "he felt so unembarrassed,"[157] Kondo seems unable to voice his happiness in a wider circle of friends. His desire to "walk with [Don] and shout, 'He is mine!' "[158] remains a dream vision which he does not dare turn into reality. In "Who Asks This Thing?" which seems to be the only extant Renaissance poem in which Nugent explicitly refers to men-loving men, the presumably male speaker dares to "wear [his] love for all to see."[159] This courage has consequences for both him and his apparently closeted partner, as the poem's framing statements—"I walk alone and lone must be . . . / He walks alone who walks in love with me"—indicate. The speaker's uncompromising openness means that he is "bound," identified, as might be said, as a gay man and restricted by a society aware of his transgressive desire, while his explicitly male beloved "is, sadly, free." Though restrictive, openness is here presented as the better choice, as it leaves the speaker at least with a "song" of love to sing, while the closeted lover seems condemned to freedom without happiness. Openness and closetedness thus remain contested issues within Nugent's work that cannot simply be categorized as either positive or negative.

GENDER, THE SEXES, AND MASCULINITY

Nugent not only challenges boundaries of sexuality and adds complexity to apparently "simple" issues such as openness and closetedness but also puts forward a view of manhood and gender that transcends the varieties presented by the Renaissance writers discussed before. While McKay and, to a lesser degree, Hughes for various reasons emphasize masculinity and male camaraderie, opposing them to effeminate stereotypes of men-loving men, Nugent refuses to seek apologies or camouflages for his representation of various types of same-sex-interested men, thereby denying the validity of clichés. As a consequence, none of the gay "types" such as "fairies" or "wolves" prominent in McKay's or Hughes's work are present in Nugent's writing. The one figure that has characteristics similar to a fairy is Carus. A fragile, white young man, Carus is emotional and does not hold back his tears, yet he is nonetheless not specifically described as effeminate, beauty being his main feature.

While masculinity is not an issue in Nugent's depiction of male characters, one factor linking men in Nugent's work which can be said to be implicitly connected to masculinity is their class status. In contrast to McKay's working-class characters, who derive much of their "manly" or phallic power from this background, Nugent's characters are never seen to engage in physical work: The disciples study, the Magi fulfill their royal duties, Kondo survives presumably because of the generosity of his apparently wealthy lovers, and Alex seems to be constantly on the verge of starvation but nevertheless refuses to work. Considering Nugent's affinity with the styles of aestheticism and decadence and the central position of the concept of beauty in his work, it seems as if Nugent to some extent followed Oscar Wilde in what Sinfield describes as Wilde's "dream ticket: a conjunction of art and the leisure class, in opposition to middle-class, philistine, masculine practicality."[160] A scion of an elite family, Nugent apparently did not identify with and was not interested in the masses or the bourgeoisie of whatever racial background as literary subjects, choosing his characters from a bohemian scene and a "biblical" aristocracy, thereby incorporating aesthetic male representations instead of "realist" images into his work. Admiration for the almost stereotypically masculine body can be detected, however, in Nugent's work—for instance, in the cases of the partners of Nugent's protagonists: Beauty has "strong" legs and a "broad deep chest," Don's "profile was white and hard and chiseled," Gale's leg is "hard-muscled," and Kondo enjoys the "tingling roughness of [Gale's] cheek and chin."[161] The concept of masculinity is thus not absent in Nugent's writings—it is simply not focused on or contrasted with effeminacy.

Maleness is not necessarily a stable identity in Nugent's works. This is evident in "Narcissus,"[162] in which Nugent negates a construct fundamental to society's organization—the strict separation of the sexes. At this point, characteristics attributed by contemporary sexologists to "savage perverts"—nonwhite men and women—and decadent writers alike seem to merge in the figure of Nugent: As Julian Carter suggests, sexologists viewed both of these groups as unable to "recognize, construct, and maintain the crucial differences between sickness and health, evolution and degeneration, men and women" as "degeneration becomes 'degenderation.' "[163] In "Narcissus," the separation of the sexes is suspended as a male protagonist of the same name gazes into what seems to be water and sees a reflection which is no longer wholly male but partially female. Nugent here inverts the legend of Narcissus, which could, despite its homoerotic implications, be described as a fundamentally heterosexual plot: Narcissus, believing his mirror image to be a water nymph, drowns in the ill-fated attempt to pursue his vision of the female figure. Narcissus's reflection in Nugent's poem cannot be mistaken for a nymph, because distinctly female features—"[f]aint fair breasts"—are combined with a "male torso." While this image of a hermaphrodite body could be regarded as disturbing, Nugent presents it as attractive, its beauty being so intense that it "pained" Narcissus. "Male into female seemed to flow" and sex boundaries become irrelevant as an androgynous beauty comes into existence. This process clearly pleases Narcissus, as evident in the reflection of his smile, which, like the mirror image of his body, has become "double sexed." The figure of the hermaphrodite was a popular subject of decadent writers like Algernon Charles Swinburne, in whose poem "Hermaphroditus"[164] the incorporation of two sexes in one body is described as beautiful yet simultaneously as a symbol of sterility. Nugent, in contrast, presents this body positively as enriched as it combines the best qualities of both sexes. He thus creates a fictional "intermediate sex" that constitutes an alternative to the model envisioned by Edward Carpenter in that it does not combine emotional characteristics of one sex and sexual characteristics of the other but merges sexual characteristics of both.[165] As readers might expect, Narcissus will attempt to pursue the beautiful "double sexed" vision, his fate, as indicated by the five hyphens in the poem's last line, remaining unclear.

The crossing of gender boundaries constitutes a central theme in "Geisha Man" and is also alluded to in "Smoke, Lilies and Jade." In the latter story, Alex seeks to transgress and widen the boundaries drawn around masculinity: When passing a woman at night and smelling her perfume, he muses over the question why it was "that men wouldn't use perfumes . . . they should . . . each and every one of them liked perfumes . . . the man who denied that was a liar . . . or a coward."[166] Alex is obviously aware of the subversive meaning and forbidden status of his question, wondering what would happen "if ever he were to voice that thought," being certain that "he would be misunderstood."[167] Since perfume is categorized as a "feminine" item, Alex probably expects to be regarded as a fairy who seeks to acquire the other gender's signifiers and identifies with its sexual object choice—a description which does not fit him because he is not linked to gender inversion and, moreover, seems to be bisexual rather than gay-identified. Yet Alex seems content with his reputation as a "queer," sexually ambiguous artist brought about by his seeking of sensual pleasure.

The title of the story "Geisha Man" itself introduces the topic of the crossing of gender boundaries. Appropriating the Japanese term *geisha*—usually exclusively female-identified and denoting a sexual entertainer for men—Nugent depicts the half-Japanese Kondo as a geisha's equivalent. While Kondo is presented as less aggressive than his male partners, he is not depicted as effeminate. As the occasion of a drag ball shows, he is, however, a gifted crossdresser. Attending the ball, he wears a dazzling white-silver dress and silver slippers, thereby appropriating female signifiers. Numerous men approach him, yet no one seems to mistake him for a woman, because they recognize his dress as a "[b]eautiful costume."[168] The masked ball represents an occasion on which identities are fluid and to some extent inverted—participants include "Arab sheiks in fantastic colors," "Indian temple dancers," and "[b]oys dressed as girls and simpering sadly. Girls dressed as boys and bulging in places"—but Kondo remains a transvestite.[169] He is aware that he looks "strange" and that his is a "weird, intoxicating beauty," as is that of the other masked visitors.[170] Kondo defines female signifiers such as women's clothing as nonmasculine; at the same time, however, he regrets the fact that they are thus classified, since for him, a man, their appropriation is consequently deemed "abnormal" or "degenerate." Therefore he exclaims: "If only I had been born a woman!"[171] This desire does not mean, however, that he represents a case of what nineteenth-century homosexual apologist Karl Heinrich Ulrichs believed to be "a female mind trapped in a male body," because Kondo's statement refers only to the appropriation of female signifiers.[172] Significantly, he does not negotiate same-sex desire via gender inversion but merely fantasizes about being able "[t]o dress in flowing silks and silver and colors always. . . . With perfumes and lace"—a style of dress and behavior that would, to borrow from Judith Butler, not fit a "performance" of maleness.[173] It is noteworthy, however, that Kondo desires to dress in a feminine style yet wants to achieve a "modish mannish look"[174] in which, as might be suspected, his masculinity remains recognizable.

The drag ball represents an exceptional occasion for Kondo, who is clearly not used to cross-dressing. Realizing that Gale desires him most when he performs femaleness—an indication of Gale's heterosexuality—Kondo seems willing to give up his male outward appearance to succeed in his pursuit of Gale. After an unofficial wedding ceremony, Gale and Kondo were, as Gale remarks, "married 'in the sight of man and God,' " and Kondo becomes Gale's "wife."[175] This new role seems unproblematic for Kondo. On the one hand, his identity as Gale's wife seems respected by others—for instance, by Gale's friends, who, like the visitors of the aforementioned drag ball, are aware of his male identity. On the other hand, and more significantly, Gale enables Kondo to live out what appears to be his fantasy: While Gale performs a male role by taking care of financial issues, Kondo leads an existence as a traditionally defined woman and wife, entertaining guests, being "the most chic woman in the room,"[176] and indulging in the fabrics and colors of women's clothes which he fetishizes. It remains unknown whether Kondo would have continuously felt comfortable with his cross-dressing performance, because Gale is unable to get accustomed to the fact that Kondo is not a "real" woman. Owing to his heterosexuality, Gale can, as is revealed in the end, fully engage in only those sexual relationships that correspond to clear-cut sex and gender binaries. Kondo's homosexuality, in contrast, enables him to explore sex and gender freely, defying traditional binaries and crossing boundaries.

As remarked by Wirth, it needs to be understood that "[a]s a writer Nugent stands at the intersection of two separate literary traditions—black and gay."[177] The same indefinite quality is evident in Nugent's artistic works in which race frequently remains an insignificant and undefined factor, and in which the topics of sexuality, sex, and gender virtually never pertain to binaries. Nugent's portrayals of ambiguous sexual dissidence complicate and implicitly question not only the validity of moral boundaries but also a simplistic reliance on binaries, underlining his unique position within the chorus of gay Harlem Renaissance voices.

Conclusion

Discussing the link between homosexuality and Harlem Renaissance writers, Essex Hemphill asserts that "[t]he effort to uplift the race and prove the Negro worthy of respect precluded issues of sexuality. . . . The defeat of racism was far too important to risk compromising such a struggle by raising issues of homosexuality."[1] Even for Countée Cullen, who closely identified with the Harlem Renaissance and its aim of using the field of art and literature to improve race relations and eventually gain equality, this assessment applies only partially, as same-sex desire is not absent from his texts. For the other three writers discussed in this book, Hemphill's conclusion seems inapplicable because it is based on the wrong premise: These writers did not, as Hemphill suggests, subscribe to a philosophy of racial "uplift" as proposed partially by Renaissance intellectuals and particularly by the black bourgeoisie. Like many of their younger white contemporaries, they were attracted to the subject of sexuality for various reasons, deeming it a controversial, possibly financially rewarding, appropriate, and "real" part of their own lives and/or more generally African Americans' lives.

An exploration of these writers' politics of representation clearly complicates what might at first be assumed to be unity among Renaissance writers. Even the rather easily identifiable distinction between Cullen and the other writers who are treated in this book must be further broken up to allow an understanding of the motivations and pressures that shaped their creative processes. The question of writers' sexual identification requires the same amount of investigation and results in the recognition that a claiming of these Renaissance writers as "gay" makes sense only on a very general level of discussion. In exploring and historicizing their sexual biographies, it remains impossible to position all four writers within the clear-cut dichotomy of homo-/heterosexuality, although they are all linked to same-sex desire. Various levels of identification, ranging from the openly gay-identified Richard Bruce Nugent to the apparently sexually indefinable Langston Hughes, can be recognized and must be viewed within the context of contemporary varieties of sexuality- and gender-based negotiations of same-sex desire. These Renaissance writers' gay voices are clearly informed by their personal location within the field of sexual identifications and must be viewed particularly in light of the contemporary dominant link in public perception between homosexuality and gender inversion.

Nugent's affirmative gay identity seems reflected in his unapologetic portrayal of men-loving men in which moral, racial, sexual, and gender boundaries are crossed. The pitch of Cullen's gay voice is more subdued. Employing codes derived from the discourse of Alain Locke's gay circle, Cullen incorporated the subject of same-sex desire in his works, which, though decodable by readers familiar with these gay signifiers, remained within the sphere of "respectable" poetry particularly because of their strict formality. Hughes's and McKay's gay literary voices must be viewed in the context of their cultural politics, which were informed by their focus on issues of race and class. Particularly in Hughes's maritime works and, far more intensely, in McKay's novels, an emphasis on male camaraderie, reminiscent of Whitman's vision of a "manly love of comrades," is evident. Homosocial bonding and virility are of significance in many of these texts which can be described as "manly" narratives. Virility-based portrayals of same-sex desire are contrasted with the two authors' representations of same-sex-interested men in the context of gender inversion, ranging from sympathetic portrayals to negative depictions that, similar to sexologists' discourses, link homosexuality to degeneracy and morbidity.

As George Hutchinson indicates, Whitman figured as a model for Renaissance writers and intellectuals—on a political and, as indicated above, also on a sexual level.[2] Given what Thomas Yingling describes as an "unchallenged reading of Whitman . . . as a national, cultural, and/or philosophical spokesman" by a majority of readers, references to Whitman's concept of "manly comrades" could serve as "screens" for representations of men-loving men.[3] The same-sex context of such references would pass unsuspecting readers by, while they would be identified by those who shared what Eve Sedgwick describes as a "durable and broadly based Anglo-American definition of male homosexuality" in which Whitman's influence "was profound and decisive."[4] Clearly unaware of any sexual significance of his reference to Whitman, genteel African American critic Benjamin Brawley commented in 1932 that "most of our young Negro poets are [Whitman's] grandchildren."[5] Brawley referred to Whitman's poetic free-verse form, of course, but his statement seems equally applicable in a sexual context in which it would also encompass Cullen and McKay despite their employment of traditional poetic forms. With the exception of Nugent, the Renaissance writers treated in this book linked up to white contemporary authors by appropriating a very specific coded gay discourse that was culturally white-defined.

Renaissance writers' references to this gay discourse but also to other modes of coding same-sex desire, embedded particularly in a racial context, would have been identifiable for a contemporary, potentially interracial gay or same-sex interested readership. This is also hinted at in Blair Niles's novel *Strange Brother* (1931), whose white gay protagonist strongly identifies with Cullen's poetry and furthermore stacks Alain Locke's *The New Negro*, the Renaissance's "bible," next to works by the "priest" of contemporary gay men—Whitman. Such issues as oppression, struggle, and liberation would, in the context of Renaissance writing, almost automatically be read in a racial context, but, particularly given the space writers left by often not explicitly identifying race as their poems' topics, a transference between race and sexuality, enabling both racial and gay readings, seems possible. Revisiting Hemphill's suggestion that issues of race and representation stifled Renaissance authors' sexually dissident voices, it can thus be concluded that this assessment can be refuted for yet another reason than most of the discussed writers' lack of identification with the cause of racial "uplift." The subject matter of race by no means subordinated the topic of same-sex desire: The two issues were not mutually exclusive but, as evident in Cullen's poem "Tableau," were joined together in writers' layering of racial and sexual themes. Same-sex-interested writers shaped the Harlem Renaissance—not in the sense of a development of a specific gay aesthetic but because of their position at the heart of the movement, their involvement in a gay network that constituted a major structure within the Renaissance, and their creation of gay literary voices, which, audible to various extents, resound, reflecting the movement's diversity.

Notes

INTRODUCTION

1. Cheryl A. Wall, *Women of the Harlem Renaissance* (Bloomington: Indiana University Press, 1995); Gloria T. Hull, *Color, Sex and Poetry: Three Women Writers of the Harlem Renaissance* (Bloomington: Indiana University Press, 1987); Lorraine Roses and Ruth Elizabeth Randolph, *Harlem Renaissance and Beyond: Literary Biographies of 100 Black Women Writers, 1900–1945* (Boston: Hall, 1990).

2. Henry Louis Gates, Jr., "The Black Man's Burden," *Fear of a Queer Planet*, ed. Michael Warner (Minneapolis: University of Minnesota Press, 1993), 233.

3. For a revisionist discussion of these issues as presented in the works of various scholars of the Harlem Renaissance, see George Hutchinson, *The Harlem Renaissance in Black and White* (Cambridge, Mass.: Belknap-Harvard University Press, 1995), 14–28.

4. Alan Sinfield, *Cultural Politics—Queer Readings* (Philadelphia: University of Pennsylvania Press; London: Routledge, 1994), 61.

5. David Levering Lewis, *When Harlem Was in Vogue* (New York: Knopf, 1981), 77.

6. Gerald Early, introduction, *My Soul's High Song: The Collected Writings of Countee Cullen, Voice of the Harlem Renaissance*, ed. Gerald Early (New York: Doubleday, 1991), 19.

7. Eric Garber, "T'ain't Nobody's Bizness: Homosexuality in 1920s Harlem," *Black Men/White Men: A Gay Anthology*, ed. Michael J. Smith (San Francisco: Gay Sunshine, 1983), 7–16.

8. Kevin J. Mumford, *Interzones: Black/White Sex Districts in Chicago and New York in the Early Twentieth Century* (New York: Columbia University Press, 1997).

9. Hull; David L. Blackmore, " 'That Unreasonable Feeling': The Homosexual Subtexts of Nella Larsen's *Passing*," *African American Review* 26 (1992): 475–84; Deborah E. McDowell, " 'It's Not Safe. Not Safe at All': Sexuality in Nella Larsen's *Passing*," *The Lesbian and Gay Studies Reader*, ed. Henry Abelove, Michèle Aina Barale, and David M. Halperin (New York: Routledge, 1993), 616–25.

10. Alden Reimonenq, "Countee Cullen's Uranian 'Soul Windows,' " *Critical Essays: Gay and Lesbian Writers of Color*, ed. Emmanuel S. Nelson (New York: Harrington Park-Haworth, 1993), 143–66; Gregory Woods, "Gay Re-readings of the Harlem Renaissance Poets," *Critical Essays*, 127–42; Amitai F. Avi-Ram, "The Unreadable Black Body: Conventional Poetic Form in the Harlem Renaissance," *Genders* 7 (1990): 32–46.

11. Sinfield, 56, 5, 9.

12. Thomas E. Yingling, *Hart Crane and the Homosexual Text: New Thresholds, New Anatomies* (Chicago: University of Chicago Press, 1990), 14.

13. George Chauncey, Jr., *Gay New York: Gender, Urban Culture and the Making of the Gay Male World, 1890–1940* (New York: Basic, 1994), 12–13.

14. Reimonenq, 145.

15. Sinfield, 20.

16. James Weldon Johnson, "The Dilemma of the Negro Author," *American Mercury* 15 (1928): 477.

1. GAY HARLEM AND THE HARLEM RENAISSANCE

1. Lynn Dumenil, *Modern Temper: American Culture and Society in the 1920s* (New York: Hill and Wang, 1995), 7.

2. George Chauncey, Jr., *Gay New York: Gender, Urban Culture and the Making of the Gay Male World, 1890–1940* (New York: Basic, 1994), chapter 5; David J. Pivar, "Cleansing the Nation: The War on Prostitution, 1917–21," *Prologue* 12 (1980): 28–40. Anti-vice movements usually proceeded in the following manner: Plainclothes investigators were sent to social meeting places like clubs and bars and would then file reports on what they had seen. In some instances, arrests, usually in cooperation with the police, would be undertaken. For examples of investigations see Chauncey, 215–16, 279–80; Kevin J. Mumford, *Interzones: Black/White Sex Districts in Chicago and New York in the Early Twentieth Century* (New York: Columbia University Press, 1997), 79–80, 86–87. For censorship, see John Tebbel, *The Golden Age between Two Wars: 1920–1940* (New York: Bowker, 1978), 21–22, 635–55; "Censorship Epidemic," *Variety*, February 23, 1927: 1, 28–29.

3. Chauncey, 314–25. Regarding intensified anti-gay policing, see Chauncey, chapter 12.

4. George Chauncey, Jr., "From Sexual Inversion to Homosexuality: Medicine and the Changing Conceptualization of Female Deviance," *Salmagundi* 58–59 (1982–1983): 114–46.

5. Chauncey, *Gay New York*, 12–13.

6. Gert Hekma, " 'A Female Soul in a Male Body': Sexual Inversion in Nineteenth-Century Sexology," *Third Sex, Third Gender: Beyond Sexual Dimorphism in Culture and History*, ed. Gilbert Herdt (New York: Zone, 1994), 235. This, however, does not imply that all cross-dressers were same-sex interested.

7. Chauncey, *Gay New York*, 47.

8. Chauncey, *Gay New York*, 103. For an example of the stereotype of "mannish-looking" women, see "Women Rivals For Affection of Another Woman Battles With Knives, and One Has Head Almost Severed From Body," *New York Age*, November 27, 1926: 1, in which reference is made to a woman known as "Big Ben," whose name derives from "her unusual size and from her inclination to ape the masculine in dress and manner, and particularly in her attention to women."

9. David Levering Lewis, *When Harlem Was in Vogue* (New York: Knopf, 1981), 21–22.

10. Alain Locke, "The New Negro," *The New Negro*, ed. Alain Locke (1925; New York: Atheneum, 1992), 6.

11. Claude McKay, *Harlem: Negro Metropolis* (1940; New York: Harcourt, 1968), 16.

12. For the evolution of the concept of the "New Negro," see Henry Louis Gates, Jr., "The Trope of a New Negro and the Reconstruction of the Image of the Black," *Representations* 24 (1988): 129–55.

13. The debate on the role African American cultural production was to play in the overall context of "racial uplift" is discussed in chapter 2.

14. Chidi Ikonné, *From Du Bois to Van Vechten: The Early New Negro Literature, 1903–1926*, Contributions in Afro-American and African Studies 60 (Westport, Conn.: Greenwood, 1981), 3.

15. Steven Watson, *The Harlem Renaissance: Hub of African-American Culture, 1920–1930* (New York: Pantheon, 1995), 105.

16. Huggins, 91.

17. Carl Van Vechten, *Nigger Heaven* (New York: Knopf, 1926).

18. Advertising leaflet for Wallace Thurman and William Jourdan Rapp, *Harlem* (1929), n.d. [1929], WTP, 3, BRBML. The play was first performed in 1929. For a draft of the play, under still a different title, see Wallace Thurman and William Jourdan Rapp, " 'Cordelia the Crude': A Melodrama in 3 Acts," unpublished typescript, n.d., WTP, 1, BRBML.

19. L. A. Erenberg, *Steppin' Out: New York Nightlife and the Transformation of American Culture* (Chicago: University of Chicago Press, 1984), 255.

20. Erenberg, 255.

21. Edgar M. Grey, "Harlem after Dark," *New York Amsterdam News*, April 6, 1927: 16.

22. "White Slummer Hit Blow in Report Depicting Conditions in Harlem District," *New York Amsterdam News*, October 6, 1929: n.p.; Gilbert Osofsky, *Harlem: The Making of a Ghetto, Negro New York, 1890–1930* (New York: Harper, 1968), 146; Chauncey, *Gay New York*, 247.

23. Mumford, 85.

24. Chauncey, *Gay New York*, 170–73, 185–86.

25. Wallace Thurman, letter to Rapp, n.d. [Tuesday, May 7], WTP, 1, BRBML; Bruce Kellner, "Dill, Augustus Granville," *The Harlem Renaissance: A Historical Dictionary for the Era* (New York: Methuen; London: Routledge, 1987), 100. Thurman gave a false name and was eventually bailed out by friends. Dill's arrest had grave consequences: He lost his position at *The Crisis*.

26. Levi Hubert, "On Seventh Avenue," *Baltimore Afro-American*, December 27, 1930: 9.

27. S. P. Fullinwider, *The Mind and Mood of Black America: 20th Century Thought* (Homewood, Ill.: Dorsey Press, 1969), 132; Mumford, 154. For the COF estimate, see "White Slummer."

28. Rudolph Fisher, "The Caucasian Storms Harlem," *American Mercury* 11 (1927): 393–98; Lewis, 209–10.

29. Langston Hughes, *The Big Sea: An Autobiography* (1940; New York: Hill, 1993), 226, 226–27; Wilbur Young, "Gladys Bentley," WPC, reel 1, SCRBC, n.p.

30. Mumford, 153–54.

31. COF report quoted in "Night Clubs Found Chief Vice Centres," *New York Times*, October 14, 1929: 1.

32. "They Won't Keep Away," *New York Amsterdam News*, October 23, 1929: n.p.

33. Lillian Faderman, *Odd Girls and Twilight Lovers: A History of Lesbian Life in Twentieth-Century America* (New York: Columbia University Press, 1991), 68, 63; Chauncey, *Gay New York*, 65.

34. Faderman, 67–72.

35. Chauncey, *Gay New York*, 61.

36. "Bass Voiced 'Girl Friend' Sentenced," *New York Amsterdam News*, August 28, 1929: 2; " 'She' Turns Out to Be a 'He' in Court," *New York Amsterdam News*, February 8, 1928: 16.

37. Mumford, 88; Faderman, 68.

38. RBNP/Tapes #2.

39. Young. Gladys Bentley, who usually performed wearing a hat and tuxedo, is the most prominent example of a cross-dressing singer. While Bentley at first sight seems like the embodiment of the stereotype of the lesbian "invert," she, as Elizabeth Stavney points out, did not completely fit the description of "a gay woman in men's clothes," as she also wore "feminine" clothes, thereby deliberately mixing sex-role referents. Anne Elizabeth Stavney, "Harlem in the 1920s: A Geographical and Discursive Site of the Black and White Literary Imagination" (dissertation, University of Washington, 1994), 227, 222–29.

40. Mumford, 74–75, 84–85, 91.

41. Mumford, 85.

42. Chauncey, *Gay New York*, 244.

43. Richard Bruce Nugent, "Geisha Man," excerpt published in Thomas H. Wirth, ed., *Gay Rebel of the Harlem Renaissance: Selections from the Work of Richard Bruce Nugent* (Durham, N.C.: Duke University Press, 2002), 96–97; RBNP/Notes, December 27, 1981. The party is not described, however, as a distinct "Harlem" party; racial signifiers seem absent.

44. Mumford, 83; Faderman, 68.

45. Hughes, 229–33; Lewis, 107–108; Eric Garber, "A Spectacle in Color: The Lesbian and Gay Subculture of Jazz Age Harlem," *Hidden From History: Reclaiming the Gay and Lesbian Past*, ed. Martin Bauml Duberman, Martha Vicinus, and George Chauncey, Jr. (Harmondsworth, England: Penguin, 1991), 321–23.

46. Ruby Smith, quoted in John Gill, *Queer Noises: Male and Female Homosexuality in Twentieth-Century Music* (London: Cassell, 1995), 40; Smith, quoted in Garber, 323.

47. Lewis, 168, 167.

48. Daphne Duval Harrison, *Black Pearls: Blues Queens of the 1920s* (New Brunswick, N.J.: Rutgers University Press, 1988), 103–105; Faderman, 76–78; Gill, chapter 4; Ma Rainey, "Prove It on Me Blues," *Down in the Basement*, Milestone, MLP-2017.

49. Chauncey, *Gay New York*, 244; Young; Faderman, 73; Blair Niles, *Strange Brother* (1931; London: GMP, 1991), 57, 155. Anti-vice propaganda, however, specifically targeted lesbians, as is seen in the next part of this chapter.

50. "Mere Male Blossoms Out in Garb of Milady at Big Hamilton Lodge Ball," *New York Amsterdam News*, February 19, 1930: 3; Hughes, 273–74. Although it seems implied in many newspaper reports, not all masked participants of drag balls were sexually attracted to members of their own sex.

51. Gallant [pseudonym], "Society's 'Good Companions' Listen to Reading of Novel," *National News*, April 14, 1932: 5; Richard Bruce Nugent, "On Alexander Gumby," *Gay Rebel of the Harlem Renaissance*, 223; Garber, 323.

52. Garber, 329. See also a party description in Wallace Thurman, *Infants of the Spring* (1932; Boston: Northeastern University Press, 1992), 173–87. Note that both Thurman and Nugent spelled the term "Niggeratti," while, for instance, Hughes used "Niggerati." I have adopted Thurman and Nugent's spelling.

53. Alain Locke, letter to Richard Jenkins, n.d., GCP, 145–25, MSRC.

54. Richard Jefferson, letter to Locke, May 16, 1927, GCP, 145–25, MSRC; Jefferson, letter to Locke, n.d., GCP, 145–25, MSRC. As evident in the first of these and also in other letters, Locke heavily relied on Greek literary sources for his same-sex model. See also chapter 3, 50–52 and 63, for Locke's recommendation of literary works in the case of Cullen.

55. Countée Cullen, letters to Locke, November 24, 1923; August 26, 1923; March 3, 1923, ALP, 164–22, MSRC.

56. William C. George, letter to Locke, May 15, 1922, ALP, 164–31, MSRC. For parents' gratitude, see F. A. Cullen, letter to Locke, January 29, 1924, ALP, 164–22, MSRC; M. E. George [mother of William C. George], letter to Locke, June 4, 1922, ALP, 164–22, MSRC.

57. Locke, letter to Jefferson, n.d. [Sunday], GCP, 145–25, MSRC.

58. Locke, letter to Jefferson, n.d. [Sunday], GCP, 145–25, MSRC. Locke's "fraternity" seems quite similar to the "Order of Chaeronea," a secret "gay" society existing from the mid 1890s in England, as described by Jeffrey Weeks in *Coming Out: Homosexual Politics in Britain from the Nineteenth Century to the Present*, rev. ed. (London: Quartet, 1990), 122–27.

59. For the acceptance of heterosexual desire see, for example, Cullen, letter to Locke, May 4, 1924, ALP, 164–22, in which Cullen reports that "Langston is . . . in love . . . with a young English colored girl," or George, letter to Locke, n.d. [July 26 or 27], ALP, 164–31, MSRC, in which George assumes that "some woman will, however, cause [Locke's] heart to flutter violently."

60. Locke, letter to Lewellyn Ransom, n.d., ALP, 164–79; Cullen, letter to Locke, May 27, 1925, ALP, 164–22, MSRC.

61. Richard Bruce Nugent, letter to Locke, January 4, 1928, ALP, 164–75, MSRC; Locke, letter to Nugent, March 5, 1929, GCP, 145–25, MSRC; Radclyffe Hall, *The Well of Loneliness* (1928; London: Virago, 1992).

62. Locke, letter to Cullen, n.d., ALP, 164–22, MSRC.

63. Mumford, 84.

64. Cheryl Clarke, "The Failure to Transform: Homophobia in the Black Community," *Home Girls: A Black Feminist Anthology*, ed. Barbara Smith (New York: Kitchen Table: Women of Color, 1983), 206.

65. Clarke, 206; Faderman, 73.

66. Mumford, 84.

67. Garber, 329.

68. Hughes, 225.

69. Niles, 234.

70. Niles, 151–52.

71. RBNP/Tapes #2; Bessie Smith, "T'ain't Nobody's Bizness If I Do," *The World's Greatest Blues Singer*, Columbia GP-33.

72. Mumford, 84.

73. Sterling A. Brown, " More Odds," *Opportunity*, June 1932: 189.

74. George Hutchinson, *The Harlem Renaissance in Black and White* (Cambridge, Mass.: Belknap-Harvard University Press, 1995), 6.

75. Frederick Lewis Allen, *Only Yesterday: An Informal History of the Nineteen-Twenties* (New York: Harper, 1931), 88–89, 98–103.

76. E. Franklin Frazier, *Black Bourgeoisie: The Rise of a New Middle Class in the United States* (1957; New York: Collier, 1962), 124.

77. For prevalent stereotypes of African Americans, see, for example, James Weldon Johnson, "The Dilemma of the Negro Author," *American Mercury* 15 (1928): 478.

78. Claudia Tate, *Domestic Allegories of Political Desire: The Black Heroine's Text at the Turn of the Century* (New York: Oxford University Press, 1992), 58.

79. Hutchinson, 153; Frazier, 108–109.

80. Hazel V. Carby, "Policing the Black Woman's Body in an Urban Context," *Critical Inquiry* 18 (1992): 738–55; Thomas J. Durant, Jr. and Joyce S. Louden, "The Black Middle Class in America: Historical and Contemporary Perspectives," *Phylon* 47 (1986): 257.

81. William H. Ferris, "Ferris Scores Obscenity In Our Literature," *Pittsburgh Courier,* March 31, 1928, section 2: 8.

82. Chauncey, *Gay New York*, 135.

83. E. Franklin Frazier, "Sex Morality among Negroes," *Religious Education* 23 (1928): 448, 450.

84. Chauncey, *Gay New York*, 256.

85. Chauncey, *Gay New York*, 111–12.

86. Alice Dunbar-Nelson, "Woman's Most Serious Problem" [1927], *Speech and Power: The African-American Essay and Its Cultural Content from Polemics to Pulpit*, ed. Gerald Early, 2 vols. (Hopewell, N.J.: Ecco, 1993), 2: 225. See also "Women Workers," editorial, *Opportunity* August 1925: 226.

87. Ann Douglas, *Terrible Honesty: Mongrel Manhattan in the 1920s* (New York: Noonday, 1996), 259; "Crime in Harlem," *New York Amsterdam News*, March 13, 1929: n.p. This article suggests that "the Negro man . . . often finds it impossible, because of his color, to get a job which will enable him to meet [his family's living] expenses without the aid of his wife."

88. Kobena Mercer, *Welcome to the Jungle: New Positions in Black Cultural Studies* (New York: Routledge, 1994), 137.

89. Wallace Thurman, *The Blacker the Berry* (1929; London: X Press, 1994), 147.

90. The phenomenon of "sweetmen" may also be related to the fact that, as stated in a 1932 newspaper article, "Negroes have shown an excess of females over males in every census since 1840." "Women Aplenty," *National News*, April 14, 1932: 5.

91. Tate, 56.

92. Stavney, 128; Nella Larsen, *Quicksand* (New York: Knopf, 1928).

93. Carby, 745–46.

94. Christina Simmons, "Modern Sexuality and the Myth of Victorian Repression," *Passion and Power: Sexuality in History*, ed. Kathy Peiss and Christina Simmons (Philadelphia: Temple University Press, 1989), 169.

95. Dunbar-Nelson, 225–26; Havelock Ellis, *The Task of Social Hygiene* (Boston: Houghton, 1912), chapter 5. The drop in birth rates was largely linked to the use of birth-control methods.

96. bell hooks, *Talking Back: Thinking Feminist, Thinking Black* (Boston: South End, 1989), 121. hooks's comment is not made in specific reference to the 1920s/1930s. See also Simmons, 169.

97. Erin G. Carlston, " 'A Finer Differentiation': Female Homosexuality and the American Medical Community, 1926–1940," *Science and Homosexualities*, ed. Vernon A. Rosario (New York: Routledge, 1997), 177, 180.

98. Havelock Ellis, *Sexual Inversion* [1897], vol. 1, part 4 of Havelock Ellis, *Studies in the Psychology of Sex* (1903; New York: Random, 1942), 1: 201. *Sexual Inversion* was first published as a coauthored monograph by Havelock Ellis and John Addington Symonds. The first edition was immediately withdrawn from the market; in later editions, Symonds's name was omitted. I cite from the 1942 edition. See also Lillian Faderman, "The Morbidification of Love between Women by 19th-Century Sexologists," *Journal of Homosexuality* 4 (1978): 77.

99. Faderman, "Morbidification," 77; Weeks, 64. Note again that sexologists did not "invent" homosexuality and could not control attitudes but rather strengthened and spread notions that already existed. Chauncey, "From Sexual Inversion," 115.

100. Geraldyn Dismond, "Social Snapshots," *Inter-State Tattler*, February 22, 1929: 5. See also Abram Hill, "The Hamilton Lodge Ball," August 30, 1939, WPC, reel 4, SCRBC, 2. Women were even barred from some drag balls. See "Men Dance at Vagabonds Ball; Women Are Barred," *Baltimore Afro-American*, March 7, 1925: 20.

101. "Dr. A.C. Powell Scores Pulpit Evils," *New York Age*, November 16, 1929: 1.

102. George S. Schuyler, "Views and Reviews," *Pittsburgh Courier*, March 5, 1927, section 2: 8.

103. Frazier, *Bourgeoisie*, 77.

104. Frazier, *Bourgeoisie*, 146.

105. "Women Rivals."

106. "Women Rivals."

107. "Women Rivals."

108. Chauncey, "From Sexual Inversion," 144–45. For an explicit example of a description of lesbians as "man-haters," see "Evelyn Addams, 1 Yr. And Deporta-

tion: Boss of Eve's in Village Sold 'Dirty' Book—Man-Hater Besides," *Variety*, July 7, 1926: 33. Note that a refraining from socializing with the other sex was also regarded as suspicious for men who could be described as "woman-haters." See Rudolph Fisher, *The Conjure-Man Dies* (1932; London: X Press, 1995), 15.

109. Ralph Matthews, "Are Pansies People?" *Baltimore Afro-American*, April 2, 1932: 3. Matthews claims this description to be a quote from Buddy Browning, "Fag Balls Exposed," *Broadway Brevities*, March 14, 1932: 12. It seems, however, that while his article contains sections from "Fag Balls," this particular depiction was not contained in the *Brevities* piece. Note the close connection made between drug and alcohol consumption and sexual "deviance" that is also evident in "Women Rivals."

110. Thurman, *Berry*, 108; Carby, 741. See also Faderman, *Odd Girls*, 69–70.

111. Thurman, *Berry*, 108.

112. Thurman, *Berry*, 109.

113. "Uncle Held for Special Sessions Charged with Corrupting Boy's Morals," *New York Amsterdam News*, December 8, 1926: 2. See also "Alleged Degenerate Held As Boy Cries," *Baltimore Afro-American*, February 18, 1928: 10; Estelle B. Freedman, " 'Uncontrolled Desires': The Response to the Sexual Psychopath, 1920–1960," *Journal of American History* 74 (1987–1988): 83–106.

114. Browning/Matthews; "Dr. A.C. Powell"; Chauncey, *Gay New York*, 254.

115. Matthews.

116. "Dr. Powell's Crusade against Abnormal Vice Is Approved," *New York Age*, November 23, 1929: 1. For congenital theories concerning lesbianism, see Faderman, "Morbidification," 76–82.

117. Pivar, 29, 32.

118. Osofsky, 140–43.

119. Magnus Hirschfeld, *Homosexuality in Men and Women* [1914], excerpt reprinted in Jonathan Ned Katz, *Gay American History: Lesbians and Gay Men in the U.S.A.* (New York: Harper, 1985), 51. Hirschfeld recounts the blaming of Italians and Asian immigrants. For xenophobia in the United States during the 1920s, see Dumenil, 204–207.

120. Browning/Matthews.

121. Browning/Matthews.

122. Bulletin #1480: Sexual Perversion Cases in New York City Courts, Committee of Fourteen Records, 88, Manuscripts and Archives Division, New York Public Library, Astor, Lenox and Tilden Foundations, 1. Note also that other "explanations" for the increase in convictions for disorderly conduct, such as urbanization, are mentioned.

123. Bulletin #1480.

124. James Weldon Johnson, *Negro Americans, What Now?* (1938; New York: AMS, 1971), 29–30; Berta Gilbert, "Harlem Churches Refute Night Life Charges," article, n.d., AGC, 40, CURBML, n.p.

125. Edward Margolies, *Native Sons: A Critical Study of Twentieth-Century Negro American Authors* (Philadelphia: Lippincott, 1968), 31.

126. "They Won't Keep Away."

127. Terence E. Williams, "Queer People of Greenwich Village Converting Harlem into Isle of Lesbos, Charge," *Pittsburgh Courier*, March 17, 1928, section 2: 1.

128. "Will the Plague Spread?" article, n.d., AGC, 40, CURBML, n.p.; Williams.

129. "Masquerade Ball Draws 5,000 People," *New York Amsterdam News*, February 20, 1929: 2. See also "Down the Avenue," *New York Amsterdam News*, December 1, 1926: 11; Chauncey, *Gay New York*, 260. For the participation of white men from a white perspective, see Charles Ford and Parker Tyler, *The Young and Evil* (1933; London: GMP, 1989).

130. Chauncey, *Gay New York*, 248. There seem to be no reports on arrests of women in newspapers.

131. "Rev. Hightower Leads Raids On Vice in Hill," *Pittsburgh Courier*, March 31, 1928, section 1: 8.

132. "Rev. Hightower."

133. "Citizens Claim That Lulu Belle Club on Lenox Avenue Is Notorious Dive," *New York Amsterdam News*, February 15, 1928: 1. Such arrests could lead to suicides: Chauncey, *Gay New York*, 250.

134. "Rev. Hightower." There was a dispute within the church about ministers taking action against vice. Chauncey, *Gay New York*, 255–56.

135. Faderman, *Odd Girls*, 76.

136. Lewis, 76. For rumors about Cullen, see "Best Man Sails with Groom," *Baltimore Afro-American*, n.d. [1928]: n.p.

137. Wallace Thurman, letter to William Jourdan Rapp, n.d. [Tuesday, May 7], WTP, 1 BRBML.

138. Langston Hughes, letter to Alain Locke, n.d. [Friday], ALP, 164–38, MSRC.

139. Locke, letter to Cullen, n.d. [1923?], CCP, 3, ARC. See also Cullen, letter to Locke, August 26, 1923, ALP, 164–22, MSRC, in which Cullen advises Locke against meeting up with a male lover in Washington, reminding him that "there are some people in Washington who would give their hope of heaven for a chance to hurt you."

140. Gloria T. Hull, *Color, Sex and Poetry: Three Women Writers of the Harlem Renaissance* (Bloomington: Indiana University Press, 1987), 12.

141. For the concept of the "open secret," see David A. Miller, *The Novel and the Police* (Berkeley: University of California Press, 1988), 205–206.

142. Eric Garber, " 'T'ain't Nobody's Bizness': Homosexuality in 1920s' Harlem," *Black Men/White Men: A Gay Anthology*, ed. Michael J. Smith (San Francisco: Gay Sunshine, 1983), 14.

2. WRITING IN THE HARLEM RENAISSANCE

1. Alain Locke, "Negro Youth Speaks," *The New Negro*, ed. Alain Locke (1925; New York: Atheneum, 1992), 48, 48–49.

2. James Weldon Johnson, ed., *The Book of American Negro Poetry* (New York: Harcourt, 1922).

3. Gloria T. Hull, *Color, Sex and Poetry: Three Women Writers of the Harlem Renaissance* (Bloomington: Indiana University Press, 1987), 165–66. For an example of young writers' relationships with Johnson, who was addressed as "Godmother," see Wallace Thurman, letter to Georgia Douglas Johnson, n.d., GDJP, 162–2, MSRC.

4. Langston Hughes, *The Big Sea: An Autobiography* (1940; New York: Hill, 1993), 218.

5. W.E.B. Du Bois, "Opinion of W.E.B. Du Bois," *Crisis* April 1920: 299.

6. George Hutchinson, *The Harlem Renaissance in Black and White* (Cambridge, Mass.: Belknap-Harvard University Press, 1995), 167.

7. Langston Hughes, letter to Alain Locke, n.d. [c. May 1923], ALP, 164–38, MSRC.

8. Charles S. Johnson, letter to Alain Locke, March 4, 1924, ALP, 164–40, MSRC.

9. Alain Locke, letter to Walter White, n.d. [1924?], WWP, 91, NAACP, LC.

10. Walter White, letter to Claude McKay, May 20, 1925, WWP, 93, NAACP, LC; Walter White, letter to Rudolph Fisher, February 14, 1925, WWP, 92, NAACP, LC.

11. "An Opportunity for Negro Writers," editorial, *Opportunity* September 1924: 258. Already in 1912, Du Bois organized a short-story competition in *The Crisis*. In contrast to 1920s' events, this was not a regular or greatly publicized contest. Arnold Rampersad, *The Art and Imagination of W.E.B. Du Bois* (Cambridge, Mass.: Harvard University Press, 1988), 185.

12. Chidi Ikonné, *From Du Bois to Van Vechten: The Early New Negro Literature, 1903–1926*, Contributions in Afro-American and African Studies 60 (Westport, Conn.: Greenwood, 1981), 103–105.

13. Ralph D. Story, "Patronage and the Harlem Renaissance: You Get What You Pay For," *CLA Journal* 32 (1989): 290.

14. Charles W. Scruggs, "Alain Locke and Walter White: Their Struggle for Control of the Harlem Renaissance," *Black American Literature Forum* 14 (1980): 98.

15. Hull, 7.

16. Hull, 8; Arnold Rampersad, *The Life of Langston Hughes*, 2 vols. (New York: Oxford University Press, 1988), 1: 66–71. It must be stressed that Hughes was a promising and popular writer and therefore would have represented a suitable candidate on account of his reputation alone.

17. RBNP/Notes, October 3, 1982. See Hull 7–8.

18. RBNP/Notes, January 16, 1982.

19. Rampersad, *The Life*, 1: 156–81; Robert E. Hemenway, *Zora Neale Hurston: A Literary Biography* (London: Camden, 1986), 104–35; Story.

20. James Weldon Johnson, "Race Prejudice and the Negro Artist," *Harper's Monthly Magazine* 157 (1928): 769.

21. W.E.B. Du Bois, "Truth and Beauty," *Crisis* November 1922: 7.

22. "A Note on the New Literary Movement," editorial, *Opportunity* March 1926: 81; Alain Locke similarly described the field of "cultural competition" as a "relatively free and unblockable avenue." Alain Locke, "The High Cost of Prejudice," *Forum* 78 (1927): 502, 506.

23. Hutchinson, 8.

24. John Tebbel, *The Golden Age between Two Wars: 1920–1940* (New York: Bowker, 1978), 23.

25. Hutchinson, 126. For an overview of Harlem Renaissance works and their publishers, see Bruce Kellner, ed., *The Harlem Renaissance: A Dictionary for the Era* (New York: Methuen; London: Routledge, 1987), 407–13.

26. "The New Generation," editorial, *Opportunity*, March 1924: 68.

27. The campaign is discussed in Harry E. Davis, letter to Walter White, 6 May 1924, WWP, 91, NAACP, LC.

28. W.E.B. Du Bois, "Criteria of Negro Art," *Crisis*, April 1927: 70; Du Bois, "Our Monthly Sermon," *Crisis*, April 1929: 125; Sterling A. Brown, "Our Literary Audience" [1930], *A Son's Return: Selected Essays of Sterling A. Brown*, ed. Mark A. Sanders (Boston: Northeastern University Press, 1996), 139–40.

29. Locke, "High Cost," 502. For the concept of a "double audience," see James Weldon Johnson, "The Dilemma of the Negro Author," *American Mercury* 15 (1928): 477–81.

30. "A Note," 80.

31. James Weldon Johnson, preface, *The Book of American Negro Poetry*, ed. James Weldon Johnson (New York: Harcourt, 1922), vii.

32. Johnson, preface, viii.

33. Jonathan Dollimore, *Sexual Dissidence from Augustine to Wilde, Freud to Foucault* (Oxford: Clarendon, 1991), 54.

34. Johnson, preface, viii.

35. Charles S. Johnson quoted in Hutchinson, 176.

36. James Weldon Johnson, "The Larger Success," *Southern Workman,* September 1923: 435; Houston A. Baker, Jr., *Modernism and the Harlem Renaissance* (Chicago: University of Chicago Press, 1987), 75–81; Hutchinson, 31.

37. Walter White, letter to Dr. Turner, June 10, 1924, WWP, 91, NAACP, LC.

38. "An Opportunity," 258.

39. Richard Dyer, *The Matter of Images: Essays on Representations* (London: Routledge, 1993), 141.

40. Locke, "High Cost," 507. For the concept of the "Talented Tenth," see W.E.B. Du Bois, "The Talented Tenth" [1903], *Negro Protest Thought in the Twentieth Century,* ed. Francis L. Broderick and August Meier (Indianapolis: Bobbs, 1965), 48.

41. Alain Locke, *The Negro in America,* Reading with a Purpose 68 (Chicago: American Library Association, 1933), 47.

42. Writing for the *Pittsburgh Courier,* Theodore Hernandez, for instance, discussed Renaissance writers "whose splendid work in literature has produced favorable reactions not only to themselves but to the race in quarters of thought the world over." Theodore Hugh Hernandez, "Why Read Negro Literature?" *Pittsburgh Courier,* February 13, 1932, section 2: 3. The definition of writers' responsibilities exceeded the boundaries of black America: Interpreted according to an ideology of African American exceptionalism, Renaissance writers were deemed "the advanceguard of the African peoples." Locke, "The New Negro," *The New Negro,* 14.

43. Hutchinson, 49.

44. W.E.B. Du Bois, "Criteria of Negro Art," *Crisis,* October 1926: 296. Du Bois, as should be noted, also made less extreme comments regarding the use of propaganda.

45. Cary D. Wintz, *Black Culture and the Harlem Renaissance* (Houston: Rice University Press, 1988), 106–108; Ralph L. Pearson, "Combatting Racism with Art: Charles S. Johnson and the Harlem Renaissance," *American Studies* 18 (1977): 132.

46. Alain Locke, "Beauty Instead of Ashes" [1928], *The Critical Temper of Alain Locke: A Selection of His Essays on Art and Culture,* ed. Jeffrey C. Stewart (New York: Garland, 1983), 24; Alain Locke, "Art or Propaganda?" *Harlem* 1 (1928): 12.

47. Locke, "New Negro," 11.

48. Locke, "Negro Youth," 50.

49. Hutchinson, 30.

50. Baker; Paul Gilroy, *Black Atlantic: Modernity and Double Consciousness* (Cambridge, Mass.: Harvard University Press, 1993).

51. Hutchinson, 119.

52. Richard Bruce [Richard Bruce Nugent], "Smoke, Lilies and Jade," *Fire!!* 1 (1926): 33–39. Note that the title of this piece has sometimes been misspelled as "Smoke, Lillies and Jade."

53. Charles S. Johnson, "Jazz Poetry and Blues," *Carolina Magazine,* May 1928: 18.

54. Alain Locke, "Color Line: Inside and Out," review of *Plum Bun,* by Jessie Fauset, and *The Blacker the Berry,* by Wallace Thurman, *Survey* 62 (1929): 325.

55. Eunice Hunton Carter, review of *The Blacker the Berry,* by Wallace Thurman, *Opportunity,* May 1929: 162–63.

56. Wallace Thurman, "This Negro Literary Renaissance," "Aunt Hagar's Children," unpublished typescript, n.d., WTP, 1, BRBML, 4.

57. Aubrey Bowser, "Black Realism," review of *The Blacker the Berry,* by Wallace Thurman, *New York Amsterdam News,* February 13, 1929: 16.

58. Bowser.

59. Benjamin Brawley, "The Negro Literary Renaissance," *Southern Workman,* March 1927: 183.

60. "Thinking Black," review of *Home to Harlem*, by Claude McKay, quoted in Marcus Garvey, " 'Home to Harlem,' Claude McKay's Damaging Book, Should Earn Wholesale Condemnation of Negroes," *Negro World*, September 29, 1928: 1.

61. Jack B. Moore, *W.E.B. Du Bois*, Twayne United States Authors Series 399 (Boston: Twayne, 1981), 110.

62. W.E.B. Du Bois, "Opinion of W.E.B. Du Bois," *Crisis*, May 1925: 9. See also Moore, 109.

63. Thomas Fortune, "We Must Make Literature to Make Public Opinion," *Negro World*, November 22, 1924: 4; Aubrey Bowser, "The Two-Dollar Woman Out Again," *New York Amsterdam News*, November 28, 1928: n.p. The *Negro World* was from 1918 to 1933 the weekly publication of Marcus Garvey and his Universal Negro Improvement Association.

64. Moore 96. Moore makes this comment in reference to Du Bois.

65. James O. Hopson, "Negro Writers in White Magazines," *Pittsburgh Courier*, February 20, 1932, section 2: 2.

66. Cary D. Wintz, "Series Introduction," *The Harlem Renaissance 1920–1940*, ed. Cary D. Wintz, 7 vols. (New York: Garland, 1996), 1–7: x. Despite the age difference, White can, given his alignment with the older Renaissance writers, also be counted among this group.

67. Deborah E. McDowell, " 'It's Not Safe. Not Safe at All': Sexuality in Nella Larsen's *Passing*," *The Lesbian and Gay Studies Reader*, ed. Henry Abelove, Michèle Aina Barale, and David M. Halperin (New York: Routledge, 1993), 618; Ann DuCille, *The Coupling Convention: Sex, Text, and Tradition in Black Women's Fiction* (New York: Oxford University Press, 1993), for example, on Larsen and Fauset: 66–109. For critics' classification of these writers as bourgeois and "respectable," see, for example, Robert Bone, *The Negro Novel in America* (New Haven, Conn.: Yale University Press, 1958), 101–106. There were exceptions among female writers like Hurston and Gwendolyn Bennett, who contributed to highly contested literary ventures like the magazine *Fire!!*, a publication which is discussed in more detail in this chapter.

68. Steven Watson, *The Harlem Renaissance: Hub of African-American Culture, 1920–1930* (New York: Pantheon, 1995), 79; Regarding Cullen's not belonging to the Niggeratti group, see Eleonore van Notten, *Wallace Thurman's Harlem Renaissance*, Costerius New Series 93 (Amsterdam, The Netherlands: Rodopi, 1994), 145.

69. "Surrounded by His Books, Countee Cullen Is Happy," article, n.d. [October 23, 1925?], CCP, scrapbook 2, ARC, n.p.

70. "Surrounded."

71. Countee Cullen, "The Dark Tower," *Opportunity*, March 1928: 90.

72. "The Negro in Art: How Shall He Be Portrayed—A Symposium," *Crisis*, August 1926: 193.

73. Countee Cullen, "The Dark Tower," *Opportunity*, July 1927: 210; Locke quoted in Cullen, "Dark Tower," July 1927: 210.

74. Countee Cullen, "Countee Cullen," *Caroling Dusk: An Anthology of Verse by Negro Poets*, ed. Countee Cullen (New York: Harper, 1927), 179.

75. Henry Louis Gates, Jr., "The Black Man's Burden," *Fear of a Queer Planet*, ed. Michael Warner (Minneapolis: University of Minnesota Press, 1993), 230.

76. McKay, letter to Harold Jackman, August 1, 1927, CMKP, 6, BRBML.

77. Claude McKay, *A Long Way from Home* (1937; New York: Harcourt, 1970), 115.

78. Langston Hughes, "Says Race Leaders, Including Preachers, Flock to Harlem Cabarets," *Pittsburgh Courier*, April 16, 1927, section 1: 8.

79. Hughes, *Big Sea*, 228; McKay, *Long Way*, 322.

80. Hughes, letter to Thurman, n.d., WTP, 1, BRBML.
81. Claude McKay, letter to Harold Jackman, n.d., CMKP, 6, BRBML. Thurman thanked McKay for his encouraging comments on *Fire!!*. See Notten, 158.
82. "Fire" open letter, n.d., ADP, 1, SCRBC; McKay, letter to White, June 15, 1925, WWP, 93, NAACP, LC.
83. Wallace Thurman, editorial, *Harlem* 1 (1928): 22.
84. Granville Hicks, "The New Negro: An Interview with Wallace Thurman," *Churchman*, April 30, 1927: 10.
85. McKay, letter to Jackman, March 31, 1928, CMKP, 6, BRBML.
86. Scruggs, 97. The poem in question was "White House," which Locke changed to "White Houses" for his anthology *The New Negro*. Claude McKay, "White Houses," *The New Negro*, 134.
87. Alain Locke, review of *Infants of the Spring*, by Wallace Thurman, n.d., ALP, 164–134, MSRC, 1.
88. Thurman, "This Negro Literary Renaissance," 2–3; Langston Hughes, *The Weary Blues* (New York: Knopf, 1926).
89. Hughes, letter to McKay, May 28, 1927, CMKP, 2, BRBML; Langston Hughes, *Fine Clothes to the Jew* (New York: Knopf, 1927).
90. J. A. Rogers, "Rogers Calls Langston Hughes' Book of Poems 'Trash,' " review of *Fine Clothes to the Jew*, by Langston Hughes, *Pittsburgh Courier*, February 12, 1927, section 1: 4; review of *Fine Clothes to the Jew*, by Langston Hughes, *Chicago Whip*, February 26, 1927: n.p.
91. Benjamin Brawley, letter to A. Epstein [representing Alfred A. Knopf, Inc.], n.d., LHP, 20, BRBML; Langston Hughes, *Not Without Laughter* (1931; New York: Simon & Schuster, 1995).
92. "Infants of Spring," review of *Infants of the Spring*, by Wallace Thurman, *Abbott's Monthly Review*, April 1932: 51; W.E.B. Du Bois, "Two Novels," review of *Passing*, by Nella Larsen and *Home to Harlem*, by Claude McKay, *Crisis*, June 1928: 202; Wallace Thurman, *Infants of the Spring* (1932; Boston: Northeastern University Press, 1992); Claude McKay, *Home to Harlem* [1928], *Classic Fiction of the Harlem Renaissance*, ed. William L. Andrews (New York: Oxford University Press, 1994), 105–237.
93. William H. Ferris, "Ferris Scores Obscenity in Our Literature," *Pittsburgh Courier*, March 31, 1928, section 2: 8; Garvey.
94. Allison Davis, "Our Negro 'Intellectuals,' " *Crisis,* August 1928: 268; W.E.B. Du Bois, review of *Nigger Heaven*, by Carl Van Vechten, *Crisis,* December 1926: 81.
95. "A Note," 80; Alain Locke, "1928: A Retrospective Review," *Opportunity,* January 1929: 8.
96. Ferris; Davis, 269. Cullen was also included in Davis's remarks.
97. Davis, 269; Bowser, "Two-Dollar"; Du Bois, review of *Nigger Heaven*, 81.
98. George W. Jacobs [George S. Schuyler], "New Yorker Flays McKay's Book, 'Home to Harlem,' " *Pittsburgh Courier*, April 7, 1928, section 2: 8; Ferris.
99. Aubrey Bowser, "Invincible Laughter," review of *Not Without Laughter*, by Langston Hughes, *New York Amsterdam News*, July 23, 1930: 20; George S. Schuyler, "Views and Reviews," *Pittsburgh Courier*, March 24, 1928, section 2: 8. The latter statement's anti-Semitic tone can probably be linked to the fact that parts of Harlem's entertainment industry were owned by Jews.
100. See, for example, Hughes, letter to McKay, March 5, 1928, CMKP, 2, BRBML, in which Hughes anticipates harsh reactions to McKay's *Home to Harlem*.
101. Thurman, "This Negro Literary Renaissance," 3; Hughes, letter to Thurman, n.d. [Sunday], WTP, 1, BRBML; Watson, 91.

102. For positive comments see, for example, "A Challenge to the Negro," *Bookman*, November 1926: 258–59; Robert T. Kerlin, "Conquest by Poetry," *Southern Workman*, June 1927: 284. For negative comments see, for example, Aubrey Bowser, "An Example for Harlem Writers: The Saturday Evening Quill," *New York Amsterdam News*, June 20, 1928: 20; Brawley, "Negro Literary Renaissance," 178–79, 183.

103. Claude McKay, "A Negro to His Critics," *New York Herald Tribune Books*, March 6, 1932: 1.

104. While *The Crisis* reached a circulation of about 100,000 and *Opportunity* about 10,000, the *Pittsburgh Courier*, for instance, reached up to 250,000 copies. Dennis B. Downey, "*The Crisis*" and "*Opportunity*," *Harlem Renaissance Dictionary*, 86–87 and 273–74; David Stameshkin, "*Pittsburgh Courier*," *Harlem Renaissance Dictionary*, 183–84; Walter C. Daniel, *Black Journals of the United States* (Westport, Conn.: Greenwood, 1982).

105. Donald Jeffrey Hayes, "Youth Flays Critics for Prudish Attacks On 'Realism,' " *Chicago Defender*, April 21, 1928, section 2: 1; Rogers.

106. Thurman, letter to Hughes, n.d. [Friday], LHP, 150, BRBML; " 'The End of Harlem,' " *New York News*, May 25, 1929: n.p.; Wallace Thurman and William Jourdan Rapp, *Harlem* (1929).

107. Thurman, letter to Rapp, n.d., WTP, 1, BRBML.

108. "New Generation."

109. Alain Locke, review of *Sex Expression in Literature*, by V. F. Calverton, *Opportunity*, February 1926: 58.

110. Du Bois, quoted in Moore, 109.

111. W.E.B. Du Bois and Alain Locke, "The Younger Literary Movement," *Crisis*, February 1924: 161.

112. Du Bois, "Two Novels," 202. For a similar list, see Du Bois, review of *God Sends Sunday*, by Arna Bontemps, *Crisis*, September 1931: 304.

113. Rogers.

114. George Chauncey, Jr., "From Sexual Inversion to Homosexuality: Medicine and the Changing Conceptualization of Female Deviance," *Salmagundi* 58–59 (1982–1983): 134.

115. George S. Schuyler, "Lights and Shadows of the Underworld—Studying the Social Outcasts: II. The Folk Farthest Down," *Messenger*, August 1923: 787.

116. Aubrey Bowser, review of *Banjo*, by Claude McKay, *New York Amsterdam News*, May 8, 1929: 20.

117. Bowser, review of *Banjo*.

118. Bowser, "Two-Dollar Woman"; Bowser, "Black Realism."

119. W.M.K. [William M. Kelley], "Langston Hughes—the Sewer Dweller," review of *Fine Clothes to the Jew*, by Langston Hughes, *New York Amsterdam News*, February 9, 1927: 22; Ferris.

120. Ferris.

121. Ferris.

122. Bowser, "Example for Harlem Writers."

123. Thurman, editorial, 21.

124. Brawley, "Negro Literary Renaissance," 178.

125. Brawley, "Negro Literary Renaissance," 179.

126. Cullen did not like Thurman, but, as Nugent recalled, he was fond of Nugent. RBNP/Tapes #10. Moreover, he liked Hughes.

127. Fred Bair, letter to Countée Cullen, n.d. [April 18, 1929], CCP, 1, ARC.

128. W.E.B. Du Bois, "The Looking Glass," *Crisis*, January 1927: 158.

129. Countee Cullen, "The Dark Tower," *Opportunity*, January 1927: 25.

130. Cullen, "Dark Tower," January 1927: 25.

131. Locke, "Fire: A Negro Magazine," *Survey* 58 (1927): 563.

132. Julian Carter, "Normality, Whiteness, Authorship: Evolutionary Sexology and the Primitive Pervert," *Science and Homosexualities*, ed. Vernon A. Rosario (New York: Routledge, 1997), 155–76.

133. Notten, 144.

134. For Locke's recommendations of literature, see Locke, letter to Cullen, March 15, 1923, CCP, 3, ARC; Cullen, letter to Locke, March 3, 1923, ALP, 164–22, MSRC.

135. Hughes, "Says Race."

136. Claude McKay, letter to Arthur A. Schomburg, April 28, 1925, AASP, 5, SCRBC. McKay refers to his novel "Color Scheme"—presumably the precursor of *Home to Harlem*—which was never published.

137. Hughes, for instance, believed *Home to Harlem* to be "so damned real!" Hughes, letter to McKay, March 5, 1928, CMKP, 2, BRBML.

138. Notten, 138.

139. Wallace Thurman, "Cordelia the Crude," *Fire!!* 1 (1926): 5–6.

140. Michael L. Cobb, "Insolent Racing, Rough Narrative: The Harlem Renaissance's Impolite Queers," *Callaloo* 23 (2000): 343. Cobb made this comment in specific reference to Nugent's "Smoke, Lilies and Jade."

141. Nugent, quoted in Charles Michael Smith, "Bruce Nugent: Bohemian of the Harlem Renaissance," *In the Life: A Black Gay Anthology*, ed. Joseph Beam (Boston: Alyson, 1986), 214.

142. Thurman, "This Negro Literary Renaissance," 13.

143. James Weldon Johnson, "Negro Authors and White Publishers," *Crisis,* July 1929: 229.

144. Fauset, quoted in "Publisher Denies Prejudice against Negro Writers," *Pittsburgh Courier*, July 27, 1929, section 1: 12.

145. J. A. Rogers, "The Critics: Do They Tell the Truth?" *Messenger*, December 1926: 365.

146. William H. Ferris, " 'Individuality' Is Race's Greatest Need," *Pittsburgh Courier*, November 27, 1926, section 1: 8.

147. Ferris, "Ferris Scores."

148. Ferris, "Ferris Scores."

149. Langston Hughes, letter, *Crisis,* September 1928: 302; Hughes, letter to McKay, September 13, 1928, CMKP, 2, BRBML.

150. McKay, "Negro to His Critics," 6.

151. McKay, letter to Jackman, May 19, 1928, CMKP, 6, BRBML.

152. Amritjit Singh, *The Novels of the Harlem Renaissance: Twelve Black Writers 1923–1933* (University Park: Pennsylvania State University Press, 1976), 25; Wayne F. Cooper, *Claude McKay: Rebel Sojourner in the Harlem Renaissance—A Biography* (New York: Schocken, 1990), 242.

153. Thurman, "Tribute," "Aunt Hagar's Children," 1.

154. James Weldon Johnson, "Negro Authors," 229; "Publisher Denies Prejudice."

155. Harold Jackman, letter to Countée Cullen, February 10, 1930, CCP, 3, ARC. At this stage, the manuscript had a different title—"The [Christ?] in the Cloud." Arna Bontemps, *God Sends Sunday* (New York: Harcourt, 1931).

156. Du Bois, review of *God Sends Sunday*. For further hints about this matter, see Arna Bontemps, "The Awakening: A Memoir," *The Harlem Renaissance Remembered: Essays Edited with a Memoir*, ed. Arna Bontemps (New York: Dodd, 1972), 25–26.

157. Hutchinson, 347–50.

158. Hughes, "Says Race."

159. Thurman, letter to Rapp, August 1, 1929, WTP, 1, BRBML.

160. Thurman, letter to Rapp, August 1, 1929, WTP, 1, BRBML.

161. Thurman, letter to Rapp, August 1, 1929, WTP, 1, BRBML.

162. Wallace Thurman, *The Blacker the Berry* (1929; London: X Press, 1994). This does not imply, however, that Thurman did not portray transgressive sexualities in his novels.

163. Wallace Thurman, "Negro Poets and Their Poetry" [1928], *Black Writers Interpret the Harlem Renaissance*, ed. Cary D. Wintz (New York: Garland, 1996), 78; Baker, 85–87.

164. Hughes, *Big Sea*, 235.

165. Notten, 132.

166. Gwendolyn Bennett, letter to Countée Cullen, August 28, 1925, CCP, 1, ARC.

167. Stanley Coben, *Rebellion against Victorianism: The Impetus for Cultural Change in 1920s America* (New York: Oxford University Press, 1991). For Renaissance participants' discussions of literary topics see, for example, Wallace Thurman, letter to Harold Jackman, n.d. [August 30, 1930], WTP, 1, BRBML; Thurman, letter to Jackman, n.d. [midnight, Thursday], WTP, 1, BRBML.

168. Locke, "Fire"; Coben, 59. See also McKay, letter to Jackman, March 31, 1928, CMKP, 6, BRBML, where McKay explains: "I do not find [my characters] more sexy than the characters of white modern authors, Hardy, Joyce, Morand, . . . "

169. James Levin, *The Gay Novel in America* (New York: Garland, 1991), 27.

170. Container 4: 1920–1950, SSVP, LC.

171. Notten, 137. For the inspiration for *Fire!!* from white little magazines, see Locke, "Fire."

172. Smith, 214.

173. Tebbel, 8–9, 404.

174. Thurman, "This Negro Literary Renaissance," 3.

175. George S. Schuyler, "The Negro-Art Hokum," *Nation*, June 16, 1926: 662.

176. Langston Hughes, "The Negro Artist and the Racial Mountain," *Nation*, June 23, 1926: 693.

177. "Fire," open letter.

178. Notten, 139–47.

179. Hughes, "The Negro Artist," 694.

180. Notten, 158–67.

3. COUNTÉE CULLEN

1. Houston A. Baker, Jr., *A Many-Colored Coat of Dreams: The Poetry of Countee Cullen*, Broadside Critics Series 4 (Detroit: Broadside, 1974), 18.

2. David Levering Lewis, *When Harlem Was in Vogue* (New York: Knopf, 1981), 77.

3. Countée Cullen, letter to Alain Locke, June 17, 1923, ALP, 164–22, MSRC.

4. Wallace Thurman, "This Negro Literary Renaissance," "Aunt Hagar's Children," unpublished typescript, n.d., WTP, 1, BRBML, 9.

5. Steven Watson, *The Harlem Renaissance: Hub of African-American Culture, 1920–1930* (New York: Pantheon, 1995), 48.

6. Wallace Thurman, "Negro Artists and the Negro," *New Republic* 52 (1927): 39.

7. Geraldyn Dismond, "Through the Lorgnette," *Pittsburgh Courier*, May 28, 1927, section 2: 1.

8. Jean Wagner, *Black Poets of the United States: From Paul Laurence Dunbar to Langston Hughes*, trans. Kenneth Douglas (Urbana: University of Illinois Press, 1973), 284–87. For further varying statements about other personal information, see Gerald Early, introduction, *My Soul's High Song: The Collected Writings of Countee Cullen, Voice of the Harlem Renaissance*, ed. Gerald Early (New York: Doubleday, 1991), 6–7.

9. Harold Jackman, untitled report (for Sister M. Margaret), August 27, 1960, GCP, 145–13, MSRC; Harold Jackman, letter to Cullen, September 20, 1929, CCP, 3, ARC.

10. Lewis, 76.

11. Dismond.

12. Wagner, 287.

13. Lewis, 76.

14. Cullen, quoted in Lester A. Walton, "Protests Holding Negro Artist to Racial Themes," *New York World*, May 15, 1927: 16.

15. Dismond.

16. Cullen, letter to Jackman, February 22, 1926, CCP, 2, BRBML.

17. Cullen, letter to Locke, August 26, 1923, ALP, 164–22, MSRC. Looking at the women Cullen dated—for example, Fiona Braithwaite, daughter of well-known literary figure William Stanley Braithwaite, and Yolande Du Bois, daughter of the most prominent contemporary African American—the impression that he tried to marry a woman of high social standing who would enhance his reputation seems corroborated.

18. For rumors about Cullen's homosexuality, see "Best Man Sails with Groom," *Baltimore Afro-American*, n.d. [1928]: n.p.; Gerald Early, "Three Notes toward a Cultural Definition of the Harlem Renaissance," *Callaloo* 14 (1991): 145. For Cullen's relationship with Atkinson, see Alden Reimonenq, "Countee Cullen's Uranian 'Soul Windows,' " *Critical Essays: Gay and Lesbian Writers of Color*, ed. Emmanuel S. Nelson (New York: Harrington Park-Haworth, 1993), 159–62.

19. Early, introduction, 19.

20. Lewis, 77; Monika Plessner suggests a link between Cullen's suicide-themed poems and his homosexuality. Monika Plessner, *Ich bin der dunklere Bruder: Die Literatur der schwarzen Amerikaner. Von den Spirituals bis zu James Baldwin. Eine Einführung* (Hagen, Germany: Linnepe, 1977), 200; Reimonenq, 152–53.

21. Cullen, letter to Locke, May 4, 1924, ALP, 164–22, MSRC.

22. Cullen, letter to Locke, November 1, 1924, ALP, 164–22, MSRC.

23. Charles W. Scruggs, "Alain Locke and Walter White: Their Struggle for Control of the Harlem Renaissance," *Black American Literature Forum* 14 (1980): 94.

24. Cullen, letter to Locke, March 3, 1923, ALP, 164–22, MSRC; Edward Carpenter, *Ioläus: An Anthology of Friendship*, 2nd enl. ed. (London: Swan; Manchester, England: Clarke, 1906); Reimonenq, 144.

25. Cullen, letter to Locke, August 26, 1923, ALP, 164–22, MSRC; Cullen, letter to Locke, June 8, 1923, ALP, 164–22, MSRC; Cullen to Locke, October 27, 1924, ALP, 164–22, MSRC.

26. Cullen, letter to Locke, March 3, 1923, ALP, 164–22, MSRC.

27. Cullen, letter to Locke, March 3, 1923, ALP, 164–22, MSRC.

28. For instance, Cullen closes a letter to Atkinson with "Yo te . . . tan mucho." The all-revealing word *quiero*—"I love" in Spanish—is omitted. Cullen, letter to Richard Atkinson, August 1, 1937, CCP, 1, BRBML; Reimonenq, 159.

29. Cullen, letter to Locke, March 3, 1923, ALP, 164–22, MSRC.

30. Cullen, letter to Locke, July 29, 1924, ALP, 164–22, MSRC. Locke, in contrast, closely followed sexologists' works and was willing to discuss "[his] own ho-

mosexual experiences and temperament." Locke, letter to Richard Jenkins, n.d., GCP, 145–25, MSRC.

31. Jonathan Dollimore, *Sexual Dissidence: Augustine to Wilde, Freud to Foucault* (Oxford: Clarendon, 1991), 54.

32. Locke, letter to Cullen, n.d. [1923?], CCP, 3, ARC.

33. Locke, letter to Cullen, n.d. [1923?], CCP, 3, ARC.

34. Countée Cullen, "To France," *My Soul's High Song*, 245. Cullen expressed a similar attitude toward France in his French composition notebook: "In Paris I find everything that appeals to me: lights, noises in the night, places where one has fun according to one's liking, a sympathetic and tolerant world. . . ." Cullen, quoted in Michel Fabre, *From Harlem to Paris: Black American Writers in France, 1840–1980* (Urbana: University of Illinois Press, 1991), 82.

35. Cullen, letter to Jackman, n.d., CCP, 1, BRBML. Cullen here states his belief that much of French literature was "obscene. French authors go too far."

36. For a fictional work by Cullen see, for example, Countee Cullen, *One Way to Heaven* (New York: Harper, 1932).

37. Reimonenq, 153. Reimonenq here borrows Houston Baker's term.

38. Reimonenq, 158.

39. Cullen himself indicated that his poem "The Spark," in which gender is not specified, could be read in a gay context. Cullen, letter to Locke, March 30, 1925, ALP, 164–22, MSRC; Countée Cullen, "The Spark," *Copper Sun* (New York: Harper, 1927), 31–32; Reimonenq, 154–55.

40. Rictor Norton, "Ganymede Raped: Gay Literature—The Critic as Censor" [1974], *Gay Roots: Twenty Years of Gay Sunshine—An Anthology of Gay History, Sex, Politics, and Culture*, ed. Winston Leyland (San Francisco: Gay Sunshine, 1991), 329–30.

41. Cullen, letter to Jackman, February 22, 1926, CCP, 2, BRBML.

42. Nathan Irvin Huggins, *Harlem Renaissance* (London: Oxford University Press, 1971), 164.

43. Countee Cullen, "Countee Cullen," *Caroling Dusk: An Anthology of Verse by Negro Poets*, ed. Countee Cullen (New York: Harper, 1927), 179.

44. Locke, letter to Langston Hughes, n.d., LHP, 92, BRBML.

45. Allison Davis, "Our Negro 'Intellectuals,' " *Crisis,* August 1928: 269.

46. Charles S. Johnson, "The Negro Enters Literature," *Carolina Magazine,* May 1927: 44.

47. Countee Cullen, *The Medea and Some Poems* (New York: Harper, 1935).

48. "A Negro Renaissance," *New York Herald Tribune,* May 7, 1925: 16.

49. Margaret Sperry, "Countee P. Cullen, Negro Boy Poet, Tells His Story," *Brooklyn Daily Eagle,* February 10, 1924: n.p.

50. Darwin T. Turner, *In a Minor Chord: Three Afro-American Writers and Their Search for Identity* (Carbondale: Southern Illinois University Press; London: Feffer, 1971), 67. Note in this context that Cullen also could not be accused of writing to fulfill the demands of a white patron, as he, in contrast to most prominent Renaissance writers, never had a patron. For patronage and the Harlem Renaissance, see, for example, Ralph D. Story, "Patronage and the Harlem Renaissance: You Get What You Pay For," *CLA Journal* 32 (1989): 284–95.

51. Cullen, quoted in "Negro Wins Prize in Poetry Contest," *New York Times,* December 2, 1923, section 2: 1. For further insights into Cullen's problematic attitude toward "racial" subject matter in his work, see Cullen, letter to Jackman, January 6, 1925, CCP, 2, BRBML.

52. Countée Cullen, "Heritage," *Color* (New York: Harper, 1925), 36–41.

53. Cullen, "Heritage" 36, 38.

54. Cullen, "Heritage" 36.

55. David Bergman, "The African and the Pagan in Gay Black Literature," *Sexual Sameness: Textual Differences in Lesbian and Gay Writing*, ed. Joseph Bristow (London: Routledge, 1992), 164.

56. Cullen, "Heritage," 37; Bergman, 163.

57. Cullen, "Heritage," 38.

58. Cullen, "Heritage," 39.

59. Cullen, "Heritage," 39.

60. Cullen, "Heritage," 39; Bergman, 164. Note also Cullen's description of Hughes after his return from Africa: "Langston is back from his African trip looking like a virile brown god. . . ." Cullen, letter to Locke, November 24, 1923, ALP, 164–22, MSRC.

61. Cullen, "Heritage," 39–40.

62. Blair Niles, *Strange Brother* (1931; London: GMP, 1991), 234. See also Peter Burton, introduction, *Strange Brother*, 3, in which he indicates that Niles may have been conscious of the gay link between her protagonist and Cullen. For the concept of African Americans' "double consciousness," see W.E.B. Du Bois, *The Souls of Black Folk* (1903; New York: Penguin, 1989).

63. Countée Cullen, "The Black Christ," *My Soul's High Song*, 207–36.

64. Alden Reimonenq, "Cullen, Countee," *The Gay and Lesbian Heritage: A Reader's Companion to the Writers and Their Works, from Antiquity to the Present* (New York: Holt, 1995), 185.

65. Stephen Wayne Foster, "Beauty's Purple Flame: Some Minor American Gay Poets, 1786–1936," *Homosexual Themes in Literary Studies*, Studies in Homosexuality 8, ed. Wayne R. Dynes and Stephen Donaldson (New York: Garland, 1992), 141; Cullen, "Black Christ," 215.

66. Cullen, "Black Christ," 215.

67. Gregory Woods, "Gay Re-readings of the Harlem Renaissance Poets," *Critical Essays*, 132.

68. Cullen, "Black Christ," 229, 232.

69. Ellis Hanson, *Decadence and Catholicism* (Cambridge, Mass.: Harvard University Press, 1997), 273–74.

70. Cullen, "Black Christ," 233.

71. Cullen, "Black Christ," 234.

72. Isaac William Brumfield, "Race Consciousness in the Poetry and Fiction of Countee Cullen" (dissertation, University of Illinois at Urbana–Champaign, 1977), 90.

73. Cullen, "Black Christ," 232.

74. Woods, 132. Cullen characterized or, as might also be said, coded his relationship with Jackman along similar lines: "I feel toward him as David toward Jonathan." Cullen, letter to Locke, January 7, 1924, ALP, 164–22, MSRC. According to Arna Bontemps, Cullen and Jackman were called "the David and Jonathan of the Harlem twenties." Arna Bontemps, "The Awakening: A Memoir," *The Harlem Renaissance Remembered: Essays Edited with a Memoir*, ed. Arna Bontemps (New York: Dodd, 1972), 12.

75. Countée Cullen, "The Shroud of Color," *My Soul's High Song*, 97–103.

76. Reimonenq, "Uranian," 154.

77. Countée Cullen, "Judas Iscariot," *Color*, 90–94.

78. Patrick Cockburn, "Sealed with a Loving Kiss," review of *Judas: Betrayer or Friend of Jesus?* by William Klassen, *Independent on Sunday* (London), March 23, 1997: 4.

79. Xavier Mayne [Edward Irenaeus Prime Stevenson], *The Intersexes: A History of Simisexualism as a Problem in Social Life* (n.p.: privately printed, 1908), 259.

Note that Richard Bruce Nugent also wrote a story in which same-sex desire links Judas and Jesus. See chapter 6, 129.

80. Cullen, "Judas," 90.

81. Judges, 19: 22.

82. Cullen, "Judas," 91.

83. Cullen, "Judas," 91.

84. Cullen, "Judas," 92.

85. Cullen, "Judas," 92.

86. Cullen, "Judas," 92.

87. Cullen, "Judas," 93.

88. Cullen, letter to Locke, May 12, 1924, ALP, 164–22, MSRC: "I do wish you and Langston could get together and understand one another. . . ."; Cullen, letter to Locke, November 1, 1924, ALP, 164–22, MSRC.

89. Cullen, "Judas," 94, 92.

90. Cullen, letter to Locke, March 3, 1923, ALP, 164–22, MSRC.

91. Edward Carpenter, *Love's Coming-of-Age* [1896], *Edward Carpenter: Selected Writings*, 3 vols. (London: GMP, 1984), 1: 96. As also indicated later in this chapter, Cullen read *Love's Coming-of-Age*—presumably following Locke's recommendation. Cullen, letter to Locke, September 30, 1923, ALP, 164–22, MSRC. For a failed attempt by Cullen to establish a physical relationship, see Cullen, letter to Locke, March 3, 1923, ALP, 164–22, MSRC. For Cullen's need for sexual satisfaction, see Cullen, letter to Locke, October 27, 1924, ALP, 164–22, MSRC, as discussed hereafter.

92. Cullen, letter to Locke, October 27, 1924, ALP, 164–22, MSRC. The "E.W." mentioned was presumably Renaissance writer Eric Walrond.

93. Reimonenq, "Uranian," 153.

94. Countée Cullen, "To a Brown Boy," *Color*, 8.

95. Watson 54; Arnold Rampersad, *The Life of Langston Hughes*, 2 vols. (New York: Oxford University Press, 1988), 1: 63. The dedication was not included in the poem's publication in *Color*.

96. Countée Cullen, "Youth Sings a Song of Rosebuds," *My Soul's High Song*, 167.

97. Robert Herrick, "To the Virgins, to make much of Time" [1648], *The Poems of Robert Herrick*, ed. L. C. Martin (London: Oxford University Press, 1965), 84; Alan Richter, *Sexual Slang: A Compendium of Offbeat Words and Colorful Phrases from Shakespeare to Today* (1993; New York: HarperPerennial, 1995), 188.

98. Cullen, letter to Locke, April 11, 1924, ALP, 164–22, MSRC.

99. Cullen, letter to Locke, April 11, 1924, ALP, 164–22, MSRC.

100. Cullen, letter to Locke, May 15, 1925, ALP, 164–22, MSRC.

101. Countée Cullen, "Advice to Youth," *Color*, 80. An earlier, handwritten copy of the poem was dedicated to Harold Jackman: CCP, 14, ARC. Note also that the word "Lad," included in the poem, is reminiscent of A. E. Housman's gay poetry.

102. Cullen, letter to Locke, September 30, 1923, ALP, 164–22, MSRC. The woman in question is presumably Yolande Du Bois, whom Cullen met in August 1923.

103. Guillaume Brown, letter to Cullen, July 21, 1927, CCP, 1, ARC.

104. Cullen, letter to Jackman, October 7, 1925, CCP, 1, BRBML.

105. Brown, letter to Cullen, July 21, 1927, CCP, 1, ARC.

106. E. Anthony Rotundo, *American Manhood: Transformations in Masculinity from the Revolution to the Modern Era* (New York: Basic, 1993), 88.

107. Cullen, "Advice to Youth."

108. Countée Cullen, "Suicide Chant," *Color*, 87–88; Countée Cullen, "Saturday's Child," *Color*, 18.

109. Cullen, "Saturday's Child."

110. Cullen, "Suicide Chant."

111. Baker, 18; Lewis, 76; Alan Shucard, *Countee Cullen*, Twayne's United States Authors Series 470 (Boston: Twayne, 1984), 61–62.

112. Countée Cullen, "The Love Tree," *My Soul's High Song*, 155.

113. Genesis, 3: 22.

114. John Addington Symonds, quoted in Eve Kosofsky Sedgwick, *Between Men* (New York: Columbia University Press, 1985), 212.

115. Countée Cullen, "For a Virgin," *Color*, 49; Countée Cullen, "For a Wanton," *Color*, 65.

116. Countée Cullen, "Portrait of a Lover," *Copper Sun*, 47–48; Countée Cullen, "Magnets," *My Soul's High Song*, 241.

117. Jonathan Ned Katz, *Gay/Lesbian Almanac: A New Documentary* (1983; New York: Carroll, 1994), 147; Carl Westphal, "Die contrare Sexualempfindung, Symptom eines neuropathischen (psychopathischen) Zustandes," *Archiv für Psychiatrie und Nervenkrankheiten* 2 (1869): 73–108.

118. Cullen, "Portrait," 47.

119. Cullen, "Portrait," 47.

120. Cullen, "Portrait," 47.

121. Alfred Douglas, quoted in H. Montgomery Hyde, ed., *The Trials of Oscar Wilde: Regina (Wilde) v. Queensberry, Regina v. Wilde and Taylor* (London: Hodge, 1948), 257.

122. Cullen, "Portrait," 47.

123. Cullen, "Portrait," 47.

124. Cullen, "Portrait," 47.

125. Countée Cullen, "Ultimatum," *My Soul's High Song*, 171.

126. Countée Cullen, "For One Who Gayly Sowed His Oats," *Color*, 61.

127. For the possible homosexual significance of the term *gay* in the early twentieth century, see George Chauncey, Jr., *Gay New York: Gender, Urban Culture and the Making of the Gay Male World, 1890–1940* (New York: Basic, 1994), 16–17.

128. Cullen, "Ultimatum."

129. Countée Cullen, "More Than a Fool's Song," *My Soul's High Song*, 169.

130. Dollimore, 14. Dollimore chooses Oscar Wilde as an example of this strategy.

131. Reimonenq, "Uranian," 157.

132. Countée Cullen, "Love's Way," *My Soul's High Song*, 161.

133. Countée Cullen, "Sonnet," *My Soul's High Song*, 247; Cullen, "Love's Way."

134. Cullen, "Love's Way."

135. Cullen, letter to Locke, August 26, 1923, ALP, 164–22, MSRC.

136. Cullen, letter to Locke, September 30, 1923, ALP, 164–22, MSRC.

137. Carpenter, *Love's Coming-of-Age*, 135.

138. Countée Cullen, "Uncle Jim," *My Soul's High Song*, 143; Cullen, "Tableau," *Color*, 12.

139. Cullen, letters to Locke, June 21, 1923; September 30, 1923; August 26, 1923, ALP, 164–22, MSRC. Reimonenq misinterprets Cullen's reference to the "German trip," contained in the last letter listed here, as a coded expression referring to a relationship with a German student. Locke and Cullen actually undertook travel plans, and Cullen was to take part in a student exchange program. For Locke's involvement with a German *Wandervogel*, see various letters sent to Locke by Rudolf Dressler in ALP, 164–26, MSRC. For homosexual currents in the *Wandervogel* movement, see Ulfried Geuter, *Homosexualität in der deutschen Jugendbewe-*

gung: Jugendfreundschaft und Sexualität im Diskurs von Jugendbewegung, Psycho-analyse und Jugendpsychologie am Beginn des 20. Jahrhunderts (Frankfurt am Main: Suhrkamp, 1994).

140. Countee P. Cullen, "The League of Youth," *Crisis*, August 1923: 167.

141. Bruce Kellner, "Gumby, [Levi Sandy] Alexander," *The Harlem Renaissance: A Historical Dictionary for the Era* (New York: Methuen; London: Routledge, 1987), 147; Alexander Gumby, "To . . . . You," unpublished typescript, n.d., AGC, "Gumby's Autobiography & Scrapbook," scrapbook 2, CURBML.

142. Cullen, "League of Youth," 167.

143. Cullen, "Uncle Jim."

144. Countée Cullen, "Spring Reminiscence," *Color*, 84; Cullen, "Uncle Jim."

145. Katz, 146–47. Ulrichs believed that an *Urning*, a term he also used to de-scribe himself, represented the case of a female "soul" trapped in a male body. Amer-ican medical writers used the term *Urnings*.

146. John Keats, *Complete Poems* (London: Softback, 1993), 135.

147. Woods, 135.

148. Reimonenq, "Uranian," 149–50. According to Jessie Fauset, Duff was "affil-iated" with the *Liberator*. Jessie Fauset, letter to Langston Hughes, May 17, 1922, LHP, 57, BRBML.

149. Cullen, "Tableau."

150. D. Dean Shackleford, "The Poetry of Countée Cullen," *Masterpieces of African-American Literature* (New York: HarperCollins, 1992), 383.

151. Kevin J. Mumford, *Interzones: Black/White Sex Districts in Chicago and New York in the Early Twentieth Century* (New York: Columbia University Press, 1997), 76. Woods also speaks of "homosexual miscegenation" in the context of Cullen's "Tableau." Woods, 135.

152. Reimonenq, "Uranian," 150.

153. Reimonenq, "Uranian," 150.

154. Walt Whitman, "We Two Boys Together Clinging," *Walt Whitman: The Complete Poems* (London: Penguin, 1975), 162. Reimonenq suggests a link to Walt Whitman, "In Paths Untrodden" [1867], *Walt Whitman*, 146; Reimonenq, "Uran-ian," 150–51.

155. Walt Whitman, *Democratic Vistas*, [1871], excerpt reprinted in *Ioläus*, 178.

156. Carpenter, quoted in George B. Hutchinson, "The Whitman Legacy and the Harlem Renaissance," *Walt Whitman: The Centennial Essays*, ed. Ed Folsom (Iowa City: University of Iowa Press, 1994), 204.

157. Cullen, letter to Locke, April 30, 1923, ALP, 164–22, MSRC.

158. Wagner, 313. Wagner here refers to "Tableau."

159. Reimonenq, "Uranian," 158.

160. Owen Dodson, "Countee Cullen (1903–1946)," *Phylon* 7 (1946): 20.

4. LANGSTON HUGHES

1. Margaret Perry, *Silence to the Drums: A Survey of the Literature of the Harlem Renaissance*, Contributions in Afro-American and African Studies 18 (West-port, Conn.: Greenwood, 1976), 45.

2. Review of *Fine Clothes to the Jew*, by Langston Hughes, *Chicago Whip*, Feb-ruary 26, 1927: n.p.; Skip G. Gates, "Of Negroes Old and New" [1974], *Analysis and Assessment, 1940–1979*, ed. Cary D. Wintz (New York: Garland, 1996), 209.

3. Alain Locke, "The Weary Blues," review of *The Weary Blues*, by Langston Hughes, *Palms*, January 1926: 25; Margaret Larkin, "A Poet for the People—A Re-

view," review of *Fine Clothes to the Jew,* by Langston Hughes, *Opportunity,* March 1927: 84; W.M.K. [William M. Kelley], "Langston Hughes—the Sewer Dweller," review of *Fine Clothes to the Jew,* by Langston Hughes, *New York Amsterdam News,* February 9, 1927: 22; Benjamin Brawley, "The Negro Literary Renaissance," *Southern Workman,* March 1927: 182.

4. Langston Hughes, "The Negro Artist and the Racial Mountain," *Nation,* June 23, 1926: 693.

5. Hughes, quoted in Steven C. Tracy, *Langston Hughes and the Blues* (Urbana: University of Illinois Press, 1988), 114.

6. Nathan Irvin Huggins, *Harlem Renaissance* (London: Oxford University Press, 1971), 227.

7. Langston Hughes, *The Big Sea: An Autobiography* (1940; New York: Hill, 1993), 3–4, 98; Arnold Rampersad, "The Origins of Poetry in Langston Hughes," *Southern Review* 21 (1985): 696.

8. George Hutchinson, *The Harlem Renaissance in Black and White* (Cambridge, Mass.: Belknap-Harvard University Press, 1995), 118–20, 414–16.

9. Henry Louis Gates, Jr., "The Black Man's Burden," *Fear of a Queer Planet,* ed. Michael Warner (Minneapolis: University of Minnesota Press, 1993), 237.

10. Arnold Rampersad, *The Life of Langston Hughes,* 2 vols. (New York: Oxford University Press, 1988); Faith Berry, *Langston Hughes: Before and Beyond Harlem* (Westport, Conn.: Hill, 1983).

11. *Looking for Langston,* dir. Isaac Julien, Sankofa, 1989; Essex Hemphill, introduction, *Brother to Brother: New Writings by Black Gay Men,* ed. Essex Hemphill (Boston: Alyson, 1991), xxv–xxvi. Poems by Hughes are printed in, for instance, Michael J. Smith, ed., *Black Men/White Men: A Gay Anthology* (San Francisco: Gay Sunshine, 1983), 30.

12. Wallace Thurman, letter to Hughes, n.d. [Friday], LHP, 150, BRBML.

13. RBNP/Notes, December 4, 1983; Nugent, paraphrased in Neil Miller, *Out of the Past: Gay and Lesbian History from 1869 to the Present* (London: Vintage, 1995), 153.

14. Rampersad, *The Life,* 1: 46; Carl Van Vechten, quoted in Miller, 153. Further Renaissance figures shared their view. See, for example, Louise Thompson, quoted in Rampersad, *The Life* 1: 196.

15. Rampersad, *The Life,* 1: 77. The same lack of documentation can be observed in Berry, 38.

16. Seth Clark Silberman, "Looking for Richard Bruce Nugent and Wallace Henry Thurman: Reclaiming Black Male Same-Sexualities in the New Negro Movement," *In Process* 1 (1996): 54.

17. Hilton Als, "Negrofaggotry," *Black Film Review* 5 (1989): 18.

18. Alden Reimonenq, "Hughes, Langston (1902–1967)," *The Gay and Lesbian Heritage: A Reader's Companion to the Writers and Their Works, from Antiquity to the Present* (New York: Holt, 1995), 374.

19. Berry, 184.

20. Reimonenq, 374–75.

21. For the distinction between sexual practice and identity see Thomas S. Weinberg, "On 'Doing' and 'Being' Gay: Sexual Behavior and Homosexual Male Self-Identity," *Journal of Homosexuality* 4 (1978): 143–56.

22. Berry, 150–51; Reimonenq, 375.

23. Rampersad, *The Life,* 1: 66–71.

24. Alain Locke, letter to Hughes, n.d., LHP, 92, BRBML.

25. Countée Cullen, letter to Locke, June 8, 1923, ALP, 164–22, MSRC.

26. Hughes, letter to Locke, April 6, 1923, ALP, 164–38, MSRC; Hughes, letter to Locke, n.d. [c. May 1923], ALP, 164–38, MSRC.

27. Hughes, letter to Locke, April 6, 1923, ALP, 164–38, MSRC; Hughes, letter to Cullen, April 7, 1923, BRBML.

28. George Chauncey, Jr., *Gay New York: Gender, Urban Culture and the Making of the Gay Male World, 1890–1940* (New York: Basic, 1994), 12–13; Alan Sinfield, *Cultural Politics—Queer Reading* (Philadelphia: University of Pennsylvania Press; London: Routledge, 1994), 12–14.

29. For Hughes's heterosexual interests, see Rampersad, *The Life,* for example, 1: 86–87, 264–65.

30. bell hooks, *Yearning: Race, Gender and Cultural Politics* (Boston: South End; London: Turnaround, 1991), 196.

31. Reimonenq, 374.

32. Rampersad, *The Life,* 1: 289; Charles I. Nero, "Re/Membering Langston: Homophobic Textuality and Arnold Rampersad's *Life of Langston Hughes,*" *Queer Representations: Reading Lives, Reading Culture,* ed. Martin Duberman (New York: New York University Press, 1997), 194.

33. Als, 18.

34. Reimonenq, 375.

35. Reimonenq, 375.

36. hooks, 197.

37. Tracy, 224.

38. Tracy, 198, and see 194. Compared with many contemporary blues songs, Hughes's verses seem moderate. Comments of contemporary genteel black critics, however, suggest the opposite: J. A. Rogers, "Rogers Calls Hughes' Book of Poems 'Trash,' " review of *Fine Clothes to the Jew,* by Langston Hughes, *Pittsburgh Courier,* February 12, 1927, sec. 1: 4.

39. hooks, 200.

40. Langston Hughes, "Poem [2]," *The Collected Poems of Langston Hughes,* ed. Arnold Rampersad (New York: Vintage, 1994), 52.

41. In *Black Men/White Men,* 30, the theory is put forward that the dedication was for Ferdinand Smith, "a merchant seaman, born in Jamaica." Berry claims that "F.S." was a man to whom Hughes "had his most intense emotional attachment" (Berry, 185). Rampersad does not corroborate these theories. Rampersad, *The Life,* 1: 403–404.

42. The issue of "softness" is also addressed in Anne Borden, "Heroic 'Hussies' and 'Brilliant Queers': Genderracial Resistance in the Works of Langston Hughes," *African American Review* 28 (1994): 341.

43. Gates, "Black Man's Burden," 234.

44. Jessie Fauset, review of *The Weary Blues,* by Langston Hughes, *Crisis,* March 1926: 239. For a well-known example of this literary tradition, see Alfred Tennyson, "In Memoriam A.H.H." [1833], *Poems and Plays* (London: Oxford University Press, 1968), 230–66.

45. Rampersad, *The Life,* 1: 62.

46. Langston Hughes, "Desire," *Collected Poems,* 105; Gregory Woods, "Gay Re-readings of the Harlem Renaissance Poets," *Critical Essays: Gay and Lesbian Writers of Color,* ed. Emmanuel S. Nelson (New York: Harrington Park-Haworth, 1993), 138.

47. hooks, 193.

48. Langston Hughes, "Star Seeker," *Collected Poems,* 64. Hughes's poem "Pictures to the Wall" ([1926], *Collected Poems,* 79) similarly, though in a more negative tone, features "bitter, forgotten dreams."

49. Langston Hughes, "The Dream Keeper," *Collected Poems*, 45.

50. Countée Cullen, "For a Poet," *My Soul's High Song: The Collected Writings of Countee Cullen, Voice of the Harlem Renaissance*, ed. Gerald Early (New York: Anchor, 1991), 109; Hughes, "Dream Keeper."

51. Amitai F. Avi-Ram, "The Unreadable Black Body: 'Conventional' Poetic Form in the Harlem Renaissance," *Genders* 7 (1990): 39–43; Hughes, "Dream Keeper."

52. Langston Hughes, "Shadows," *Collected Poems*, 34.

53. Woods, 134. Woods makes this comment in reference to Cullen's poem "From the Dark Tower," which he reads as "celebrating the hidden 'twilight world' of homosexuality"; Countée Cullen, "From the Dark Tower," *My Soul's High Song*, 139.

54. For an example of contemporary portrayals of gay men, see André Tellier, *Twilight Men* (New York: Greenberg, 1931).

55. Langston Hughes, "Our Land," *Collected Poems*, 32–33.

56. Langston Hughes, "Joy," *Collected Poems*, 63.

57. Borden, 343.

58. Walt Whitman, "Song of Myself," *Walt Whitman: The Complete Poems*, ed. Francis Murphy (London: Penguin, 1975), 685.

59. Woods, 136.

60. Woods, 136.

61. Langston Hughes, "To Beauty," *Collected Poems*, 75.

62. Alan Richter, *Sexual Slang: A Compendium of Offbeat Words and Colorful Phrases from Shakespeare to Today* (1993; New York: HarperPerennial, 1995), 242.

63. Richard Bruce [Richard Bruce Nugent], "Smoke, Lilies and Jade," *Fire!!* 1 (1926): 33–39.

64. Hughes, "To Beauty."

65. Woods, 139.

66. Hughes, *Big Sea*, 98.

67. Hughes, *Big Sea*, 10.

68. Chauncey, 16.

69. Chauncey, 78.

70. Cullen, letter to Locke, June 17, 1923, ALP, 164–22, MSRC; Cullen, letter to Locke, November 24, 1923, ALP, 164–22, MSRC.

71. Richard Bruce Nugent, "Lighting FIRE!!," insert to *Fire!!* (1926; Metuchen, N.J.: Fire!!, 1981), n.p.

72. Chauncey, 78.

73. Alan Sinfield observes this definition of effeminacy for the late nineteenth century, but it also seems valid here. Sinfield, 15.

74. Hughes, *Big Sea*, 127; Judith Butler, *Gender Trouble* (New York: Routledge, 1990), 140.

75. Chauncey, 79.

76. Chauncey, 80.

77. Butler, 136.

78. Hughes, *Big Sea*, 108.

79. Hughes, *Big Sea*, 4, 5.

80. Langston Hughes, "The Little Virgin," *Messenger*, November 1927: 327.

81. Hughes, *Big Sea*, 114–15.

82. Rampersad, *The Life*, 1: 215–22.

83. Hughes, "Little Virgin," 327.

84. Walt Whitman, "For You O Democracy" [1867], *Walt Whitman*, 150.

85. Jacob Stockinger, quoted in Thomas E. Yingling, *Hart Crane and the Homosexual Text: New Thresholds, New Anatomies* (Chicago: University of Chicago Press, 1990), 27; Nero, 194. For Hughes's holding on to Whitman's *Leaves of Grass*, see Rampersad, *The Life*, 1: 72.

86. Langston Hughes, "Long Trip," *Collected Poems*, 97.

87. Tracy, 180, 194.

88. Borden, 344.

89. Chidi Ikonné, *From Du Bois to Van Vechten: The Early New Negro Literature, 1903–1926*, Contributions in Afro-American and African Studies 60 (Westport, Conn.: Greenwood, 1981), 166–67; Langston Hughes, "Bodies in the Moonlight," *Messenger*, April 1927: 105–106; Langston Hughes, "Luani of the Jungles," *Harlem* 1 (1928): 7–11. Rampersad also underlines the exceptional, "franker revelation of aspects of the libido" evident in these stories. Rampersad, *The Life*, 1: 139.

90. Hughes, "Bodies," 106; Hughes, "Luani," 9.

91. Woods, 128.

92. Langston Hughes, "When Sue Wears Red," *Collected Poems*, 30; Rampersad, *The Life*, 1: 37.

93. Hughes, "Bodies," 105.

94. Hughes, "Bodies," 105.

95. Langston Hughes, "The Young Glory of Him: A Tragic Romance on Tropic Seas," *Messenger*, June 1927: 177–78.

96. Hughes, "Young Glory," 177–78.

97. Hughes, "Young Glory," 177.

98. Hughes, *Big Sea*, 4.

99. Hughes, *Big Sea*, 111.

100. Hughes, *Big Sea*, 111.

101. Hughes, *Big Sea*, 112.

102. Hughes, *Big Sea*, 112.

103. Hughes, *Big Sea*, 112.

104. Hughes, "Young Sailor," *Collected Poems*, 62.

105. Woods, 130.

106. Langston Hughes, "Boy," *Carolina Magazine*, May 1928: 38.

107. See chapter 3, 88.

108. For sailors' sexual transgressions, see Chauncey, 78.

109. Langston Hughes, "Port Town," *Collected Poems*, 97.

110. Hughes, *Big Sea*, 107.

111. Woods, 130.

112. Chauncey, 178.

113. Hughes, "Water-Front Streets," *Collected Poems*, 96.

114. Woods, 129.

115. For the early-twentieth-century use of the term *gay* in a homosexual context, see Chauncey, 16–17.

116. Woods, 130.

117. Woods, 130.

118. Hughes, *Big Sea*, 7.

119. Hughes, *Big Sea*, 7.

120. Georges-Michel Sarotte, *Like a Brother, Like a Lover: Male Homosexuality in the American Novel and Theatre from Herman Melville to James Baldwin*, trans. Richard Miller (Garden City, N.Y.: Anchor-Doubleday, 1978), 73.

121. Hughes, "Little Virgin," 327; Herman Melville, *White Jacket, or The World in a Man-of-War* (1850; Boston: Page, 1950).

122. Hughes, "Little Virgin," 327; Herman Melville, *Redburn: His First Voyage* (1849; Boston: Page, 1924).

123. Hughes, "Little Virgin," 328.

124. Hughes, *Big Sea*, 4.

125. Hughes, *Big Sea*, 4.

126. Arnold Rampersad, introduction, *Big Sea*, xvi.

127. Hughes, *Big Sea*, 7.

128. Hughes, *Big Sea*, 8.

129. Locke, letter to Richard Jenkins, n.d., GCP, 145–25, MSRC; Hughes, *Big Sea*, 8; David Bergman, "The African and the Pagan in Gay Black Literature," *Sexual Sameness: Textual Differences in Lesbian and Gay Writing*, ed. Joseph Bristow (London: Routledge, 1992), 165. Bergman also lists another incident as indicating sexual ambiguity: In *The Big Sea*, Hughes cannot specify whether Mohammedans are male or female. Bergman, 164–65.

130. Rampersad, *The Life* 1: 80. Bergman suggests that Hughes's disgust was perhaps caused "by the openness of the sodomy. Or was it the low wages?" Bergman, 164.

131. Hughes, *Big Sea*, 226.

132. Langston Hughes, *Little Ham* [1935], *Five Plays of Langston Hughes*, ed. Webster Smalley (Bloomington: Indiana University Press, 1968), 63, 71; Langston Hughes, *Not Without Laughter* (1931; New York: Simon & Schuster, 1995), 244, 105.

133. Borden, 335, 338.

134. Langston Hughes, "Lover's Return," *Collected Poems*, 125; Langston Hughes, "Hard Daddy," *Collected Poems*, 124.

135. Tracy, 117.

136. hooks, 194; Langston Hughes, "Suicide," *Collected Poems*, 82; Langston Hughes, "Lament over Love," *Collected Poems*, 69–70; Langston Hughes, "Midwinter Blues," *Collected Poems*, 65.

137. Langston Hughes, "Young Prostitute," *Collected Poems*, 33; Langston Hughes, "Ruby Brown," *Collected Poems*, 73.

138. Langston Hughes, "Café: 3 a.m.," *Collected Poems*, 406; Langston Hughes, "Blessed Assurance," *Something in Common and Other Stories* (New York: Hill, 1963), 227–32.

139. Borden, 339.

140. Borden, 339.

141. Hughes, "Blessed Assurance," 227.

142. Hughes, "Blessed Assurance," 227.

143. Rampersad, *The Life* 2: 334; Nero, 192.

144. Borden, 339.

145. Hughes, "Blessed Assurance," 228.

146. Borden, 339.

147. Hughes, *Little Ham*, 68–69. Berry also mentions Hughes's stereotyping in *Little Ham* (Berry, 243). For the connection between the concept of effeminacy and misogyny, see Sinfield, 15.

148. Jean Wagner, *Black Poets of the United States: From Paul Laurence Dunbar to Langston Hughes*, trans. Kenneth Douglas (Urbana: University of Illinois Press, 1973), 425: Hughes "established as his specialty the portrayal of a half-world peopled with unwed mothers and prostitutes, pimps, homosexuals, and drug addicts, together with drunks, gamblers, bad men, and killers."

149. Hughes, *Not Without*, 217.

150. Hughes, *Not Without*, 217.

151. Hughes, *Not Without*, 282; Roger Rosenblatt, *Black Fiction* (Cambridge, Mass.: Harvard University Press, 1974), 82.

152. Hughes, *Not Without*, 283.

153. Hughes, *Not Without*, 282; Buddy Browning, "Fag Balls Exposed," *Broadway Brevities*, March 14, 1932: 12. The newspaper comment is made in reference to drag ball participants and visitors yet seems applicable here, as Sandy's attacker displays obvious signs of gender inversion and could thus be regarded as a fairy.

154. Hughes, *Not Without*, 283.

155. Hughes, *Big Sea*, 156.

156. Rampersad, *The Life* 1: 85; "Women Rivals for Affection of Another Woman Battles with Knives, and One Has Head Almost Severed from Body," *New York Age*, November 27, 1926: 1. See also chapter 1, 17–20.

157. Hughes, *Big Sea*, 156.

158. Hughes, *Big Sea*, 156–57.

159. Rampersad, *The Life* 1: 221.

160. Darwin T. Turner, "Langston Hughes as Playwright," *Roots and Rituals: The Search for Identity—The Image Makers: Plays and Playwrights*, ed. Errol Hill (Englewood Cliffs, N.J.: Prentice-Hall, 1980), 144, 147.

161. Compare with Thurman as discussed in chapter 2, 44.

162. Jemie Onwuchewka, *Langston Hughes: An Introduction to the Poetry* (New York: Columbia University Press, 1976), 24; Allen D. Prowle, "Langston Hughes," *Poetry and Drama*, ed. C.W.E. Bigsby (Deland, Fla.: Everett-Edwards, 1969), 81.

163. Geraldyn Dismond, "Social Snapshots," *Inter-State Tattler*, February 22, 1929: 5.

164. Hughes, *Big Sea*, 273.

165. Jonathan Dollimore, *Sexual Dissidence: Augustine to Wilde, Freud to Foucault* (Oxford: Clarendon, 1991), 31.

166. " 'Y'Mus Come Ovah!' Sez Cops," *Inter-State Tattler*, March 10, 1932: 2.

167. Reimonenq, 375.

5. CLAUDE MCKAY

1. Steven Watson, *The Harlem Renaissance: Hub of African-American Culture, 1920–1930* (New York: Pantheon, 1995), 32.

2. Langston Hughes, "The Twenties: Harlem and Its Negritude," *African Forum* 1 (1966): 11; Claude McKay, *Harlem Shadows* (New York: Harcourt, 1922). McKay had already published another sonnet collection, *Spring in New Hampshire, and other poems* (London: Richards, 1920), which was, however, almost completely contained in *Harlem Shadows*.

3. Claude McKay, *Home to Harlem* [1928], *Classic Fiction of the Harlem Renaissance*, ed. William L. Andrews (New York: Oxford University Press, 1994), 105–237; Claude McKay, *Banjo: A Story without a Plot* (1929; New York: Harcourt, 1957); Carl Van Vechten, *Nigger Heaven* (New York: Knopf, 1926).

4. George W. Jacobs [George S. Schuyler], "New Yorker Flays McKay's Book, 'Home to Harlem,' " *Pittsburgh Courier*, April 7, 1928, section 2: 8.

5. Harold Jackman, letter to McKay, April 22, 1928, CMKP, 3, BRBML.

6. P. S. Chauhan, "Rereading Claude McKay," *CLA Journal* 34 (1990): 71.

7. McKay retrospectively stated: "I was an older man and not regarded as a member of the renaissance. . . ." Claude McKay, *A Long Way from Home* (1937; New York: Harcourt, 1970), 321.

8. This interest seems also evident in McKay's visit to the Soviet Union in 1922–1923, during which he attended the Fourth Congress of the Third Communist

International. Wayne F. Cooper, *Claude McKay: Rebel Sojourner in the Harlem Renaissance—A Biography* (New York: Schocken, 1990), 171–92.

9. Claude McKay, "Birthright" [1922], review of *Birthright*, by T. S. Stribling, *The Passion of Claude McKay: Selected Poetry and Prose, 1912–1948*, ed. Wayne F. Cooper (New York: Schocken, 1973), 74.

10. McKay, letter to Jackman, May 9, 1928, CMKP, 6, BRBML.

11. Claude McKay, *Songs of Jamaica* (Kingston, Jamaica: Gardner, 1912); Claude McKay, *Constab Ballads* (London: Watts, 1912).

12. McKay, letter to Jackman, January 14, 1927, CMKP, 6, BRBML.

13. McKay, letter to Arthur A. Schomburg, n.d. [1925], AASP, 5, SCRBC.

14. Cooper, *Rebel Sojourner*, 150; Henry Lee Moon, "Claude McKay Comes Home to Harlem after Spending Ten-Year Exile on 2 Continents," *New York Amsterdam News*, February 7, 1934: 1. Unknown to most, McKay had married in 1914 but had quickly separated from his wife. Cooper, *Rebel Sojourner*, 70–76.

15. Alain Locke, "Spiritual Truancy," review of *A Long Way from Home*, by Claude McKay, *New Challenge* 2 (1937): 84.

16. McKay rejected White's advice to submit his manuscripts to the recently established Viking Press: "I should prefer a more underlined firm." McKay, letter to Walter White, June 15, 1925, WWP, 93, NAACP, LC.

17. McKay, letter to White, n.d. [1925?], WWP, 93, NAACP, LC. For one example of many more "begging letters" McKay sent from Europe, see copy of McKay, letter to Com. Campbell, January 7, 1924, WWP, 91, NAACP, LC.

18. McKay, letter to Jackman, March 31, 1928, CMKP, 6, BRBML.

19. Harper and Brothers Publishers, letter to William Aspenwall Bradley, July 11, 1927, CMKP, 2, BRBML; Block, quoted in McKay, letter to White, September 7 [1925?], WWP, 93, NAACP, LC.

20. McKay, letter to Schomburg, August 14, 1924, AASP, 5, SCRBC.

21. McKay, letter to White, October 15, 1925, WWP, 93, NAACP, LC. This is again a reference to "Color Scheme." McKay and Eastman remained close friends.

22. Harper and Brothers, letter to Bradley, July 11, 1927, CMKP, 2, BRBML.

23. Cooper, *Rebel Sojourner*, 253–54. McKay insisted on the restoration of his original text.

24. Claude McKay, "Romance in Marseilles," typescript, 1930, CMKP, 6, SCRBC. McKay changed the working title of this manuscript several times. Cooper, *Rebel Sojourner*, 286. The novel is scheduled to be published in 2003 by the University of Exeter Press as *Romance in Marseille, and three short stories*.

25. Cooper, *Rebel Sojourner*, 268–69.

26. Watson 32; Emmanuel Nelson, "Critical Deviance: Homophobia and the Reception of James Baldwin's Fiction," *Journal of American Culture* 14 (1991): 92.

27. Cooper, *Rebel Sojourner*, 75. Cooper also considers bisexuality an option.

28. Charles Ford, letter to McKay, August 8, 1938, CMKP, 2, BRBML.

29. It must be emphasized that the correspondence dates from 1938. This can be of significance, considering McKay's sometimes dramatic changes in attitude—for instance, concerning religion. Cooper, *Rebel Sojourner*, 351–69.

30. Tyrone Tillery, *Claude McKay: A Black Poet's Struggle for Identity* (Amherst: University of Massachusetts Press, 1992), 12.

31. McKay, *Long Way*, 243.

32. Carpenter purchased a farm outside Sheffield, and Jekyll left Europe to live in the mountains of Jamaica. Cooper can only speculate about Jekyll's same-sex interests, yet the parallels between Jekyll's and Carpenter's lifestyles point in such a direction. Cooper, *Rebel Sojourner*, 23–24, 29–30. For Carpenter, see Jeffrey Weeks,

Coming Out: Homosexual Politics in Britain from the Nineteenth Century to the Present, rev. ed. (London: Quartet, 1990), chapter 6.

33. Cooper, *Rebel Sojourner*, 30–31.

34. Claude McKay, *My Green Hills of Jamaica and Five Jamaican short Stories*, ed. Mervyn Morris (Kingston, Jamaica: Heinemann [Caribbean], 1979).

35. McKay, *Green Hills*, 66.

36. McKay, *Green Hills*, 67.

37. McKay, *Green Hills*, 68.

38. Eve Kosofsky Sedgwick, *Between Men* (New York: Columbia University Press, 1985), 1–5; Cooper, *Rebel Sojourner*, 95–96. Interestingly, Jean Toomer similarly formed many such intense male bonds. See for instance the relationship between Toomer and the white writer Waldo Frank. Siobhan B. Somerville, *Queering the Color Line: Race and the Invention of Homosexuality in American Culture* (Durham, N.C.: Duke University Press), 158–60.

39. There is evidence of the by now familiar coding: McKay, for instance, speaks of a "fraternal understanding" between him and Locke. McKay, letter to Locke, June 4, 1927, ALP, 164–67, MSRC. Discussing difficulties Locke encountered with a male partner, McKay suggested a "highly preserved and guarded emotion" as the only way to cope and concentrate on one's creative potential. McKay, letter to Locke, May 1, 1924, ALP, 164–67, MSRC.

40. Michel Fabre, *From Harlem to Paris: Black American Writers in France, 1840–1980* (Urbana: University of Illinois Press, 1991), 99. Locke usually seems to have chosen men from student circles as sexual partners.

41. McKay, *Long Way*, 46.

42. McKay, *Long Way*, 49, 50.

43. McKay, *Long Way*, 51.

44. McKay, *Long Way*, 313. For a similar comment on Locke's alleged weakness, see McKay, letter to Locke, October 7, 1924, ALP, 164–67, MSRC.

45. McKay, *Long Way*, 252.

46. Alan Sinfield, *Cultural Politics—Queer Reading* (Philadelphia: University of Pennsylvania Press; London: Routledge, 1994), 35. Sinfield underlines that "it is un-American not to be manly."

47. McKay, *Long Way*, 108.

48. For E. M. Forster's and Carpenter's linking of the two issues, see John Fletcher, "Forster's Self-Erasure: Maurice and the Scene of Masculine Love," *Sexual Sameness: Textual Differences in Lesbian and Gay Writing*, ed. Joseph Bristow (London: Routledge, 1992), 64–90; Alan Sinfield, *The Wilde Century: Effeminacy, Oscar Wilde and the Queer Moment* (London: Cassell, 1994), chapter 6.

49. McKay, *Long Way*, 360.

50. McKay, letter to White, September 7 [1925?], WWP, 93, NAACP, LC. See also Claude McKay, "A Negro to His Critics," *New York Herald Tribune Books*, March 6, 1932: 1, in which he suggests that "respectable Negro opinion and criticism" tend to "emasculate the colored aspirant."

51. Cooper, *Rebel Sojourner*, 101; Wallace Thurman, "Negro Poets and Their Poetry" [1928], *Black Writers Interpret the Harlem Renaissance*, ed. Cary D. Wintz (New York: Garland, 1996), 78. Thurman here specifically refers to McKay's poem "If We Must Die" (1919).

52. Cooper, *Rebel Sojourner*, 131.

53. Cooper, *Rebel Sojourner*, 131; Josephine Herbst, quoted in Tillery, 12.

54. Two poems which are set into a racial context and seem furthermore given to gay readings are discussed later in this chapter. A short discussion of McKay's pre-Renaissance poetic work also follows.

55. Cooper, *Rebel Sojourner*, 75. Note A. L. McLeod's observation that only three poems in McKay's poetry volumes clearly establish a heterosexual context. A. L. McLeod, "An Ideal Woman: Claude McKay's Composite Image," *Claude McKay: Centennial Studies*, ed. A. L. McLeod (New Delhi, India: Sterling, 1992), 73.

56. Claude McKay, "Rest in Peace," Claude McKay, *Selected Poems of Claude McKay* (New York: Bookman, 1953), 77.

57. Cooper, *Rebel Sojourner*, 75.

58. Cooper, *Rebel Sojourner*, 75.

59. Claude McKay, "The Barrier," *Selected Poems*, 80; Claude McKay, "One Year After," *Selected Poems*, 105. The latter poem consists of two separate sections.

60. Gregory Woods, "Gay Re-readings of the Harlem Renaissance Poets," *Critical Essays: Gay and Lesbian Writers of Color*, ed. Emmanuel S. Nelson (New York: Harrington Park-Haworth, 1993), 134. Woods here refers to "The Barrier." McKay, "One Year After."

61. Woods, 134.

62. Alexander Gumby, "To . . . . You," unpublished typescript, n.d., AGC, "Gumby's Autobiography & Scrapbook," scrapbook 2, CURBML.

63. Claude McKay, "Courage," *Selected Poems*, 109. Woods also suggests the validity of racial and gay readings. Woods, 134–35.

64. Walt Whitman, *Leaves of Grass (I) and Democratic Vistas* (London: Dent, 1912), 348.

65. Claude McKay, "If We Must Die," *Selected Poems*, 36; McKay, "Courage," 109. Woods links "If We Must Die" to "homosexual oppression." Woods, 133.

66. Claude McKay, "I Know My Soul," *Selected Poems*, 56.

67. Amitai F. Avi-Ram, "The Unreadable Black Body: Conventional Poetic Form in the Harlem Renaissance," *Genders* 7 (1990): 36.

68. McKay, "One Year After," 105.

69. McKay, *Long Way*, 150.

70. Claude McKay, "Honeymoon," "New Poems," unpublished typescript, n.d., CMKP, 10, BRBML, 39. Cooper lists a poem titled "Honeymoon" in his bibliography of McKay's works. I could not certify whether the typescript I had access to is identical with the poem published in *Milwaukee Arts Monthly* 1 (1922): 8.

71. Walt Whitman, "Song of Myself" [1855], *Walt Whitman: The Complete Poems*, ed. Francis Murphy (London: Penguin, 1975), 685.

72. Woods, 139; Alden Reimonenq, "The Harlem Renaissance," *The Gay and Lesbian Literary Heritage: A Reader's Companion to the Writers and Their Works, from Antiquity to the Present* (New York: Holt, 1995), 360.

73. Nathan Irvin Huggins, *Harlem Renaissance* (London: Oxford University Press, 1971), 219; Woods, 139.

74. Tracy Graham McCabe, "Resisting Primitivism: Race, Gender, and Power in Modernism and the Harlem Renaissance" (dissertation, University of Wisconsin-Madison, 1994), 3.

75. McCabe, 151.

76. McCabe, 2.

77. Timothy S. Chin, " 'Bullers' and 'Battymen': Contesting Homophobia in Black Popular Culture and Contemporary Caribbean Literature," *Callaloo* 20 (1997): 130.

78. Juda Charles Bennett, "Translating Race: The Passing Figure in American Literature" (dissertation, Washington University, 1994), 28.

79. McKay, *Home*, 220. The issue addressed in this song also features prominently in Wallace Thurman, *The Blacker the Berry* (1929; London: X Press, 1994).

80. Bennett, 28.

81. McKay, *Banjo*, 278. For another positive yet color-conscious description of a white man, see *Banjo*, 127.

82. McKay, *Banjo*, 112.

83. McKay, *Banjo*, 170, 255, and see 161–62.

84. For the link established between blackness and vitality, see Richard Dyer, *The Matter of Images: Essays on representations* (London: Routledge, 1993), 152–53.

85. Huggins, 124–25. Huggins specifically refers to *Home to Harlem*.

86. Chauhan comments that "[s]exual indulgence . . . [is] virtually the only activity permitted in this Harlem." Chauhan, 78.

87. McKay, *Banjo*, 212.

88. McKay, *Home*, 126. For McKay's use of food metaphors relating to Harlem and black women, see Sidney H. Bremer, "Home in Harlem, New York: Lessons from the Harlem Renaissance Writers," *PMLA* 105 (1990): 49. McKay admitted to a somewhat more positive portrayal of Harlem. McKay, letter to Jackman, March 31, 1928, CMKP, 6, BRBML.

89. McKay, *Banjo*, 235; McKay, *Long Way*, 277. On the group's Pan-African character, see James R. Giles, *Claude McKay*, Twayne United States Authors Series 271 (Boston: Twayne, 1976), 85.

90. McKay, *Banjo*, 57–58.

91. McKay, *Banjo*, 10; Aubrey Bowser, "Dirt for Art's Sake," review of *Home to Harlem*, by Claude McKay, *New York Amsterdam News*, March 21, 1928: 20. Note also Bennett's comment that Jake's "blackness is sexualized and he in turn sexualizes color." Bennett, 26.

92. Claude McKay, *Banana Bottom* (1933; New York: Harvest-Harcourt, 1961), 27. Jake and his partner Felice, in contrast, reproduce successfully.

93. Chin, 131.

94. Huggins, 123.

95. McKay, *Home*, 179.

96. McKay, *Home*, 180.

97. McKay, *Banjo*, 322; McKay, *Home*, 209; Barbara Griffin, "The Fragmented Vision of Claude McKay: A Study of His Works" (dissertation, University of Maryland-College Park, 1989), 236.

98. McKay, *Home*, 182.

99. For Ray's heterosexual desire see McKay, *Home*, 206; McKay, *Banjo*, 283. As will be discussed later, this does not imply that Ray is not same-sex-interested.

100. McKay, *Banjo*, 323.

101. McKay, *Banjo*, 164.

102. McKay, *Banjo*, 252; Michael B. Stoff, "Claude McKay and the Cult of Primitivism," *The Harlem Renaissance Remembered: Essays Edited with a Memoir*, ed. Arna Bontemps (New York: Dodd, 1972), 134, 138–39.

103. Jacobs [Schuyler].

104. McKay, *Banjo*, 252; Jacobs [Schuyler].

105. Jonathan Dollimore, *Sexual Dissidence: Augustine to Wilde, Freud to Foucault* (Oxford: Clarendon, 1991), 14.

106. McKay, *Banjo*, 252.

107. McKay, *Banjo*, 314. For a similar statement, see McKay, *Home*, 178.

108. McKay, *Home*, 216, and see 215–16; Robert M. Greenberg, "Idealism and Realism in the Fiction of Claude McKay," *CLA Journal* 24 (1981): 247.

109. McKay, *Banjo*, 325.

110. McKay, *Banjo*, 253.

111. McKay, *Home*, 146.

112. McKay, *Home*, 146.

113. McKay, *Home*, 118; McKay, *Banjo*, 105.

114. McKay, *Banana Bottom*, 175.

115. McKay, *Banana Bottom*, 174–75; Chin, 131.

116. Griffin, 166.

117. McKay, *Long Way*, 337.

118. McKay, *Banjo*, 206.

119. McKay, *Banjo*, 206. McKay includes an example of such a racially motivated inhibition with the brothel-keeper Madame Laura, who "ain't got no loving inclination for any skin but chocolate." McKay, *Home*, 182.

120. Heather A. Hathaway, "Cultural Crossings: Migration, Generation, and Gender in Writings by Claude McKay and Paule Marshall" (dissertation, Harvard University, 1993), 84.

121. McKay, *Banjo*, 205.

122. McKay, *Home*, 120.

123. McKay, *Home*, 118. Rose wants to be hit by Jake. She is portrayed as inferior to the "brown" Felice: "[Rose's] spirit lacked the charm and verve, the infectious joy." McKay, *Home*, 120; Giles, 79.

124. McKay, *Banjo*, 208.

125. McKay, *Banjo*, 208.

126. McKay, *Banjo*, 209; Giles, 79.

127. McKay, *Banjo*, 209.

128. McKay, *Banjo*, 214.

129. McKay, *Banjo*, 214.

130. Griffin, 251.

131. McKay, *Banjo*, 211. For an example of McKay's use of animal imagery in a black context, see McKay, *Home*, 236.

132. McKay, *Banjo*, 211.

133. McKay, *Banjo*, 211. Note the similarity of these comments to those made by black intellectuals, such as James Weldon Johnson, who feared for the survival of African Americans' allegedly wholesome sexuality. See chapter 1, 21–22.

134. McKay, *Banjo*, 213.

135. McKay, *Banjo*, 211.

136. McKay, *Long Way*, 316.

137. McKay, *Long Way*, 316. The term *morale* is used by McKay. For the link between steam baths and a homosexual subculture as evident in the case of New York, see George Chauncey, *Gay New York: Gender, Urban Culture and the Making of the Gay Male World, 1890–1940* (New York: Basic, 1994), 207–26.

138. Claude McKay, "Boy Prostitute," unpublished manuscript, n.d., ALP, 164–86, MSRC. It must be noted that this copy of the poem is in Locke's handwriting, but the name *Claude McKay* is noted below the poem. In light of McKay and Locke's "fraternal understanding," it is possible that McKay gave the poem to Locke, who copied it onto another sheet, maybe to circulate it among other members of his gay network—apparently a common practice.

139. Claude McKay, "Alfonso, Dressing to Wait At Table, Sings," *Selected Poems*, 76. The poem's title is abbreviated in McKay's *Selected Poems*, in which it is, deviating from its original as published in *Harlem Shadows*, listed as "Alfonso, Dressing to Wait At Table." Woods reads this poem in a homoerotic context. Woods, 131–32.

140. McKay, "Boy Prostitute."

141. McKay, *Home*, 184–85. McKay fell ill with syphilis in 1923. Cooper, *Rebel Sojourner*, 199–200. It is furthermore interesting to note that he in 1920 described

syphilis as a "disease peculiar to white and yellow peoples; where it is known among the blacks it has been carried thither by the whites." Claude McKay, "A Black Man Replies," letter [1920], *The Passion of Claude McKay*, 56.

142. Chin, 130, 131. As an example, Chin refers to Squire Gensir, a white middle-aged English character in *Banana Bottom*, who seems clearly modeled after Walter Jekyll. This character, however, is, in line with McKay's intimate and apparently happy relationship with Jekyll, portrayed positively. His same-sex interest may be alluded to implicitly—he describes himself as "not a marrying man"—yet unlike, for instance, the visitors of bathhouses or the occultists McKay depicts, he is in no way linked to "perversion."

143. Chin, 130–32.

144. McKay, *Home*, 139.

145. McKay, *Home*, 139.

146. McKay, *Home*, 108.

147. Claude McKay, "Harlem Glory," typescript, n.d. [c. 1937–1940], CMKP, 2, SCRBC, 49. It is emphasized that the impersonator is not effeminate himself. There are also published versions of this novel, such as *Harlem Glory: A Fragment of Aframerican Life* (Chicago: Kerr, 1990). I quote from the typescript.

148. McKay, *Banjo*, 210.

149. McKay, "Romance in Marseilles," 157; McKay, *Banjo*, 196–97.

150. McKay, *Banjo*, 210.

151. McKay, *Home*, 115.

152. McKay, *Home*, 116.

153. McKay, *Home*, 144.

154. McKay, *Home*, 115.

155. McKay, *Banjo*, 196, 87, 87.

156. McKay, *Banjo*, 299.

157. Cooper, *Rebel Sojourner*, 268. Cooper describes a scene from "Romance in Marseilles" which, despite having some similarities to the one discussed here, nevertheless varies in several details. However, he also appears to have used the manuscript held at the SCRBC.

158. McKay, "Romance," 148, 123.

159. McKay, "Romance," 123.

160. McKay, "Romance," 156.

161. McKay, "Romance," 154.

162. McKay, "Romance," 156.

163. McKay, "Romance," 123.

164. McKay, "Romance," 159.

165. McKay, "Romance," 157.

166. McKay, "Romance," 160.

167. Weeks, 62.

168. McKay, *Home*, 139.

169. McKay, *Home*, 139.

170. Chauncey, 89.

171. McKay, *Home*, 207. Nevertheless, there appears to be some overlapping of their sexual interests, as "normal" men occasionally have sexual contacts with pansies.

172. Chauncey, 87.

173. McKay, *Home*, 138.

174. Chauncey, 87.

175. McKay, *Home*, 209, and see 197.

176. McKay, *Home*, 219, 138.

177. Alain Locke, letter to Charlotte Mason, n.d. [1928], ALP, 164–68, MSRC. Other white and black contemporaries made similar comments: Langston Hughes, letter to McKay, March 5, 1928, CMKP, 2, BRBML; John R. Chamberlain, "When Spring Comes to Harlem," review of *Home to Harlem*, by Claude McKay, *New York Times Book Review*, March 11, 1928: 5.

178. McKay paraphrased in J. A. Rogers, " 'Ahead of Its Time': McKay Defends Book, *Home to Harlem*," *New York Amsterdam News*, April 10, 1929: 20. For a similar statement, see McKay, quoted in Cooper, *Rebel Sojourner*, 221.

179. For the audience's potential knowledge about "wolves," see Bowser, who mentions "an invert capable of disinterested friendship" in his review of *Home to Harlem*.

180. McKay, *Home*, 224–25.

181. Susy's friend is described as "a putty-skinned mulattress with purple streaks on her face. Two of her upper front teeth had been knocked out and her lower lip slanted pathetically leftward." McKay, *Home*, 127.

182. McKay, *Home*, 126.

183. McKay, *Home*, 155.

184. McKay, *Long Way*, 310.

185. McKay, *Long Way*, 310.

186. McKay, *Long Way*, 310.

187. Lillian Faderman, *Surpassing the Love of Men: Romantic Friendship and Love Between Women from the Renaissance to the Present* (London: Junction, 1981), 17.

188. McKay, *Home*, 155.

189. McKay, "Romance," 70.

190. McKay, "Romance," 70.

191. Giles, 116; Claude McKay, "Highball," *Gingertown* (New York: Harper, 1932), 117, 130, 117.

192. Giles, 116.

193. McKay, "Highball," 106.

194. McKay, "Highball," 117.

195. McKay, "Highball," 128.

196. Joseph Sheridan Le Fanu, "Carmilla" [1872] (New York: Scholastic, 1971). One might get the impression that Myra is presented as guided by Dinah in her evil. Responsibility would thus to some extent be lifted from Myra's shoulders. This impression seems mainly linked to the fact that the story is told from the perspective of Nation, who for most of the story is convinced of his wife's innocence.

197. Giles, 74. It must be noted that McKay's portrayal of women seems transformed in *Banana Bottom*, in which female characters, as exemplified in Bita, the protagonist, are presented more positively and as reconciling figures.

198. For women as a foil, see Hathaway, 82.

199. Judith Butler, *Gender Trouble* (New York: Routledge, 1990), 140–41.

200. McKay, *Banjo*, 27.

201. Cora Kaplan, " 'A Cavern Opened in My Mind': The Poetics of Homosexuality and the Politics of Masculinity in James Baldwin," *Representing Black Men*, ed. Marcellus Blount and George P. Cunningham (New York: Routledge, 1996), 32.

202. McKay, *Home*, 149.

203. There is, however, a scene in *Banjo* in which a sailor hits and kicks a woman with Banjo and Ray's approval; but the woman is presented as "deserving" her physical punishment because of her provocation of the sailor. It would presumably have

been "unmanly" for him to endure the woman's behavior without retaliation. McKay, *Banjo*, 99–100.

204. McKay, *Home*, 149.

205. McKay, *Home*, 149.

206. McKay, *Home*, 149; Hazel V. Carby, "Policing the Black Woman's Body in an Urban Context," *Critical Inquiry* 18 (1992): 750.

207. Sweetmen are however once mentioned in a completely different context in *Banjo*, where Ray regards them as products of the corruption of black integrity. McKay, *Banjo*, 211–12.

208. McKay, *Home*, 143. As a consequence of his failure to dominate his woman, Zeddy discovers that "in his own circles in Harlem he had become something of a joke." McKay, *Home*, 137. The far more sophisticated "Yaller Prince" also eventually fails, as his lovers find out about his promiscuity. McKay, *Home*, 214–15.

209. McKay, *Home*, 120.

210. Hathaway, 82.

211. McKay, *Home*, 191.

212. McKay, *Home*, 200.

213. McKay, *Home*, 231.

214. McKay, *Home*, 187.

215. McKay, *Home*, 187; Butler, 140. Butler's italics.

216. McKay, *Banjo*, 306. Jake states that he "liked it."

217. Hathaway, 85.

218. McKay, *Banjo*, 98.

219. McKay, *Banjo*, 32.

220. Giles, 75. Note, however, that even a French prostitute can apparently sometimes "[rise] over her passion for gain." McKay, *Banjo*, 280.

221. McKay, *Banjo*, 206. For similar statements, see McKay, *Home*, 117, 131.

222. In his earlier poetic work, in contrast, McKay evokes an image of women as victims of capitalism—particularly in "Harlem Shadows" (1922). Claude McKay, "Harlem Shadows," *Selected Poems*, 60.

223. McKay, *Home*, 131.

224. McKay, *Banjo*, 206; Hathaway, 87. Jake even equates women with what he regards as cruel sex, deploring men's dependence on "[t]he wild, shrieking mad woman that is sex. . . ." McKay, *Home*, 232.

225. McKay, *Home*, 117. In *Home to Harlem* and *Banjo*, however, this does not imply what Chin in the context of his discussion of *Banana Bottom* describes as a reproductive norm set up by McKay. Chin, 131.

226. McKay, *Home*, 131; Giles, 74; McKay, *Home*, 232. For interracial clashes between men about women, see McKay, *Home*, 131, and McKay, *Banjo*, 36–37.

227. Claude McKay, "When I Pounded the Pavement," *Gingertown*, 203–20.

228. McKay, *Green Hills*, 67.

229. Sedgwick, 207.

230. McKay, "When I," 207.

231. McKay, "When I," 208.

232. McKay, "When I," 208.

233. McKay, "When I," 208.

234. Whitman, *Democratic Vistas*, 348.

235. Claude McKay, "To Bennie" (1912), *Songs of Jamaica*, 127; McKay, "Bennie's Departure" (1912), *Constab Ballads*, 15–22; McKay, "Consolation" (1912), *Constab Ballads*, 23–25.

236. Cooper, *Rebel Sojourner*, 46.

237. McKay, "When I," 208.

238. McKay, "When I," 209.

239. McKay, "When I," 203.

240. McKay, "When I," 212; Whitman, *Democratic Vistas*, 348.

241. McKay, *Banjo*, 32, and see 29–31, 46.

242. McKay, *Banjo*, 14.

243. McKay, *Home*, 168.

244. McKay, *Home*, 209. Billy claims that Ray and Jake are "soft."

245. McKay, *Home*, 209; McKay, *Banjo*, 292.

246. McKay, *Banjo*, 293.

247. McKay, *Banjo*, 34.

248. McKay, *Banjo*, 34.

249. McKay, *Banjo*, 34.

250. Claude McKay, "Sukee River," *Selected Poems*, 17; Claude McKay, "Home Thoughts," *Selected Poems*, 21.

251. McKay, "Sukee River," 17.

252. Woods describes this poem as a "celebration of the physical activities of boys." Woods, 136.

253. McKay, *Banjo*, 235.

254. McKay, *Home*, 166.

255. McKay, *Banjo*, 67, 284.

256. McKay, *Banjo*, 283. Ray has a similar drug-induced vision that involves "slim, naked negresses" but also "gleaming-skinned black boys bearing goblets of wine and obedient eunuchs waiting in the offing," which is described in McKay, *Home*, 166.

257. Claude McKay, "The Prince of Porto Rico," *Gingertown*, 32–54.

258. McKay, "Porto Rico," 32.

259. McKay, "Porto Rico," 33.

260. McKay, "Porto Rico," 33.

261. McKay, "Porto Rico," 40.

262. McKay, "Porto Rico," 38.

263. McKay, *Home*, 144.

264. Sedgwick, 2.

265. Sedgwick, 1.

266. For gay readings as "haunting possibilities" see Sinfield, *Cultural Politics*, 20.

267. George E. Kent, "The Soulful Way of Claude McKay," *Black World*, November 1970: 48.

268. McKay, *Banjo*, 326.

269. Kent, 48.

270. Cooper, *Rebel Sojourner*, 75; Chin, 129.

271. McCabe, 173.

272. Kobena Mercer, *Welcome to the Jungle: New Positions in Black Cultural Studies* (New York: Routledge, 1994), 158.

273. bell hooks, *Black Looks: Race and Representation* (Boston: South End, 1992), 98.

6. RICHARD BRUCE NUGENT

1. Mark Helbling and Bruce Kellner, "Nugent, Richard Bruce," *The Harlem Renaissance: A Historical Dictionary for the Era* (New York: Methuen; London: Routledge, 1987), 269.

2. RBNP/Tapes, #5.

3. Richard Bruce [Richard Bruce Nugent], "Smoke, Lilies and Jade," *Fire!!* 1 (1926): 33–39.

4. Bruce Nugent [Richard Bruce Nugent], "Sahdji," *The New Negro*, ed. Alain Locke (1925; New York: Atheneum, 1992), 113–14.

5. RBNP/Tapes, #7.

6. RBNP/Tapes, #7.

7. Thomas H. Wirth, introduction, *Gay Rebel of the Harlem Renaissance: Selections from the Work of Richard Bruce Nugent*, ed. Thomas H. Wirth (Durham, N.C.: Duke University Press, 2002), 41–42.

8. RBNP/Tapes, #6.

9. RBNP/Tapes, #7.

10. Thomas H. Wirth, "Richard Bruce Nugent," *Black American Literature Forum* 19 (1985): 16.

11. Nugent played a minor part in the successful production of the play *Porgy*— a time-consuming occupation, as the cast toured the United States and England in 1929. Wirth, introduction, 15.

12. RBNP/Notes, February 17, 1982; RBNP/Tapes, #8; Eric Garber, "Richard Bruce Nugent," *Afro-American Writers from the Harlem Renaissance to 1940*, Dictionary of Literary Biography 51 (Detroit: Gale, 1987), 213. See also David Levering Lewis, *When Harlem Was in Vogue* (New York: Knopf, 1981), 196, 150, where Lewis describes Nugent as a "self-conscious decadent" and an "*enfant terrible.*"

13. Carl Van Vechten, letter to Langston Hughes [1927], *Letters of Carl Van Vechten*, ed. Bruce Kellner (New Haven, Conn.: Yale University Press, 1987), 96.

14. James V. Hatch, "An Interview with Bruce Nugent—Actor, Artist, Writer, Dancer," *Artists and Influences* 1 (1982): 93.

15. Richard Bruce [Richard Bruce Nugent], "Shadow," *Opportunity*, October 1925: 296; RBNP/Tapes, #2.

16. RBNP/Tapes, #5, #6. Nugent, as should be noted, was deeply disappointed by Locke's rejection of his drawing.

17. Richard Bruce [Richard Bruce Nugent], "Richard Bruce," *Caroling Dusk: An Anthology of Verse by Negro Poets*, ed. Countee Cullen (New York: Harper, 1927), 206.

18. RBNP/Tapes, #7; Nugent, letter to Alain Locke, n.d. [January 24, 1929], ALP, 164–75, MSRC. Nugent here describes his creative process of drawing.

19. Nugent, letter to Locke, n.d., ALP, 164–75, MSRC.

20. RBNP/Tapes #10. Thurman lived together with his long-term white lover Harald Jan Stefansson but apparently also had female lovers. He insisted that he was not homosexual. Eleonore van Notten, *Wallace Thurman's Harlem Renaissance*, Costerius New Series 93 (Amsterdam: Rodopi, 1994), 205–207, 209–10.

21. Nugent, letter to Locke, n.d. [January 24, 1929], ALP, 164–75, MSRC.

22. RBNP/Notes, April 24, 1983; R[ichard] v[on] Krafft-Ebing, *Psychopathia Sexualis, with Especial Reference to Antipathic Sexual Instinct: A Medico-Forensic Study* (1892; London: Rebman, 1901). The book was first published in German in 1886.

23. Richard Bruce Nugent, "Gentleman Jigger," unpublished typescript, n.d., RBNP, chapter 1, 10.

24. RBNP/Tapes, #3.

25. RBNP/Notes, December 28, 1981. Nugent frequently used the name *Richard Bruce*, but he is also listed as *Bruce Nugent* and sometimes used pseudonyms such as *Gary George*. It is significant to note that Nugent's choice of the name *Richard*

Bruce only appears to be a sign of his willingness to adapt to social norms: While the name *Nugent* had no social cachet, *Bruce* indicated his link to the traditional Bruce family.

26. Personal communication with Thomas H. Wirth, February 15, 1999. For Nugent's heterosexual encounter, see RBNP/Tapes, #3.

27. Neil Miller, *Out of the Past: Gay and Lesbian History from 1869 to the Present* (London: Vintage, 1995), 139–40.

28. Wirth, introduction, 34–35.

29. RBNP/Tapes #2, #3.

30. Nugent, quoted in Charles Michael Smith, "Bruce Nugent: Bohemian of the Harlem Renaissance," *In the Life: A Black Gay Anthology*, ed. Joseph Beam (Boston: Alyson, 1986), 219.

31. RBNP/Notes, April 23, 1983.

32. RBNP/Tapes, #2. As Nugent recalled, his open pursuit of homosexual affairs was deemed too outrageous in Washington's black elite circles.

33. Nugent, "Gentleman," chapter 1, 10.

34. Nugent, letter to Locke, n.d. [January 24, 1929], ALP, 164–75, MSRC.

35. Garber, 213. Alden Reimonenq similarly assumes that "[t]he long life of Richard Bruce Nugent . . . produced very few literary monuments. . . ." Alden Reimonenq, "The Harlem Renaissance," *The Gay and Lesbian Heritage: A Reader's Guide to the Writers and Their Works, from Antiquity to the Present* (New York: Holt, 1995), 360.

36. Nugent, letter to Locke, n.d. [January 24, 1929], ALP, 164–75, MSRC.

37. Georgia Douglas Johnson, letter to Richard Bruce Nugent, n.d., AGC, scrapbook 101, CURBML; Richard Bruce Nugent, "Geisha Man," excerpt published in *Gay Rebel of the Harlem Renaissance*, 90–111; Richard Bruce Nugent, "Beyond Where the Star Stood Still," *Crisis*, December 1970: 405–408; communication with Wirth, March 3, 2002.

38. Nugent, letter to Johnson, n.d., GDJP, 162–1, MSRC.

39. Wirth, introduction, 61.

40. Richard Bruce Nugent, illustration [male head], *Opportunity*, March 1926: cover page.

41. RBNP/Notes, December 28, 1981. For Nugent's community involvement, see Wirth, introduction, 37.

42. RBNP/Tapes, #4; RBNP/Tapes, #1.

43. For "passing" experiences from a female perspective, see, for example, Jessie Fauset, *Plum Bun: A Novel without a Moral* (New York: Stokes, 1929), and Nella Larsen, *Passing* (New York: Knopf, 1929).

44. RBNP/Tapes, #5. For a fictional treatment of intraracial prejudices, see Wallace Thurman, *The Blacker the Berry* (1929; London: X Press, 1994).

45. The series is printed in Wirth, *Gay Rebel of the Harlem Renaissance*, 67–70.

46. Nugent, quoted in Thomas H. Wirth, "FIRE!! in Retrospect," insert to *Fire!!* (1926; Metuchen, N.J.: Fire!!, 1981), n.p. See also Nugent's depiction of the scene with Du Bois in Jeff Kisseloff, *You Must Remember This: An Oral History of Manhattan from the 1890s to World War II* (San Diego: Harcourt, 1989), 288, in which he recalls that Du Bois made a specific reference to homosexuality.

47. Nugent, "Sahdji," 113.

48. Nugent, "Sahdji," 113.

49. Richard Bruce Nugent, "Bastard Song," *Gay Rebel of the Harlem Renaissance*, 89–90. It is unclear when exactly the poem was written (presumably around 1930).

50. RBNP/Tapes, #9.

51. Nugent, "Bastard Song," 90.

52. Nugent, "Bastard Song," 90.

53. Nugent, "Bastard Song," 90.

54. Nugent, "Bastard Song," 90.

55. Nugent, "Bastard Song," 89.

56. See, for instance, Edward Carpenter's *The Intermediate Sex: A Study of Some Transitional Types of Men and Women* (London: Swan; Manchester: Clarke, 1908).

57. Bruce, "Shadow."

58. Gregory Woods, "Gay Re-readings of the Harlem Renaissance Poets," *Critical Essays: Gay and Lesbian Writers of Color*, ed. Emmanuel S. Nelson (New York: Harrington Park-Haworth, 1993), 127.

59. RBNP/Tapes, #2.

60. Ralph Matthews, "Are Pansies People?" *Baltimore Afro-American*, April 2, 1932: 3.

61. Manthia Diawara, "The Absent One: The Avant-Garde and the Black Imaginary in *Looking for Langston*," *Representing Black Men*, ed. Marcellus Blount and George P. Cunningham (New York: Routledge, 1996), 208; *Looking for Langston*, dir. Isaac Julien, Sankofa, 1989.

62. Nugent, "Smoke," 38.

63. Nugent, "Smoke," 34.

64. RBNP/Tapes, #2.

65. Richard Bruce Nugent, "Tunic with a Thousand Pleats," unpublished typescript, n.d., RBNP; Richard Bruce Nugent, "The Now Discordant Song of Bells," *Gay Rebel of the Harlem Renaissance*, 122–30.

66. Nugent, "Tunic," 16.

67. Nugent, "Tunic," 7, 8; Nugent, "Bells," 126, 127.

68. Nugent, "Bells," 129, 128.

69. Nugent, "Bells," 127; Nugent, "Tunic," 5.

70. Nugent, "Tunic," 5.

71. Nugent, "Tunic," 9.

72. Nugent, "Bells," 126.

73. Nugent, "Bells," 124.

74. Nugent, "Bells," 128; Joris-Karl Huysmans, *Against Nature (A rebours)*, trans. Margaret Mauldon, ed. Nicholas White (1884; Oxford: Oxford University Press, 1998).

75. Théophile Gautier, quoted in Holbrook Jackson, *The Eighteen Nineties: A Review of Art and Ideas at the Close of the Nineteenth Century* (1913; Hassocks, England: Harvester, 1976), 136.

76. Nugent, "Beyond," 407, 406, 406, 406, 407, respectively. The biblical figure Caspar is spelled "Casper" by Nugent. For another example of a play of colors, see Richard Bruce Nugent, "Slender Length of Beauty," *Gay Rebel of the Harlem Renaissance*, 130–39, particularly the description of Salome's dance, 137–38.

77. Jackson, 138.

78. Richard Bruce Nugent, "Tree with Kerioth-Fruit," *Gay Rebel of the Harlem Renaissance*, 139–46.

79. Nugent, quoted in Smith, 214. Nugent makes this comment in reference to "Smoke, Lilies and Jade."

80. Richard Bruce Nugent, "And Rose (McClendon)," unpublished typescript, n.d., RBNP, 1.

81. Nugent, "Smoke," 37.

82. Nugent, "Bells," 126, 123; Nugent, "Beyond," 408.

83. Nugent, "Beyond," 405–408.

84. Jesus is described as a "poet." Nugent, "Kerioth-Fruit," 140.

85. Nugent, "Kerioth-Fruit," 140.

86. Nugent, "Kerioth-Fruit," 141.

87. Nugent, "Kerioth-Fruit," 141.

88. Nugent, "Kerioth-Fruit," 140.

89. Nugent, "Kerioth-Fruit," 140.

90. Nugent, "Kerioth-Fruit," 144.

91. Nugent, "Kerioth-Fruit," 144.

92. Nugent, "Kerioth-Fruit," 143.

93. Nugent, "Kerioth-Fruit," 143.

94. Xavier Mayne [Edward Irenaeus Prime Stevenson], *The Intersexes: A History of Simisexualism as a Problem in Social Life* (n.p.: privately printed, 1908), 259. For further information on Stevenson and *The Intersexes*, see Byrne R. S. Fone, *A Road to Stonewall: Male Homosexuality and Homophobia in English and American Literature, 1750–1969* (New York: Twayne, 1995), 195–201.

95. Nugent, "Kerioth-Fruit," 143.

96. Wirth, introduction, 45.

97. Nugent, "Kerioth-Fruit," 139.

98. Nugent, "Kerioth-Fruit," 143.

99. Nugent, "Kerioth-Fruit," 144.

100. Nugent, "Kerioth-Fruit," 144.

101. Nugent, "Bells," 128.

102. Personal communication with Wirth, February 15, 1999.

103. Nugent, "Kerioth-Fruit," 145.

104. Nugent, "Kerioth-Fruit," 141.

105. Wirth, introduction, 45.

106. Nugent, "Bells," 128, 130.

107. Nugent, "Bells," 130.

108. Michael L. Cobb, "Insolent Racing, Rough Narrative: The Harlem Renaissance's Impolite Queers," *Callaloo* 23 (2000): 343, 344.

109. Richard Bruce Nugent, "I Am Twenty Five," unpublished typescript, n.d. [c. 1931], RBNP; "Geisha Man," 91.

110. Nugent, "Geisha Man," 91. There is also a strong aural level to Kondo's perception of male bodies. See, for instance, "Geisha Man," 91: "Music is beauty in tones, and a body is one tone. Oh, to make a searing chord! A searing chord of bodies garnered from the night."

111. Nugent, "Geisha Man," 91.

112. Nugent, "Gentleman Jigger," "Orini" excerpt, 1.

113. Nugent, "Smoke," 37.

114. Wirth, introduction, 44. Wirth refers to "Smoke, Lilies and Jade."

115. Nugent, "Geisha Man," 99.

116. Nugent, "Smoke," 38; Nugent, "Geisha Man," 108.

117. Nugent, "Smoke," 37.

118. Nugent, "Smoke," 38.

119. Nugent, "Geisha Man," 97, 101, and see 106.

120. Nugent, "Geisha Man," 99.

121. Nugent, "Geisha Man," 93.

122. Nugent, "Geisha Man," 103.

123. Nugent, "Geisha Man," 108.

124. RBNP/Tapes, #9; RBNP/Notes, April 23, 1983; Nugent, letter to Locke, n.d., ALP, 164–75, MSRC.

125. Helbling and Kellner; Wirth, "Nugent," *Black American Literature Forum*, 16.

126. Nugent, "Smoke," 36.

127. Nugent, "Geisha Man," 106.

128. Nugent, "Geisha Man," 97.

129. Shawn Stewart Ruff, introduction, *Go the Way Your Blood Beats: An Anthology of Lesbian and Gay Fiction by African-American Writers*, ed. Shawn Stewart Ruff (New York: Holt, 1996), xxvi.

130. Nugent, "Smoke," 39; Nugent, "Geisha Man," 97: "It's very possible for one person to care for more than one."

131. RBNP/Tapes, #8.

132. Fone, 272.

133. RBNP/Tapes, #7.

134. Wirth, introduction, 28–32. As Alan Sinfield points out, it must be noted that nineteenth-century writers involved in the aesthetic movement did not necessarily work within a modern sexual framework, which makes the assumption of their use of a "coded language" a hazardous venture. Alan Sinfield, *The Wilde Century: Effeminacy, Oscar Wilde and the Queer Moment* (London: Cassell, 1994), 89–105.

135. Edmund Wilson, *The Shores of Light: A Literary Chronicle of the Twenties and Thirties* (London: Allen, 1952), 70.

136. Ellis Hanson, *Decadence and Catholicism* (Cambridge, Mass.: Harvard University Press, 1997), 23.

137. Sinfield, 96.

138. Garber, 220.

139. Lewis, 197.

140. Garber, 220; Seth Clark Silberman, "Lighting the Harlem Renaissance aFire!!: Embodying Richard Bruce Nugent's Bohemian Politic," *The Greatest Taboo: Homosexuality in Black Communities*, ed. Delroy Constanine-Simms (Los Angeles: Alyson, 2001), 267.

141. Cobb, 345.

142. Cobb, 345.

143. Nugent, "Smoke," 39.

144. Nugent, "Geisha Man," 109.

145. Nugent, "Geisha Man," 109.

146. Nugent, "Geisha Man," 91.

147. André Tellier, *Twilight Men* (New York: Greenberg, 1931).

148. Nugent, "Geisha Man," 100.

149. Nugent, "Geisha Man," 91.

150. Nugent, "Geisha Man," 91.

151. Nugent, "Geisha Man," 91. For a discussion of "Tableau," see chapter 3, 65–67.

152. Nugent, "Geisha Man," 91.

153. RBNP/Tapes, #10.

154. Nugent, "Geisha Man," 97.

155. Nugent, "Geisha Man," 93.

156. Nugent, "Geisha Man," 97.

157. Nugent, "Smoke," 38.

158. Nugent, "Geisha Man," 94.

159. Richard Bruce Nugent, "Who Asks This Thing?" *Gay Rebel of the Harlem Renaissance*, 90.

160. Sinfield, 98.

161. Nugent, "Smoke," 37; Nugent, "Geisha Man," 99, 106, 107.

162. Richard Bruce Nugent, "Narcissus," *Trend* 1 (1933): 127.

163. Julian Carter, "Normality, Whiteness, Authorship: Evolutionary Sexology and the Primitive Pervert," *Science and Homosexualities*, ed. Vernon A. Rosario (New York: Routledge, 1997), 164. Carter partially paraphrases Barbara Spackman.

164. Algernon Charles Swinburne, "Hermaphroditus," *Poems and Ballads* (London: Hotten, 1866), 91–93.

165. Carpenter.

166. Nugent, "Smoke," 35.

167. Nugent, "Smoke," 35.

168. Nugent, "Geisha Man," 101.

169. Nugent, "Geisha Man," 100, 101, 101.

170. Nugent, "Geisha Man," 101.

171. Nugent, "Geisha Man," 100.

172. For further information on Ulrichs, see Hubert Kennedy, *Ulrichs: The Life and Works of Karl Heinrich Ulrichs, Pioneer of the Modern Gay Movement* (Boston: Alyson, 1988).

173. Nugent, "Geisha Man," 100; Judith Butler, *Gender Trouble* (New York: Routledge, 1990), 140.

174. Nugent, "Geisha Man," 100.

175. Nugent, "Geisha Man," 104, 109.

176. Nugent, "Geisha Man," 109.

177. Wirth, introduction, 40.

CONCLUSION

1. Essex Hemphill, introduction, *Brother to Brother: New Writings by Black Gay Men*, ed. Essex Hemphill (Boston: Alyson, 1991), xxix.

2. George B. Hutchinson, "The Whitman Legacy and the Harlem Renaissance," *Walt Whitman: The Centennial Essays*, ed. Ed Folsom (Iowa City: University of Iowa Press, 1994), 201–16.

3. Thomas E. Yingling, *Hart Crane and the Homosexual Text: New Thresholds, New Anatomies* (Chicago: University of Chicago Press, 1990), 27. One of the earliest attacks on Whitman seems to have been Mark Van Doren's essay "Walt Whitman, Stranger" (1935), in which he disputed Whitman's "manly" reputation by claims about his "fastidious, eccentric and feminine character." Mark Van Doren, quoted in Alan Sinfield, *Cultural Politics—Queer Reading* (Philadelphia: University of Pennsylvania Press; London: Routledge, 1994), 35.

4. Eve Kosofsky Sedgwick, *Between Men* (New York: Columbia University Press, 1985), 203.

5. Benjamin Brawley, "Art Is Not Enough," *Southern Workman*, December 1932: 313.

Bibliography

UNPUBLISHED MATERIAL

ARCHIVES AND PRIVATE COLLECTIONS

Amistad Research Center (ARC), Tulane University, New Orleans, Louisiana
    Countée Cullen Papers (CCP)
    Correspondence
    Cullen, Countée, "Advice to Youth," ms., n.d., Box 14
    "Surrounded by His Books, Countee Cullen Is Happy," art., n.d. [October 23, 1925?], scrapbook 2, n.p.

Beinecke Rare Book and Manuscript Library (BRBML), Yale University, New Haven, Connecticut
    James Weldon Johnson Memorial Collection
      Claude McKay Papers (CMKP)
        Correspondence
        McKay, Claude, "Honeymoon," "New Poems," unpublished typescript, n.d., Box 10, 39
      Countée Cullen Papers (CCP)
        Correspondence
      James Weldon Johnson Papers (JWJP)
        Correspondence
      Langston Hughes Papers (LHP)
        Correspondence
      Wallace Thurman Papers (WTP)
        Correspondence
        Advertising leaflet for Wallace Thurman and William Jourdan Rapp, *Harlem* (1929), n.d. [1929], Box 3
        Thurman, Wallace, "Aunt Hagar's Children," unpublished typescript, n.d. [completed 1929], Box 1
        "Mr. Van Vechten's Jurors"
        "This Negro Literary Renaissance"
        "Tribute"
        Thurman, Wallace, and William Jourdan Rapp, " 'Cordelia the Crude': A Melodrama in 3 Acts," unpublished typescript, n.d., Box 1

Columbia University, Rare Book and Manuscript Library (CURBML), New York, New York
    Alexander Gumby Collection (AGC)
      Correspondence
      Gilbert, Berta, "Harlem Churches Refute Night Life Charges," art., n.d., Box 40, n.p.
      Gumby, Alexander, "To . . . . You," unpublished typescript, n.d., "Gumby's Autobiography & Scrapbook," scrapbook 2
      "Will the Plague Spread," art., n.d., Box 40, n.p.

Richard Bruce Nugent Papers (RBNP), Private Collection of Thomas H. Wirth, Elizabeth, New Jersey
  RBNP/Notes: Notes by Thomas H. Wirth summarizing meetings and telephone conversations with Richard Bruce Nugent, 1981–1984
  RBNP/Tapes: Audiotape recordings of interviews with Richard Bruce Nugent conducted by Thomas H. Wirth, 1983
  Unpublished typescripts
    "And Rose (McClendon)," n.d. [late 1930s]
    "Gentleman Jigger," n.d. [excerpts, partially paginated, classified as "Harlem Renaissance writing" by Thomas H. Wirth]
    "I Am Twenty Five," n.d. [c. 1931]
    "Tunic with a Thousand Pleats," n.d. [late 1920s]

Library of Congress, Manuscript Division, Washington, D.C.
  NAACP Collection, Walter White Papers (WWP, NAACP, LC)
  Correspondence
  Society for the Suppression of Vice Papers (SSVP, LC)
  Container 4: 1920–1950

Moorland-Spingarn Research Center, Howard University, Washington, D.C.
  Alain Locke Papers (ALP)
  Correspondence
    Locke, Alain, rev. of *Infants of the Spring*, by Wallace Thurman. n.d., Box 164-134
    McKay, Claude, "Boy Prostitute," unpublished manuscript, n.d., Box 164-186
  Georgia Douglas Johnson Papers (GDJP)
  Correspondence
  Glenn Carrington Papers (GCP)
  Correspondence
    Jackman, Harold, untitled report (for Sister M. Margaret), August 7, 1960, Box 145-13

The New York Public Library, Manuscript and Archives Division, Astor, Lenox, and Tilden Foundations, New York, New York
  Committee of Fourteen Records
    Bulletin #1480: Sexual Perversion Cases in New York City Courts, Box 88

Manuscripts, Archives and Rare Books Division, Schomburg Center for Research in Black Culture, The New York Public Library, Astor, Lenox and Tilden Foundations, New York, New York
  Aaron Douglas Papers (ADP)
    "Fire" open letter, n.d., Box 1
  Arthur A. Schomburg Papers (AASP)
    Correspondence
  Claude McKay Papers (CMKP)
    Correspondence
    "Harlem Glory," typescript, n.d. [c. 1937–1940], Box 2
    "Romance in Marseilles," typescript, n.d. [1930], Box 6
  Writers' Program Collection (WPC)
    Hill, Abram, "The Hamilton Lodge Ball," August 30, 1939, reel 4
    Young, Wilbur, "Gladys Bentley," n.d., reel 1

Theses and Unpublished Papers

Bennett, Juda Charles. "Translating Race: The Passing Figure in American Literature." Dissertation, Washington University, 1994.
Brumfield, Isaac William. "Race Consciousness in the Poetry and Fiction of Countee Cullen." Dissertation, University of Illinois at Urbana-Champaign, 1977.
Griffin, Barbara. "The Fragmented Vision of Claude McKay: A Study of His Works." Dissertation, University of Maryland–College Park, 1989.
Hathaway, Heather A. "Cultural Crossings: Migration, Generation, and Gender in Writings by Claude McKay and Paule Marshall." Dissertation, Harvard University, 1993.
McCabe, Tracy Graham. "Resisting Primitivism: Race, Gender, and Power in Modernism and the Harlem Renaissance." Dissertation, University of Wisconsin–Madison, 1994.
Stavney, Anne Elizabeth. "Harlem in the 1920s: A Geographical and Discursive Site of the Black and White Literary Imagination." Dissertation, University of Washington, 1994.

PUBLISHED PRIMARY AND SECONDARY SOURCES

"Alleged Degenerate Held As Boy Cries." *Baltimore Afro-American*, February 18, 1928: 10.
Allen, Frederick Lewis. *Only Yesterday: An Informal History of the Nineteen-Twenties*. New York: Harper, 1931.
Als, Hilton. "Negrofaggotry." *Black Film Review* 5 (1989): 18–19.
Anderson, Jervis. *Harlem: The Great Black Way, 1900–1950*. London: Orbis, 1982.
Avi-Ram, Amitai F. "The Unreadable Black Body: 'Conventional' Poetic Form in the Harlem Renaissance." *Genders* 7 (1990): 32–46.
Baker, Houston A., Jr. *A Many-Colored Coat of Dreams: The Poetry of Countee Cullen*. Broadside Critics Series 4. Detroit: Broadside, 1974.
———. *Modernism and the Harlem Renaissance*. Chicago: University of Chicago Press, 1987.
"Bass Voiced 'Girl Friend' Sentenced." *New York Amsterdam News*, August 28, 1929: 2.
Bergman, David. "The African and the Pagan in Gay Black Literature." *Sexual Sameness: Textual Differences in Lesbian and Gay Writing*. Ed. Joseph Bristow. London: Routledge, 1992. 148–69
Berry, Faith. *Langston Hughes: Before and Beyond Harlem*. Westport: Hill, 1983.
"Best Man Sails With Groom." *Baltimore Afro-American*, n.d. [1928]: n.p.
Blackmore, David L. " 'That Unreasonable Restless Feeling': The Homosexual Subtexts of Nella Larsen's *Passing*." *African American Review* 26 (1992): 475–84.
Bone, Robert. *The Negro Novel in America*. New Haven, Conn.: Yale University Press, 1958.
Bontemps, Arna. "The Awakening: A Memoir." *The Harlem Renaissance Remembered: Essays Edited with a Memoir*. Ed. Arna Bontemps. New York: Dodd, 1972. 1–26.
———. *God Sends Sunday*. New York: Harcourt, 1931.
Borden, Anne. "Heroic 'Hussies' and 'Brilliant Queers': Genderracial Resistance in the Works of Langston Hughes." *African American Review* 28 (1994): 333–45.

Bowser, Aubrey. "Black Realism." Rev. of *The Blacker the Berry*, by Wallace Thurman. *New York Amsterdam News*, February 13, 1929: 16.

———. Rev. of *Banjo*, by Claude McKay. *New York Amsterdam News*, May 8, 1929: 20.

———. "Dirt For Art's Sake." Rev. of *Home to Harlem*, by Claude McKay. *New York Amsterdam News*, March 21, 1928: 20.

———. "An Example for Harlem Writers: The Saturday Evening Quill." *New York Amsterdam News*, June 20, 1928: 16.

———. "Invincible Laughter." Rev. of *Not Without Laughter*, by Langston Hughes. *New York Amsterdam News*, July 23, 1930: 20.

———. "The Two-Dollar Woman Out Again." *New York Amsterdam News*, November 28, 1928: n.p.

Brawley, Benjamin. "Art Is Not Enough." *Southern Workman*, December 1932: 489–94.

———. "The Negro Literary Renaissance." *Southern Workman*, March 1927: 177–84.

Bremer, Sidney H. "Home in Harlem, New York: Lessons from the Harlem Renaissance Writers." *PMLA* 105 (1990): 47–56.

Brown, Sterling A. "More Odds." *Opportunity*, June 1932: 188–89.

———. "Our Literary Audience." [1930]. *A Son's Return: Selected Essays of Sterling A. Brown*. Ed. Mark A. Sanders. Boston, Mass.: Northeastern University Press, 1996. 139–48.

Browning, Buddy. "Fag Balls Exposed." *Broadway Brevities*, March 14, 1932: 12.

Bruce, Richard [Richard Bruce Nugent]. "Richard Bruce." *Caroling Dusk: An Anthology of Verse by Negro Poets*. Ed. Countee Cullen. New York: Harper, 1927. 205–206.

———. "Shadow." *Opportunity*, October 1925: 296.

———. "Smoke, Lilies and Jade." *Fire!!* 1 (1926): 33–39.

Burton, Peter. Introduction. *Strange Brother*. By Blair Niles. 1931. London: GMP, 1991. i–v.

Butler, Judith. *Gender Trouble*. New York: Routledge, 1990.

Carby, Hazel V. "Policing the Black Woman's Body in an Urban Context." *Critical Inquiry* 18 (1992): 738–55.

Carlston, Erin G. " 'A Finer Differentiation': Female Homosexuality and the American Medical Community, 1926–1940." *Science and Homosexualities*. Ed. Vernon A. Rosario. New York: Routledge, 1997. 177–96.

Carpenter, Edward. *The Intermediate Sex: A Study of Some Transitional Types of Men and Women*. London: Swan; Manchester: Clarke, 1908.

———. *Ioläus: An Anthology of Friendship*. 2nd enl. ed. London: Swan; Manchester: Clarke, 1906.

———. *Love's Coming-of-Age*. [1896]. *Edward Carpenter: Selected Writings*. 3 vols. Vol. 1. London: GMP, 1984. 95–183.

Carter, Eunice Hunton. Rev. of *The Blacker the Berry*, by Wallace Thurman. *Opportunity*, May 1929: 162.

Carter, Julian. "Normality, Whiteness, Authorship: Evolutionary Sexology and the Primitive Pervert." *Science and Homosexualities*. Ed. Vernon A. Rosario. New York: Routledge, 1997. 155–76.

"Censorship Epidemic." *Variety*, February 23, 1927: 1, 28–29.

"A Challenge to the Negro." *Bookman*, November 1926: 258–59.

Chamberlain, John R. "When Spring Comes to Harlem." Rev. of *Home to Harlem*, by Claude McKay. *New York Times Book Review*, March 11, 1928: 5.

Chauhan, P. S. "Rereading Claude McKay." *CLA Journal* 34 (1990): 68–80.

Chauncey, George, Jr. "From Sexual Inversion to Homosexuality: Medicine and the Changing Conceptualization Of Female Deviance." *Salmagundi* 58–59 (1982–1983): 114–46.

———. *Gay New York: Gender, Urban Culture and the Making of the Gay Male World, 1890–1940.* New York: Basic, 1994.

Chin, Timothy S. " 'Bullers' and 'Battymen': Contesting Homophobia in Black Popular Culture and Contemporary Caribbean Literature." *Callaloo* 20 (1997): 127–41.

"Citizens Claim That Lulu Belle Club on Lenox Avenue Is Notorious Dive." *New York Amsterdam News*, February 15, 1928: 1.

Clarke, Cheryl. "The Failure to Transform: Homophobia in the Black Community." *Home Girls: A Black Feminist Anthology.* Ed. Barbara Smith. New York: Kitchen Table: Women of Color, 1983. 197–208.

Cobb, Michael L. "Insolent Racing, Rough Narrative: The Harlem Renaissance's Impolite Queers." *Callaloo* 23 (2000): 328–51.

Coben, Stanley. *Rebellion against Victorianism: The Impetus for Cultural Change in 1920s America.* New York: Oxford University Press, 1991.

Cockburn, Patrick. "Sealed with a Loving Kiss." Rev. of *Judas: Betrayer or Friend of Jesus?* by William Klassen. *Independent on Sunday* (London), March 23, 1997: 4–5.

Cooper, Wayne F. *Claude McKay: Rebel Sojourner in the Harlem Renaissance—A Biography.* New York: Schocken, 1990.

"Crime in Harlem." *New York Amsterdam News*, March 13, 1929: n.p.

Cullen, Countee. *See also* Cullen, Countee P.

Cullen, Countee. *Color.* New York: Harper, 1925.

———. *Copper Sun.* New York: Harper, 1927.

———. "Countee Cullen." *Caroling Dusk: An Anthology of Verse by Negro Poets.* Ed. Countee Cullen. New York: Harper, 1927. 179.

———. "The Dark Tower." *Opportunity,* January 1927: 25.

———. "The Dark Tower." *Opportunity,* July 1927: 210.

———. "The Dark Tower." *Opportunity,* March 1928: 90.

———. *The Medea and Some Poems.* New York: Harper, 1935.

———. *My Soul's High Song: The Collected Writings of Countee Cullen, Voice of the Harlem Renaissance.* Ed. Gerald Early. New York: Anchor, 1991.

———. *One Way to Heaven.* New York: Harper, 1932.

Cullen, Countee P. "The League of Youth." *Crisis,* August 1923: 167–68.

Daniel, Walter C. *Black Journals of the United States.* Westport, Conn.: Greenwood, 1982.

Davis, Allison. "Our Negro 'Intellectuals.' " *Crisis,* August 1928: 268–69, 284–86.

Diawara, Manthia. "The Absent One: The Avant-Garde and the Black Imaginary in *Looking for Langston.*" *Representing Black Men.* Ed. Marcellus Blount and George P. Cunningham. New York: Routledge, 1996. 205–24.

Dismond, Geraldyn. "Social Snapshots." *Inter-State Tattler,* February 22, 1929: 5.

———. "Through the Lorgnette." *Pittsburgh Courier,* May 28, 1927, section 2: 1.

Dodson, Owen. "Countee Cullen (1903–1946)." *Phylon* 7 (1946): 20.

Dollimore, Jonathan. *Sexual Dissidence: Augustine to Wilde, Freud to Foucault.* Oxford: Clarendon, 1991.

Douglas, Ann. *Terrible Honesty: Mongrel Manhattan in the 1920s.* New York: Noonday, 1996.

Downey, Dennis B. *"The Crisis." The Harlem Renaissance: A Historical Dictionary for the Era.* New York: Methuen; London: Routledge, 1987. 86–87.

———. *"Opportunity." The Harlem Renaissance: A Historical Dictionary for the Era.* New York: Methuen; London: Routledge, 1987. 273–74.

"Dr. A.C. Powell Scores Pulpit Evils." *New York Age,* November 16, 1929: 1.

"Dr. Powell's Crusade against Abnormal Vice Is Approved." *New York Age,* November 23, 1929: 1.

Du Bois, W.E.B. "Criteria of Negro Art." *Crisis,* October 1926: 290–97.

———. "Criteria of Negro Art." *Crisis,* April 1927: 70.

———. "The Looking Glass." *Crisis,* January 1927: 158.

———. "Opinion of W.E.B. Du Bois." *Crisis,* April 1920: 298–99.

———. "Opinion of W.E.B. Du Bois." *Crisis,* May 1925: 7–10.

———. "Our Monthly Sermon." *Crisis,* April 1929: 125.

———. Rev. of *God Sends Sunday,* by Arna Bontemps. *Crisis,* September 1931: 304.

———. Rev. of *Nigger Heaven,* by Carl Van Vechten. *Crisis,* December 1926: 81–82.

———. *The Souls of Black Folk.* 1903. New York: Penguin, 1989.

———. "The Talented Tenth." [1903]. *Negro Protest Thought in the Twentieth Century.* Ed. Francis L. Broderick and August Meier. Indianapolis: Bobbs, 1965. 40–48.

———. "Truth and Beauty." *Crisis,* November 1922: 7–8.

———. "Two Novels." Rev. of *Passing,* by Nella Larsen, and *Home to Harlem,* by Claude McKay. *Crisis,* June 1928: 202.

Du Bois, W.E.B., and Alain Locke. "The Younger Literary Movement." *Crisis,* February 1924: 161–63.

DuCille, Ann. *The Coupling Convention: Sex, Text, and Tradition in Black Women's Fiction.* New York: Oxford University Press, 1993.

Dumenil, Lynn. *Modern Temper: American Culture and Society in the 1920s.* New York: Hill, 1995.

Dunbar-Nelson, Alice. "Woman's Most Serious Problem." [1927]. *Speech and Power: The African-American Essay and Its Cultural Content, from Polemics to Pulpit.* Ed. Gerald Early. 2 vols. Vol. 1. Hopewell, N.J.: Ecco, 1993. 224–27.

Durant, Thomas J., Jr., and Joyce S. Louden. "The Black Middle Class in America: Historical and Contemporary Perspectives." *Phylon* 47 (1986): 253–63.

Dyer, Richard. *The Matter of Images: Essays on Representations.* London: Routledge, 1993.

Early, Gerald. Introduction. *My Soul's High Song: The Collected Writings of Countee Cullen, Voice of the Harlem Renaissance.* Ed. Gerald Early. New York: Doubleday, 1991. 3–73.

———. "Three Notes toward a Cultural Definition of the Harlem Renaissance." *Callaloo* 14 (1991): 136–49.

Ellis, Havelock. *Sexual Inversion.* [1897]. Vol. 1, pt. 4 of *Studies in the Psychology of Sex.* By Havelock Ellis. 2 vols. 1903. New York: Random, 1942.

———. *The Task of Social Hygiene.* Boston, Mass.: Houghton, 1912.

Erenberg, L. A. *Steppin' Out: New York Nightlife and the Transformation of American Culture.* Chicago: University of Chicago Press, 1984.

"Evelyn Addams, 1 Yr. And Deportation: Boss of Eve's in Village Sold 'Dirty' Book—Man-Hater Besides." *Variety,* July 7, 1926: 33.

Fabre, Michel. *From Harlem to Paris: Black American Writers in France, 1840–1980.* Urbana: University of Illinois Press, 1991.

Faderman, Lillian. "The Morbidification of Love between Women by 19th-Century Sexologists." *Journal of Homosexuality* 4 (1978): 73–90.

———. *Odd Girls and Twilight Lovers: A History of Lesbian Life in Twentieth-Century America.* New York: Columbia University Press, 1991.

———. *Surpassing the Love of Men: Romantic Friendship and Love between Women from the Renaissance to the Present.* London: Junction, 1981.

Fauset, Jessie. *Plum Bun: A Novel without a Moral.* New York: Stokes, 1929.

———. Rev. of *The Weary Blues,* by Langston Hughes. *Crisis,* March 1926: 239.

Ferris, William H. "Ferris Scores Obscenity in Our Literature." *Pittsburgh Courier,* March 31, 1928, section 2: 8.

———. " 'Individuality' Is Race's Greatest Need." *Pittsburgh Courier,* November 27, 1926, section 1: 8.

Fisher, Rudolph. "The Caucasian Storms Harlem." *American Mercury* 11 (1927): 393–98.

———. *The Conjure-Man Dies.* 1932. London: X Press, 1995.

Fletcher, John. "Forster's Self-Erasure: *Maurice* and the Scene of Masculine Love." *Sexual Sameness: Textual Differences in Lesbian and Gay Writing.* Ed. Joseph Bristow. London: Routledge, 1992. 64–90.

Fone, Byrne R. S. *A Road to Stonewall: Male Homosexuality and Homophobia in English and American Literature, 1750–1969.* New York: Twayne, 1995.

Ford, Charles, and Parker Tyler. *The Young and Evil.* 1933. London: GMP, 1989.

Fortune, Thomas. "We Must Make Literature to Make Public Opinion." *Negro World,* November 22, 1924: 4.

Foster, Stephen Wayne. "Beauty's Purple Flame: Some Minor American Gay Poets, 1786–1936." *Homosexual Themes in Literary Studies.* Studies in Homosexuality 8. Ed. Wayne R. Dynes and Stephen Donaldson. New York: Garland, 1992. 141–44.

Frazier, E. Franklin. *Black Bourgeoisie: The Rise of a New Middle Class in the United States.* 1957. New York: Collier, 1962.

———. "Sex Morality among Negroes." *Religious Education* 23 (1928): 447–50.

Freedman, Estelle B. " 'Uncontrolled Desires': The Response to the Sexual Psychopath, 1920–1960." *Journal of American History* 74 (1987–1988): 83–106.

Fullinwider, S. P. *The Mind and Mood of Black America: 20th Century Thought.* Homewood, Ill.: Dorsey, 1969.

Gallant [pseud.]. "Society's 'Good Companions' Listen to Reading of Novel." *National News,* April 14, 1932: 5.

Garber, Eric. "Richard Bruce Nugent." *Afro-American Writers from the Harlem Renaissance to 1940.* Dictionary of Literary Biography 51. Detroit: Gale, 1987. 213–21.

———. "A Spectacle in Color: The Lesbian and Gay Subculture of Jazz Age Harlem." *Hidden from History: Reclaiming the Gay and Lesbian Past.* Ed. Martin Bauml Duberman, Martha Vicinus, and George Chauncey, Jr. Harmondsworth: Penguin, 1991. 318–31.

———. " 'T'ain't Nobody's Bizness': Homosexuality in 1920s' Harlem." *Black Men/White Men: A Gay Anthology.* Ed. Michael J. Smith. San Francisco: Gay Sunshine, 1983. 7–16.

Garvey, Marcus. " 'Home to Harlem,' Claude McKay's Damaging Book, Should Earn Wholesale Condemnation of Negroes." *Negro World,* September 29, 1928: 1.

Gates, Henry Louis, Jr. "The Black Man's Burden." *Fear of a Queer Planet.* Ed. Michael Warner. Minneapolis: University of Minnesota Press, 1993. 230–38.

———. "The Trope of a New Negro and the Reconstruction of the Image of the Black." *Representations* 24 (1988): 129–55.

Gates, Skip G. "Of Negroes Old and New." [1974]. *Analysis and Assessment, 1940–1979.* New York: Garland, 1996. Vol. 6 of *The Harlem Renaissance 1920–1940.* Ed Cary D. Wintz. 198–210. 7 vols.

Geuter, Ulfried. *Homosexualität in der deutschen Jugendbewegung: Jugendfreundschaft und Sexualität im Diskurs von Jugendbewegung, Psychoanalyse und Jugendpsychologie am Beginn des 20. Jahrhunderts.* Frankfurt am Main: Suhrkamp, 1994.

Giles, James R. *Claude McKay.* Twayne United States Authors Series 271. Boston, Mass.: Twayne, 1976.

Gill, John. *Queer Noises: Male and Female Homosexuality in Twentieth-Century Music.* London: Cassell, 1995.

Gilroy, Paul. *Black Atlantic: Modernity and Double Consciousness.* Cambridge, Mass.: Harvard University Press, 1993.

Greenberg, Robert M. "Idealism and Realism in the Fiction of Claude McKay." *CLA Journal* 24 (1981): 237–61.

Grey, Edgar M. "Harlem after Dark." *New York Amsterdam News,* April 6, 1927: 16.

Hall, Radclyffe. *The Well of Loneliness.* 1928. London: Virago, 1992.

Hanson, Ellis. *Decadence and Catholicism.* Cambridge, Mass.: Harvard University Press, 1997.

Harrison, Daphne Duval. *Black Pearls: Blues Queens of the 1920s.* New Brunswick, N.J.: Rutgers University Press, 1988.

Hatch, James V. "An Interview with Bruce Nugent—Actor, Artist, Writer, Dancer." *Artists and Influences* 1 (1982): 81–104.

Hayes, Donald Jeffrey. "Youth Flays Criticism for Prudish Attack on 'Realism.' " *Chicago Defender,* April 21, 1928, section 2: 1.

Hekma, Gert. " 'A Female Soul in a Male Body': Sexual Inversion in Nineteenth-Century Sexology." *Third Sex, Third Gender: Beyond Sexual Dimorphism in Culture and History.* Ed. Gilbert Herdt. New York: Zone, 1994. 213–39.

Helbling, Mark, and Bruce Kellner. "Nugent, Richard Bruce." *The Harlem Renaissance: A Historical Dictionary for the Era.* New York: Methuen; London: Routledge, 1987. 269.

Hemenway, Robert E. *Zora Neale Hurston: A Literary Biography.* London: Camden, 1986.

Hemphill, Essex. Introduction. *Brother to Brother: New Writings by Black Gay Men.* Ed. Essex Hemphill. Boston, Mass.: Alyson, 1991. xv–xxxi.

Hernandez, Theodore Hugh. "Why Read Negro Literature?" *Pittsburgh Courier,* February 13, 1932, section 2: 3.

Herrick, Robert. *The Poems of Robert Herrick.* Ed. L. C. Martin. London: Oxford University Press, 1965.

Hicks, Granville. "The New Negro: An Interview with Wallace Thurman." *Churchman,* April 30, 1927: 10–11.

hooks, bell. *Black Looks: Race and Representation.* Boston, Mass.: South End, 1992.

———. *Talking Back: Thinking Feminist, Thinking Black.* Boston, Mass.: South End, 1989.

———. *Yearning: Race, Gender and Cultural Politics.* Boston, Mass.: South End; London: Turnaround, 1991.

Hopson, James O. "Negro Writers in White Magazines." *Pittsburgh Courier,* February 20, 1932, section 2: 2.

Hubert, Levi. "On Seventh Avenue." *Baltimore Afro-American,* December 27, 1930: 9.

Huggins, Nathan Irvin. *Harlem Renaissance.* London: Oxford University Press, 1971.

Hughes, Langston. *The Big Sea: An Autobiography.* 1940. New York: Hill, 1993.

———. "Bodies in the Moonlight." *Messenger,* April 1927: 105–106.

———. "Boy." *Carolina Magazine,* May 1928: 38.

———. *The Collected Poems of Langston Hughes.* Ed. Arnold Rampersad. New York: Vintage, 1994.

———. *Fine Clothes to the Jew.* New York: Knopf, 1927.

———. Letter. *Crisis,* September 1928: 302.

———. *Little Ham.* [1935]. *Five Plays of Langston Hughes.* Ed. Webster Smalley. Bloomington: Indiana University Press, 1968. 43–112.

———. "The Little Virgin." *Messenger,* November 1927: 327–28.

———. "Luani of the Jungles." *Harlem* 1 (1928): 7–11.

———. "The Negro Artist and the Racial Mountain." *Nation,* June 23, 1926: 692–94.

———. *Not Without Laughter.* 1931. New York: Simon & Schuster, 1995.

———. "Says Race Leaders, Including Preachers, Flock to Harlem Cabarets." *Pittsburgh Courier,* April 16, 1927, section 1: 8.

———. *Something in Common and Other Stories.* New York: Hill, 1963.

———. "The Twenties: Harlem and Its Negritude." *African Forum* 1 (1966): 11–20.

———. *The Weary Blues.* New York: Knopf, 1926.

———. "The Young Glory of Him: A Tragic Romance on Tropic Seas." *Messenger,* June 1927: 177–78.

Hull, Gloria T. *Color, Sex and Poetry: Three Women Writers of the Harlem Renaissance.* Bloomington: Indiana University Press, 1987.

Hutchinson, George. *The Harlem Renaissance in Black and White.* Cambridge, Mass.: Belknap-Harvard University Press, 1995.

Hutchinson, George B. "The Whitman Legacy and the Harlem Renaissance." *Walt Whitman: The Centennial Essays.* Ed. Ed Folsom. Iowa City: University of Iowa Press, 1994. 201–16.

Huysmans, Joris-Karl. *Against Nature (A rebours).* Trans. Margaret Mauldon. Ed. Nicholas White. 1884. Oxford: Oxford University Press, 1998.

Hyde, H. Montgomery. Ed. *The Trials of Oscar Wilde: Regina (Wilde) v. Queensberry, Regina v. Wilde and Taylor.* London: Hodge, 1948.

Ikonné, Chidi. *From Du Bois to Van Vechten: The Early New Negro Literature, 1903–1926.* Contributions in Afro-American and African Studies 60. Westport, Conn.: Greenwood, 1981.

"Infants of Spring." Rev. of *Infants of the Spring,* by Wallace Thurman. *Abbott's Monthly Review,* April 1932: 51.

Jackson, Holbrook. *The Eighteen Nineties: A Review of Art and Ideas At the Close of the Nineteenth Century.* 1913. Hassocks, England: Harvester, 1976.

Jacobs, George W. [George S. Schuyler]. "New Yorker Flays McKay's Book, 'Home To Harlem.' " *Pittsburgh Courier,* April 7, 1928, section 2: 8.

Johnson, Charles S. "Jazz Poetry and Blues." *Carolina Magazine,* May 1928: 16–19.

———. "The Negro Enters Literature." *Carolina Magazine,* May 1927: 3–9, 44–48.

Johnson, James Weldon. Ed. *The Book of American Negro Poetry.* New York: Harcourt, 1922.

———. "The Dilemma of the Negro Author." *American Mercury* 15 (1928): 477–81.

———. "The Larger Success." *Southern Workman,* September 1923: 427–36.

———. *Negro Americans, What Now?* 1938. New York: AMS, 1971.

——. "Negro Authors and White Publishers." *Crisis,* July 1929: 228–29.

——. Preface. *The Book of American Negro Poetry* Ed. James Weldon Johnson. New York: Harcourt, 1922. vii–xlviii.

——. "Race Prejudice and the Negro Artists." *Harper's Monthly Magazine* 157 (1928): 769–76.

Julien, Isaac. Dir. *Looking for Langston.* Sankofa, 1989.

Kaplan, Cora. " 'A Cavern Opened in My Mind': The Poetics of Homosexuality and the Politics of Masculinity in James Baldwin." *Representing Black Men.* Ed. Marcellus Blount and George P. Cunningham. New York: Routledge, 1996. 27–54.

Katz, Jonathan Ned. *Gay American History: Lesbians and Gay Men in the U.S.A.* New York: Harper, 1985.

——. *Gay/Lesbian Almanac: A New Documentary.* 1983. New York: Carroll, 1994.

Keats, John. *Complete Poems.* London: Softback, 1993.

Kellner, Bruce. "Dill, Augustus Granville." *The Harlem Renaissance: A Historical Dictionary for the Era.* New York: Methuen; London: Routledge, 1987. 100–101.

——. "Gumby, [Levi Sandy] Alexander." *The Harlem Renaissance: A Historical Dictionary for the Era.* New York: Methuen; London: Routledge, 1987. 147–48.

——. Ed. *The Harlem Renaissance: A Historical Dictionary for the Era.* New York: Methuen; London: Routledge, 1987.

K[elley], W[illiam] M. "Langston Hughes—the Sewer Dweller." Rev. of *Fine Clothes to the Jew,* by Langston Hughes. *New York Amsterdam News,* February 9, 1927: 22.

Kennedy, Hubert. *Ulrichs: The Life and Works of Karl Heinrich Ulrichs, Pioneer of the Modern Gay Movement.* Boston, Mass.: Alyson, 1988.

Kent, George E. "The Soulful Way of Claude McKay." *Black World,* November 1970: 37–51.

Kerlin, Robert T. "Conquest by Poetry." *Southern Workman,* June 1927: 282–84.

Kisseloff, Jeff. *You Must Remember This: An Oral History of Manhattan from the 1890s to World War II.* San Diego: Harcourt, 1989.

Krafft-Ebing, R[ichard] v[on]. *Psychopathia Sexualis, with Especial Reference To Antipathic Sexual Instinct: A Medico-Forensic Study.* 1892. London: Rebman, 1901.

Larkin, Margaret. "A Poet for the People—A Review." Rev. of *Fine Clothes to the Jew,* by Langston Hughes. *Opportunity,* March 1927: 84.

Larsen, Nella. *Passing.* New York: Knopf, 1929.

——. *Quicksand.* New York: Knopf, 1928.

Le Fanu, Joseph Sheridan. *Carmilla.* [1872]. New York: Scholastic, 1971.

Levin, James. *The Gay Novel in America.* New York: Garland, 1991.

Lewis, David Levering. *When Harlem Was in Vogue.* New York: Knopf, 1981.

Locke, Alain. "Art or Propaganda?" *Harlem* 1 (1928): 12.

——. "Beauty Instead of Ashes." [1928]. *The Critical Temper of Alain Locke: A Selection of His Essays on Art and Culture.* Ed. Jeffrey C. Stewart. New York: Garland, 1983. 24–25.

——. "Color Line: Inside and Out." Rev. of *Plum Bun,* by Jessie Fauset, and *The Blacker the Berry,* by Wallace Thurman. *Survey* 62 (1929): 325.

——. "Fire: A Negro Magazine." *Survey* 58 (1927): 563.

——. "The High Cost of Prejudice." *Forum* 78 (1927): 500–10.

——. *The Negro in America.* Reading with a Purpose 68. Chicago: American Library Association, 1933.

———. "Negro Youth Speaks." *The New Negro*. Ed. Alain Locke. 1925. New York: Atheneum, 1992. 47–53.

———. "The New Negro." *The New Negro*. Ed. Alain Locke. 1925. New York: Atheneum, 1992. 3–16.

———. Rev. of *Sex Expression in Literature*, by V. F. Calverton. *Opportunity,* February 1926: 57–58.

———. "Spiritual Truancy." Rev. of *A Long Way from Home*, by Claude McKay. *New Challenge* 2 (1937): 81–85.

———. "The Weary Blues." Rev. of *The Weary Blues*, by Langston Hughes. *Palms* January 1926: 25–28.

———. "1928: A Retrospective Review." *Opportunity,* January 1929: 8–11.

McDowell, Deborah E. " 'It's Not Safe. Not Safe at All': Sexuality in Nella Larsen's *Passing.*" *The Lesbian and Gay Studies Reader*. Ed. Henry Abelove, Michèle Aina Barale, and David M. Halperin. New York: Routledge, 1993. 616–25.

McKay, Claude. *Banana Bottom*. 1933. New York: Harvest-Harcourt, 1961.

———. *Banjo: A Story without a Plot*. 1929. New York: Harcourt, 1957.

———. "Birthright." [1922]. Rev. of *Birthright*, by T. S. Stribling. *The Passion of Claude McKay: Selected Poetry and Prose, 1912–1948*. Ed. Wayne F. Cooper. New York: Schocken, 1973. 73–76.

———. "A Black Man Replies." Letter. [1920]. *The Passion of Claude McKay: Selected Poetry and Prose, 1912–1948*. Ed. Wayne F. Cooper. New York: Schocken, 1973. 54–57.

———. *Constab Ballads*. London: Watts, 1912.

———. *Gingertown*. New York: Harper, 1932.

———. *Harlem Glory: A Fragment of Aframerican Life*. Chicago: Kerr, 1990.

———. *Harlem: Negro Metropolis*. 1940. New York: Harcourt, 1968.

———. *Harlem Shadows*. New York: Harcourt, 1922.

———. *Home to Harlem*. [1928]. *Classic Fiction of the Harlem Renaissance*. Ed. William L. Andrews. New York: Oxford University Press, 1994. 105–237.

———. *A Long Way from Home*. 1937. New York: Harcourt, 1970.

———. *My Green Hills of Jamaica and Five Jamaican Short Stories*. Ed. Mervyn Morris. Kingston, Jamaica: Heinemann (Caribbean), 1979.

———. "A Negro to His Critics." *New York Herald Tribune Books*, March 6, 1932: n.p.

———. *Selected Poems of Claude McKay*. New York: Bookman, 1953.

———. *Songs of Jamaica*. Kingston, Jamaica: Gardner, 1912.

———. *Spring in New Hampshire, and Other Poems*. London: Richards, 1920.

———. "White Houses." *The New Negro*. Ed. Alain Locke. 1925. New York: Atheneum, 1992. 134.

McLeod, A. L. "An Ideal Woman: Claude McKay's Composite Image." *Claude McKay: Centennial Studies*. Ed. A. L. McLeod. New Delhi, India: Sterling, 1992. 70–81.

Margolies, Edward. *Native Sons: A Critical Study of Twentieth-Century Negro American Authors*. Philadelphia: Lippincott, 1968.

"Masquerade Ball Draws 5,000 People." *New York Amsterdam News*, February 20, 1929: 2.

Matthews, Ralph. "Are Pansies People?" *Baltimore Afro-American*, April 2, 1932: 3.

Mayne, Xavier [Edward Irenaeus Prime Stevenson]. *The Intersexes: A History Of Simisexualism as a Problem in Social Life*. N.p.: privately printed, 1908.

Melville, Herman. *Redburn: His First Voyage*. 1849. Boston, Mass.: Page, 1924.

————. *White Jacket, or The World in a Man-of-War*. 1850. Boston, Mass.: Page, 1950.

"Men Dance at Vagabonds Ball; Women Are Barred." *Baltimore Afro-American*, March 7, 1925: 20.

Mercer, Kobena. *Welcome to the Jungle: New Positions in Black Cultural Studies.* New York: Routledge, 1994.

"Mere Male Blossoms Out in Garb of Milady at Big Hamilton Lodge Ball." *New York Amsterdam News*, February 19, 1930: 3.

Miller, David A. *The Novel and the Police*. Berkeley: University of California Press, 1988.

Miller, Neil. *Out of the Past: Gay and Lesbian History from 1869 to the Present.* London: Vintage, 1995.

Moon, Henry Lee. "Claude McKay Comes Home to Harlem after Spending Ten-Year Exile on 2 Continents." *New York Amsterdam News*, February 7, 1934: 1.

Moore, Jack B. *W.E.B. Du Bois*. Twayne United States Authors Series 399. Boston, Mass.: Twayne, 1981.

Mumford, Kevin J. *Interzones: Black/White Sex Districts in Chicago and New York in the Early Twentieth Century*. New York: Columbia University Press, 1997.

"A Negro Renaissance." *New York Herald Tribune*, May 7, 1925: 16.

"Negro Wins Prize In Poetry Contest." *New York Times*, December 2, 1923, section 2: 1.

Nelson, Emmanuel. "Critical Deviance: Homophobia and the Reception of James Baldwin's Fiction." *Journal of American Culture* 14 (1991): 91–96.

Nero, Charles I. "Re/Membering Langston: Homophobic Textuality and Arnold Rampersad's *Life of Langston Hughes*." *Queer Representations: Reading Lives, Reading Culture*. Ed. Martin Duberman. New York: New York University Press, 1997. 188–96.

"The New Generation." Editorial. *Opportunity*, March 1924: 68.

"Night Clubs Found Chief Vice Centres." *New York Times*, 14 Oct. 1929: 1.

Niles, Blair. *Strange Brother*. 1931. London: GMP, 1991.

Norton, Rictor. "Ganymede Raped: Gay Literature—the Critic as Censor." [1974]. *Gay Roots: Twenty Years of Gay Sunshine—An Anthology of Gay History, Sex, Politics, and Culture*. Ed. Winston Leyland. San Francisco: Gay Sunshine, 1991. 328–36.

"A Note on the New Literary Movement." Editorial. *Opportunity*, March 1926: 80–81.

Notten, Eleonore van. *Wallace Thurman's Harlem Renaissance*. Costerius New Series 93. Amsterdam, The Netherlands: Rodopi, 1994.

Nugent, Bruce [Richard Bruce Nugent]. "Sahdji." *The New Negro*. Ed. Alain Locke. 1925. New York: Atheneum, 1992. 113–14.

Nugent, Richard Bruce. See also Nugent, Bruce and Bruce, Richard.

Nugent, Richard Bruce. "Beyond Where the Star Stood Still." *Crisis*, December 1970: 405–408.

————. *Gay Rebel of the Harlem Renaissance: Selections from the Work of Richard Bruce Nugent*. Ed. Thomas H. Wirth. Durham, N.C.: Duke University Press, 2002.

————. Illus. [male head]. *Opportunity* March 1926: cover page.

————. "Lighting FIRE!!" Insert to *Fire!!* 1926. Metuchen, N.J.: Fire!!, 1981. n.p.

————. "Narcissus." *Trend* 1 (1933): 127.

Onwuchekwa, Jemie. *Langston Hughes: An Introduction to the Poetry*. New York: Columbia University Press, 1976.

"An Opportunity for Negro Writers." Editorial. *Opportunity*, September 1924: 258.

Osofsky, Gilbert. *Harlem: The Making of a Ghetto, Negro New York, 1890–1930.* New York: Harper, 1968.

Pearson, Ralph L. "Combatting Racism with Art: Charles S. Johnson and the Harlem Renaissance." *American Studies* 18 (1977): 123–34.

Perry, Margaret. *Silence to the Drums: A Survey of the Literature of the Harlem Renaissance.* Contributions in Afro-American and African Studies 18. Westport, Conn.: Greenwood, 1976.

Pivar, David J. "Cleansing the Nation: The War on Prostitution, 1917–21." *Prologue* 12 (1980): 28–40.

Plessner, Monika. *Ich bin der dunklere Bruder: Die Literatur der schwarzen Amerikaner. Von den Spirituals bis zu James Baldwin. Eine Einführung.* Hagen, Germany: Linnepe, 1977.

Prowle, Allen D. "Langston Hughes." *Poetry and Drama.* Ed. C. W. E. Bigsby. Deland, Fla.: Everett-Edwards, 1969. Vol. 2 of *The Black American Writer.* 77–87. 2 vols.

"Publisher Denies Prejudice against Negro Writers." *Pittsburgh Courier,* July 27, 1929, section 1: 12.

Rainey, Ma. "Prove It on Me Blues." *Down in the Basement.* Milestone MLP-2017.

Rampersad, Arnold. *The Art and Imagination of W.E.B. Du Bois.* Cambridge, Mass.: Harvard University Press, 1988.

———. Introduction. *The Big Sea: An Autobiography.* By Langston Hughes. 1940. New York: Hill, 1993. xiii–xxvi.

———. *The Life of Langston Hughes.* 2 vols. New York: Oxford University Press, 1988.

———. "The Origins of Poetry in Langston Hughes." *Southern Review* 21 (1985): 695–705.

Reimonenq, Alden. "Countee Cullen's Uranian 'Soul Windows.' " *Critical Essays: Gay and Lesbian Writers of Color.* Ed. Emmanuel S. Nelson. New York: Harrington Park-Haworth, 1993. 143–66.

———. "Cullen, Countee." *The Gay and Lesbian Heritage: A Reader's Companion to the Writers and Their Works, from Antiquity to the Present.* New York: Holt, 1995. 185–86.

———. "The Harlem Renaissance." *The Gay and Lesbian Heritage: A Reader's Companion to the Writers and Their Works, from Antiquity to the Present.* New York: Holt, 1995. 358–61.

———. "Hughes, Langston (1902–1967)." *The Gay and Lesbian Heritage: A Reader's Companion to the Writers and Their Works, from Antiquity to the Present.* New York: Holt, 1995. 374–75.

"Rev. Hightower Leads Raids on Vice in Hill." *Pittsburgh Courier,* March 31, 1928, section 1: 8.

Rev. of *Fine Clothes to the Jew,* by Langston Hughes. *Chicago Whip,* February 26, 1927: n.p.

Richter, Alan. *Sexual Slang: A Compendium of Offbeat Words and Colorful Phrases from Shakespeare to Today.* 1993. New York: HarperPerennial, 1995.

Rogers, J. A. " 'Ahead of Its Time': McKay Defends Book, *Home to Harlem.*" *New York Amsterdam News,* April 10, 1929: 20.

———. "The Critics: Do They Tell the Truth?" *Messenger,* December 1926: 365.

———. "Rogers Calls Langston Hughes' Book of Poems 'Trash.' " Rev. of *Fine Clothes to the Jew,* by Langston Hughes. *Pittsburgh Courier,* February 12, 1927, section 1: 4.

Rosenblatt, Roger. *Black Fiction.* Cambridge, Mass.: Harvard University Press, 1974.

Roses, Lorraine, and Ruth Elizabeth Randolph. *Harlem Renaissance and Beyond: Literary Biographies of 100 Black Women Writers, 1900–1945.* Boston, Mass.: Hall, 1990.

Rotundo, E. Anthony. *American Manhood: Transformations in Masculinity from the Revolution to the Modern Era.* New York: Basic, 1993.

Ruff, Shawn Stewart. Introduction. *Go the Way Your Blood Beats: An Anthology of Lesbian and Gay Fiction by African-American Writers.* Ed. Shawn Stewart Ruff. New York: Holt, 1996. xxi–xxix.

Sarotte, Georges-Michel. *Like a Brother, Like a Lover: Male Homosexuality in the American Novel and Theatre from Hermann Melville to James Baldwin.* Trans. Richard Miller. Garden City, N.Y.: Anchor-Doubleday, 1978.

Schuyler, George S. *See also* Jacobs, George W.

Schuyler, George S. "Lights and Shadows of the Underworld—Studying the Social Outcasts: II. The Folk Farthest Down." *Messenger,* August 1923: 787–88, 796–97.

———. "The Negro-Art Hokum." *Nation,* June 16, 1926: 662–63.

———. "Views and Reviews." *Pittsburgh Courier,* March 5, 1927, section 2: 8.

———. "Views and Reviews." *Pittsburgh Courier,* March 24, 1928, section 2: 8.

Scruggs, Charles. W. "Alain Locke and Walter White: Their Struggle for Control of the Harlem Renaissance." *Black American Literature Forum* 14 (1980): 91–99.

Sedgwick, Eve Kosofsky. *Between Men.* New York: Columbia University Press, 1985.

Shackleford, D. Dean. "The Poetry of Countée Cullen." *Masterpieces of African-American Literature.* New York: HarperCollins, 1992. 382–86.

" 'She' Turns Out to Be a 'He' in Court." *New York Amsterdam News,* February 8, 1928: 16.

Shucard, Alan. *Countee Cullen.* Twayne's United States Authors Series 470. Boston, Mass.: Twayne, 1984.

Silberman, Seth Clark. "Lighting the Harlem Renaissance aFire!!: Embodying Richard Bruce Nugent's Bohemian Politic." *The Greatest Taboo: Homosexuality in Black Communities.* Ed. Delroy Constanine-Simms. Los Angeles: Alyson, 2001. 254–73.

———. "Looking for Richard Bruce Nugent and Wallace Henry Thurman: Reclaiming Black Male Same-Sexualities in the New Negro Movement." *In Process* 1 (1996): 53–73.

Simmons, Christina. "Modern Sexuality and the Myth of Victorian Repression." *Passion and Power: Sexuality in History.* Ed. Kathy Peiss and Christina Simmons. Philadelphia: Temple University Press, 1989. 157–77.

Sinfield, Alan. *Cultural Politics—Queer Reading.* Philadelphia: University of Pennsylvania Press; London: Routledge, 1994.

———. *The Wilde Century: Effeminacy, Oscar Wilde and the Queer Moment.* London: Cassell, 1994.

Singh, Amritjit. *The Novels of the Harlem Renaissance: Twelve Black Writers 1923–1933.* University Park: Pennsylvania State University Press, 1976.

Smith, Bessie. "T'ain't Nobody's Biz-ness If I Do." *The World's Greatest Blues Singer.* Columbia GP-33.

Smith, Charles Michael. "Bruce Nugent: Bohemian of the Harlem Renaissance." *In the Life: A Black Gay Anthology.* Ed. Joseph Beam. Boston, Mass.: Alyson, 1986. 209–20.

Smith, Michael J. Ed. *Black Men/White Men: A Gay Anthology.* San Francisco: Gay Sunshine, 1983.

Somerville, Siobhan B. *Queering the Color Line: Race and the Invention of Homosexuality in American Culture*. Durham, N.C.: Duke University Press, 2000.

Sperry, Margaret. "Countee P. Cullen, Negro Boy Poet, Tells His Story." *Brooklyn Daily Eagle*, February 10, 1924: n.p.

Stameshkin, David. "*Pittsburgh Courier*." *The Harlem Renaissance: A Historical Dictionary for the Era*. New York: Methuen; London: Routledge, 1987. 283–84.

Stoff, Michael B. "Claude McKay and the Cult of Primitivism." *The Harlem Renaissance Remembered: Essays Edited with a Memoir*. Ed. Arna Bontemps. New York: Dodd, 1972. 126–46.

Story, Ralph D. "Patronage and the Harlem Renaissance: You Get What You Pay For." *CLA Journal* 32 (1989): 284–95.

Strauss, Gerald H. "Cane." *Masterpieces of African-American Literature*. New York: HarperCollins, 1992. 91–94.

Swinburne, Algernon Charles. *Poems and Ballads*. London: Hotten, 1866.

Tate, Claudia. *Domestic Allegories of Political Desire: The Black Heroine's Text at the Turn of the Century*. New York: Oxford University Press, 1992.

Tebbel, John. *The Golden Age between Two Wars: 1920–1940*. New York: Bowker, 1978. Vol. 3 of *A History of Book Publishing in the United States*. 4 vols. 1972–81.

Tellier, André. *Twilight Men*. New York: Greenberg, 1931.

Tennyson, Alfred. *Alfred Tennyson, Poems and Plays*. London: Oxford University Press, 1968.

"They Won't Keep Away." *New York Amsterdam News*, October 23, 1929: n.p.

Thurman, Wallace. *The Blacker the Berry*. 1929. London: X Press, 1994.

———. "Cordelia the Crude." *Fire!!* 1 (1926): 5–6.

———. Editorial. *Harlem* 1 (1928): 21–22.

———. *Infants of the Spring*. 1932. Boston, Mass.: Northeastern University Press, 1992.

———. "Negro Artists and the Negro." *New Republic* 52 (1927): 37–39.

———. "Negro Poets and Their Poetry." [1928]. *Black Writers Interpret the Harlem Renaissance*. New York: Garland, 1996. Vol. 3 of *The Harlem Renaissance 1920–1940*. Ed. Cary D. Wintz. 70–82. 7 vols.

Thurman, Wallace, and William Jourdan Rapp. *Harlem*. 1929.

Tillery, Tyrone. *Claude McKay: A Black Poet's Struggle for Identity*. Amherst: University of Massachusetts Press, 1992.

Tracy, Steven C. *Langston Hughes and the Blues*. Urbana: University of Illinois Press, 1988.

Turner, Darwin T. *In a Minor Chord: Three Afro-American Writers and Their Search for Identity*. Carbondale: Southern Illinois University Press; London: Feffer, 1971.

———. "Langston Hughes as Playwright." *Roots and Rituals: The Search for Identity—The Image Makers: Plays and Playwrights*. Ed. Errol Hill. Englewood Cliffs, N.J.: Prentice-Hall, 1980. Vol. 1 of *The Theater of Black Americans: A Collection of Critical Essays*. 136–47. 2 vols.

"Uncle Held for Special Sessions Charged with Corrupting Boy's Morals." *New York Amsterdam News*, December 8, 1926: 2.

Van Vechten, Carl. *Letters of Carl Van Vechten*. Ed. Bruce Kellner. New Haven, Conn.: Yale University Press, 1987.

———. *Nigger Heaven*. New York: Knopf, 1926.

Wagner, Jean. *Black Poets of the United States: From Paul Laurence Dunbar to Langston Hughes*. Trans. Kenneth Douglas. Urbana: University of Illinois Press, 1973.

Wall, Cheryl A. *Women of the Harlem Renaissance*. Bloomington: Indiana University Press, 1995.

Walton, Lester A. "Protests Holding Negro Artist to Racial Themes." *New York World*, May 15, 1927: 16.

Watson, Steven. *The Harlem Renaissance: Hub of African-American Culture, 1920–1930*. New York: Pantheon, 1995.

Weeks, Jeffrey. *Coming Out: Homosexual Politics in Britain from the Nineteenth Century to the Present*. Rev. ed. London: Quartet, 1990.

Weinberg, Thomas S. "On 'Doing' and 'Being' Gay: Sexual Behavior and Homosexual Male Self-Identity." *Journal of Homosexuality* 4 (1978): 143–56.

Westphal, Carl. "Die conträre Sexualempfindung, Symptom eines neuropathischen (psychopathischen) Zustandes." *Archiv für Psychiatrie und Nervenkrankheiten* 2 (1869): 73–108.

"White Slummer Hit Blow in Report Depicting Conditions in Harlem District." *New York Amsterdam News*, October 6, 1929: n.p.

Whitman, Walt. *Walt Whitman: The Complete Poems*. Ed. Francis Murphy. London: Penguin, 1975.

Williams, Terence E. "Queer People Of Greenwich Village Converting Harlem into Isle of Lesbos, Charge." *Pittsburgh Courier*, March 17, 1928, section 2: 1.

Wilson, Edmund. *The Shores of Light: A Literary Chronicle of the Twenties and Thirties*. London: Allen, 1952.

Wintz, Cary D. *Black Culture and the Harlem Renaissance*. Houston, Tex.: Rice University Press, 1988.

———. "Series Introduction." *The Harlem Renaissance 1920–1940*. Ed. Cary D. Wintz. Vols. 1–7. New York: Garland, 1996. ix–xii. 7 vols.

Wirth, Thomas H. "FIRE!! in Retrospect." Insert to *Fire!!* 1926. Metuchen, N.J.: Fire!!, 1981. n.p.

———. Introduction. *Gay Rebel of the Harlem Renaissance: Selections from the Work of Richard Bruce Nugent*. Ed. Thomas H. Wirth. Durham, N.C.: Duke University Press. 1–61.

———. "Richard Bruce Nugent." *Black American Literature Forum* 19 (1985): 16–17.

"Women Aplenty." *National News*, April 14, 1932: 5.

"Women Rivals for Affection of Another Woman Battles with Knives, and One Has Head Almost Severed from Body." *New York Age*, November 27, 1926: 1.

"Women Workers." Editorial. *Opportunity*, August 1925: 226.

Woods, Gregory. "Gay Re-readings of the Harlem Renaissance Poets." *Critical Essays: Gay and Lesbian Writers of Color*. Ed. Emmanuel S. Nelson. New York: Harrington Park-Haworth, 1993. 127–42.

Yingling, Thomas E. *Hart Crane and the Homosexual Text: New Thresholds, New Anatomies*. Chicago: University of Chicago Press, 1990.

" 'Y'Mus Come Ovah!' Sez Cops." *Inter-State Tattler*, March 10 1932: 2.

Index

"Advice to Youth" (Cullen), 58, 163*n*101
Africa, 7, 34, 154*n*42, 162*n*60; in Harlem Renaissance works, 36, 53–54, 77, 78, 79, 83, 102, 120, 124–25
African Americans: attitudes toward homosexuality, 14–23; concerns about black female sexuality, 16–20, 39–40; stereotypes of, 8, 15, 17, 30, 36, 39, 43, 99; working class, 4, 5, 9, 11, 14, 15, 16, 17, 18, 29, 30, 36, 38, 39, 46, 68, 72, 86, 89, 99
Against Nature (Huysmans), 127
Alexander, Lewis, 14
"Alfonso, Dressing To Wait At Table, Sings" (McKay), 103, 176*n*139
Atkinson, Edward, 50, 160*n*28
Audiences, 3–4, 25, 28–29, 30, 32, 34, 36, 40, 42, 44, 45, 52, 54, 61, 62, 65, 66, 67, 79–80, 86, 89, 96, 178*n*179

Baker, Houston, 29, 44, 48, 59, 161*n*37
Banana Bottom (McKay), 98, 100–101, 177*n*142, 178*n*197, 179*n*225
Banjo (McKay), 39, 88, 90, 96–106, 110, 112–13, 115–18, 178–79*n*203, 179*nn*207,225
"The Barrier" (McKay), 94, 174*nn*59,60
"Bastard Song" (Nugent), 125, 182*n*49
Beardsley, Aubrey, 40, 120
Bennett, Gwendolyn, 45, 155*n*67
"Bennie's Departure" (McKay), 114, 115
Bentley, Gladys, 11, 83, 147*n*39
Berry, Faith, 69, 70, 166*n*15, 167*n*41, 170*n*147
"Beyond Where the Star Stood Still" (Nugent), 123, 127
The Big Sea (Hughes), 68, 76, 77, 79, 80, 81–83, 86, 87, 170*n*129
Bisexuality, 10, 89, 90, 91, 93, 110, 117, 122–23, 135, 140, 172*n*27
Black bourgeoisie, 14–19, 22–24, 32, 34, 37, 38, 39, 42, 45, 46, 48, 89, 142
"The Black Christ" (Cullen), 54–56
The Blacker the Berry (Thurman), 17, 19–20, 44, 174*n*79, 182*n*44
"Blessed Assurance" (Hughes), 84
Blues, 11–12, 15, 68, 72, 78, 83–84, 101, 167*n*38
"Bodies in the Moonlight" (Hughes), 78–79

Bonds, Caska, 12
Bonner, Embry, 12
Bontemps, Arna, 43–44, 162*n*74; *God Sends Sunday*, 43–44, 158*n*155
Bowser, Aubrey, 39, 178*n*179
"Boy" (Hughes), 80
"Boy Prostitute" (McKay), 103, 176*n*138
Braithwaite, Fiona, 49, 160*n*17
Braithwaite, William S., 49, 160*n*17
Brawley, Benjamin, 32, 35, 40, 143
Brown, Guillaume, 58–59
Buffet flats, 11, 23, 100
Bulldykers/Bulldaggers, 11, 18, 39, 20, 100, 108
Burden of representation, 4, 5, 25, 30, 32–47 passim, 68–69, 71, 120–21, 142, 144, 154*n*42
Butler, Judith, 76–77, 110, 112, 140

Cabell, James Branch, 45, 126
"Café: 3 a.m." (Hughes), 84, 85
Cane (Toomer), 38
"Carmilla" (Le Fanu), 110
Carpenter, Edward, 50–51, 57, 63, 67, 91, 139, 172*n*32; *Ioläus: An Anthology of Friendship*, 50, 52, 66; *Love's Coming-of-Age*, 63, 163*n*91
Censorship, 6, 37, 42, 45, 51, 69, 72, 89–90, 118, 124, 133, 172*n*23
Chauncey, George, 3, 6, 7, 11, 12, 16, 39, 76, 77, 107
Chesnutt, Charles W., 25
"Color Scheme" (McKay), 90, 158*n*136
Committee of Fourteen (COF), 6, 9, 10, 21
Constab Ballads (McKay), 113
Cooper, Wayne, 43, 90, 91, 93–94, 114, 118, 172*n*32, 174*n*70, 177*n*157
"Cordelia the Crude" (Thurman), 41–42, 46
"Courage" (McKay), 94–95
The Crisis (magazine), 9, 26, 27, 28, 37, 40, 53, 147*n*25, 153*n*11, 157*n*104
Critics, contemporary, 4, 18–19, 23, 25, 27, 29, 30–33, 35–37, 38–43, 44, 46, 53, 67, 68, 88, 89, 96, 98, 99, 143, 167*n*38, 173*n*50
Cross-dressing, 6, 7, 10, 11, 18, 22, 82, 87, 104, 135, 140–41, 146*nn*6,8, 147*n*39. *See also* Drag balls

Cullen, Countée, 2, 3, 4, 23, 34, 43, 44, 48–67, 68, 69, 70, 71, 75, 76, 89, 93, 121, 124, 126, 142, 143, 144, 149*n*59, 156*n*96, 157*n*126, 161*n*50, 162*n*60, 164–65*n*139; "Advice to Youth," 58, 163*n*101; and Alain Locke, 12, 13, 14, 33, 41, 50–51, 52, 58, 63, 70–71, 143, 148*n*54, 152*n*139, 163*n*91, 164–65*n*139; "The Black Christ," 54–56; and *Fire!!*, 40, 41; "For a Poet," 74; "For a Virgin," 60; "For a Wanton," 60; "For One Who Gayly Sowed His Oats," 62, 80; "From the Dark Tower," 168*n*53; and Harold Jackman, 23, 49, 50, 54, 162*n*74, 163*n*101; "Heritage," 53–54, 61; homosexuality of, 2, 4, 50, 51; "Judas Iscariot," 56–57, 60, 128; and Langston Hughes, 58, 70–71, 157*n*126; "The Love Tree," 59–60, 61; "Love's Way," 63; "Magnets," 60–61, 63; *The Medea and Some Poems*, 53; "More Than a Fool's Song," 62–63; "Portrait of a Lover," 60, 61; religious theme in the works of, 52–57, 60, 62, 63, 67; "Saturday's Child," 59; "The Shroud of Color," 56; "The Spark," 161*n*39; "Spring Reminiscence," 64; "Suicide Chant," 59, 60; "Tableau," 63, 65–67, 136, 144; "To a Brown Boy," 58, 59; "To France," 51; "Ultimatum," 62, 80; "Uncle Jim," 63, 64–65; and women, 49–50, 52, 160*n*17, 163*n*102; "Youth Sings of Rosebuds," 58
Cullen, Frederick, 49

Davis, Allison, 53
Democratic Vistas (Whitman), 66, 94
"Desire" (Hughes), 73
Dill, Augustus Granville, 9, 147*n*25
Dodson, Owen, 67
Dollimore, Jonathan, 29, 51, 62, 99
Douglas, Aaron, 34
Drag balls, 12, 18, 19, 21, 22, 83, 87, 135, 140, 148*n*50, 150*n*100, 171*n*153
"Drawings for Mulattoes" (Nugent), 124
"The Dream Keeper" (Hughes), 74
Du Bois, W.E.B., 8, 26, 27, 28, 30–32, 33, 35, 38, 40, 44, 120, 124, 153*n*11, 182*n*46
Du Bois, Yolande, 50, 160*n*17, 163*n*102
Duff, Donald, 65, 67, 165*n*148
Dunbar, Paul Laurence, 25
Dunbar-Nelson, Alice, 16
Dunham, Albert, 14

Early, Gerald, 2, 50
Eastman, Max, 90, 91, 172*n*21
Effeminacy, 6, 7, 11, 12, 51, 76, 82, 83, 84, 85, 86, 93, 99, 104–106, 107, 108, 117, 138, 139, 168*n*73, 170*n*147, 177*n*147. *See also* Fairies; Pansies
Eliot, T. S., 31
Ellis, Havelock, 18; *Sexual Inversion*, 150*n*98
Europe, 21, 71, 88, 92, 98, 101, 172*nn*17,32
Faderman, Lillian, 10, 22, 108
Fairies, 7, 10, 12, 18, 20, 82, 84, 85–86, 87, 107, 138, 139. *See also* Pansies
Fauset, Jessie, 26, 33, 41, 42, 73, 165*n*148
Ferris, William, 39, 43
Fine Clothes to the Jew (Hughes), 35, 37, 43
Fire!!, 37, 39–42, 44–47, 89, 120, 121, 155*n*67, 156*n*81
Fisher, Hank, 125
Fisher, Rudolph, 147*n*28
"For a Poet" (Cullen), 74
"For a Virgin" (Cullen), 60
"For a Wanton" (Cullen), 60
"For One Who Gayly Sowed His Oats" (Cullen), 62, 80
Ford, Charles, 90–91
France, 21, 51, 102, 116, 161*n*34
Frank, Waldo, 173*n*38
Frazier, E. Franklin, 15, 16, 19
Freud, Sigmund, 18, 28, 90
"From the Dark Tower" (Cullen), 168*n*53

Garber, Eric, 2, 14, 123, 135
Garvey, Marcus, 29, 32, 36, 75, 155*n*63
Gates, Henry Louis, 1, 34, 69, 73
Gautier, Théophile, 127
Gay Harlem Renaissance network. *See* Locke, Alain
"Geisha Man" (Nugent), 123, 128, 131–34, 135–37, 138, 139, 140–41, 148*n*43, 184*n*110
Gender inversion, 4, 7, 11, 13, 19–20, 22, 81–87 passim, 104–10 passim, 138–41 passim, 143, 147*n*39, 171*n*153, 178*n*179. *See also* Bulldykers/Bulldaggers; Cross-dressing; Effeminacy; Fairies; Homosexuality, stereotypes in Harlem Renaissance works; Pansies
"Gentleman Jigger" (Nugent), 122, 123, 132
God Sends Sunday (Bontemps), 43–44, 158*n*155
Greenwich Village, 11, 12, 22, 88, 120

Grimké, Angelina Weld, 2, 23
Gumby, L. S. Alexander, 12, 64, 94; "To . . . . You," 94

Hall, Radclyffe, 13; *The Well of Loneliness*, 13
"Hard Daddy" (Hughes), 83
Harlem (Thurman and Rapp), 37, 147*n*18
Harlem: A Forum of Negro Life (magazine), 34, 46–47
"Harlem Glory" (McKay), 104, 106, 177*n*147
Harlem Renaissance: creation and aims of, 3, 4, 8, 25–30, 153*n*22. *See also* Racial uplift, concept of
Harlem Shadows (McKay), 88, 89, 171*n*2, 176*n*139
"Harlem Shadows" (McKay), 179*n*222
Harris, Frank, 45; *My Life and Loves*, 45
Hayes, Donald, 14, 37
Hemingway, Ernest, 92
Hemphill, Essex, 142, 144
"Heritage" (Cullen), 53–54, 61
"Hermaphroditus" (Swinburne), 139
"Highball" (McKay), 109–10, 178*n*196
Hirschfeld, Magnus, 151*n*119
"Home Thoughts" (McKay), 116
Home to Harlem (McKay), 32, 35–36, 38, 39, 41, 43, 88, 96–109, 110–13, 115–18, 158*n*137, 175*nn*85,91, 179*nn*208,225, 180*n*256
Homosexuality: African Americans' attitudes toward, 14–23; clergy's attitude toward, 18, 20, 22, 152*n*134; contamination theory, 20–22; Greek model of, 12, 50–51, 64, 70, 91, 130, 148*n*54; policing efforts, 8–9, 10, 14, 15, 20, 22, 23, 123, 146*n*2, 147*n*25, 151*n*122, 152*n*130,133; stereotypes in Harlem Renaissance works, 19–20, 81–87, 104–10, 135, 138
"Honeymoon" (McKay), 95–96, 174*n*70
hooks, bell, 17–18, 71, 72, 73, 84, 118–19
Housman, A. E., 48, 163*n*101
Hughes, Langston, 2, 3, 4–5, 9, 14, 26, 27, 31, 33, 34, 35, 36, 37, 38, 39, 41, 44, 46, 68–87, 88, 89, 121, 122, 126, 143, 149*n*59, 158*n*137, 162*n*60, 170*nn*129,130; *The Big Sea*, 68, 76, 77, 79, 80, 81–83, 86, 87, 170*n*129; and Alain Locke, 14, 27, 70–71, 163*n*88; "Blessed Assurance," 84; and the blues, 68, 72, 78, 83–84, 167*n*38; "Bodies in the Moonlight," 78–79; "Boy," 80; "Café: 3 a.m.," 84, 85; and

Countée Cullen, 58, 70–71, 157*n*126; "Desire," 73; "The Dream Keeper," 74; *Fine Clothes to the Jew*, 35, 37, 43; "Hard Daddy," 83; "Joy," 75; "Lament over Love," 84; *Little Ham*, 83, 85, 86, 170*n*147; "Little Virgin," 77, 82; "Long Trip," 78; "Lover's Return," 83; "Luani of the Jungles," 78, 86; maritime themes in the works of, 76–83, 143; "Midwinter Blues," 84; *Not Without Laughter*, 35, 83, 85–86, 87, 171*n*153; "Our Land," 74–75, 81; and patronage, 27, 28, 71, 153*n*16; "Pictures to the Wall," 167*n*48; "Poem [2]," 72–73, 167*n*41; poetry of, 68, 72–76, 78, 80–81, 83, 84, 85, 93, 125, 167*nn*41,48; "Port Town," 80–81; "Red Silk Stockings," 39; representation of women in the works of, 38, 39, 41, 77, 78–79, 82, 83–84, 86–87; "Ruby Brown," 84; sexuality of, 69–71, 142; "Shadows," 74; "Star Seeker," 73; "Suicide," 84; "To Beauty," 75–76; "Water-Front Streets," 81; *The Weary Blues*, 35; "When Sue Wears Red," 78; "The Young Glory of Him," 79; "Young Prostitute," 84; "Young Sailor," 80
Hull, Gloria, 1, 23, 27
Hurston, Zora Neale, 27, 28, 34, 46, 155*n*67
Hutchinson, George, 16, 30, 31, 44, 143
Huysmans, Joris-Karl, 120, 127, 134; *Against Nature*, 127

"I Am Twenty Five" (Nugent), 131
"I Know My Soul" (McKay), 95
"If We Must Die" (McKay), 94, 173*n*51, 174*n*65
"In Memoriam A.H.H." (Tennyson), 167*n*44
"In Paths Untrodden" (Whitman), 165*n*154
Infants of the Spring (Thurman), 35, 44, 148*n*52
Interracial relationships, 2, 10–11, 12, 54–55, 63–67, 89, 94, 95, 101, 125–27, 165*n*151
The Intersexes (Stevenson), 56, 129
Ioläus: An Anthology of Friendship (Carpenter), 50, 52, 66

Jackman, Harold, 13, 23, 43, 49, 50, 52, 54, 59, 88, 162*n*74, 163*n*101
Jekyll, Walter, 91, 172*n*32, 177*n*142
Johnson, Charles S., 26, 29, 30, 31, 53

Johnson, Georgia Douglas, 23, 26, 123, 152*n*3
Johnson, James Weldon, 4, 21, 25, 26, 29, 30, 31, 33, 42, 43, 88, 176*n*133
Journals, African American. *See The Crisis; Fire!!; Harlem: A Forum of Negro Life; Opportunity*
"Joy" (Hughes), 75
Joyce, James, 45, 159*n*168; *Ulysses*, 45
"Judas Iscariot" (Cullen), 56–57, 60, 128
Julien, Isaac, 69, 73, 126; *Looking for Langston*, 69, 73, 126

Keats, John, 48, 64
Krafft-Ebing, Richard von, 122; *Psychopathia Sexualis*, 122, 181*n*22

"Lament over Love" (Hughes), 84
Larsen, Nella, 2, 17, 33
Le Fanu, Joseph Sheridan, 110; "Carmilla," 110
Leaves of Grass (Whitman), 77
Lesbianism, 2, 3, 4, 7, 10, 11, 12, 13, 17–20, 21, 22, 23, 39, 86–87, 125, 146*n*8, 147*n*39, 148*n*49, 150–51*n*108; literary representation of in Harlem Renaissance works, 19–20, 39, 83, 84, 86, 103, 108–10, 118, 135
Liberator (magazine), 28, 89, 165*n*148
Literary contests, 27, 153*n*11
Little Ham (Hughes), 83, 85, 86, 170*n*147
Little Review, 45
"Little Virgin" (Hughes), 77, 82
Locke, Alain, 1, 23, 26, 27–28, 30, 31, 33, 35, 38, 40, 41, 43, 45, 48, 49, 50, 51, 52, 53, 58, 63, 65, 89, 92, 123, 149*n*59, 160–61*n*30, 164–65*n*139, 173*n*40; and Claude McKay, 13, 35, 91–92, 156*n*86, 173*n*39, 176*n*138; and Countée Cullen, 12, 13, 14, 33, 41, 50–51, 52, 58, 63, 70–71, 143, 148*n*54, 152*n*139, 163*n*91, 164–65*n*139; gay network of, 12–14, 23, 27, 50–51, 70, 91, 122, 143, 144, 148*n*54, 149*n*59, 173*n*39, 176*n*138; and Langston Hughes, 14, 27, 70–71, 163*n*88; *The New Negro*, 35, 37, 120, 121, 144, 156*n*86; and Richard Bruce Nugent, 12, 13, 14, 27–28, 121, 122, 123
"Long Trip" (Hughes), 78
A Long Way From Home (McKay), 91, 92–93, 99, 101, 102–103, 106, 108
Looking for Langston (Julien), 69, 73, 126
"The Love Tree" (Cullen), 59–60, 61

"Lover's Return" (Hughes), 83
Love's Coming-of-Age (Carpenter), 63, 163*n*91
"Love's Way" (Cullen), 63
"Luani of the Jungles" (Hughes), 78, 86

McClendon, Rose, 128
McKay, Claude, 2, 3, 5, 8, 27, 88–119, 124, 126, 143, 156*n*81, 171*n*7, 171–72*n*8, 172*n*14,16,29, 173*n*50; and Alain Locke, 13, 35, 91–92, 156*n*86, 173*n*39, 176*n*138; "Alfonso, Dressing To Wait At Table, Sings," 103, 176*n*139; *Banana Bottom*, 98, 100–101, 177*n*142, 178*n*197, 179*n*225; *Banjo*, 39, 88, 90, 96–106, 110, 112–13, 115–18, 178–79*n*203, 179*n*207,225; "The Barrier," 94, 174*n*59,60; "Bennie's Departure," 114, 115; "Boy Prostitute," 103, 176*n*138; and censorship, 89–90, 118, 172*n*23; "Color Scheme," 90, 158*n*136; *Constab Ballads*, 113; "Courage," 94–95; "Harlem Glory," 104, 106, 177*n*147; *Harlem Shadows*, 88, 89, 171*n*2, 176*n*139; "Harlem Shadows," 179*n*222; "Highball," 109–10, 178*n*196; "Home Thoughts," 116, 180*n*252; *Home to Harlem*, 32, 35–36, 38, 39, 41, 43, 88, 96–109, 110–13, 115–18, 158*n*137, 175*nn*85,91, 179*nn*208,225, 180*n*256; "Honeymoon," 95–96, 174*n*70; "I Know My Soul," 95; "If We Must Die," 94, 173*n*51, 174*n*65; and Jamaica, 88, 89, 91, 98, 100, 113, 114, 116; *A Long Way From Home*, 91, 92–93, 99, 101, 102–103, 106, 108; *My Green Hills of Jamaica*, 91, 113; "One Year After," 94, 95; poetry of, 88, 89, 91, 93–96, 103, 113, 116, 143, 174*n*55; and primitivism, 5, 43, 89, 91, 92, 96–103 passim, 112, 118; "The Prince of Porto Rico," 117; representation of women in the works of, 39, 98, 101, 108–13, 115, 118, 175*n*88, 176*n*119,123, 178*n*181,196,197, 178–79*n*203, 179*n*220,222,224; "Rest in Peace," 93–94; "Romance in Marseilles," 90, 104, 105–106, 109, 172*n*24, 177*n*157; sexuality of, 13, 89, 90–91, 93; *Songs of Jamaica*, 113; *Spring in New Hampshire, and other poems*, 171*n*2; "Sukee River," 116; "When I Pounded the Pavement," 113–15; "White Houses," 156*n*86

"Magnets" (Cullen), 60–61, 63
Maritime themes in Harlem Renaissance works, 76–83, 98, 106, 115, 116–17, 143
Masculinity, 13, 16–17, 73, 76–77, 78, 80–83, 84, 85, 87, 92–93, 96, 99, 100, 104–108, 110–12, 113, 117, 118–19, 132, 138–40, 143, 146n8, 178–79n203. *See also* Effeminacy; Primitivism; Sweetbacks/Sweetmen; Whitman, Walt, male camaraderie as envisioned by; Wolves
Mason, Charlotte, 27–28
The Medea and Some Poems (Cullen), 53
Melville, Herman, 82; *Redburn*, 82; *White Jacket*, 82
Mencken, H. L., 28, 45, 126
"Midwinter Blues" (Hughes), 84
Miscegenation. *See* Interracial relationships
Misogyny, 27, 77, 110, 117, 170n147
Modernism, 31–32, 42–47, 69, 120
"More Than a Fool's Song" (Cullen), 62–63
Mumford, Kevin, 2, 9, 10, 11, 14, 65–66
My Green Hills of Jamaica (McKay), 91, 113
My Life and Loves (Harris), 45

"Narcissus" (Nugent), 138–39
National Association for the Advancement of Colored People (NAACP), 9, 26, 28
National Urban League (NUL), 26, 28
The New Negro (Locke), 35, 37, 120, 121, 144, 156n86
New Republic, 28
New York Amsterdam News, 9, 10, 20
Nigger Heaven (Van Vechten), 8, 36, 88
"Niggeratti," 34–47 passim, 88, 89, 121, 148n52
"Niggeratti Manor," 12, 120
Niles, Blair, 14, 54, 144, 162n62; *Strange Brother*, 14, 54, 144, 162n62
Not Without Laughter (Hughes), 35, 83, 85–86, 87, 171n153
"The Now Discordant Song of Bells" (Nugent), 126–27, 128, 130–31
Nugent, Richard Bruce, 3, 5, 10–11, 12, 13, 14, 44–45, 46, 69, 120–41, 142, 143, 157n126, 181–82n25, 182n35; and Alain Locke, 12, 13, 14, 27–28, 121, 122, 123; "Bastard Song," 125, 182n49; "Beyond Where the Star Stood Still," 123, 127; Bible stories of, 126–31, 132, 138, 184n84; bohemian-

ism of, 14, 121–22, 123; "Drawings for Mulattoes," 124; "Geisha Man," 123, 128, 131–34, 135–37, 138, 139, 140–41, 148n43, 184n110; "Gentleman Jigger," 122, 123, 132; "I Am Twenty Five," 131; "Narcissus," 138–39; "The Now Discordant Song of Bells," 126–27, 128, 130–31; poetry of, 121, 125–26, 136, 137, 138–39; "Sahdji," 120, 121, 124–25; sexuality of, 13, 122–23, 142; "Shadow," 121, 125–26, 136; "Slender Length of Beauty," 183n76; "Smoke, Lilies and Jade," 31, 40, 41–42, 45, 46, 76, 120, 121, 122, 124, 126, 128, 131–32, 133, 134, 135, 136, 137, 138, 139–40, 154n52, 184n114; "Tree with Kerioth-Fruit," 128, 129, 130; "Tunic with a Thousand Pleats," 126–27; as visual artist, 121–22, 123, 124, 128, 181n16; and Wallace Thurman, 12, 41–42, 45, 120, 121, 122, 124; "Who Asks This Thing?" 137

"One Year After" (McKay), 94, 95
Opportunity (magazine), 26, 27, 40, 121, 124, 157n104
"Our Land" (Hughes), 74–75, 81

Paganism, 52–54, 61, 67
Pansies, 6, 11, 20, 51, 87, 104–106, 107, 126, 177n171. *See also* Fairies
Passing, racial, 124
Patronage, 25, 27–28, 71, 108, 153n16, 161n50
Perry, Edward, 62
"Pictures to the Wall" (Hughes), 167n48
Pittsburgh Courier, 157n104
"Poem [2]" (Hughes), 72–73, 167n41
"Port Town" (Hughes), 80–81
"Portrait of a Lover" (Cullen), 60, 61
Pound, Ezra, 69
Powell, Adam Clayton, 18, 20, 22
Primitivism, 5, 8, 21, 36, 42–43, 53, 56, 74–75, 89, 91, 92, 96–103 passim, 112, 118
"The Prince of Porto Rico" (McKay), 117
Propaganda, use of in African American literature, 30–31, 33, 154n44
Prostitution, 9, 10, 16, 21, 39; in Harlem Renaissance works, 38, 39, 41–42, 72, 81, 84, 86, 98, 99, 102, 103, 104, 109, 110, 111, 112, 113, 115, 170n148, 179n220
Psychopathia Sexualis (Krafft-Ebing), 122, 181n22

Publishers, 25, 26, 27, 28, 35, 36, 42, 43–44, 89–90, 123–24, 172*n*16

Quicksand (Larsen), 17

Racial uplift, concept of, 8, 17, 19, 89, 121, 142, 144
Rainey, Ma, 148*n*48
Rampersad, Arnold, 69, 70, 71, 73, 77, 82, 83, 84, 86, 167*n*41, 169*n*89
Ransom, Lewellyn, 13, 50
Rapp, William Jourdan, 37, 44; *Harlem*, 37
Readers. *See* Audiences
"Red Silk Stockings" (Hughes), 39
Redburn (Melville), 82
Reimonenq, Alden, 2, 3, 50, 52, 55, 56, 57, 66, 67, 69, 70, 71–72, 87, 96, 164*n*139, 165*n*154, 182*n*35
Rent parties, 8, 11
"Rest in Peace" (McKay), 93–94
Robertson, Ida, 50
Rogers, J. A., 35, 37, 42
"Romance in Marseilles" (McKay), 90, 104, 105–106, 109, 172*n*24, 177*n*157
"Ruby Brown" (Hughes), 84

"Sahdji" (Nugent), 120, 121, 124–25
Sailors. *See* Maritime themes in Harlem Renaissance works
Sandburg, Carl, 31, 32, 69
Sappho, 108–109, 135
"Saturday's Child" (Cullen), 59
Schomburg, Arthur, 89, 90
Schuyler, George, 18–19, 39, 46, 88, 99
Sedgwick, Eve, 91, 113, 117, 143
Sexology, 7, 12, 18, 19, 20, 41, 60–61, 65–66, 106, 139, 143, 150*n*99, 160*n*30. *See also* Ellis, Havelock
Sexual Inversion (Ellis), 150*n*98
"Shadow" (Nugent), 121, 125–26, 136
"Shadows" (Hughes), 74
"The Shroud of Color" (Cullen), 56
Sinfield, Alan, 1, 2, 3, 134, 138, 168*n*73, 173*n*46, 185*n*134
"Slender Length of Beauty" (Nugent), 183*n*76
Smith, Bessie, 11
"Smoke, Lilies and Jade" (Nugent), 31, 40, 41–42, 45, 46, 76, 120, 121, 122, 124, 126, 128, 131–32, 133, 134, 135, 136, 137, 138, 139–40, 154*n*52, 184*n*114
Society for the Suppression of Vice (SSV), 6, 45
"Song of Myself" (Whitman), 75, 96

"Song of the Open Road" (Whitman), 70
Songs of Jamaica (McKay), 113
"The Spark" (Cullen), 161*n*39
Speakeasies, 6, 9, 10, 11, 17, 23, 39, 98, 105
Spring in New Hampshire, and other poems (McKay), 171*n*2
"Spring Reminiscence" (Cullen), 64
"Star Seeker" (Hughes), 73
Stefansson, Harald Jan, 181*n*20
Stevenson, Edward, 56, 129; *The Intersexes*, 56, 129
Strange Brother (Niles), 14, 54, 144, 162*n*62
"Suicide" (Hughes), 84
"Suicide Chant" (Cullen), 59, 60
"Sukee River" (McKay), 116, 180*n*252
Sweetbacks/Sweetmen, 8, 17, 111, 150*n*90, 179*nn*207,208
Swinburne, Algernon Charles, 139; "Hermaphroditus," 139
Symonds, John Addington, 60, 150*n*98
Syphilis, 103, 176–77*n*141

"Tableau" (Cullen), 63, 65–67, 136, 144
Talented Tenth, 30, 33, 48, 120
Taylor, Edward, 55
Tellier, André, 136; *Twilight Men*, 136, 168*n*54
Tennyson, Alfred, 32, 48, 167*n*44; "In Memoriam A.H.H.," 167*n*44
Thompson, Louise, 23, 166*n*14
Thurman, Wallace, 8, 9, 23, 32, 37, 44, 48, 69, 93, 124, 147*n*25, 148*n*52, 157*n*126, 159*n*162, 173*n*51; *The Blacker the Berry*, 17, 19–20, 44, 174*n*79, 182*n*44; "Cordelia the Crude," 41–42, 46; and *Fire!!*, 37, 40, 41–42, 45–46, 156*n*81; *Harlem*, 37; *Infants of the Spring*, 35, 44, 148*n*52; and Richard Bruce Nugent, 12, 41–42, 45, 120, 121, 122, 124; sexuality of, 23, 181*n*20
"To a Brown Boy" (Cullen), 58, 59
"To Beauty" (Hughes), 75–76
"To France" (Cullen), 51
"To . . . . You" (Gumby), 94
Toomer, Jean, 14, 38, 173*n*38; *Cane*, 38
"Tree with Kerioth-Fruit" (Nugent), 128, 129, 130
"Tunic With a Thousand Pleats" (Nugent), 126–27
Twilight Men (Tellier), 136, 168*n*54
Tyler, Parker, 120

Ulrichs, Karl Heinrich, 64, 140, 165*n*145

"Ultimatum" (Cullen), 62, 80
Ulysses (James Joyce), 45
"Uncle Jim" (Cullen), 63, 64–65

Van Vechten, Carl, 8, 27, 36, 43, 69, 88, 96, 121; *Nigger Heaven*, 36, 88

Walker, A'Lelia, 11
Walrond, Eric, 57, 163*n*92
Wandervogel movement, 63, 164–65*n*139
Watch and Ward Society (Boston), 45
"Water-Front Streets" (Hughes), 81
"We Two Boys Together Clinging" (Whitman), 66
The Weary Blues (Hughes), 35
The Well of Loneliness (Hall), 13
Westphal, Carl, 60–61
Wheatley, Phillis, 25
"When I Pounded the Pavement" (McKay), 113–15
"When Sue Wears Red" (Hughes), 78
White, Walter, 26, 30, 88, 89, 155*n*66, 172*n*16
"White Houses" (McKay), 156*n*86
White Jacket (Melville), 82
Whitman, Walt, 12, 51, 52, 60, 66–67, 69, 70, 71, 75, 77, 87, 91, 94, 96, 114, 115, 143, 144; *Democratic Vistas*, 66, 94; "In Paths Untrodden," 165*n*154,

Leaves of Grass, 77; male camaraderie as envisioned by, 12–13, 51, 66–67, 77–78, 83, 87, 94, 96, 113–15, 118, 143; "Song of Myself," 75, 96; "Song of the Open Road," 70; "We Two Boys Together Clinging," 66. *See also* Locke, Alain, gay network of
"Who Asks This Thing?" (Nugent), 137
Wilde, Oscar, 40, 51, 61, 91, 138, 164*n*130
Wirth, Thomas, 121, 122–23, 124, 129, 130, 131, 132, 133, 141
Wolves, 106–108, 138, 177*n*171, 178*n*179
Women writers: African American, 1, 2, 3, 23, 26, 27, 33. *See also* Bennett, Gwendolyn; Dunbar-Nelson, Alice; Fauset, Jessie; Grimké, Angelina Weld; Hurston, Zora Neale; Johnson, Georgia Douglas; Wheatley, Phillis
Woods, Gregory, 2, 55, 65, 73, 74, 75, 76, 78, 80, 81, 94, 96, 125, 165*n*151, 174*nn*63,65, 176*n*139, 180*n*252

The Young and Evil (Ford and Tyler), 90, 151*n*129
"The Young Glory of Him" (Hughes), 79
"Young Prostitute" (Hughes), 84
"Young Sailor" (Hughes), 80
"Youth Sings of Rosebuds" (Cullen), 58

A. B. Christa Schwarz is an independent scholar and lives in Germany.